Pocket Guide to Cardiovascular Diseases

PRESENTED TO

DR. KEITH EVANS

WITH COMPLIMENTS

AND BEST WISHES.

BARRY JACKSON

(SANOFI)

Pocket Guide to Cardiovascular Diseases

Edward K. Chung, MD, FACP, FACC
Director of the Heart Station
Director, Cardiac Stress Testing Center
Thomas Jefferson University Hospital;
Professor of Medicine
Jefferson Medical College
Philadelphia, Pennsylvania

Dennis A. Tighe, MD, FACP, FACC
Director, Noninvasive Cardiology
Baystate Medical Center
Springfield, Massachusetts;
Assistant Professor of Medicine
Tufts University School of Medicine
Boston, Massachusetts

b

**Blackwell
Science**

© 1999 by Blackwell Science, Inc.

Editorial Offices:
Commerce Place, 350 Main Street, Malden, Massachusetts 02148, USA
Osney Mead, Oxford OX2 0EL, England
25 John Street, London WC1N 2BL, England
23 Ainslie Place, Edinburgh EH3 6AJ, Scotland
54 University Street, Carlton, Victoria 3053, Australia

Other Editorial Offices:
Blackwell Wissenschafts-Verlag GmbH, Kurfürstendamm 57, 10707 Berlin,
    Germany
Blackwell Science KK, MG Kodenmacho Building, 7-10 Kodenmacho Nihom-
bashi, Chuo-ku, Tokyo 104, Japan

Distributors:

USA
  Blackwell Science, Inc.
  Commerce Place
  350 Main Street
  Malden, Massachusetts 02148
  (Telephone orders: 800-215-1000 or 781-388-8250; fax orders: 781-388-8270)

Canada
  Login Brothers Book Company
  324 Saulteaux Crescent
  Winnipeg, Manitoba, R3J 3T2
  (Telephone orders: 204-224-4068)

Australia
  Blackwell Science Pty, Ltd.
  54 University Street
  Carlton, Victoria 3053
  (Telephone orders: 03-9347-0300; fax orders: 03-9349-3016)

Outside North America and Australia
  Blackwell Science, Ltd.
  c/o Marston Book Services, Ltd.
  P.O. Box 269
  Abingdon
  Oxon OX14 4YN
  England
  (Telephone orders: 44-01235-465500; fax orders: 44-01235-465555)

Acquisitions: Christopher Davis
Production: Irene Herlihy
Manufacturing: Lisa Flanagan
Typeset by Best-set Typesetter Ltd., Hong Kong
Printed and bound by Edwards Brothers Inc.

Printed in the United States of America
99 00 01 02 5 4 3 2 1

The Blackwell Science logo is a trade mark of Blackwell Science Ltd., regis-
tered at the United Kingdom Trade Marks Registry

Library of Congress Cataloging-in-Publication Data
Chung, Edward K.
    Pocket guide to cardiovascular diseases / Edward K. Chung,
Dennis A. Tighe.
      p.   cm.
    Includes bibliographical references and index.
    ISBN 0-86542-508-6
    1. Cardiovascular system—Diseases—Handbooks, manuals, etc.   I.
Tighe, Dennis A.   II. Title.
    RC669.25 .C48 1999
    616.1—dc21   98-45297
                                                        CIP

To my wife Lisa, our children Linda and Christopher, and our grandchildren Nicholas and Jacqueline

—Edward K. Chung

To my wife Leslie, and our children Elizabeth and Alexander

—Dennis A. Tighe

Contents

Preface

The primary intention of *Pocket Guide to Cardiovascular Diseases* is to describe common cardiovascular disorders that are frequently encountered in our daily practice. Thus, the purpose of this publication is by no means to discuss in-depth various subjects in medicine nor to describe in detail all cardiovascular diseases.

The content is intended to be clinical, concise, and practical so that the *Pocket Guide* will provide all readers with up-to-date materials that will assist them directly in the care of their patients with common cardiovascular problems. It can be said that we never have sufficient time to read in-depth the standard textbooks and various journals when presented with a clinical cardiovascular problem. In addition, it may not be absolutely necessary for medical students, house staff, and noncardiac physicians to read many oversized textbooks in cardiology.

The format of this pocket guide is organized into an outline structure in order to provide all necessary information in the diagnosis as well as management of common cardiovascular disorders without spending much time. Thus, the *Pocket Guide* will be particularly valuable to medical house staff, primary care physicians (family physicians, emergency room physicians, internists), and cardiology fellows. In addition, medical students and cardiac care nurses will benefit greatly by reading this pocket guide for a better understanding of various cardiovascular problems.

My co-author, Dennis A. Tighe, deserves special

recognition for his outstanding, extremely educational chapters on many difficult subjects.

I am also grateful to the contributors who have written excellent chapters dealing with various cardiovascular problems. In addition, I would like to express my sincere appreciation to my personal secretary, Maureen Gamble, for her valuable assistance in the *Pocket Guide*'s completion. The endless cooperation of the staff of Blackwell was, of course, indispensable. Lastly, I owe deep gratitude and appreciation to my father, Dr. Il-Chun Chung, who has always provided proper guidance and inspiration for me.

Edward K. Chung
Bryn Mawr, PA

Contributors

Edward K. Chung, MD, FACP, FACC
Director of the Heart Station
Director, Cardiac Stress Testing Center
Thomas Jefferson University Hospital;
Professor of Medicine
Jefferson Medical College
Philadelphia, Pennsylvania

James R. Cook, MD, FACC
Associate Director, Cardiac Electrophysiology
Director of Electrocardiography
Baystate Medical Center
Springfield, Massachusetts;
Assistant Professor of Medicine
Tufts University School of Medicine
Boston, Massachusetts

Howard J. Eisen, MD, FACP, FACC
Medical Director, Cardiac Transplant Program
Director, Heart Failure Intensive Care Unit
Temple University Hospital;
Professor of Medicine and Physiology
Temple University School of Medicine
Philadelphia, Pennsylvania

James B. Kirchhoffer, MD, FACC
Acting Chief, Cardiology Division
Director, Cardiac Electrophysiology
Baystate Medical Center
Springfield, Massachusetts;
Assistant Professor of Medicine

Tufts University School of Medicine
Boston, Massachusetts

Yvonne M. Paris, MD
Pediatric Cardiologist
Department of Pediatrics
Baystate Medical Center
Springfield, Massachusetts;
Assistant Professor of Pediatrics
Tufts University School of Medicine
Boston, Massachusetts

Ileana L. Piña, MD, FACC
Director, Heart Failure Program
Director, Cardiac Rehabilitation
Temple University Hospital;
Associate Professor of Medicine
Temple University School of Medicine
Philadelphia, Pennsylvania

Mark N. Porway, MD, FACC
Medical Director, Cardiac Inpatient Services
Associate Director, Cardiac Catheterization Laboratory
Baystate Medical Center
Springfield, Massachusetts;
Assistant Professor of Medicine
Tufts University School of Medicine
Boston, Massachusetts

Dennis A. Tighe, MD, FACP, FACC
Director, Noninvasive Cardiology
Baystate Medical Center
Springfield, Massachusetts;
Assistant Professor of Medicine
Tufts University School of Medicine
Boston, Massachusetts

Howard H. Weitz, MD, FACP, FACC
Director, Division of Cardiology
Thomas Jefferson University Hospital;
Clinical Associate Professor of Medicine
Jefferson Medical College
Philadelphia, Pennsylvania

Abbreviations

AAA	abdominal aortic aneurysm
AAD	anti-arrhythmic drug
ABC	Airway, Breathing, Circulation
ABE	acute bacterial endocarditis
ABI	ankle-brachial index
ACC	American College of Cardiology
ACE	angiotensin-converting enzyme
ACLS	advanced cardiac life support
AF	atrial fibrillation
AFFIRM	Atrial Fibrillation Follow-up Investigation of Rhythm Management
AHA	American Heart Association
AIDS	acquired immunodeficiency syndrome
AIVR	accelerated idioventricular rhythm
AMP	adenosine monophosphate
ANA	antinuclear antibody
ANP	atrial natriuretic peptide
AP	anterior-posterior
APC	atrial premature contraction
APD	action potential duration
APSAC	anistreplase
aPTT	activated partial thromboplastin time
AR	aortic regurgitation
ARB	angiotensin II receptor-1 blocker
ARF	acute rheumatic fever
ARVD	arrhythmogenic right ventricular cardio-myopathy/dysplasia
AS	aortic stenosis
ASA	acetylsalicylic acid (aspirin)

ASD	atrial septal defect
ASO	antistreptolysin O
AT	atrial tachycardia
AV	atrioventricular (node)
AVC	aberrant ventricular conduction
AVID	Antiarrhythmics Versus Implantable Defibrillators
AVJT	atrioventricular junctional tachycardia
AVNRT	atrioventricular nodal reentrant tachycardia
AVP	arginine vasopressin
BARI	Bypass Angioplasty Revascularization Investigation (trial)
BASIS	Basel Antiarrhythmic Study of Infarct Survival
BAV	balloon aortic valvuloplasty
BBBB	bilateral bundle branch block
BHEG	British Heart Electrical Group
BLS	basic life support
BMV	balloon mitral valvuloplasty
BP	blood pressure
BUN	blood urea nitrogen
CABG	coronary artery bypass grafting
CAD	coronary artery disease
CAMIAT	Canadian Amiodarone Myocardial Infarction Arrhythmia Trial
CAPS	Cardiac Arrhythmia Pilot Study
CASS	Coronary Artery Surgery Study
CAST	Cardiac Arrhythmia Suppression Trial
CBC	complete blood count
CC	cubic centimeter
CCB	calcium channel blocker
CCS	Canadian Cardiovascular Society
CCU	coronary care unit
CHF	congestive heart failure
CHF-STAT	Survival Trial of Antiarrhythmic Therapy in Congestive Heart Failure
CI	Cardiac Index
CMV	cytomegalovirus
CNS	central nervous system
CO	cardiac output
CPK	creatinine phosphokinase

CPR	cardiopulmonary resuscitation
CSRT	corrected sinus node recovery time
CSS	carotid sinus stimulation
CT	computed tomography
CVP	central venous pressure
CXR	chest x-ray
DBP	diastolic blood pressure
DC	direct current
DCA	directional coronary atherectomy
DCM	dilated cardiomyopathy
dL	deciliter
DSA	digital subtraction angiography
DVT	deep venous thrombosis
EBCT	electron beam (ultrafast) CT
ECC	emergency cardiac care
ECG	electrocardiogram
ED	Emergency Department
EMD	electromechanical dissociation
EMS	emergency medical services
EP	electrophysiology
EPS	electrophysiologic study
ERP	effective refractory period
ESR	erythrocyte sedimentation rate
ESVEM	Electrophysiologic Study Versus Electro-cardiographic Monitoring
ETT	exercise tolerance test
FDA	Food and Drug Administration (U.S.)
FU	fluorouracil
GAS	group A streptococci
GES	graded elastic stockings
GESICA	Grupo de Estudio de la Sobrevida en la Insuficiecia Cardiaca en Argentina
GI	gastrointestinal
GU	genitourinary
HCM	hypertrophic cardiomyopathy
HDL	high density lipoprotein
HELLP	hemolysis, elevated liver function tests, low platelets (syndrome)
HIV	human immunodeficiency virus
HLA	human lymphocyte antigens
HPV	herpesvirus
HR	heart rate

HTN	hypertension
HV	His bundle-ventricular
IABP	intra-aortic balloon counterpulsation
ICD	implanted cardioverter-defibrillator
ICH	intracerebral hemorrhage
IE	infective endocarditis
IHSS	idiopathic hypertrophic subaortic stenosis
IL	interleukin
ILVT	idiopathic left ventricular tachycardia
IMA	internal mammary artery
IMPACT	International Mexiletine and Placebo Anti-arrhythmic Coronary Trial
INR	international normalized ratio
IPC	intermittent pneumatic compression
IPG	impedance plethysmography
ISA	intrinsic sympathomimetic activity
IV	intravenous
IVC	inferior vena cava
IVCD	intraventricular conduction delay
IVDA	intravenous drug abuse(r)
JER	junctional escape rhythm
JT	junctional tachycardia
kg	kilogram
L	liter
LA	left atrial
LAE	left atrial enlargement
LAFB	left anterior fascicular block
LAO	left anterior oblique
LBBB	left bundle branch block
LDH	lactate dehydrogenase
LDL	low density lipoprotein
LGL	Lown-Ganong-Levine (syndrome)
LMWH	low molecular weight heparin
LPFB	left posterior fascicular block
LQTS	long QT syndrome
LV	left ventricle
LVEDP	left ventricular end-diastolic pressure
LVEDV	left ventricular end-diastolic volume
LVEF	left ventricular ejection fraction
LVH	left ventricular hypertrophy
LVOT	left ventricular outflow tract

MADIT	Multicenter Automatic Defibrillator Implantation Trial
MAP	mean arterial pressure
MAT	multifocal atrial tachycardia
MBC	minimal bactericidal concentration
meq	milliequivalent
MET	metabolic equivalent
mg	milligram
MHC	major histocompatibility complex
MI	myocardial infarction
MIC	minimal inhibitory concentration
min	minute
mL	milliliter
MR	mitral regurgitation
MRA	magnetic resonance angiography
MRI	magnetic resonance imaging
MS	mitral stenosis
MUSTT	Multicenter Unsustained Tachycardia Trial
MV	mitral valve
MVP	mitral valve prolapse
MVPS	mitral valve prolapse syndrome
NAPA	*N*-acetylprocainamide
NASPE	North American Society of Pacing and Electrophysiology
NE	norepinephrine
ng	nanogram
NPO	non per os (nothing by mouth)
NTG	nitroglycerin
NVE	native valve endocarditis
NYHA	New York Heart Association
OCP	oral contraceptive pill
PA	pulmonary artery
PAT	paroxysmal atrial tachycardia
PCWP	pulmonary capillary wedge pressure
PDA	patent ductus arteriosus
PEA	pulseless electrical activity
PE	pulmonary embolism
PET	positron emission tomography
PFO	patent foramen ovale
pg	picogram
PND	paroxysmal nocturnal dyspnea

PR	pulmonic regurgitation
PRA	plasma renin activity
PS	pulmonary stenosis
PTCA	percutaneous transluminal coronary angioplasty
PTRA	percutaneous transluminal renal angioplasty
PV	pulmonic valve
PVE	prosthetic valve endocarditis
PVOD	pulmonary vascular obstructive disease
PVR	pulmonary vascular resistance
RA	right atrium
RAA	renin-angiotensin-aldosterone system
RAD	right axis deviation
RAO	right anterior oblique
RBBB	right bundle branch block
RCM	restrictive cardiomyopathy
RF	radiofrequency (catheter ablation)
RHD	rheumatic heart disease
RMVT	repetitive monomorphic ventricular tachycardia
r-PA	reteplase
rt-PA	recombinant tissue plasminogen activator
RV	right ventricle
RVH	right ventricular hypertrophy
RVMI	right ventricular myocardial infarction
RVOT	right ventricular outflow tract
SA	sinoatrial
SACT	sinoatrial conduction time
SAM	systolic anterior motion
SBE	subacute bacterial endocarditis
SBP	systolic blood pressure
SCD	sudden cardiac death
SGOT	serum glutamic-oxaloacetic transaminase
SK	streptokinase
SLE	systemic lupus erythematosus
sp.	species
SPAF-I	Stroke Prevention in Atrial Fibrillation Trial
SSS	sick sinus syndrome
SVC	superior vena cava
SVR	systemic vascular resistance

SVT	supraventricular tachycardia
TAA	thoracic aortic aneurysm
TB	tuberculosis
TEE	transesophageal echocardiography
TFB	trifascicular block
TNF	tumor necrosis factor
TPR	total peripheral resistance
TR	tricuspid regurgitation
TS	tricuspid stenosis
TSPI	toe systolic pressure index
TTE	transthoracic echocardiography
TV	tricuspid valve
VAD	ventricular assist device
VEB	ventricular escape beat
VF	ventricular fibrillation
VPC	ventricular premature contraction
VSD	ventricular septal defect
VT	ventricular tachycardia
WPW	Wolff-Parkinson-White (syndrome)

Coronary Artery Disease

Dennis A. Tighe
Mark N. Porway
Edward K. Chung

Coronary artery disease (CAD) is the leading cause of morbidity and mortality in Western society. Each year almost 700,000 Americans die from complications of CAD, and more than 1 million myocardial infarctions (MI) occur. The economic impact of CAD on American society exceeded $90 billion in 1997. Atherosclerosis is a progressive disease that most often produces clinical symptoms in middle to late adulthood. Depending on the severity of the underlying lesions and biologic triggers, a spectrum of clinical syndromes ranging from stable angina pectoris to acute coronary syndromes and ischemic sudden death may occur. This chapter reviews the clinical syndromes associated with CAD, diagnostic approaches, and the available therapeutic options.

Risk Factors for Coronary Artery Disease

Because CAD is the leading cause of death and morbidity in the United States, the identification of risk factors that may contribute to and/or accelerate the atherosclerotic process has great public health implications.

It is not uncommon for a patient without a single risk factor to suffer from the complications of CAD; however, the majority of patients coming to clinical attention possess one or more of the established risk factors.

1

Major Risk Factors

Hereditary (Genetic) Factor
- Familial aggregation of CAD is well established.
- Premature development (age less than 55 years) of CAD among first-degree relatives increases the risk two to fivefold of an individual developing CAD.

Diabetes Mellitus
- Diabetes has macrovascular and microvascular effects on the heart.
- Age-adjusted death rates for diabetics are twice those of nondiabetics. The vast majority of excess mortality is due to CAD.
- Other risk factors such as hyperlipidemia, hypertension (HTN), and obesity frequently coexist.

Cigarette Smoking
- Cigarette smoking enhances the risk of developing atherosclerosis by a variety of mechanisms including altered lipid metabolism, increased coronary vasomotor tone, altered hematologic parameters, endothelial cell dysfunction, and diminished response to antihypertensive agents.

Hypertension
- HTN is associated with increased morbidity and mortality from stroke and CAD. Treatment of HTN has led to a significant decline in vascular mortality over the past three decades.

Hyperlipidemia
- The risk of MI and cardiovascular death increases sharply above a total cholesterol level exceeding 240 mg/dL.
- It is important to fractionate serum lipids. Low serum high density lipoprotein (HDL <35 mg/dL), increased low density lipoprotein (LDL), and increased lipoprotein(a) are associated with increased risk for the development of CAD.

Level of Physical Activity
- Lack of regular physical activity is a risk factor for development of CAD.
- The mechanism of benefit afforded by regular

physical activity is multifactorial and involves improved glucose tolerance, increased HDL levels, decreased LDL levels, lesser incidence of obesity, and improved HTN control.

Obesity

- Obesity, defined as body weight greater than 20% to 30% above ideal body weight, adversely affects health and decreases longevity.
- Obese patients frequently possess other risk factors for CAD including HTN, hyperlipidemia, and impaired glucose tolerance.
- The distribution of body fat plays an important role. Intra-abdominal fat deposition poses a greater cardiovascular risk than peripheral obesity.

Other Potential Risk Factors

Estrogen Deficiency

- Premenopausal women have a lower incidence of CAD compared to men of similar age that is believed to be secondary to differences in the relative levels of estrogens and androgenic hormones.

Oral Contraceptive Pills (OCPs)

- OCPs contain both estrogen and progesterone in varying combinations. Their use per se does not increase cardiovascular risk.
- In patients with past thromboembolic events, other coronary risk factors, and advanced age, OCPs may increase the risk of a vascular event and should be used with caution.

Ethanol Consumption

- Alcohol use, in moderate amounts, may decrease the risk of developing CAD. The consumption of red wine has been shown to be associated with a lower risk of CAD. This benefit may extend to other forms of alcohol.
- Excessive ethanol consumption has a number of negative effects on the heart and may increase the risk of development of coronary atherosclerosis through alterations of lipid metabolism and increased levels of BP.

Psychosocial Stress

- A statistical association between emotional distress and the development of CAD has not been firmly established.

Homocysteine

- Homocysteine is an intermediate formed during the metabolism of methionine. Metabolism of methionine is complex, and is dependent on cofactors which include vitamins B6 and B12 and folic acid.
- Interest in homocysteine as a risk factor for CAD stems from the observation that patients with homocysteinuria, a rare autosomal recessive disease, experience a very high incidence of premature vascular disease.
- Among patients with premature CAD, elevated plasma homocysteine levels have been found.

CHRONIC STABLE ANGINA PECTORIS

Myocardial ischemia results from an imbalance between myocardial oxygen demand and supply. The heart, as an aerobic organ, relies upon oxidative metabolism for energy generation and can only incur a small oxygen debt.

Myocardial oxygen consumption (demand) sets the ischemic threshold and has three primary determinants:

1. Heart rate (HR)
2. Systolic wall tension
3. Myocardial contractility
   Myocardial oxygen supply is dependent on the oxygen carrying capacity of the blood and coronary blood flow.

- *Coronary blood flow* in turn is dependent on a number of independent factors including the driving gradient from the aorta to the resistance vessels, the coronary collateral circulation, extravascular compressive forces, hormonal and neural influences on vasomotor tone, autoregulation, and the functional integrity of the endothelium.
- Under basal conditions, coronary stenosis in excess of

80 to 90% luminal diameter is required to compromise flow; whereas with exertion, a narrowing exceeding 60% to 70% diameter can cause myocardial ischemia.

Clinical Presentation

History

Exertional chest discomfort, relieved by rest, is the hallmark of angina pectoris.

Description of Discomfort

- The discomfort ("pain") is characteristically described as a dull or heavy sensation but may be sharp or burning in nature.
- It is typically retrosternal, but it may radiate to the neck, jaw, teeth, arms, interscapular region, or upper abdomen.
- Anginal discomfort tends to be remarkably reproducible with certain levels of physical activity, and generally lasts 1 to 5 minutes.

Associated Symptoms

- Associated symptoms may include shortness of breath, nausea, vomiting, and diaphoresis.

Causes

- Precipitating causes include physical exertion, emotional distress, exposure to cold weather, recumbent position (angina decubitus), postprandial state, and smoking.

Relief

- Angina is usually abolished by rest or within 1 to 2 minutes by nitroglycerin.

Comments

- Significant limitations exist in regards to the history for angina pectoris. Numerous noncoronary cardiac and noncardiac disorders may cause discomfort clinically indistinguishable from angina pectoris (Table 1-1).
- A significant number of patients have episodes of silent myocardial ischemia or atypical symptoms

Table 1-1. Noncoronary Differential Diagnosis of Chest Pain

Noncoronary Cardiac Causes
Acute pericarditis
Pulmonary embolism
Severe pulmonary HTN
Dissecting hematoma of the thoracic aorta
Mitral valve prolapse syndrome
Aortic valve disease
Myocarditis and cardiomyopathy
Cardiac vasculitis
Myocardial contusion

Pulmonary Causes
Spontaneous pneumothorax
Pleuritis
Pneumonitis

Gastrointestinal Causes
Gastroesophageal reflux disease
Esophageal spasm
Esophageal rupture
Biliary colic
Peptic ulcer disease
Hiatus hernia
Acute pancreatitis
Achalasia

Musculoskeletal and Neural Causes
Tietze's syndrome
Cervical radiculopathy
Thoracic outlet syndrome
Dermatomal herpes zoster
Chest wall injury

Neuropsychiatric Causes
Depression
Neurocirculatory asthenia (anxiety)
Malingering

such as dyspnea or nausea. This is especially true among the elderly and those with diabetes.
- Some patients may significantly curtail activity to minimize episodes of chest discomfort or be limited by vascular claudication.
- Fleeting episodes of pain (lasting only a few seconds) or prolonged chest discomfort (lasting many hours to days) are not usually due to CAD.

Physical Examination

The physical examination should have two goals:

1. Detect signs of cardiovascular disease.
2. Search for clues that may implicate a noncoronary cause of chest discomfort.

Specific Checks

- Pulse contour should be assessed for signs of adequate perfusion. Vascular bruits should be sought.
- Particular attention should be directed to the cardiac examination especially for murmurs, signs of pulmonary HTN, gallops sounds, rubs, and an LV apical lift (associated with dyskinetic myocardium).
- The eye grounds should be carefully evaluated to exclude effects of chronic HTN or diabetes on the retina.
- Corneal arcus and xanthelasma are correlated with abnormalities of plasma lipid metabolism; however, these signs are nonspecific in older individuals.
- Tendinous xanthoma is indicative of a lipid disorder.
- Pulmonary auscultation may reveal signs of central congestion.

Diagnostic Testing

Electrocardiogram (ECG)

- The resting ECG is often normal in patients with stable angina not having pain at the time of the test.
- In patients with silent myocardial ischemia or prior MI, abnormal Q waves, abnormalities of the T wave (such as peaking or inversion), and ST segment changes may be present.
- During episodes of spontaneous pain, horizontal or downsloping ST segment depression of ≥1 mm is highly indicative of myocardial ischemia in the absence of resting ST segment abnormalities.
- ST segment elevation is noted during episodes of variant (Prinzmetal's) angina.

Exercise ECG (Stress) Test

Purpose

- The exercise ECG is the most widely used test to diagnose CAD. It is most effectively applied in patients with an intermediate pretest likelihood of CAD.
- In patients with known CAD, the exercise ECG can be utilized to determine the response to therapy and/or determine long-term prognosis based on the extent of exercise performed.

Protocol

- The various exercise protocols are designed to gradually increase myocardial workload. The standard Bruce multistage protocol or its modified version is most commonly used.

Accuracy

- For all patients referred for testing, the sensitivity and specificity of the exercise ECG is approximately 60% to 70%.
- Test accuracy is increased when multivessel disease is present, when symptoms typical of angina occur, with greater degrees of ST segment depression, and when adverse hemodynamic findings occur.
- Use of this test in those with a high or low pretest likelihood of CAD may lead to false-negative or false-positive results, respectively, as shown by the application of Bayes' theorem.

Interpretation

- The diagnosis of myocardial ischemia is suggested by the development of ≥1 mm horizontal or downsloping ST segment depression (in the absence of resting ST abnormalities) persisting 80 msec or more after the J-point during exercise or in the recovery period—especially if typical chest discomfort is reproduced.
- Multivessel CAD is suggested by exercise-induced hypotension (decline in SBP ≥10 mm Hg), severe ST depression (≥2 mm) at a low workload (≤5 METS), failure to increase heart rate to >120 bpm (off beta-blockers), and persistent ST segment depression in 5

or more leads lasting ≥5 minutes into the postexercise recovery period.

- Inconclusive tests warrant further testing (myocardial imaging, pharmacologic stress, or coronary arteriography) to confirm a diagnosis of CAD.

Myocardial Imaging

- Myocardial imaging techniques (radionuclide perfusion agents, echocardiography) provide noninvasive assessment of myocardial blood flow and/or global and regional myocardial function during stress.
- Imaging techniques enhance the sensitivity and specificity of the exercise ECG test and should be utilized when the exercise test is nondiagnostic or false-positive or false-negative results are anticipated.

Radionuclide perfusion

Protocol

- Currently available perfusion agents include thallium-201, technetium-99m sestamibi, technetium-99m tetrafosmin, and technetium-99m teboroxime.
- Thallium-201 and technetium-99m sestamibi are the most widely used.
- The perfusion agent is administered at peak stress.
- With thallium-201, imaging must commence within 10 minutes after stress. Delayed (rest) images are obtained 3 to 4 hours later.
- With technetium-99m sestamibi, separate rest and stress injections are required. Poststress imaging usually begins within 1 hour of injection; resting images are obtained on another day or in a separate session on the same day.

Interpretation

- Perfusion defects are assessed on both a qualitative and quantitative basis. Defects that are present after stress and that improve or are not present at rest are considered to represent ischemic myocardium. Persistent (fixed) defects noted on both the rest and poststress scans may represent scarred myocardium.
- Persistent defects noted on the delayed (rest) thallium scan must be interpreted with caution as

approximately 50% will redistribute on 24-hour delayed or re-injection imaging, indicating viable myocardium.

- In addition to diagnosing CAD, perfusion imaging can confer important information about long-term prognosis—especially the extent of perfusion abnormality present and number of myocardial segments involved. High-risk scans are identified by stress-induced lung uptake of radioisotope, LV cavity dilatation, and a multivessel disease pattern on quantitative assessment.

Stress echocardiography

- Stress echocardiography (with either physical exercise or pharmacologic simulation—especially dobutamine) is gaining popularity for the assessment of CAD because of its portability, the lack of exposure to ionizing radiation, the brief amount of imaging time required to perform a full test compared to perfusion agents, and its ability to yield rapid reports.
- The major limitation of stress echocardiography is that inadequate transthoracic images are obtained in as many as 10% of patients.

Protocol

- Images are obtained at baseline, during stress (as in the case of dobutamine), and immediately after stress (in the case of exercise).

Interpretation

- The normal response to stress is thickening and hypercontractile wall motion in all myocardial regions.
- An abnormal stress echocardiogram is indicated by the development of a new regional wall motion abnormality or failure of a region to augment with stress.
- Potentially viable myocardium can be accurately assessed by dobutamine echocardiography. A "biphasic response," augmented contractility at low dose ($\leq 10\,\mu g/kg/min$) with subsequent deterioration of function at higher infused doses, is characteristic of hibernating myocardium.

Alternate Diagnostic Testing

For patients unable to exercise adequately, other modes of stress testing are available.

Pharmacologic Testing Available agents include vasodilators (dipyridamole, adenosine) and positive inotropic agents (dobutamine, arbutamine).

- **Vasodilators.** Dipyridamole and adenosine are potent intravenous (IV) vasodilators which can increase coronary blood flow four- to fivefold over basal levels. Flow heterogeneity is produced between normal arterial beds which dilate maximally in response to vasodilator infusion, and those subtended by stenotic arteries which dilate less. ST segment depression during vasodilator infusion is a highly specific, but insensitive, marker for the diagnosis of CAD.
- **Dobutamine.** Dobutamine is a synthetic catecholamine with positive inotropic and chronotropic effects. A graded infusion of dobutamine (2.5 µg/kg/min up to 50 µg/kg/min with supplemental atropine if target heart rate is not achieved) is used. Myocardial ischemia is indicated by a reversible nuclear scan defect (if perfusion agents are used) or development of a new regional wall motion abnormality and/or failure of appropriate augmentation on echocardiography.
- **Arbutamine.** Like dobutamine, arbutamine is a synthetic catecholamine. A computer-controlled, HR-feedback ("closed-loop") IV delivery system is designed to infuse arbutamine according to the rate of the HR increase (HR slope) up to a predetermined target HR. The side effect profile and clinical efficacy of arbutamine appear similar to dobutamine. Due to high cost, arbutamine has found limited clinical use.

Concomitant myocardial imaging is required with all pharmacologic stress testing agents because ST segment shifts are infrequent.

Detection of Coronary Artery Calcification Fluoroscopy, helical CT scanning, and electron beam (ultrafast) CT scanning can identify coronary calcium.

Electron beam (ultrafast) CT scanning (EBCT) EBCT can localize calcium and quantify its amount or volume. In addition, EBCT can detect smaller and less dense calcium deposits as compared to the other techniques.

- Among patients with chest pain, the absence of calcium on EBCT implies the absence of significant angiographic coronary stenosis, but does not exclude the presence of atherosclerosis.
- The presence of calcium on EBCT implies the presence of atherosclerotic plaque and may indicate increased risk of a coronary event in the following 2 to 5 years. EBCT does not localize the site of coronary stenosis.

Cardiac Catheterization Coronary angiography and left ventriculography are indicated when a definitive diagnosis of CAD is required.

Indications
- Indications for coronary arteriography in patients with stable angina include poor control of angina with medical therapy, a change in the usual pattern of angina, a markedly abnormal result of a stress test, atypical symptoms with equivocal results on noninvasive testing, certain high-risk occupations, and occasionally for employment or insurance purposes.

Precautions
- Cardiac catheterization is associated with a 0.05% to 0.1% incidence of death, MI, or stroke and a 0.6% incidence of vascular complications.

Results
- Among patients with stable angina, the incidence of critical narrowing ($\geq$70% of the luminal diameter by visual estimate) involving one, two, or three major epicardial coronary arteries is approximately 25% for each category. Approximately 5% to 10% have critical narrowing ($\geq$50% of the luminal diameter) of the left main coronary artery. Nonobstructive disease is found in 15% to 20%.

Treatment

The therapy of stable angina is directed at a number of aspects:

1. Identification of underlying atherosclerotic risk factors
2. Assessment of the extent of underlying disease and LV function to identify patients at highest risk of a future cardiac event
3. Nonpharmacologic therapies aimed at changes in lifestyle
4. Specific pharmacologic therapies
5. Revascularization procedures

Identification and Modification of Coronary Risk Factors

Major risk factors for coronary atherosclerosis should be identified. In particular, remediable risk factors such as smoking, HTN, hyperlipidemia, obesity, and inactivity should be modified to the extent possible. The physician should involve patients in the therapy of their disease.

- Referral to a dietitian and smoking cessation programs may help to reinforce compliance.
- Advise the patient to avoid activities that provoke chest discomfort.
- Advise the patient about the appropriate level of physical exertion and work activities that may be performed. For example, sexual activity is equivalent to climbing one flight of stairs at a normal pace; with appropriate precautions (including premedication with nitroglycerin in some cases), it may be undertaken with safety in the majority of patients.
- Instruct patients in the proper use of their medications and when to seek medical attention (for example, with an escalation of, or change in, symptom complex).

Identification of High Risk Patients The physician must define the extent of underlying CAD and LV function to formulate an accurate prognosis for the patient.

- Stress ECG and nuclear perfusion studies (as described above) can be predictors of prognosis.
- Left main or three-vessel disease with marked LV dysfunction as demonstrated by cardiac catheterization is also a predictor of adverse outcome.

Pharmacologic Therapy

Angina pectoris is caused by an imbalance between myocardial oxygen supply and demand. Pharmacologic therapy is directed at modifying the factors that can augment myocardial oxygen supply or reduce myocardial oxygen demand.

Table 1-2 lists the currently available pharmacologic therapies.

Table 1-2. Pharmacologic Therapy of Angina Pectoris

Drug	Trade Name	Dose Range (mg)	Frequency
Nitrates			
Isosorbide dinitrate	Isordil, Dilatrate, Sorbitrate	10–60	three or four times daily
Isosorbide mononitrate	Imdur; Ismo, Monoket	30–240; 20	once daily; twice daily 7 hours apart
Nitroglycerin transdermal	Deponit, Nitrodur, Transdermnitro	2.5–20	once daily
Nitroglycerin sublingual	Nitro-stat, Nitrolingual spray; Isordil, Sorbitrate	0.3–0.4; 2.5–5	as needed; as needed
Beta-Blocking Drugs			
Acebutolol[a,b]	Sectral	200–600	twice daily
Atenolol[a]	Tenormin	25–100	once daily
Betoxolol[a]	Kerlone	10–20	once daily
Bisoprolol[a]	Zebeta	2.5–20	once daily
Carteolol[b]	Cartrol	2.5–10	once daily
Esmolol[a]	Breviblock	500 µg/kg (load); 100–300 µg/kg/min (maintenance)	IV infusion
Labetolol[c]	Trandate, Normodyne	100–1200	twice daily
Metoprolol[a]	Lopressor	25–200	twice daily

Table 1-2. (continued)

Table 1-2. (continued) Pharmacologic Therapy of Angina Pectoris

Drug	Trade Name	Dose Range (mg)	Frequency
Metoprolol, long acting[a]	Toprol XL	50–400	once daily
Nadolol	Corgard	40–320	once daily
Penbutolol	Levatol	20–80	once daily
Pindolol[b]	Visken	5–30	twice daily
Propranolol	Inderal	20–80	twice to four times daily
Propranolol, long acting	Inderal LA	80–320	once daily
Timolol	Blocadren	10–30	twice daily
Calcium Channel Blockers			
Amlodipine	Norvasc	2.5–10	once daily
Bepridil	Vascor	200–400	once daily
Diltiazem	Cardizem	30–120	three or four times daily
Diltiazem, sustained release	Cardizem SR	60–180	twice daily
Diltiazem, continuous delivery	Cardizem CD, Dilacor XR, Tiazac	120–360	once daily
Nicardipine	Cardene	20–40	three times daily
Nicardipine, long acting	Cardene SR	30–60	twice daily
Nifedipine	Procardia, Adalat	10–60	three times daily
Nifedipine, long acting	Procardia XL, Adalat CC	30–120	once daily
Verapamil	Calan, Isoptin	80–160	twice or three times daily
Verapamil, long acting	Calan SR, Isoptin SR, Verelan, Covera HS	180–480	once daily

[a] Cardioselective.

[b] ISA.

[c] Alpha- and beta-blocker.

Nitrates

- Nitrates are vasoactive agents with effects on the veins and arteries. Venodilatation increases venous capacitance, decreases venous return to the heart, and decreases systolic wall tension, lowering myocardial oxygen demand. Dilatation of arterial vessels also decreases myocardial oxygen demand. Myocardial oxygen supply is augmented in part by vasodilatation of the epicardial coronary arteries and coronary collateral circulation.

- Coronary artery spasm is relieved by nitrates.
- Nitrates can be used in the immediate and long-term therapy of angina pectoris.

Nitroglycerin

Sublingual Forms
- Sublingual nitroglycerin (NTG) as a tablet (0.3–0.4 mg) or aerosol (0.4 mg/spray) is the drug of choice for infrequent episodes of angina.
- NTG is the most important agent for an acute attack of angina due to its short onset of action (1 to 2 minutes). In the acute situation, the sublingual dose may be repeated every 5 minutes until chest discomfort is relieved or three tablets have been used. If chest discomfort is not relieved by 3 sublingual NTG tablets, the patient should be instructed to seek medical attention.

To ensure adequate potency, the tablets should be prescribed within the preceding 6 months and must not be directly exposed to sunlight.

Long-acting nitrates Long-acting nitrates may be administered by the sublingual, buccal, oral, or topical route. Tolerance to long-acting NTG preparations is a well-described clinical phenomenon, thus nitrate-free intervals should be provided.

Isosorbide dinitrate
- Isosorbide dinitrate is available as an oral preparation. Sublingual and buccal administration of isosorbide dinitrate is effective, but impractical for long-term use due to its short duration of action.
- The dinitrate form undergoes extensive first-pass hepatic metabolism.

Isosorbide mononitrate
- Isosorbide mononitrate is the active form of the dinitrate and is completely bioavailable because it does not undergo rapid hepatic degradation.

Topical Forms
- **NTG ointment** (15 mg/inch) is used in dosages of 0.5 to 2 inches every 6 to 8 hours.

- **Transdermal NTG patch systems** come in a variety of dosages and are designed to provide controlled release of NTG through a semipermeable membrane continuously over a 24-hour period.

Beta-Blocking Agents Beta-blockers bind to the myocardial β-1 receptor to competitively inhibit the binding of catecholamines to the receptor site. HR and myocardial contractility are diminished, reducing myocardial oxygen demand.

- A secondary effect of beta-blockers is lowering of BP with further beneficial effects on oxygen consumption.
- Optimal beta-blockade is achieved when symptoms are substantially diminished and the resting HR is 50 to 60 beats per minute.
- The beta-blockers are classified by their ability to selectively inhibit the β-1 receptor which predominates in the heart. Agents that inhibit only the β-1 receptor are termed *cardioselective*. Agents that also inhibit the β-2 receptor are termed *nonselective*.

Cardioselective agents Cardioselective beta-blockers theoretically do not cause bronchoconstriction and do not inhibit peripheral vasodilatation nor glycogenolysis. However, cardioselectivity is lost at higher doses.

- Currently available cardioselective agents include metoprolol, atenolol, acebutolol, betoxolol, bisoprolol, and esmolol.
- Esmolol a short-acting (half-life 9 minutes), IV, cardioselective beta-blocker is most useful in situations where longer acting agents may be contraindicated (reactive airways disease, relative hypotension) because of its short half-life.

Nonselective agents
- Nonselective agents include propranolol, nadolol, timolol, pindolol.
- Labetolol, a combined alpha- and nonselective beta-blocking agent, is useful in patients with HTN.

Intrinsic Sympathomimetic Agents (ISA) Agents with ISA offer partial agonist activity at low levels of beta-stimulation with less resultant reduction of HR and contractility.

- ISA agents may not be as effective as non-ISA drugs for nocturnal angina and in patients with severe symptoms.
- Agents without ISA cause short-term decreases in plasma HDL and increases in triglyceride levels. The long-term clinical significance is unknown.

Side effects
- Class effects include sinus bradycardia, sinus arrest, AV block, CHF, bronchoconstriction, CNS effects, sexual dysfunction, fatigue, gastrointestinal (GI) upset, and masking of insulin-induced hypoglycemic episodes.
- Agents with high lipid solubility (propranolol, metoprolol, and pindolol) may cross the blood-brain barrier causing side effects such as sleep disturbances, depression, fatigue, and weakness. If these side effects are prominent, agents with less lipid solubility may be substituted.
- Abrupt withdrawal of beta-blockers in patients with known CAD may lead to enhanced ischemia and MI.

Contraindications Contraindications to the use of beta-blockers include:

Advanced AV block without a pacemaker in place
Asthma
CHF
Severe peripheral vascular disease
Known hypersensitivity

Calcium Channel Blockers (CCBs) Alone, or in combination with nitrates, CCBs are the treatment of choice for variant angina (coronary vasospasm) and angina in patients with chronic lung disease or bronchospasm.

The CCBs approved for the treatment of angina pectoris are a heterogeneous group of compounds with varied clinical effects.

Dihydropyridine compounds The dihydropyridines (nifedipine, nicardipine, and amlodipine) have the most marked vasodilatory effect and the least effect on contractility and AV node conduction. A dihydropyridine is the CCB of choice with conduction system abnormalities and LV dysfunction.

Nifedipine
- The effective dose ranges from 30–180 mg per day.
- Side effects include headache, dizziness, peripheral edema, nausea, hypotension, and reflex tachycardia.
- Controversy surrounds the use of short-acting nifedipine preparations in moderate to high doses (>80 mg/day). An increased risk of mortality among patients with CAD is reported. Based on available data, it is prudent not to use short-acting nifedipine in ischemic heart disease. This recommendation does not appear to apply to long-acting dihydropyridines and other classes of CCBs.

Nicardipine and amlodipine
- Nicardipine and amlodipine have side effect profiles similar to long-acting nifedipine preparations.
- Doses of 60–120 mg per day of nicardipine are generally effective in patients with chronic angina. Amlodipine is administered as a once daily dose of 5–10 mg.

Verapamil   Verapamil, a papaverine derivative, has the most pronounced depressive effects on AV nodal conduction and contractility and the least vasodilatory effect.

- Verapamil is supplied in oral and IV forms, but only the oral form is approved for use in angina. Effective daily dose ranges from 120–480 mg.
- Side effects include headache, hypotension, constipation, CHF, symptomatic bradycardia, and nausea. Verapamil can increase serum digoxin levels by approximately 70%, increase cyclosporin levels, and cause profound AV block or worsen CHF when used in combination with beta-blockers.

Diltiazem   Diltiazem, a benzothiazepine derivative, has physiologic effects intermediate between the dihydropyridines and verapamil.

- Diltiazem is available in oral and IV forms. Only the oral preparations are approved for use in angina. Effective doses range between 120 and 480 mg per day.
- Diltiazem can have profound effects on AV node conduction and may exacerbate CHF. Diltiazem also may increase serum lithium and cyclosporin levels and its use should be monitored closely in patients receiving concomitant beta-blocker therapy.

Bepridil   Bepridil, a potent vasodilator, has profound electrophysiologic (EP) effects which include slowing of the HR, prolongation of ventricular and atrial effective refractory periods, and QT-interval prolongation.

- Because of its marked EP effects, including the risk of torsades de pointes, bepridil is currently indicated only for patients who have failed to respond optimally to or who are intolerant of other anti-anginal medications.
- Frequent ECGs are indicated to monitor the QT interval.

Aspirin (ASA)   ASA (75–325 mg every day) has been demonstrated to decrease the risk of future coronary events among treated patients (some with prior cardiac events). Therefore, ASA use is probably indicated in patients with chronic angina without a prior cardiac event.

Estrogen Replacement Therapy

Rationale
- Epidemiologic study reveals that women who experience menopause prior to age 40 years have a fourfold higher incidence of CAD compared to women of the same age who have not undergone menopause.
- Estrogen replacement therapy is associated with an approximately 44% risk reduction for cardiac events.

Side Effects
- The use of estrogen (such as premarin 0.625 mg/d) in postmenopausal women must be tempered by potential side effects including increased risk of

endometrial cancer (in the presence of intact uterus), uterine bleeding, and increased risk of breast cancer. Addition of a progestin compound to estrogen may decrease the risk of endometrial cancer and bleeding, but the cardiovascular benefit of estrogen may be compromised.

Revascularization Therapy

Revascularization procedures include catheter-based interventions—percutaneous transluminal coronary angioplasty (PCTA), laser angioplasty, rotational atherectomy, excisional (directional) coronary atherectomy, extraction atherectomy, metallic expandable intracoronary stents—and coronary artery bypass surgery (CABG).

Catheter-Based Interventions PTCA and other catheter-based interventions can be used in patients showing objective evidence of ischemia and anatomy suitable for revascularization.

Standard percutaneous transluminal coronary angioplasty (PTCA) Among patients with single vessel CAD and exercise induced myocardial ischemia, standard PTCA offers earlier and more complete relief of angina and better exercise tolerance as compared to maximal medical therapy. However, PTCA has offered no survival advantage over medical therapy. Higher cost and a higher frequency of early complications are encountered in those undergoing PTCA.

- **Rate of Success:** PTCA success is related to factors specific to the lesion types and patient characteristics.

Lesion Types

ACC/AHA type A lesions (discrete, readily accessible, noncalcified) have an anticipated success rate in excess of 90%.

ACC/AHA type B lesions (tubular, eccentric, moderately tortuous, and calcified) have a success rate of 60% to 90%.

ACC/AHA type C lesions (diffuse, complex, total occlusion >3 months) have a success rate of <60%.

Characteristics of Low-Risk Patients

Age <70 years

Male
Single-vessel and single-lesion CAD
No CHF
LV ejection fraction >40%
Stable pattern of angina
Type A lesion of <90% luminal diameter

Characteristics of Increased-Risk Patients
Age >70 years
Female
Multivessel and multilesional CAD
History of CHF
Diabetes mellitus
LV ejection fraction <40%
Left main equivalent CAD
Type B or C lesions
PTCA for unstable angina or immediately following
   thrombolytic therapy

- **Procedural success rate:** Procedural "success rate" is
  usually defined as achievement of a ≥20% change in
  luminal diameter with the final diameter stenosis
  being <50% and without the occurrence of death,
  acute MI, or need for emergent CABG.

- **Complications:** Major complications of PTCA
  include:
  Death (1%)
  MI (1% to 5%)
  Need for emergent CABG (1% to 3%)
  Abrupt closure (4% to 8%)
  Coronary artery spasm
  - *Abrupt Closure.* The availability of the intra-
    coronary stent has significantly reduced the risk of
    abrupt closure and the need for emergent CABG.
  - *Restenosis.* Restenosis due to intimal hyperplasia
    and elastic recoil occurs in 30% to 50% of patients
    within 6 months of the procedure. No adjunctive
    medical therapy to date has decreased the
    incidence of restenosis.

Adjunctive use of glycoprotein IIb-IIIa inhibitors
Recent attention has been focused on the use of a new
class of antiplatelet agents directed against the platelet

glycoprotein IIb-IIIa receptor (responsible for platelet aggregation).

- Abciximab (Reopro) has been shown to decrease the incidence of major adverse events during higher-risk catheter-based interventions.
- Numerous trials involving IIb-IIIa inhibitors are currently under way for various coronary syndromes, including both stable and unstable angina, as well as with and without thrombolytic agents for treatment of ST elevation MIs.

Laser angioplasty and rotational coronary atherectomy
Laser angioplasty and rotational coronary atherectomy devices debulk atheromatous plaques and may also affect plaque compliance.

- Rotational atherectomy has been shown to be particularly effective when treating lesions that are long, heavily calcified, ostial in location, or involving bifurcations. The use of these devices often requires adjunctive PTCA to achieve an acceptable angiographic result.
- Laser angioplasty and rotational atherectomy appear to offer no advantage in terms of restenosis as compared to standard PTCA but these procedures may allow attempts at lesions not favorable for PTCA.

Balloon-expandable intra-coronary stents Balloon-expandable intra-coronary stents act as intravascular scaffolds to maintain initial lumen gain and prevent elastic recoil after PTCA.

Advantages
- Stenting increases the initial gain in lumen diameter and diminishes elastic recoil as compared to standard PTCA.
- Data indicate improved clinical outcome, less need for revascularization procedures, and a lower rate of angiographic restenosis at 6 to 7 months for de novo stented lesions as compared to standard PTCA (22% to 32% versus 32% to 42%). Clinical and angiographic outcomes up to 3 years following

stenting are favorable compared to standard PTCA.

- A stent can also be used as a "bail-out" device for failed PTCA with threatened abrupt vessel closure due to intimal dissection.
- Stents can also be implanted in stenotic saphenous vein graft lesions with good procedural success, although restenosis rates remain high.
- Stent implantation via the radial artery has been reported to be safe and may potentially allow stents to be placed on an outpatient basis.

Limitations
- Current limitations include the risk of subacute stent thrombosis and the requirement for a vessel diameter of 3 mm or more.

Treatment
- Predilatation of the lesion with a PTCA balloon is required prior to stent deployment.
- Intravascular ultrasound, as an adjunctive procedure at the time of stenting, may aid optimal stent deployment and improve short-term outcome.
- Combined antiplatelet therapy (ticlopidine, 250 mg twice a day, and aspirin, 325 mg daily) has been shown to reduce vascular and bleeding complications following stent placement as compared to high-intensity anticoagulation. Ticlopidine is continued for 2 to 4 weeks following implantation and then stopped. Blood counts should be obtained weekly during therapy because neutropenia is a side effect of ticlopidine. ASA is continued indefinitely.

Directional coronary atherectomy (DCA) DCA devices allow lesion debulking and mechanical removal of atheromatous plaque. Adjunctive PTCA is not absolutely required, but it may be needed to produce an "optimal" angiographic result.

- Trials have shown that DCA, when compared to standard PTCA, leads to an initially larger acute gain in lumen size and a slight trend toward decreased rate of angiographic restenosis.

- DCA is associated with more procedure-related complications, and clinical outcome does not appear to be superior to standard PTCA.

Coronary Artery Bypass Surgery (CABG) CABG surgery is indicated in patients with significant narrowing of the left main coronary artery, triple-vessel CAD with LV dysfunction, single or double-vessel CAD involving the proximal anterior descending artery, refractory angina despite adequate medical therapy, lesions not amenable to PTCA, and in failed attempts at catheter-based interventions.

Advantages
- The Coronary Artery Surgery Study (CASS) has demonstrated a survival advantage for patients with chronic angina with left main stenosis and triple-vessel CAD with LV dysfunction who undergo CABG as opposed to continuing medical therapy. In addition to this survival advantage, patients also achieve symptomatic improvement for many years.
- A subgroup analysis of the BARI study indicates that among diabetics with multivessel CAD presenting for a first revascularization procedure, CABG is associated with significantly lower mortality at 5 years as compared to PTCA.

Limitations and Complications
Morbidity and Mortality: Morbidity and mortality due to the operative procedure are related to age, underlying LV function, renal function, diabetes mellitus, and emergency nature of the operation.

Perioperative Complications: Perioperative complications include MI (2% to 5%), deep venous thrombosis and pulmonary embolism, wound infection, cerebrovascular accidents and other serious CNS dysfunction (6%), conduction disturbances, bleeding, and renal dysfunction.

Vein Graft Patency: Saphenous vein graft patency rates depend upon the age of the vein graft.
- *Postoperative period:* Approximately 5 to 10% of vein grafts become thrombotically occluded in the early postoperative period.

- *1 Year:* As many as 15 to 20% of vein grafts occlude by 1 year. Intimal hyperplasia appears to be responsible for vein graft occlusion between 1 month and 1 year.
- *10 Years:* By 10 years, approximately 50% of vein grafts patent at 5 years have become occluded by a process indistinguishable from coronary atherosclerosis.

IMA Graph Patency: The internal mammary artery (IMA) is rarely involved with atherosclerosis. When used to bypass to a coronary artery, atherosclerotic changes occur in less than 10% of IMA grafts at 10 years after CABG, a significant advantage over vein grafting.

Minimally invasive cardiac surgery   "Minimally invasive" cardiac surgery—performed without median sternotomy and need for cardiopulmonary bypass—is being performed in selected patients. Preliminary data indicate that this technique is feasible and allows early hospital discharge and rapid convalescence.

Transmyocardial Laser Revascularization Among patients with severe CAD not amenable to PTCA or CABG, the creation of full thickness channels through the myocardium in the diseased vascular territory by a laser may bring relief of angina. This procedure remains experimental.

PTCA versus CABG Prospective trials comparing patients with multivessel CAD treated with PTCA or CABG have shown that primary end-points, such as death and Q wave MI, occurred with similar frequency in both groups during follow-up.

- PTCA-treated patients experienced more angina, required more medication, and needed additional revascularization procedures more often.
- CABG surgery is still indicated for patients with significant left main coronary disease, multivessel disease with involvement of the proximal left anterior descending artery, or triple-vessel disease with impaired LV systolic function because surgery improves survival in these situations.
- CABG may be favored among diabetics with

multivessel disease who are candidates for a first revascularization procedure.

- A strategy combining minimally invasive CABG with PTCA (so-called "hybrid revascularization") needs further evaluation, but may be an effective alternative to standard CABG for properly selected patients.

UNSTABLE ANGINA PECTORIS

Unstable angina represents an intermediate syndrome between chronic angina pectoris and MI. A variety of clinical syndromes may be classified as unstable angina:

- Angina of increased frequency and severity (crescendo pattern) superimposed on a pattern of prior stable angina
- Rest angina (within 1 week)
- New onset angina (within 1 to 2 months)
- Angina following recent MI (>24 hours)
- Variant (Prinzmetal's) angina

Unstable angina represents a serious clinical condition associated with increased risk (approximately 15%) of subsequent MI in certain patient subsets. Prognosis is poorest among patients with resting chest discomfort and ischemic ECG changes. Table 1-3 classifies the risk characteristics of patients presenting with symptoms suggesting unstable angina.

Clinical Presentation

History

Description of Pain The predominant complaint is chest discomfort similar in location and character to that of exertional angina. The discomfort is frequently more intense and may last for 20 minutes or more.

- An increased frequency of angina, increased usage of sublingual NTG, or chest discomfort occurring with less physical exertion is often noted.

Classification The Canadian Cardiovascular Society (CCS) Classification of angina is a useful scheme to categorize patients based on provoking factors and limits to usual activity.

Table 1-3. Short-Term Risk of Death or Nonfatal MI in Patients Presenting with Symptoms Suggesting Unstable Angina

High Risk
At least one of the following features must be present:
- Prolonged ongoing (>20 min) rest pain
- Pulmonary edema
- Angina with new/worsening mitral regurgitation murmur
- Rest angina with dynamic ST changes >1 mm
- Angina with S_3 or rales
- Angina with hypotension

Intermediate Risk
No high-risk feature is present, but must have one of the following:
- Rest angina resolved, but not low likelihood of CAD
- Rest angina (>20 min or relieved with rest or NTG)
- Angina with dynamic T wave changes
- Nocturnal angina
- New onset CCSC III or IV angina in the past 2 weeks
- Q waves or ST depression >1 mm in multiple leads
- Age >65 years

Low Risk
No high or intermediate risk feature is present, but must have one of the following:
- Increased angina frequency, severity, or duration
- Angina provoked at a lower threshold
- New onset angina within 2 weeks to 2 months
- Normal or unchanged ECG

CCSC: Canadian Cardiovascular Society Classification; NTG: nitroglycerin
Reproduced with permission from: Braunwald E, et al. Diagnosing and managing unstable angina. Circulation 1994;90:617. Copyright 1994, American Heart Association.

- **Class I** angina is provoked by prolonged exertion with no limitation of ordinary activities.
- **Class II** angina occurs after walking >2 blocks and is associated with slight limitation of ordinary activity.
- **Class III** angina occurs with minimal exertion (walking <2 blocks) and is associated with significant impairment of ordinary activity.
- **Class IV** is resting angina.

Risk Factors
- Multiple risk factors for CAD are often present.
- Other factors such as anemia, infection, fever, thyroid dysfunction, or progression of other cardiac diseases

which may precipitate unstable angina should be sought.

Physical Examination

The physical examination is similar to that of patients with chronic stable angina.

A higher incidence of LV dysfunction may be present, especially among patients with post-MI angina.

Laboratory Examination

Laboratory Tests

- Laboratory values are similar to those in patients with stable angina.
- Enzymatic evidence of acute myocardial necrosis is not present.
- Cardiac troponin T or I may rise above normal levels with a severe episode of unstable angina. Elevated cardiac troponin levels identify a subset of patients at increased risk of cardiac events.

ECG

- Transient episodes of ST segment depression or elevation and T wave inversion are common.
- As the acute ischemic episode is treated, ECG changes usually revert to baseline.
- ECG changes persisting beyond 12 to 24 hours suggest a non-Q wave MI.
- Patients with resting chest discomfort associated with transient ST segment deviation have a higher incidence of MI, death, or need for revascularization during the current hospitalization compared to those without such changes.

Diagnostic Tests

Exercise ECG (Stress) Test   Exercise testing is contraindicated in patients with active unstable angina. After medical stabilization for at least 48 hours, stress testing can be safely performed in many patients.

- Patients with a normal resting ECG and no evidence of ischemia during an exercise test of adequate workload have a low coronary event rate over the ensuing 5 years.

- Patients with inducible ischemia should be referred for coronary angiography.

Coronary Arteriography　Depending upon the population studied, findings among patients with unstable angina may vary considerably (Table 1-4).

- Among patients with progressive angina superimposed upon chronic stable angina, a high incidence of left main and three-vessel CAD is found.
- Among patients with new onset angina without prior stable angina, a higher incidence of single-vessel disease is noted.

Table 1-4. Likelihood of Significant CAD in Patients with Unstable Angina

High Likelihood
Any of the following features:
- Known history of CAD
- Definite angina: men >60, or women >70 years
- Hemodynamic or ECG changes with pain
- Variant angina
- ST increase or decrease >1 mm
- Marked symmetrical T wave inversion in multiple precordial leads

Intermediate Likelihood
Absence of high likelihood features and any of the following:
- Definite angina: men <60, or women <70 years
- Probable angina: men >60, or women >70 years
- Probably not angina in diabetics, or in nondiabetics with >2 other CAD risk factors
- Extracardiac vascular disease
- ST depression 0.5–1.0 mm
- T wave inversion >1 mm in leads with dominant R waves

Low Likelihood
Absence of high or intermediate likelihood features but may have:
- Chest pain, probably not angina
- One CAD risk factor not including diabetes
- T wave flattened or inverted <1 mm in leads with dominant R waves
- Normal ECG

Reproduced with permission from: Braunwald E, et al. Diagnosing and managing unstable angina. Circulation 1994;90:616. Copyright 1994, American Heart Association.

Findings

- The coronary collateral circulation appears less well developed compared to those with stable angina.
- Approximately 15% to 20% of patients referred for coronary angiography with unstable angina have nonobstructive disease.
- Coronary angiography exhibits eccentric stenoses with a narrow neck or overhanging edges (Ambrose type II lesion) in 70% of patients with unstable angina as opposed to a 16% incidence with stable angina pectoris.
- Intraluminal, hazy filling defects consistent with coronary thrombus are noted in many patients. The highest incidence is noted among those with resting chest discomfort within 24 hours of catheterization.
- Left ventriculography usually reveals preserved systolic function, except in those patients who have suffered a previous MI or those with ongoing ischemia at the time of study.

Therapy

The major goal of therapy is to prevent MI and its complications and allow stabilization of the atherosclerotic plaque.

- High-risk patients should be admitted to a monitored unit, placed on strict bed rest, and treated with an intense medical regimen that includes supplemental oxygen (if needed), NTG, heparin (IV most commonly used although subcutaneous low molecular weight heparin (enoxaparin) has documented efficacy), ASA, and beta-blocker. A CCB may be added if needed, or may be substituted for the beta-blocker if contraindications are present.
- Lower-risk patients should be admitted to an intermediate monitored unit. All patients should receive ASA, beta-blockers (provided no contraindications are present), and nitrates. Heparin is not mandatory.
- Patients failing adequate medical therapy should be

referred for coronary arteriography and possible revascularization.

- Patients with continuing chest discomfort refractory to maximal medical therapy and unable to undergo urgent coronary angiography should have intra-aortic balloon counterpulsation as an attempt to stabilize the clinical situation.
- Underlying disease states which may affect the imbalance between myocardial oxygen supply and demand must be promptly identified and treated.
- Serial ECGs and cardiac enzymes should be obtained.
- Low-risk patients and those stabilized on medical therapy without further ischemia or high-risk characteristics should undergo a stress test prior to discharge. If ischemia is induced, coronary angiography should be performed.

Pharmacologic Therapy

Nitrates IV NTG, starting at a dose of 10–20 µg/min and titrated upward (maximum dose usually 200–300 µg/min) as allowed by changes in BP and adequacy of peripheral organ perfusion, should be administered to all patients with acute, severe unstable angina at least for the first 24 hours or until the clinical situation has stabilized. Tolerance to IV NTG begins within 24 hours and may require dosage adjustment.

Topical NTG ointment may be applied for less severe forms of unstable angina.

Beta-Blocking Agents Beta-blockers reduce symptoms of recurrent ischemia when combined with other anti-anginal agents and decrease the occurrence of MI in patients with unstable angina. Unless otherwise contraindicated, beta-blockers should be administered to all patients.

Calcium Channel Blockers As monotherapy, CCBs have not been demonstrated to decrease the risk of MI and death in patients with unstable angina. These agents should be used when contraindications to beta-blockers exist or as additional medical therapy in cases of refractory angina.

Antiplatelet Agents   ASA (81–1300 mg per day) use has been demonstrated to decrease the incidence of cardiac events by approximately 50%.

- ASA should be considered standard therapy of unstable angina. Although the optimal therapeutic dose is unknown, most physicians would recommend 325 mg per day.
- Ticlopidine (250 mg twice a day) or clopidogrel (75 mg per day) should be substituted if a true allergy to ASA use exists.
- Other antiplatelet agents (sulfinpyrazone and dipyridamole) have no clear benefit alone or in combination with ASA for the treatment of unstable angina.

Anticoagulant Therapy   IV heparin, alone or in combination with ASA, has been shown to significantly reduce the incidence of ischemic complications associated with unstable angina. In general, administration of heparin should continue for a prolonged period (48 to 96 hours) to stabilize the disrupted plaque, if the clinical situation allows.

Complications
- Premature discontinuation of IV heparin may lead to reactivation of the unstable plaque and recurrent ischemia.
- The major complication of heparin therapy is bleeding. The activated partial thromboplastin time (aPTT) must be closely monitored.
- Another complication, heparin-induced thrombocytopenia, can occur in a significant number of patients and thus the platelet count should be followed.

Glycoprotein IIb-IIIa inhibitors   Two recently completed trials indicate that IV tirofiban (in addition to ASA) used either as an alternative or as an adjunct to IV heparin may reduce ischemic events in patients with unstable angina or non-Q wave MI.

Thrombolytic Therapy   Initial enthusiasm for thrombolytic therapy in unstable angina has declined because clinical trials have demonstrated no advantage over standard medical therapy.

Interventional Therapy

PTCA   PTCA can be performed safely and with high primary success rate in patients with unstable angina. Emergency PTCA is indicated among patients with ongoing myocardial ischemia despite optimal medical therapy and suitable coronary anatomy.

Procedure-related complication rates for emergency PTCA occur at approximately twice the rate as for elective PTCA in a stable patient. Following successful PTCA, the long-term success rate and restenosis rate are similar to elective PTCA.

CABG   CABG is the treatment of choice for patients with left main stenosis, triple-vessel CAD, and diminished LV systolic function.

- Emergent CABG is associated with twice the risk of mortality and MI compared to patients undergoing elective surgery.

ACUTE MYOCARDIAL INFARCTION (MI)

More than 1 million Americans suffer an MI each year. One-third experience sudden death outside the hospital. MI is associated with an in-hospital mortality rate of 6% to 10%; those discharged from the hospital have a similar mortality within 1 year.

Since the 1960s, the mortality rate from MI has progressively declined owing to a fall in the incidence of infarction and improved survival once the patient has sustained MI. Significant contributors to this decline in mortality include:

Development of the coronary care unit.
Improvement in community emergency medical
   services.
Recognition and modification of coronary risk factors.
Improved medical and interventional therapies.

Pathophysiology

MI is characterized by irreversible ischemic injury and necrosis of myocardial tissue.

Atherosclerotic MI: In the vast majority of acute MIs, a ruptured eccentric atherosclerotic coronary plaque with superimposed occlusive coronary thrombosis is found.

Nonatherosclerotic MI: A small minority of MIs are nonatherosclerotic. The differential diagnosis includes coronary artery and myocardial trauma; embolism to the coronary artery; coronary artery vasculitis; congenital anomalies of the coronary arteries; prolonged coronary vasospasm; dissection of the thoracic aorta; coronary artery dissection; hypercoagulable states; cocaine abuse; iatrogenic (cardiac catheterization, CABG); and medication withdrawal.

Pathologic Types

On the basis of gross pathologic examination, two major types of MI can be distinguished: transmural and non-transmural (subendocardial) infarction.

It must be noted that the clinical designations "Q wave" and "non-Q wave" MI do not completely correlate with the pathologic descriptions transmural and subendocardial.

Transmural Infarction

- Transmural MI involves necrosis of ≥50% of the ventricular wall thickness.
- Transmural MI most often is associated with complete thrombotic occlusion and involvement of a single-vessel distribution.

Nontransmural Infarction

- Nontransmural (subendocardial) MI involves <50% of wall thickness.
- Nontransmural MI frequently occurs in the setting of patent but severely diseased coronary arteries and may represent early spontaneous thrombolysis of a total thrombotic occlusion.
- In general, the coronary collateral circulation is developed more extensively with subendocardial MI, as compared to transmural MI.

Q wave versus non-Q wave MI   Non-Q wave MI accounts for 30% to 40% of all MIs. It has a somewhat different clinical course and natural history, as compared to Q wave MI:

- Non-Q wave MIs tend to occur in older patients.
- A higher percentage of patients with non-Q MI are women.
- Patients with non-Q MI more often have experienced a prior cardiac event.
- Angiography soon after non-Q MI demonstrates an infrequent occurrence of total coronary occlusion as compared to Q wave MI.
- Non-Q infarct size tends to be smaller and the in-hospital incidence of CHF and severe ventricular arrhythmia is less.
- Short-term mortality is roughly one-half that associated with a Q wave MI.

The long-term morbidity and mortality for non-Q wave MI equals or exceeds that of Q wave MI. A higher incidence of recurrent angina, MI, and death has been noted at 1-year follow-up.

Pathologic changes in MI   Gross pathologic changes do not occur until approximately 6 hours after the onset of MI. Over the ensuing 1 to 2 weeks, gradual thinning of the infarct zone occurs. Within 2 to 3 months, the necrotic myocardium is gradually replaced by collagen fibers and scar tissue.

- In the majority of cases, MI only involves the LV, however RV and atrial infarction may also occur.
- Infarction of the RV is most often associated with inferior/inferoposterior MI in the setting of a proximal right coronary artery occlusion. Isolated RVMI with a normal right coronary artery is unusual, but may occur in the setting of chronic RV pressure overload and rarely with occlusion of the left anterior descending artery.
- Atrial infarction occurs in approximately 15% of autopsy proven cases of MI.

Clinical Features

The history and physical examination, while being complete, must focus on salient features. Evaluation of the patient should be completed within 10 minutes of the arrival in the emergency department (ED). An overly detailed evaluation can waste valuable time needed for instituting appropriate medical or interventional therapy.

History

The history should elicit symptoms and risk factors for CAD, determine any possible noncoronary cause for the chest pain (see Table 1-1), and determine possible contraindications to thrombolytic therapy.

Classic Symptoms Many patients develop prodromal symptoms of increasing angina over a period of days to weeks prior to suffering an acute MI.

Type of Pain: The classic symptom of acute MI is prolonged and intense chest discomfort, described as crushing, oppressive, heavy, or constricting.

Duration: The discomfort usually lasts more than 30 minutes.

Location: Usually retrosternal in location, the pain may radiate to the ulnar aspect of the left arm, jaw, teeth, neck, shoulders, or interscapular area.

Associated Symptoms: Diaphoresis, nausea, vomiting, and dyspnea.

A circadian variation in the time of onset of acute MI has been identified. The peak incidence occurs at approximately 9 AM and a secondary peak occurs at 8 PM. To explain this early morning peak, alterations in blood viscosity and endogenous tissue plasminogen activator level, increased platelet aggregation, and increased catecholamine levels have been identified. The early morning peak is blunted in those receiving beta-blockers or ASA.

Atypical Presentations Any discussion of symptoms must emphasize that the classic features of acute MI may *not* be present in all patients. The chest discomfort may be atypical and/or associated symptoms may predominate—especially among the elderly and diabetics.

- Silent MI occurs in 25% to 35% of cases.
- Over 20% of patients lack prodromal symptoms and present with acute MI or sudden cardiac death as their first clinical manifestation of CAD.

- Other presentations of acute MI may include:
  CHF
  Syncope due to ventricular arrhythmia
  Weakness
  Peripheral embolization from an LV mural thrombus
  Stroke
  Confusion
  Sweating

Physical Examination

General Appearance

- Patients often appear pale, anxious, and restless.
- Diaphoresis is very common and the skin is usually cool and clammy.
- Levine's sign—a clenched fist over the midsternal area—strongly suggests cardiac discomfort.

Hemodynamic Status For patients with suspected acute MI, rapid assessment of hemodynamic status should be a main priority.

Heart Rate

- The HR may vary from severe bradycardia to tachycardia depending on the location of the infarction and the underlying LV function.
- Marked sinus bradycardia or AV junctional escape rhythm can be associated with an inferior MI.

Blood Pressure

- Although the majority of patients suffering an acute MI are normotensive, BP may be elevated or depressed.
- Cardiogenic shock is present when SBP remains below 90 mm Hg with evidence of diminished CO and pulmonary congestion.

Respiratory Rate

- Respiratory rate can be variable. Most patients hyperventilate soon after the onset of pain. Following relief of pain and anxiety, the respiratory rate usually returns to the normal range.
- Patients with CHF may continue to have an increased respiratory rate.

Temperature

- Low-grade fever (38° to 39°C) is common within the first 48 hours after MI.
- Temperature gradually returns to the normal range by the end of the first week.

Neck Vessels

- The height of the jugular venous pulsation reflects RA and RV diastolic pressures. Jugular venous pressure is elevated in patients with RV dysfunction and is usually very prominent and associated with Kussmaul's sign in patients with RVMI. The presence of cannon A waves suggests AV dissociation while a prominent V wave implies significant TR.
- The contour of the carotid artery pulsation provides a gross estimation of LV stroke volume. A small, brief pulse suggests diminished CO, whereas pulsus alternans is associated with severe LV dysfunction.

Pulmonary Examination

- The majority of patients with acute MI have a normal pulmonary examination.
- A normal pulmonary examination in association with hypotension and jugular venous hypertension may suggest RVMI or cardiac tamponade due to myocardial rupture.
- Pulmonary rales are associated with increased LA pressure and LV dysfunction.

The Killip classification (Table 1-5) relates the degree of pulmonary congestion at the time of presentation to in-hospital mortality.

Table 1-5. Killip Classification of Acute Myocardial Infarction

Class	Clinical Findings	In-Hospital Mortality
I	No pulmonary rales/S_3 not present	6% to 8%
II	Pulmonary rales <50% of lung fields	15% to 30%
III	Pulmonary edema	35% to 45%
IV	Cardiogenic shock	80% to 100%

Cardiac Examination

- The most common findings are tachycardia and/or S_4 secondary to diminished LV compliance.
- Precordial palpation may reveal an apical systolic bulge characteristic of dyskinetic LV myocardium or a preexisting LV aneurysm.
- A third heart sound is associated with a greater degree of LV dysfunction.
- Pericardial friction rubs can be auscultated in patients with transmural MI. Friction rubs are characteristically evanescent in nature.
- Careful note should be made of any heart murmur auscultated because new murmurs developing within the first week post-MI may represent a serious mechanical complication of MI.

Peripheral Pulses and Extremities   Because atherosclerosis is a systemic disease, the peripheral arteries should be examined for pulse contour, strength, and the presence of bruits.

- Particular attention should be paid to the femoral pulsations because cardiac catheterization may be needed on an emergent basis.
- Peripheral edema is a sign of chronic RV failure.
- Cyanosis, in the setting of acute MI, implies diminished CO.

Laboratory Evaluation

ECG   The ECG is the most valuable initial test in patients with suspected MI (Table 1-6). It should be recorded simultaneously with the history and promptly interpreted.

Because the changes associated with MI are evolutionary, ECGs should be obtained at the following times:

1. Initially.
2. With changes in clinical status.
3. In a serial fashion.

Evolution seen on the ECG may help to distinguish MI from other causes of chest pain. We must emphasize that only 60% of initial ECGs are diagnostic of acute MI—

Table 1-6. ECG Diagnostic Criteria of Myocardial Infarctions

Diagnostic Criteria of Various Myocardial Infarctions

1. **Anteroseptal MI:** Q or QS waves in leads V_{1-3}.
2. **Anterior (localized) MI:** Q or QS waves in leads V_{1-4}.
3. **Anterolateral MI:** Q or QS waves in leads I, aVL, and V_{4-6}.
4. **High lateral MI:** Q or QS waves in leads I and aVL.
5. **Extensive anterior MI:** Q or QS waves in leads I, aVL, and V_{1-6}.
6. **Diaphragmatic (inferior) MI:** Q or QS waves in II, III, and aVF.
7. **Posterior MI:** Tall (or relatively tall) R waves in leads V_{1-2}.
8. **Right Ventricular MI:** ST elevation in lead V_{4R} and/or ST elevation in leads V_1–V_3 which diminishes from V_1–V_3.

Diagnostic Criteria of Abnormal Q Waves

1. Width of Q wave >0.04 sec.
2. Depth of Q wave >25% of R wave.

serial tracings increase the sensitivity to greater than 90%.

ECG manifestations of acute MI

- The earliest manifestation of acute MI is the primary T wave change (tall, somewhat peaked T waves with a broad base) (Fig 1-1). Primary T wave changes do not occur for several minutes after the onset of chest discomfort and are associated with potentially reversible ischemia.
- With ongoing ischemia, ST segment elevation occurs in the leads that reflect the injured area.
- Reciprocal ST segment depression occurs in leads opposite to the area of injury.
- Loss of R wave amplitude and the development of Q waves occur with irreversible ischemic injury (infarction).

Vessel involvement ECG patterns of MI suggest a specific vessel involvement:

- Anterior and anteroseptal MI patterns are associated with left anterior descending involvement (Figs 1-2 and 1-3).
- Inferior (Fig 1-4) and RVMI (Fig 1-5) patterns are associated with occlusion of the right coronary artery.

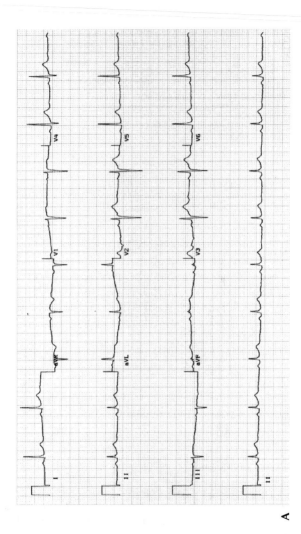

A

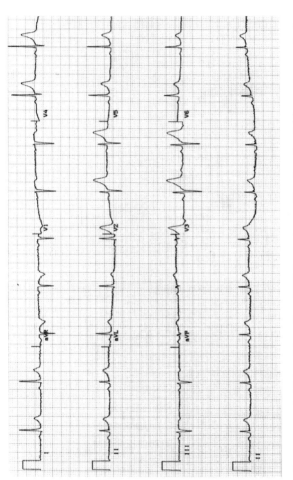

Figure 1-1. (*A*) Normal baseline ECG in patient with chronic stable angina pectoris. (*B*) Same patient as in *A*. Hyperacute T waves (most prominent in leads $V_2 - V_5$) are present during chest pain.

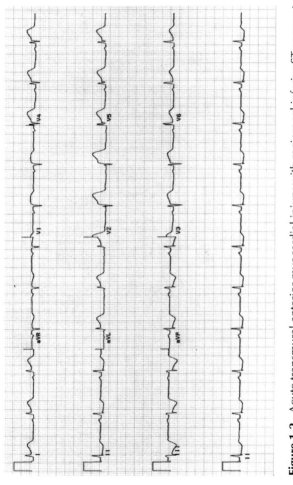

Figure 1-2. Acute transmural anterior myocardial injury with reciprocal inferior ST segment depression.

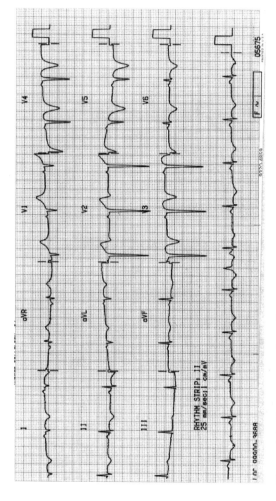

Figure 1-3. Recent anterolateral Q wave myocardial infarction.

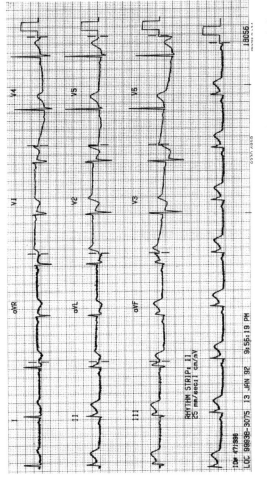

Figure 1-4. Acute inferior myocardial infarction with reciprocal anterior precordial ST segment depression.

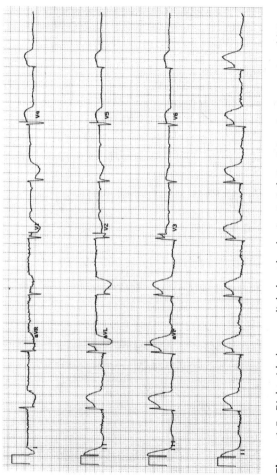

Figure 1-5. Right-sided precordial chest leads. Acute inferior injury is present. In addition, ST segment elevation in lead V_{4R} indicates right ventricular injury.

- Posterior and lateral MI patterns are associated with involvement of the circumflex artery (Fig 1-6).
- A high lateral MI pattern is associated with occlusion of diagonal branches of the left anterior descending artery (Fig 1-7).

Left bundle branch block. ECG patterns suggesting acute MI in the setting of LBBB are presented in Table 1-7. These findings are highly specific, but have moderate to poor sensitivity.

Right bundle branch block. The presence of RBBB does not interfere with the interpretation of the surface ECG for changes associated with acute MI.

Non-Q wave MI. Non-Q wave MI is characterized by T wave inversion and/or ST segment depression without the (subsequent) development of pathologic Q waves (Figs 1-8 and 1-9).

RVMI. RVMI most often occurs in the setting of inferior MI. RVMI is suggested by ST segment elevation that is most prominent in leads V_1, V_2, and V_{4R} (see Fig 1-5).

Posterior MI. Posterior MI is suggested by ST segment depression in the anterior precordial leads and a tall R wave in lead V_1.

Atrial MI. Atrial MI is characterized by PR segment elevation or depression in association with atrial arrhythmias.

Pseudo-infarction. Causes of pseudo-MI patterns include WPW, HCM, pulmonary embolism, ventricular hypertrophy, anterior and posterior hemiblock, diffuse intramyocardial disease, and acute GI conditions such as cholecystitis and pancreatitis.

Table 1-7. ECG Criteria Suggesting the Diagnosis of Acute MI in the Setting of LBBB

1. ST segment elevation ≥ 1 mm that is concordant with (in the same direction as) the QRS complex.
2. ST segment depression ≥ 1 mm in lead V_1, V_2, or V_3.
3. ST segment elevation ≥ 5 mm that is discordant with (in the opposite direction from) the QRS complex.

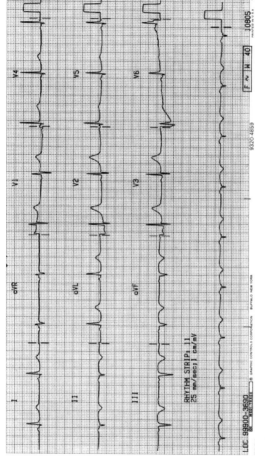

Figure 1-6. Inferior-posterior-lateral Q wave myocardial infarction.

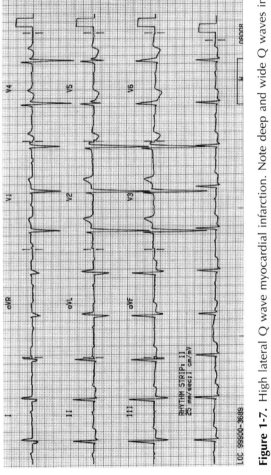

Figure 1-7. High lateral Q wave myocardial infarction. Note deep and wide Q waves in leads I and avL.

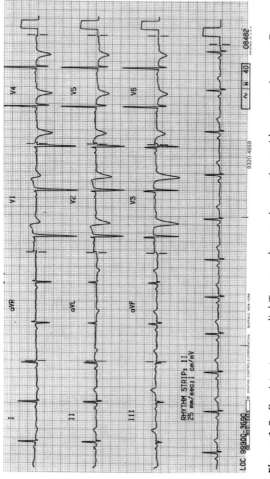

Figure 1-8. Persistent precordial T wave changes in a patient with an anterior non-Q wave MI.

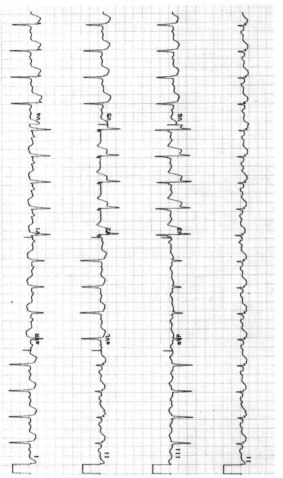

Figure 1-9. Persistent severe ST segment depression is present in many leads during chest pain. Subsequent angiography revealed a severe left mainstem stenosis.

Chest X-ray The CXR is an important test if it can be obtained promptly.

- Cardiomegaly, pulmonary congestion, and pleural effusion may be noted.
- Most importantly, attention should be paid to the cardiomediastinal silhouette and aortic knob if dissecting aneurysm of the thoracic aorta is suspected.

Cardiac Enzymes Irreversibly injured myocytes release intracellular enzymes into the blood in a characteristic pattern which can be assayed to diagnose acute MI, but these enzymatic makers only diagnose MI *after* the fact. Therefore, if clinical suspicion is strong, therapy should begin prior to enzymatic confirmation.

A single set of cardiac enzymes is not of sufficient sensitivity to exclude a diagnosis of MI in borderline instances. Serial enzyme determinations should be obtained to note the typical plasma profile associated with each enzyme during the course of acute MI.

Creatinine phosphokinase (CPK) and isoenzymes Three electrophoretic isoenzymes of CPK have been identified:

1. BB, primarily present in brain tissue.
2. MM, primarily found in skeletal muscle.
3. MB, predominantly present in cardiac muscle but also found in small amounts in the tongue, small intestine, diaphragm, and skeletal muscle.

Enzyme Marker Kinetics: Total CPK values typically rise approximately 6 to 10 hours after the onset of chest pain, peak at 24 hours, and return to normal levels at 48 to 72 hours.
- To enhance diagnostic sensitivity, samples of total CPK and CPK-MB levels and CPK-MB mass assay should be obtained on presentation, at 12 hours, and 24 hours later.
- In patients having successful reperfusion, the total CPK and MB isoenzymes peak earlier and exhibit a rapid washout from the blood.

Potential Sources of Error:
- If the patient presents more than 24 to 48 hours after the onset of chest discomfort, CPK levels may not be diagnostic of acute MI. Either cardiac troponin T or I levels or lactate dehydrogenase levels should be obtained.
- False-positive elevations of CPK-MB levels can occur with renal failure, hypothyroidism, skeletal muscle disease, ethanol intoxication, myocarditis, myocardial trauma, intramuscular injection, seizure activity, DC countershock, and "macro-CPK."

Lactate dehydrogenase (LDH) isoenzymes In some centers, total LDH levels and isoenzyme determination are still used for enzymatic confirmation of recent MI when the patient presents relatively late in the clinical course. Five electrophoretic isoenzymes of LDH have been identified.

Enzyme Marker Kinetics: LDH levels typically begin to exceed the normal range 24 to 36 hours after the onset of infarction, peak at 3 to 6 days, and return slowly to normal levels by 10 to 14 days.
- Of the electrophoretic isoenzymes of LDH, an LDH_1/LDH_2 ratio exceeding 0.8 is highly specific for the diagnosis of acute MI.

Potential Sources of Error:
- In general, LDH isoenzymes should not be routinely obtained unless the CPK values are indeterminate or the patient presents 24 to 48 hours after symptom onset.
- False-positive elevations of LDH occur in association with megaloblastic anemias, hemolysis, renal infarction, and germ cell tumors.

Other Serum Markers In an effort to establish a bio-chemical diagnosis of MI at an earlier point in time after the onset of chest pain or to make a more specific diagnosis, new serum markers of myocardial necrosis have been identified.

CPK-MB isoforms CPK-MB exists in two subforms in blood: MB_1 and MB_2.

Enzyme Marker Kinetics: An absolute $CPK\text{-}MB_2$ level $\geq 1.0\,U$ per liter and a ratio of $CPK\ MB_2/MB_1 \geq 1.5$ have enhanced sensitivity and specificity for the diagnosis of MI within 6 hours of symptom onset as compared to standard CPK-MB measurements.

Potential Sources of Error: False-positive results have been noted in patients with muscular dystrophy and severe skeletal muscle injury.

Myoglobin

Enzyme Marker Kinetics: Myoglobin is abnormally elevated in serum within 2 hours of MI. The diagnostic sensitivity is superior to CPK-MB at this early time.

Potential Sources of Error:
- Myoglobin is rapidly cleared from plasma.
- False-positive results are found in patients with skeletal muscle injury and renal failure.

Cardiac troponins T and I Cardiac troponins are very specific markers of myocardial cell injury. Monoclonal antibodies directed against cardiac troponins T and I have been developed. The role of these new serum markers of myocardial necrosis is evolving, and they may have specific applications in certain patient subgroups. At the present time, the standard marker for the enzymatic diagnosis of acute MI remains CPK-MB.

Enzyme Marker Kinetics: Troponins T and I can be detected in serum within 4 hours of MI onset.

Potential Sources of Error: Circulating troponin can also be detected in patients with unstable angina; therefore, the specificity of the troponin assay is somewhat reduced.

Other Laboratory Tests

Leukocytes Leukocytosis in the range of 12,000–15,000/mm^3 is common after acute MI. The white cell count peaks on the second or third day after MI and typically returns to normal values within 1 week.

Erythrocyte Sedimentation Rate (ESR) The ESR rises 48 to 72 hours after MI and may remain elevated for ≥ 3 weeks.

Myocardial Scintigraphy

Infarct-avid imaging Infarct-avid imaging with ^{99m}technetium (Tc) pyrophosphate or indium antimyosin antibody scanning remains positive for up to 1 week following acute MI.

- With the development of improved serum markers, infarct-avid imaging is rarely used today to diagnose MI; however, these radionuclide tests are indicated in patients presenting after 48 hours with a clinical history suggestive of MI in whom the ECG and serum enzyme determinations are nondiagnostic.
- An MI is diagnosed by discrete, rather than diffuse, myocardial tracer uptake.

Perfusion imaging ^{99m}Tc sestamibi, a myocardial perfusion agent that redistributes minimally, can be injected prior to thrombolytic therapy to estimate the area of myocardium at risk.

- Administration of a second dose many hours following treatment can document reperfusion and myocardial salvage.

Echocardiography Echocardiography allows rapid and accurate determination of global and regional systolic function.

- A new wall motion abnormality, characterized by a lack of systolic thickening and either akinetic or dyskinetic motion, is characteristic of acute MI. Echocardiography is extremely useful in the ED to triage patients with chest pain and normal ECG, as patients with completely normal wall motion have a very low incidence of acute MI.

Therapy of Patients with Acute MI

For clinical purposes, patients with acute MI are subdivided into two groups:

1. Patients with ST segment elevation/LBBB MI. These patients benefit from reperfusion therapy (thrombolysis or PTCA).
2. Patients without ST elevation or LBBB MI. Current

data do not support acute reperfusion therapy for these patients.

The initial medical treatment of both subgroups, however, is similar.

1. The history and physical examination and evaluation of the ECG should be completed within 10 minutes of patient arrival at the ED.
2. IV access and continuous ECG monitoring should be accomplished in all patients.
3. All patients should receive stool softeners and a mild anxiolytic agent to help diminish myocardial work.
4. All patients with suspected acute MI should be admitted to a monitored unit.

   Low-risk patients (those with a normal ECG despite a classic history of chest discomfort) can be admitted to an intermediate monitored unit as their in-hospital complication risk is only in the range of 1%.

   Higher risk patients and those with hemodynamic instability should be admitted to the coronary care unit.

The goals of therapy of acute MI include:

- Alleviation of pain
- Assessment of hemodynamic status
- Limitation of the extent of myocardial necrosis
- Monitoring for complications
- Assessment of future risk

Relief of Cardiac Pain

Pain represents ongoing cardiac ischemia. In addition, pain and anxiety increase circulatory levels of catecholamines which act to increase myocardial oxygen demand. Drugs which modify the myocardial oxygen supply to demand ratio favorably may alleviate cardiac pain.

Supplemental Oxygen

Uncomplicated MI   Patients with uncomplicated MI may have arterial hypoxemia on the basis of ventilation-perfusion mismatch.

- Supplemental oxygen at low flow rates (2 to 4 liters/minute) should be provided at least during the first 2 to 3 hours for patients with uncomplicated MI.

Pulmonary congestion   Patients with evidence of pulmonary congestion exhibit more severe hypoxemia.

- Among patients with severe arterial hypoxemia due to pulmonary edema, severe CHF, or a mechanical complication of MI, supplemental oxygen alone may not suffice. Endotracheal intubation with delivery of positive pressure ventilation may be required.

Analgesic Agents   Analgesic agents decrease pain and anxiety to reduce myocardial oxygen demand.

Morphine sulfate   Morphine (2 to 5 mg IV every 5 to 30 minutes) remains the drug of choice except when a documented hypersensitivity reaction has occurred. Morphine reduces myocardial oxygen demand through its central effect to block sympathetic efferent discharge.

Meperidine   Meperidine (12.5 to 50 mg IV) possesses vagolytic properties which may confer a potential advantage over the use of morphine in patients with inferior MI.

Side effects   Side effects of narcotic agents include hypotension, relative bradycardia, and respiratory depression. Clinically, respiratory depression is infrequent in patients with pulmonary edema and ischemic chest pain.
Noloxone (0.4–2.0 mg IV) can be used to reverse the effects of these agents.

Nitrates

Treatment   Recent studies have not shown a clear mortality benefit for the administration of nitrates in the setting of acute MI, but it is our practice to administer IV NTG to the vast majority of patients with acute MI for the first 24 to 48 hours. *Exceptions:* hypotension (SBP <90 mm Hg), bradycardia (HR <50 bpm), excessive tachycardia.

- The starting dose of IV NTG is 10 μg/minute with titration upward by 10 μg every 5 to 10 minutes until

mean arterial pressure is reduced by 10% in normotensive patients and by approximately 30% (not below 140/90 mm Hg) in chronically hypertensive patients or until pain is relieved.
- The maximal effective dose of IV NTG is 200 to 300 μg/min.

Precautions
- NTG should be used with extreme caution in patients with suspected RVMI as excessive reduction of preload will not be well tolerated hemodynamically.
- Side effects of nitrate administration include hypotension and bradycardia (Bezold-Jarisch reflex), tachycardia, nausea, and vomiting.

Beta-Blockers Beta-blockers should be administered early in the course of acute MI to all patients unless a contraindication is present, as beta-blockers have a beneficial effect on morbidity and mortality during the acute phase of MI. Early administration of IV beta-blockers has been documented to reduce the rate of reinfarction, recurrent myocardial ischemia, cardiac rupture, and mortality—especially in the subgroup of patients with diabetes.

Available agents
Metoprolol. Metoprolol is administered in 5 mg doses IV every 2 to 5 minutes up to a total dose of 15 mg. The IV dose is followed by 50 mg po every 6 to 12 hours.

Propranolol. Propranolol, 1 mg IV every 1 to 2 minutes up to 0.15 mg/kg, should provide adequate beta-blockade. An oral dose of 20–80 mg every 6 to 8 hours is subsequently administered.

Esmolol. Esmolol, a short-acting IV beta-blocker, is an alternative agent for use among patients who cannot receive an oral agent or who may require a quick reversal of possible complications of beta-blocker therapy.

Precautions
- Contraindications to beta-blockade include heart rate <60 bpm, SBP <100 mm Hg, moderate to severe CHF, AV block greater than first degree, severe chronic

obstructive pulmonary disease, and reactive airways disease.

Limiting Myocardial Necrosis (Reperfusion Therapy)

Infarct size and the degree of LV dysfunction are the major determinants of prognosis in acute MI.

- Among patients suffering an ST elevation or LBBB MI, the majority ($\geq$90%) exhibit total thrombotic occlusion of the infarct-related coronary artery.
- Among patients without ST elevation or LBBB MI, the incidence of thrombotic occlusion is significantly less.

Early medical and/or interventional strategies aimed at increasing coronary blood flow should assume paramount importance.

Aspirin ASA has potent antiplatelet effects and therefore is an important agent in limiting thrombus formation. Support for the use of ASA in the acute phase of MI comes from the ISIS-2 study.

- ASA (160 mg) alone reduced the short-term mortality rate from acute MI by 20% to 30%.

Treatment

- ASA should be administered immediately to all patients in a minimum dose of 162 mg unless a previous hypersensitivity response has occurred.
- The dose of ASA should be chewed rather than swallowed to minimize the time required for systemic absorption.
- If the patient cannot take oral ASA, a rectal suppository of ASA can be given.
- For patients with documented hypersensitivity to ASA, ticlopidine (250 mg twice a day) or clopidogrel (75 mg per day) may be substituted.

Heparin Heparin accelerates the formation of complexes involving antithrombin III and several activated serine proteases to induce hypocoagulability and retard clot propagation. Heparin is an important adjunct to thrombolytic therapy (especially after therapy with fibrin-specific agents) because of the risk of reocclusion after successful thrombolysis. IV Heparin is not absolutely required when less fibrin-specific agents are used.

Treatment Heparin is administered as a 5000 U IV bolus together with or shortly after thrombolytic therapy. Subsequently, heparin is continued as an IV infusion to keep the aPTT 1.5 to 2.0 times the control value for 48 to 72 hours.

- IV heparin should be administered as soon as possible—preferably in the ED—to all patients without ST elevation or LBBB MI.
- IV heparin is also indicated for patients with anteroapical MI to reduce the risk of LV mural thrombus formation and peripheral arterial embolization.
- Subcutaneous heparin should be administered to all patients not receiving IV heparin to reduce the risk of deep venous thrombosis and pulmonary embolism.

Thrombolytic Agents Due to the high incidence of occlusive coronary artery thrombosis observed in the early stages of acute ST elevation and LBBB MI and evidence that experimental infarction could be interrupted by the restoration of coronary flow, thrombolytic agents have become the mainstay of medical therapy for acute MI (Table 1-8).

All clinically available thrombolytic agents have been demonstrated to reduce both short- and long-term mortality and improve LV function in acute MI.

Indications for thrombolytic therapy are listed in Table 1-9.

- Thrombolytic therapy is indicated for patients with ST segment elevation and new LBBB MI presenting within 12 hours of symptom onset without contraindications (Table 1-10).
- Thrombolytic therapy is not indicated for those with ST segment depression or T wave inversion.

Initiating treatment The most important factor influencing mortality is the time from symptom onset to the initiation of thrombolytic therapy. A "door to needle"

Table 1-8. Characteristics of Clinically Used Thrombolytic Agents

	SK	APSAC	rt-PA	r-PA
Half-life (min)	23	90	5	13
Fibrin specificity	+	+	+++	+++
Administration regimen	1.5 million U IV over 60 min	30 U IV bolus over 2 to 5 min	15 mg IV bolus followed by 0.75 mg/kg (not to exceed 50 mg) over 30 min, followed by 0.5 mg/kg (not to exceed 35 mg) over next 60 min	10 + 10 U double-bolus injection. Each bolus is given IV over 2 min. The second bolus follows the first by 10 min.
90-min patency	55% to 60%	55% to 73%	75% to 85%	83%
Requirement for simultaneous heparin	no	no	yes	yes
Antigenicity	yes	yes	no	no
Expense	+	+++	++++	++++

APSAC: anistreplase; r-PA: reteplase, recombinant; rt-PA: alteplase, recombinant; SK: streptokinase.

Table 1-9. Indications to Initiate Thrombolytic Therapy

1. Ischemic symptoms lasting greater than 20 minutes.
2. Total duration of symptoms lasting less than or equal to 12 hours and not responding to standard medical therapy.
3. Greater than or equal to 1 mm of ST segment elevation in at least 2 contiguous ECG leads.
4. Left bundle branch block (with history suggesting acute MI).
5. Greater than or equal to 2 mm of ST segment depression in ECG leads V_{1-4} and R/S ratio greater than 0.75 suggesting a true posterior MI (possible indication).
6. No contraindication to thrombolytic therapy.
7. Informed consent obtained.

Table 1-10. Contraindications to Thrombolytic
Administration

Absolute Contraindications
1. Active internal bleeding (not including menses)
2. Recent (within 2 months) intracranial or intraspinal surgery or trauma
3. Intracranial neoplasm, AVM, aneurysm
4. Known bleeding diathesis
5. Severe uncontrolled hypertension (>180/110 mm Hg) on presentation
6. Aortic dissection
7. History of hemorrhagic cerebrovascular accident at any time or other stroke within 1 year

Relative Contraindications
1. Recent major surgery (within 10 days)
2. Recent GI/GU bleeding (within 10 days)
3. Recent trauma (within 2 to 4 weeks)
4. High likelihood of cardiac thrombus
5. Bacterial endocarditis
6. Acute pericarditis
7. Pregnancy/postpartum state
8. Noncompressible puncture (within 10 days)
9. Hemostatic defects due to advanced renal or hepatic disease
10. Diabetic hemorrhagic retinopathy
11. Patient currently receiving oral anticoagulants (INR ≥ 2.0)
12. Traumatic or prolonged (>10 min) CPR

time of less than 30 minutes for initiation of therapy should be achieved. Unfortunately, only 25% to 30% of patients with ST elevation or LBBB MI receive thrombolytic therapy due to a possible contraindication or late presentation.

- After a delay of 12 to 24 hours, the benefits of thrombolytic therapy are significantly diminished.
- Administration of thrombolytic therapy ≥24 hours following symptom onset offers no benefit to the patient.

Side effects Vascular puncture should be kept to a minimum. Bleeding complications should be anticipated and managed accordingly.

Side effects include intracerebral hemorrhage (0.5% to 1.0%); other internal bleeding (GI, GU, retroperitoneal);

surface bleeding at the site of vascular puncture; allergic reactions; hypotension; and cholesterol embolization.

Intracerebral hemorrhage (ICH) is the most feared complication of thrombolytic therapy. ICH mortality approaches 50%. The risk of ICH is increased among patients with the following characteristics:

- Age >65 years
- Low body weight (<70 kg)
- HTN on presentation
- Use of rt-PA or r-PA

Streptokinase (SK) SK is an enzyme produced by beta-hemolytic streptococci that indirectly activates the fibrinolytic system by forming a complex with plasminogen, converting the inactive pro-enzyme into an effective plasminogen activator.

Advantage: SK appears to be the preferred
  thrombolytic agent for patients ≥75 years with lower-
  risk inferior MIs because of the lesser incidence of
  ICH compared to rt-PA.
Fibrin specificity: SK is not fibrin specific.
Administration protocol: The standard dose is 1.5
  million U administered IV over 60 minutes.
Results: Patency of the infarct-related artery at 90
  minutes is approximately 55% to 60%; however, a
  significant catch-up phenomenon occurs over the
  next 24 hours.
Precautions:
- For fear of allergic reaction, patients with a history of
  allergic reaction to streptococcal products or those
  who have received SK or anistreplase (APSAC)
  within the preceding 1 to 2 years must not be treated
  with SK.
- Hypotension is a significant complication of therapy
  in 1% to 10% of patients.

Tissue plasminogen activator (rt-PA) rt-PA is a naturally occurring protein which catalyzes the conversion of the inactive pro-enzyme plasminogen into the active plasmin. Because rt-PA is a naturally occurring product, there is no associated antigenicity.

Advantage: Although prior studies suggested no major differences in terms of mortality among the clinically available thrombolytic agents, the GUSTO-1 trial indicated that accelerated dose rt-PA and concomitant IV heparin provides a survival advantage over other thrombolytic regimens.

Fibrin specificity: rt-PA is fibrin specific.

Administration protocol:

"Accelerated" delivery of rt-PA is the current protocol for administration. With this protocol, a 15 mg IV bolus is given followed by infusion of 0.75 mg/kg (up to 50 mg) over the next 30 minutes. Over the ensuing 60 minutes, 0.5 mg/kg (up to 35 mg) is infused.

Results: rt-PA achieves the highest 90-minute patency rate (75% to 85%). However, it is associated with the highest rate of reocclusion, demonstrating the need for adjunctive IV heparin therapy.

Precautions: Disadvantages of rt-PA include the need for multiple IV lines to administer the drug, and its relatively complex dosing regimen.

Alterations of the molecular structure of native rt-PA are being investigated for their clinical potential for thrombolysis. In addition, the role of concomitant administration of glycoprotein IIb/IIIa inhibitors with or without rt-PA to restore early patency is being investigated.

Anistreplase (APSAC) Similar to SK, APSAC is a streptococcal product that indirectly activates the fibrinolytic system.

Advantages:

APSAC has the longest plasma half-life of the clinically available thrombolytic agents.

The main advantage of APSAC is its ease of administration.

Fibrin specificity: APSAC is intermediate in its fibrin specificity.

Administration protocol: APSAC is administered as a single 30 U IV bolus over 2 to 5 minutes.

Results: Infarct artery patency is approximately 60% at

90 minutes. As with SK, a catch-up phenomenon with enhanced patency is noted at 24 hours.

Precautions:

APSAC should not be administered to patients with a history of allergic reaction to streptococcal products or to those who have received APSAC or SK in the past 1 to 2 years.

The incidence of hypotension is significantly less as compared to SK.

Reteplase (r-PA)   r-PA is a non-glycosylated deletion mutation of TPA. Like rt-PA it is a recombinant plasminogen activator.

Fibrin specificity: r-PA is fibrin specific.

Administration protocol:

r-PA is administered as a 10 + 10 U double-bolus injection. Each bolus is given IV over 2 minutes. The second bolus is given 30 minutes after the first bolus.

IV heparin should be concomitantly administered. Heparin and r-PA are incompatible and should not be given simultaneously through the same line.

Results: Patency of the infarct artery is 83% at 90 minutes.

Precautions: The side-effect profile of r-PA is similar to rt-PA.

PTCA

PTCA can reestablish perfusion in patients with total thrombotic occlusion of a coronary artery. Three different strategies of angioplasty-based intervention are available:

1. Primary (direct) PTCA
2. Salvage (rescue) PTCA
3. Routine (elective) PTCA

The use of PTCA for treatment of acute MI depends on patient characteristics, local practice, and availability of the angioplasty team.

Primary PTCA   Primary PTCA is a strategy in which PTCA is used as a front-line technique to restore patency of the infarcted artery.

Primary PTCA may be used in the setting of a contraindication to thrombolytic therapy or as a primary strategy. Primary PTCA should be used as an alternative strategy to thrombolysis only if performed in a timely fashion (within 60 to 90 minutes after presentation) by experienced operators (those with >75 PTCA cases/year) in a high volume center (>200 PTCA cases/year).

Patients without ST elevation or LBBB MI should have cardiac catheterization and PTCA performed if ischemia is not controlled with medical therapy and suitable anatomy is present.

Success rate   Success rates varying from 88% to 99% are reported. The majority of patients achieve TIMI grade 3 flow. Reocclusion rates approximate 10%. In some cases, adjunctive intra-coronary lytic therapy is administered during or after the procedure to decrease the thrombotic burden. Two to five percent of patients referred for primary PTCA require CABG for unsuitable anatomy or complication.

Advantages   When compared to thrombolytic therapy, primary PTCA offers the following advantages:

- Overall myocardial salvage and mortality rates appear to be similar to slightly improved.
- Primary PTCA is associated with a lower stroke risk, lower rate of in-hospital ischemia, and lesser subsequent need for revascularization.
- Hospital dismissal may occur earlier and the patient's return to work may be quicker among those treated with primary PTCA.

Disadvantages   Primary PTCA presently has three major disadvantages:

- An experienced team must be constantly available.
- PTCA availability is limited to relatively few centers in the United States.
- A relatively small number of patients have been treated using a strategy of primary PTCA (compared to thrombolytic-treated patients).

Rescue PTCA   Rescue angioplasty is the use of PTCA in patients whose infarcted arteries do not show evidence of reperfusion following thrombolytic therapy.

In general, patients who receive thromblytic therapy achieve clinical reperfusion as assessed by cessation of pain, decrease in height of ST segment elevation, and reperfusion arrhythmias (such as accelerated idioventricular rhythm) within 1 hour of drug administration. Patients not achieving clinical reperfusion and having continuing pain and/or ST segment elevation should undergo cardiac catheterization and immediate PTCA if the infarct-related artery remains occluded.

Routine/Elective PTCA   Elective PTCA should be reserved for patients developing recurrent ischemia or having evidence of exercise-induced myocardial ischemia. Several studies indicate that routine PTCA following successful thrombolytic therapy leads to a higher rate of bleeding complications, mortality, and need for CABG.

Coronary artery bypass surgery (CABG)

CABG offers complete myocardial revascularization, but most centers find it logistically difficult to perform within 4 to 6 hours after the onset of infarction.

CABG is the treatment of choice in these situations:

- Patients with failed PTCA.
- Patients with left main disease.
- Patients with extensive triple-vessel disease and anatomy unsuitable for PTCA.
- Some patients with cardiogenic shock.

Complications of Acute MI

Arrhythmias

A variety of rhythm disturbances can occur in the setting of acute MI.

Bradyarrhythmias and Conduction Disturbances

Sinus bradycardia   Sinus bradycardia is the most common rhythm disturbance. It occurs in 30% to 40% of MIs. Sinus bradycardia in the setting of inferior MI is often secondary to enhanced vagal tone (Bezold-Jarisch reflex).

Treatment: Sinus bradycardia most often is a benign rhythm disturbance. For symptomatic patients (recurrent chest pain, CHF, or ventricular ectopy), atropine in 0.5 mg aliquots up to a total dose of 2.0 mg can be administered to bring the HR to greater than 60 beats/min. If unsuccessful, temporary pacing should be instituted.

First-degree AV block First-degree AV block occurs in approximately 10% of MIs. It has a benign prognosis.

Second-degree AV block Second-degree AV block develops in 4% to 10% of patients.

- Mobitz I (Wenckebach) AV block accounts for the majority of cases.
  Treatment: This form of second-degree AV block is usually benign and can be observed. For patients experiencing hemodynamic compromise, temporary pacing is required.
- Mobitz II second-degree AV block is associated with a wide QRS complex, origination from a lesion in the conduction system below the His bundle, and increased risk of progression to complete AV block.
  Treatment: Because of the risk of progression to complete AV block with unstable escape rhythm, Mobitz II AV block should be treated with a temporary demand pacemaker.

Complete AV block Complete AV block occurs in 4% to 8% of patients.

- Complete AV block in the setting of anterior MI implies a large area of necrosis and a poor prognosis.
  Treatment: Temporary pacing (transvenous preferable to transcutaneous) is indicated in this setting but mortality (70% to 80%) appears to be unaffected.
- Complete AV block associated with inferior MI is often transient in nature and associated with a narrow complex escape rhythm. In-hospital mortality is approximately 15%.

Treatment: Patients should be carefully observed if a stable escape rhythm is present. Temporary pacing is indicated if hemodynamic compromise develops.

Intraventricular conduction disturbances Intraventricular conduction disturbances (hemiblock, bundle branch block) occur in 10% to 20% of patients.

- The development of isolated hemiblock confers no increased risk of complete AV block.
- New, complete LBBB signifies a large area of myocardial necrosis and is an indication for temporary pacing.
- New bifascicular block (RBBB and LAHB or LPHB) also implies a large area of myocardial necrosis and an increased risk of complete AV block. Temporary pacing is indicated.
- New onset RBBB alone is not an indication for temporary pacing.

Indications for temporary pacing are reviewed in Table 1-11.

Table 1-11. Indications for Temporary Pacemaker Therapy in Acute MI

Definite Indications
Complete AV block
Asystole
Mobitz II AV block
New LBBB
New bifascicular block (RBBB plus left anterior or posterior hemiblock)
Alternating bundle branch block
Symptomatic bradycardia not responding to medical therapy

Probable Indications
Sinus bradycardia with hypotension not responding to medical therapy
Mobitz I AV block with hypotension not responding to medical therapy
Recurrent sinus pauses not responding to medical therapy
Overdrive ventricular or atrial pacing to extinguish tachycardia
Preexisting LBBB with new first-degree AV block
Bifascicular block of uncertain duration

Supraventricular Tachyarrhythmias

Sinus tachycardia Sinus tachycardia occurs in 25% to 33% of patients. It most frequently is associated with pain, anxiety, or hypovolemia. Persistent sinus tachycardia may signify severe LV dysfunction.

Treatment: Therapy should be directed at the underlying etiology. Judicious use of beta-blockers, except in patients with underlying CHF, is indicated.

Atrial fibrillation (AF) AF occurs in 10% to 15% of patients. Etiologies include LV failure, atrial distention, pericarditis, and atrial infarction.

Treatment: see Chapter 17

Atrial flutter Atrial flutter occurs in 1% to 3% of patients.

Treatment: Atrial flutter should be treated in a manner similar to AF.

Paroxysmal supraventricular tachycardia (SVT) Paroxysmal SVT occurs in 2% to 10% of patients. This rhythm disturbance tends to be transient and recurrent in nature. Deleterious effects are caused by increased myocardial oxygen demand and diminished diastolic time for coronary flow.

Treatment:
- Emergency therapy of hemodynamic compromise is immediate DC cardioversion.
- For more stable patients, vagal maneuvers, adenosine injection (6–12 mg IV), or IV verapamil (2.5–5.0 mg) is generally successful.

Ventricular Arrhythmias VPCs are almost universal among patients with acute MI.

Therapies Lidocaine prophylaxis is indicated for patients with frequent VPCs (>6/min), multiform VPCs, closely coupled VPCs, and nonsustained VT.

Note: The prophylactic use of lidocaine for prevention of VF is not currently recommended because suppression of VPCs does not significantly reduce overall mortality and lidocaine therapy is associated with an increased incidence of asystole.

Adjunctive therapy for ventricular ectopy includes maintenance of adequate oxygenation, beta-blockade, correction of serum electrolyte disorders, and possibly infusion of IV magnesium sulfate.

Accelerated idioventricular rhythm (AIVR) AIVR occurs in up to 20% of patients.

Treatment:
- AIVR generally has a benign prognosis and often requires no treatment. It is a well-recognized marker of reperfusion after thrombolytic therapy.
- If hemodynamic deterioration occurs due to a loss of AV synchrony, suppression of the arrhythmia with overdrive atrial pacing or IV lidocaine is indicated.

Ventricular tachycardia (VT) VT occurs in 10% to 20% patients.

- VT occurring in the first 24 to 48 hours of infarction generally has a benign long-term prognosis.
- VT occurring more than 48 hours after MI implies the presence of an arrhythmogenic substrate with possible ischemic trigger.

Treatment:
- The immediate therapy for patients with unstable hemodynamic status is synchronized DC cardioversion (100 to 360 joules). Institution of prophylactic therapy (lidocaine or procainamide) is indicated to prevent recurrence. In refractory cases, IV amiodarone is indicated.
- Lidocaine is administered as a loading bolus of 1.0–1.5 mg/kg. Additional boluses of 0.5–0.75 mg/kg every 10 minutes up to a maximum dose of 3.0 mg/kg may be given if needed. A constant infusion of 1–4 mg/min should follow loading.
- Procainamide is administered as a loading dose of 12–17 mg/kg at a rate of 20–30 mg/min. An infusion of 1–4 mg/min should follow loading.

- Amiodarone is administered as an IV bolus of 150 mg over 10 minutes, followed by a constant infusion of 1 mg/min for 6 hours, followed by a maintenance infusion of 0.5 mg/kg.
- For patients with a stable hemodynamic status, IV loading doses of lidocaine or procainamide can be administered and subsequent continuous IV infusion can be initiated.
- Correction of underlying hypokalemia, hypomagnesemia, acidosis, and hypoxia is mandatory.
- All patients without a contraindication should receive a beta-blocker.
- Patients with sustained monomorphic VT occurring more than 48 hours after infarction should undergo coronary angiography and EP testing prior to discharge. If indicated, revascularization should be accomplished. Therapy is also guided by results of the EP test.

Asymptomatic nonsustained VT   Asymptomatic non-sustained VT is a problematic issue among survivors of acute MI. Nonsustained VT is an independent predictor of post-MI mortality.

Treatment:
- Empiric antiarrhythmic drug therapy with type IA and IC agents has been documented to increase mortality over placebo-treated patients. Empiric low-dose amiodarone may improve mortality in this subgroup of patients.
- Late potentials detected with the signal-averaged ECG and depressed LV systolic function may identify a population at higher risk of subsequent sudden death and indicate the need for an invasive EP test.
- Routine EP testing is not otherwise recommended in patients with asymptomatic nonsustained VT and good LV function.
- Among patients with prior MI, LV ejection fraction ≤35%, nonsustained VT, and nonsuppressible ventricular tachyarrhythmia on EP testing, the MADIT study suggested that prophylactic therapy

with an implantable defibrillator leads to improved survival compared to drug therapy.

Ventricular fibrillation   VF occurs in approximately 8% to 10% of patients.

- Primary VF tends to occur within the first 12 hours after the onset of symptoms and appears to carry no significant adverse long-term prognosis.
- Secondary VF occurring 24 to 48 hours after infarction is generally associated with severe LV dysfunction and implies a rather poor prognosis.

Treatment:
- Immediate therapy of VF consists of asynchronous DC countershock (200 to 360 joules) followed by prophylactic IV lidocaine or procainamide for 24 to 48 hours to prevent a recurrence. IV amiodarone is indicated in refractory cases.
- Metabolic derangements should be promptly corrected.
- Cardiac catheterization and EP evaluation are indicated for survivors of secondary VF.

LV Dysfunction

Pump failure has surpassed malignant ventricular arrhythmia as the leading cause of death associated with acute MI.

Mild LV Dysfunction   Patients with mild CHF can be treated in standard fashion (see Chapter 2). Several recent studies have validated the use of ACE inhibition early (within 24 hours) after MI to inhibit infarct expansion, attenuate abnormal ventricular remodeling, and to reduce all-cause mortality. ACE-inhibitors should be given to all patients with anterior MI and those with ejection fraction less than 40%.

Patients Not Responding to Standard Therapy   For patients not responding to standard therapy, further investigation is indicated. Bedside echocardiography should be performed to evaluate LV and RV function and exclude mechanical complications of MI. If adequate transthoracic windows are not available, TEE should be considered. Invasive hemodynamic monitoring with a PA catheter may be required to optimize therapy.

Hemodynamic classifications Based on the cardiac index (CI) and pulmonary capillary wedge pressure (PCWP), hemodynamic subsets of patients with acute MI have been established which correlate with in-hospital mortality (Table 1-12).

- Patients with a CI >2.2 liters/min/m^2 usually demonstrate adequate systemic perfusion.
- Patients with a CI <1.8 liters/min/m^2 may exhibit shock.
- Patients with PCWP >18 to 20 mm Hg usually have pulmonary congestion.

Treatment For patients with a PCWP ≤15 mm Hg and a CI ≥2.2 liters/min/m^2, hypovolemia should be suspected. Judicious administration of fluid to raise the PCWP to 18–20 mm Hg is indicated.

Patients with a PCWP ≥18 mm Hg and CI ≥2.2 liters/min/m^2 are generally in CHF:

- Diuretic agents (preferably IV furosemide) and afterload reduction (usually IV NTG) is indicated to improve hemodynamic parameters.
- An oral ACE-inhibitor should be started.

For patients with PCWP <18 mm Hg and CI <2.2 liters/min/m^2:

Gentle volume expansion to increase the PCWP and consideration of a positive inotropic agent (usually dobutamine or dopamine) should improve cardiac hemodynamics.

Table 1-12. In-Hospital Mortality Rates of Hemodynamically Defined Patient Subsets with Acute MI

Subset	PCWP (mm Hg)	Cardiac Index (liters/min/m^2)	Mortality (%)
I	<18	>2.2	3
II	>18	>2.2	9
III	<18	<2.2	23
IV	>18	<2.2	55

PCWP: pulmonary capillary wedge pressure.
Adapted from: Forrester JS, Diamond G, Chatterjee K, Swan HJC. Medical therapy of acute myocardial infarction by application of hemodynamic subsets. N Engl J Med 1976;295:1356–1362, 1404–1413.

Cardiogenic Shock　 Approximately 5% to 10% of acute MI patients present with or develop cardiogenic shock.

Cardiogenic shock complicating acute MI is usually associated with necrosis ≥40% of the LV mass. Most patients have significant three-vessel CAD. Other causes of shock in the setting of acute MI include hypovolemia, RVMI, ventricular septal rupture, acute MR, and cardiac tamponade.

Although the incidence of cardiogenic shock has declined in the thrombolytic era, this subgroup of patients (PCWP >18 mm Hg and CI <1.8 liters/min/m^2), defined clinically as SBP <90 mm Hg with diminished peripheral perfusion, has an in-hospital mortality of 70% to 80%.

Medical therapy consists of positive inotropic agents (preferred agents are dopamine and dobutamine) and/or agents to support BP (neosynephrine or norepinephrine).

An IABP should also be employed. Prompt cardiac catheterization to define coronary anatomy followed by a revascularization procedure appears at this time to be the best strategy to optimize patient salvage.

Mechanical Complications

The mechanical complications of acute MI most often occur within the first week after MI. Mortality with medical therapy exceeds 90% within 2 weeks of diagnosis. Echocardiography is the procedure of choice for rapid recognition and diagnosis. Urgent surgical intervention is often indicated once a mechanical complication has been identified.

Free Wall Rupture　 Rupture of the ventricular free wall occurs in approximately 10% of fatal MIs. Over 90% involve the LV free wall. Rupture more often involves the posterior and lateral walls. Free wall rupture is associated with preexisting HTN, female sex, first MI, and corticosteroid therapy.

Presentation　 The clinical event is often heralded by recurrent chest discomfort and rapid cardiovascular collapse with electromechanical dissociation.

Treatment　 The treatment of choice is urgent pericardiocentesis followed by emergent surgical repair.

Subacute free wall rupture The syndrome of subacute free wall rupture may occur in up to 30% of patients with free wall rupture. Most often, subacute rupture is associated with inferoposterior MI.

Presentation: Echocardiographic recognition of echodense material in the pericardial space (hemorrhage) along with hypotension and bradycardia strongly suggests the diagnosis.

Treatment: Prompt pericardiocentesis is indicated. If bloody fluid is recovered, immediate surgery is indicated because the risk of recurrent bleeding and death is high.

Interventricular Septum Rupture Rupture of the interventricular septum occurs in 1% to 3% of fatal MIs.

Presentation The diagnosis is clinically suspected from the combination of:

1. Hemodynamic compromise
2. A new and loud pansystolic murmur at the left sternal border
3. Oximetric data documenting an oxygen step-up at the ventricular level

Echocardiography can rapidly identify this complication at the bedside.

Treatment In patients with severe hemodynamic compromise, an IABP should be inserted and urgent surgery performed.

Papillary Muscle Rupture Rupture of a papillary muscle (most often the posteromedial muscle because of its single blood supply from the posterior descending artery) results in acute severe MR. This complication occurs in 0.4% to 5.0% of MIs and is associated with a relatively small posterior MI.

Presentation Clinically, patients develop acute pulmonary edema, severe hypotension, and an apical murmur of MR. This complication can be readily identified with bedside echocardiography.

Treatment   An IABP should be placed and prompt surgery should be performed.

RVMI   Autopsy-proven RVMI occurs in approximately 50% of patients suffering an inferior/inferoposterior MI. However, clinically important RVMI occurs in only 10% of cases.

RVMI accompanying inferior MI is associated with a significantly higher mortality rate than uncomplicated inferior MI (25% to 30% versus 6%).

RVMI in association with anterior MI has been reported, and isolated RVMI can occur in the setting of hypertrophy and pressure overload of the RV.

Presentation

- Hypotension, elevated jugular venous pressure (often with Kussmaul's sign), and clear lungs in the setting of an inferior/inferoposterior MI suggest an RVMI.
- These patients are exquisitely preload sensitive and classically develop hypotension with administration of small nitrate doses.
- The diagnosis can be confirmed by observing ST segment elevation in ECG lead V_{4R}, volume loading to increase the level of jugular venous distention, or echocardiographic documentation of a dilated and hypokinetic RV.
- Hemodynamic data obtained from a flow-directed PA catheter reveals elevated RA mean pressure >10 mm Hg, elevated RV pressure with a classic "dip and plateau" diastolic wave form, and RA/PCWP ratio ≥0.8.

Treatment

- Depending upon the level of hemodynamic compromise, treatment includes volume loading to increase the PCWP to 16–20 mm Hg, positive inotropic agents (dobutamine is the preferred agent), or AV sequential pacing to maintain AV synchrony.
- Patients in persistent shock may benefit from cardiac catheterization and PTCA of the occluded right coronary artery.

Pericarditis (see Chapter 13)   Pericarditis occurs in 20% to 25% of patients with ST elevation MI.

Long-Term Management and Prognosis

The long-term management of patients surviving the acute phase of MI includes an assessment of existing risk factors for poor prognosis, institution of appropriate pharmacologic therapy, modification of life-style and coronary risk factors, and cardiac rehabilitation.

Risk Factor Assessment

The goal of risk factor assessment is to identify patients at high risk of suffering a future coronary event. Established risk factors for poor long-term prognosis following acute MI include:

Spontaneous or inducible myocardial ischemia
LV dysfunction (defined as an ejection fraction <40%)
More than 10 VPCs per hour
Advanced New York Heart Association (NYHA)
    classification prior to MI
Non-Q wave MI

The presence of a greater number of risk factors at the time of hospital discharge predicts higher long-term mortality.

High-risk patients with post-MI angina, complex ventricular ectopy requiring therapy, depressed LV ejection fraction (<40%), and clinical CHF are referred for cardiac catheterization.

Exercise Testing   Exercise testing after MI has several goals, including:

- Clearance of the patient for hospital discharge.
- Evaluation of the patient's ability to perform at home activities.
- Evaluation of the efficacy of medical therapy.
- Psychological reassurance to the patient.
- Risk stratification for subsequent coronary events.

Testing Strategies   Several strategies exist for exercise testing in the post-MI period.

Strategy 1: Perform a submaximal exercise ECG (with or without myocardial imaging) at 4 to 6 days after MI in the patient without complications. The target

HR is set at 120 to 130 bpm or 70% of age-predicted maximal HR. Patients without inducible ischemia should be followed up with a symptom-limited (maximal) exercise ECG test at 4 to 6 weeks. Patients should be referred for cardiac catheterization if they:

- Cannot achieve a 3 to 5 MET workload.
- Cannot achieve the target HR.
- Exhibit exercise-induced hypotension.
- Develop exercise-induced ST segment depression or angina.
- Show evidence of myocardial ischemia by imaging techniques.

Strategy 2: Perform a symptom-limited (maximal) exercise ECG test (with or without myocardial imaging) at 10 to 14 days after MI. Medical therapy is continued if no ischemia is detected. Coronary angiography should be recommended for patients who show:

- Ischemic ECG changes.
- Abnormal hemodynamic responses.
- Imaging evidence of myocardial ischemia.

Strategy 3: Discharge the clinically low-risk patient at 5 to 7 days and perform a symptom-limited exercise ECG test at 3 weeks. Medical therapy is indicated for patients without inducible ischemia. Cardiac catheterization should be performed on patients who show:

- Ischemic ECG changes
- Abnormal hemodynamic responses
- Imaging evidence of myocardial ischemia.

Pharmacologic Stress Testing For patients unable to exercise, pharmacologic stress testing (dipyridamole, adenosine, dobutamine) can be safely performed within 48 hours after MI.

Measurement of LV Ejection Fraction Resting LV ejection fraction measured 1 week after MI remains an important predictor of long-term cardiac risk. The data indicate that 1-year mortality rises precipitously when ejection fraction is less than 40%.

Assessment of Ventricular Ectopy Frequent VPCs (>10/hour) or complex ventricular ectopy has been identified an independent risk factor for increased mortality after acute MI.

Several techniques have been used to assess the significance of ventricular ectopy following MI:

Holter (ambulatory) monitoring
Signal-averaged (high-resolution) ECG
HR variability

Although the specificity of these tests is high (>90%), the positive predictive accuracy is less than 30% when these tests are used in isolation.

- Routine Holter monitor testing, signal-averaged ECG, or HR variability testing is not recommended in patients after MI.
- Among patients with frequent, complex ectopy and a positive signal-averaged ECG, invasive EP testing may be warranted, especially in the setting of depressed LV function.
- Asymptomatic nonsustained VT should not be treated empirically, given the implications of the CAST study.

Non-Q wave MI As a group, patients with non-Q wave MIs are at increased risk for adverse events during long-term follow-up.

Discharge Evaluation Prior to hospital discharge, two equally valid strategies for evaluation may be followed:

Strategy 1: Risk stratifying stable patients with a stress test prior to hospital dismissal. Patients with stress-induced ischemia are referred for coronary angiography.

Strategy 2: Performing coronary angiography without performance of a stress test.

Poor prognostic indicators prior to hospital discharge in patients with non-Q MI include:

Anterior location
Persistent ST segment depression
Patient's inability to perform a low-level ECG stress test
Recurrent angina

Pharmacologic Therapy

Beta-Blockers

Numerous studies have demonstrated that long-term administration of beta-blockers improves survival and decreases the incidence of reinfarction.

Beta-blockers should be administered to all patients except those at extremely low risk or those with a contraindication to therapy. Treatment should continue indefinitely. Agents with ISA have not demonstrated a beneficial long-term effect on mortality and morbidity.

Aspirin (ASA)   ASA significantly reduces the risk of future coronary events in post-MI patients. A dose of 75 to 325 mg per day should be administered unless a contraindication exists. Treatment should continue indefinitely.

Other antiplatelet agents have not been adequately studied to recommend their use in the post-MI setting.

Calcium Channel Blockers

- **Diltiazem.** Diltiazem has been demonstrated to reduce the incidence of coronary events for up to 14 days following non-Q wave MI. A long-term benefit from diltiazem has not been realized in patients with both Q wave and non-Q wave MIs. An adverse outcome has been shown to occur when diltiazem is used in patients with pulmonary congestion.
- **Nifedipine.** Nifedipine and other dihydropyridines have demonstrated no benefit either in the short- or long-term treatment of patients with acute MI.
- **Verapamil.** Verapamil use should be reserved for patients who cannot receive a beta-blocker. Although verapamil has been demonstrated to reduce morbidity and mortality in post-MI patients, beta-blockers have been more extensively studied and most patients who are candidates for verapamil therapy can also tolerate beta-blockers.

ACE-Inhibitors   The rationale for use of ACE-inhibitors following MI comes from observations that captopril attenuated ventricular dilatation after anterior MI.

A number of randomized clinical trials, in which a variety of oral ACE-inhibitors were used, have consistently shown that initiation of therapy within 1 to 16 days of MI favorably affects mortality, incidence of CHF, and the rate of reinfarction. LV dilatation is attenuated and LV volume is reduced among treated patients.

- The administration of an ACE-inhibitor within 24 hours of MI is indicated in the setting of acute anterior MI and/or symptomatic LV dysfunction.
- ACE-inhibitors are also indicated for patients with LV ejection fraction less than 40% regardless of symptoms, provided no contraindication to administration exists.
- Treatment should continue indefinitely among patients with persisting LV dysfunction. The benefit of ACE-inhibitors among patients without LV dysfunction and/or small inferior MI is less clear.

Oral Anticoagulants ASA alone remains the recommended antithrombotic regimen following MI. Long-term therapy with warfarin (INR 2.0 to 5.0) can reduce the risk of death and reinfarction by approximately 30%. A 55% reduction in the number of strokes has also been reported. Based on these data, warfarin can be recommended for secondary prevention of MI in patients unable to take ASA.

Oral anticoagulation is also indicated for patients with LV mural thrombus or sustained AF. The goal INR is 2.0 to 3.0.

Antioxidants To date, the use of supplemental antioxidant drugs (vitamin E, vitamin C, beta-carotene) has not been shown to have beneficial effect on the risk of future cardiovascular events.

Estrogen Replacement Therapy Among postmenopausal women, estrogen replacement therapy has been associated with a significant reduction in future cardiac events.

Coronary Risk Factor Modification

The identification and modification of risk factors for CAD is of paramount importance not only in primary prevention, but also in secondary prevention of coronary events.

Lipid Levels

Due to the known phenomenon of false lowering of lipids during the early phases of acute MI, lipid levels should be rechecked several (at least 4 to 6) weeks after the infarction (especially if they were initially in the "normal" range). Based on the complete lipid panel, further dietary counseling and/or appropriate initiation of pharmacologic therapy should begin.

- A diet low in fat and cholesterol (Step II AHA, <200 mg cholesterol/day and <7% of total calories as saturated fat) should be reviewed with all patients prior to hospital dismissal.
- Current recommendations suggest that aggressive lowering of LDL lipoprotein levels to less than 100 mg/dL be accomplished.

Other Risk Factors

Other risk factors for atherosclerosis should be aggressively modified.

Cardiac Rehabilitation

Cardiac rehabilitation is designed to improve the exercise performance, facilitate the return to normal activities, and improve the quality of life of patients with CAD. Most programs utilize a three-phase program that gradually increases physical activity over a 6-month period.

SUGGESTED READINGS

ACC/AHA Task Force Report. Guidelines for percutaneous transluminal coronary angioplasty. J Am Coll Cardiol 1993;22:2033–2054.

ACC Expert Consensus Document. Coronary artery stents. J Am Coll Cardiol 1996;28:782–794.

Andre-Fauet X, Pillot M, Leizorovicz A, et al. "Non-Q-Wave" alias "nontransmural" myocardial infarction: a specific entity. Am Heart J 1989;117:892–902.

Badiman JJ, Fuster V, Chesebro JH, Badiman L. Coronary atherosclerosis: a multifactorial disease. Circulation 1993; 87(suppl II):II-3–II-16.

Barrett-Connor E, Bush TL. Estrogen and coronary heart disease in women. JAMA 1991;265:1861–1867.

Bittl J. Advances in coronary angioplasty. N Engl J Med 1996;335:1290–1302.

Braunwald E, Brown J, Brown L, et al. Diagnosing and managing unstable angina. Circulation 1994;90:613–622.

Chung EK, Tighe DA. Pocket guide to stress testing. Boston: Blackwell Science, 1997.

DeWood MA, Spores J, Notske R, et al. Prevalence of total coronary occlusion during the early hours of transmural myocardial infarction. N Engl J Med 1980;303:897–902.

DeWood MA, Stifter WF, Simpson CS, et al. Coronary arteriographic findings soon after non-Q wave myocardial infarction. N Engl J Med 1986;315:417–423.

Every NR, Parsons LS, Hlatky M, et al. A comparison of thrombolytic therapy with primary coronary angioplasty for acute myocardial infarction. N Engl J Med 1996;335:1253–1260.

Expert Panel on Detection, Evaluation, and Treatment of High Blood Cholesterol in Adults. Summary of the second report of the National Cholesterol Education Program Expert Panel on Detection, Evaluation, and Treatment of High Blood Cholesterol in Adults. JAMA 1993;269:3015–3023.

Fischman DL, Leon MB, Baim DS, et al. A randomized comparison of coronary-stent placement and balloon angioplasty in the treatment of coronary artery disease. N Engl J Med 1994;331:496–501.

Forrester JS, Diamond G, Chatterjee K, et al. Medical therapy of acute myocardial infarction by application of hemodynamic subsets. N Engl J Med 1976;295:1356–1362,1404–1413.

Furberg CD, Psaty BM, Meyer JV. Nifedipine. Dose-related increase in mortality with coronary heart disease. Circulation 1995;92:1326–1331.

Hamm CW. New serum markers for acute myocardial infarction. N Engl J Med 1994;331:607–608.

Hamm CW, Reimers J, Ischinger T, et al. A randomized study of coronary angioplasty compared with bypass surgery in patients with symptomatic multivessel coronary artery disease. N Engl J Med 1994;331:1037–1043.

Isner JM. Right ventricular myocardial infarction. JAMA 1988;259:712–718.

Katus HA, Scheffold T, Remppis A, Zehlein J. Proteins of the troponin complex. Lab Med 1992;23:311–317.

King SB III, Lembo NJ, Weintraub WS, et al. A randomized

trial comparing coronary angioplasty with coronary bypass surgery. N Engl J Med 1994;331:1044–1050.

Lieu TA, Gurley RJ, Lundstrom RJ, Parmley WW. Primary angioplasty and thrombolysis for acute myocardial infarction: an evidence summary. J Am Coll Cardiol 1996;27:737–750.

Mayer EL, Jacobsen DW, Robinson K. Homocysteine and coronary atherosclerosis. J Am Coll Cardiol 1996;27:517–527.

Moliterno DJ, Elliott JM, Topol EJ. Randomized trials of myocardial revascularization. Curr Probl Cardiol 1995;20:121–192.

Moosvi AR, Khaja F, Villaneuva L, et al. Early revascularization improves survival in cardiogenic shock complicating acute myocardial infarction. J Am Coll Cardiol 1992;19:907–914.

Nishimura RA, Schaff HV, Gersh BJ, et al. Early repair of mechanical complications after acute myocardial infarction. JAMA 1986;256:47–50.

Opie LH, Messerli FH. Nifedipine and mortality. Grave defects in the dossier. Circulation 1995;92:1068–1073. Editorial.

Parisi AF, Folland ED, Hartigan P, et al. A comparison of angioplasty with medical therapy in the treatment of single-vessel coronary artery disease. N Engl J Med 1992;326:10–16.

Pearson T, Rappaport E, Criqui M, et al. Optimal risk factor management in the patient after coronary revascularization. A statement for healthcare professionals from an American Heart Association writing group. Circulation 1994;90:3125–3133.

Peiris AV, Sothmann MS, Hoffman RG, et al. Adiposity, fat distribution, and cardiovascular risk. Ann Intern Med 1989;110:867–872.

Pfeffer MA, Braunwald E, Moyé LA, et al. Effect of captopril on mortality and morbidity in patients with left ventricular dysfunction after myocardial infarction. N Engl J Med 1992;327:669–677.

Pfeffer MA, Lamas GA, Vaughan DE, et al. Effect of captopril on progressive ventricular dilatation after anterior myocardial infarction. N Engl J Med 1988;319:80–86.

Puleo PR, Meyer D, Wathen C, et al. Use of a rapid assay of subforms of creatine kinase MB to diagnose or rule out acute myocardial infarction. N Engl J Med 1994;331:561–566.

Ross, R. The pathogenesis of atherosclerosis: an update. N Engl J Med 1986;314:496.

Ryan TJ, Anderson JL, Antman EM, et al. ACC/AHA guidelines for the management of patients with acute myocardial infarction: a report of the American College of Cardiology/American Heart Association Task Force on practice guidelines (Committee on Management of Acute Myocardial Infarction). J Am Coll Cardiol 1996;28:1328–1428.

Sane DC, Califf RM, Topol EJ, et al. Bleeding during thrombolytic therapy for acute myocardial infarction: mechanisms and management. Ann Intern Med 1989;111:1010–1022.

Serruys PW, De Jaegere P, Kiemeneij F, et al. A comparison of balloon-expandable-stent implantation with balloon angioplasty in patients with coronary artery disease. N Engl J Med 1994;331:489–495.

Sgarbossa EB, Pinski SL, Barbagelata A, et al. Electrocardiographic diagnosis of evolving acute myocardial infarction in the presence of left bundle branch block. N Engl J Med 1996;334:481–487.

Smith P, Arnesen H, Holme I. The effects of warfarin on mortality and reinfarction after myocardial infarction. N Engl J Med 1990;323:147–152.

The EPIC Investigators. Use of a monoclonal antibody directed against the platelet glycoprotein IIb/IIIa receptor in high-risk coronary angioplasty. N Engl J Med 1994;330:956–961.

The EPILOG Investigators. Platelet glycoprotein IIb/IIIa receptor blockade and low-dose heparin during percutaneous coronary revascularization. N Engl J Med 1997;336:1689–1696.

The GUSTO Investigators. An international randomized trial comparing four thrombolytic strategies for acute myocardial infarction. N Engl J Med 1993;329:673–682.

The GUSTO IIb Angioplasty Substudy Investigators. A clinical trial comparing primary coronary angioplasty with tissue plasminogen activator for acute myocardial infarction. N Engl J Med 1997;336:1621–1628.

The Multicenter Postinfarction Research Group. Risk stratification after myocardial infarction. N Engl J Med 1983;309:331–336.

The PRISM-PLUS Study Investigators. Inhibition of the platelet glycoprotein IIb/IIIa receptor with tirofiban in unstable angina and non Q-wave myocardial infarction. N Engl J Med 1998;338:1488–1497.

The PRISM Study Investigators. A comparison of aspirin plus tirofiban with aspirin plus heparin for unstable angina. N Engl J Med 1998;338:1489–1505.

Wexler L, Brundage B, Crouse J, et al. Coronary artery calcification: pathophysiology, epidemiology, imaging methods, and clinical implications. Circulation 1996;94:1175–1192.

Congestive Heart Failure

Dennis A. Tighe
Edward K. Chung

Congestive heart failure (CHF) refers to a syndrome rather than a specific etiologic diagnosis. CHF can be defined as the pathophysiologic state in which an abnormality of cardiac function is responsible for the inability of the heart to pump blood at a rate commensurate with the requirements of the metabolizing tissues. The clinical expression of CHF involves a complex interaction between the heart, vasculature, neuroendocrine system, and other peripheral organ systems.

This chapter reviews the epidemiology, etiology, clinical evaluation, compensatory mechanisms, and therapy of CHF.

EPIDEMIOLOGY OF CHF

CHF is a common clinical syndrome associated with a poor prognosis:

- It is estimated that 1% to 2% of the noninstitutionalized adult American population has CHF.
- The incidence of CHF increases with advancing age and is more common in men than women.
- More that 1.5 million final hospital discharges with a diagnosis of CHF are listed annually. CHF is the most common hospital discharge diagnosis among the elderly.

Table 2-1. New York Heart Association Functional Classification

Class I	No limitation. Ordinary physical activity does not cause symptoms.
Class II	Slight limitation of physical activity. Ordinary physical activity will result in symptoms.
Class III	Marked limitation of physical activity. Less than ordinary activity leads to symptoms.
Class IV	Inability to carry out any activity without symptoms. Symptoms are present at rest.

- An evaluation of recent data from Framingham Heart Study reveals that mortality after CHF onset remains high (median survival of 1.7 years in men and 3.2 years in women) despite advances in the medical and surgical therapy of cardiovascular disease.

Prognosis is related to the degree of underlying myocardial dysfunction:

- Patients in New York Heart Association (NYHA) (Table 2-1) classes I and II have a 5-year mortality approximating 50%.
- Class IV patients have a 1-year mortality of 35% to 50%.

ETIOLOGY

A variety of pathophysiologic mechanisms—including loss of myocardial muscle mass, decreased intrinsic contractility, pressure overload, volume overload, and restriction of diastolic ventricular filling—contribute to the development of CHF.

Many extra-cardiac conditions and other disease processes can be precipitating causes of CHF.

The most common causes of CHF encountered clinically include:

CAD
HTN
Valvular heart disease
Cardiomyopathy

Coronary Artery Disease (CAD)

CAD accounts for the vast majority (60% to 75%) of cases of CHF. CAD has adverse effects on both systolic and diastolic ventricular function.

- Post-MI stunning and myocardial hibernation due to chronic ischemia may lead to myocardial dysfunction.
- Myocardial ischemia contributes to enhanced myocardial stiffness and diastolic dysfunction necessitating elevated pressures to maintain ventricular filling.
- LV aneurysm formation may contribute to low CO by increasing ventricular size, heightening wall stress, and causing paradoxical systolic expansion with trapping of a given volume of blood.
- The most powerful predictors of a long-term survival among patients with CAD are the degree of residual LV function as measured by the ejection fraction and the end-systolic ventricular volume.

Hypertension

Long-standing HTN causes ventricular pressure over-load. Acute, severe HTN or intermittent inadequate control of BP can cause bouts of CHF.

Valvular Heart Disease

Heart valve dysfunction (particularly that involving the left-sided valves) produces pressure or volume overload of the ventricle, and is a leading cause of CHF (see Chapter 6).

Cardiomyopathies and Myocarditis (see Chapter 12)

Dilated Cardiomyopathy (DCM)
DCM is characterized by decreased intrinsic myocardial contractility. It is often idiopathic in nature; however, secondary causes must also be considered.

Hypertrophic Cardiomyopathy (HCM)
HCM causes diastolic ventricular dysfunction. Obstructive and nonobstructive variants are recognized.

- In a subgroup of patients with late-stage HCM, ventricular dilatation and severe systolic dysfunction (a "burned-out" phase) may occur; this condition is clinically indistinguishable from a DCM.
- Hypertensive HCM of the elderly, a syndrome characterized by severe concentric LVH with dynamic ventricular function, is an important cause of pulmonary congestion in the elderly.

Restrictive Cardiomyopathy (RCM)

RCM, the least common form of heart muscle disease encountered clinically, is also characterized by abnormal diastolic ventricular filling with relatively well-preserved systolic function.

Myocarditis

Myocarditis, secondary to a variety of infectious and toxic agents, may cause CHF due to a global decline in systolic ventricular function. Myocarditis may underlie many cases of "idiopathic" DCM.

Congenital Heart Disease (see Chapter 9)

- ASD and PDA may have long-lived natural histories and present as CHF in adults.
- VSD, though less common in adults, may cause severe left heart volume overload. If unrecognized and untreated, it can lead to irreversible pulmonary vascular disease (Eisenmenger's syndrome).
- PS may cause long-standing pressure overload of the RV which manifests as systemic venous congestion with normal LV function.
- Long-term problems related to corrective operations for complex congenital heart lesions may become an increasingly common etiology of CHF as survivors now reach adulthood with increasing frequency.

Extracardiac Restriction of Filling

Mechanical processes like constrictive pericardial disease, effusive-constrictive pericarditis, and cardiac tamponade impede ventricular filling.

Extra-cardiac mass lesions, through direct extension or metastasis, may significantly impede ventricular filling and manifest as CHF.

High-output Syndromes

High-output syndromes include:

Hyperthyroidism
AV fistula
Paget's disease (bone deformation)
Dermatologic disorders
Beriberi heart disease
Chronic anemia

These syndromes cause LV volume overload with subsequent systolic dysfunction. Their effect is maximal when ventricular reserve is diminished.

Cardiac Arrhythmias

- The development of rapid AF with loss of atrial transport in the setting of ventricular dysfunction or significant valvular heart disease may exacerbate or precipitate CHF.
- Other tachyarrhythmias are poorly tolerated in patients with severe systolic and/or diastolic ventricular dysfunction due to the decline in the diastolic filling period.
- Chronic SVTs are a recognized cause of DCM.
- Marked bradyarrythmias and severe AV conduction disturbances can also result in inadequate CO which may precipitate or aggravate heart failure.

CHF Precipitating Factors

Precipitating factors for CHF refer to other disease processes which have an effect on the cardiovascular system with marginal reserve.

- Development of a second form of heart disease (for example, an MI superimposed upon cardiomyopathy or hypertensive heart disease).
- Systemic infection.
- Disease processes affecting the other organ systems:
  Lungs: pneumonia, pulmonary embolism, obstructive or restrictive lung disease, pulmonary vascular disease, sleep apnea syndrome.
  Kidneys: acute/chronic renal failure with fluid overload, renovascular HTN.

Liver: hepatic cirrhosis.
Endocrine system: hyperthyroidism, hypothyroidism, pheochromocytoma.

- The use of medications with negative inotropic and/or chronotropic effects (beta-blockers, CCBs, Type I-A antiarrhythmic drugs) and those which contribute to salt and water retention (corticosteroids, mineralocorticoids, nonsteroidal anti-inflammatory agents) should be recognized.
- Substance abuse (especially ethanol and cocaine) may precipitate CHF.

Inadequate Therapy

Inadequate therapy may contribute to "difficult to control" cases of CHF:

- The patient may not comply with diet and/or an appropriate medical regimen.
- The physician may give inadequate therapy or an incomplete diagnosis.

In addition, it must be recognized that among 30% to 40% of patients with heart failure symptoms, systolic function is normal and the primary problem lies in diastole. Treatment designed to enhance systolic function and decrease preload (digitalis, nitrates, diuretics) may have a detrimental effect.

Miscellaneous Causes

Intracavitary mass lesions (tumors, thrombus) may obstruct the pulmonary veins, large central veins, AV valves, or semilunar valves leading to diminished CO.

CLINICAL MANIFESTATIONS
Symptoms

Pulmonary Congestion
- Pulmonary congestion, manifested initially by dyspnea on exertion, is the most common symptom of CHF.
- Other symptoms such as cough, dyspnea at rest, orthopnea, and paroxysmal nocturnal dyspnea are indicative of worsening pulmonary congestion.

Venous Hypertension

Systemic venous HTN due to sodium and fluid retention and/or restricted filling of the heart can manifest as

Peripheral edema
Weight gain
Abdominal discomfort
Nocturia
Increasing abdominal girth (ascites)

Diminished Cardiac Output

Characteristic of advanced CHF are the symptoms of significantly diminished CO:

Confusion
Fatigue
Weakness
Weight loss (cachexia)
Palpitations (tachycardia)

Physical Examination

Physical findings depend on the underlying etiology and severity of cardiac dysfunction.

General Appearance and Vital Signs

Common findings of CHF include:

Anxiety
Tachypnea
Tachycardia
Weak/thready pulses
Neck vein distention

When CO is severely diminished, the following signs may be present:

Pulsus alternans
Cyanosis
Scleral icterus
Signs of cachexia

Pulmonary Examination

Common findings include:

Moist rales
Wheezing (cardiac asthma)
Dullness to percussion (pleural effusion)

Cardiovascular Examination

Common findings include:

Lateral displacement and enlargement of the apical
  impulse
Ventricular gallop rhythm
Functional murmurs of MR and TR

Pulmonary HTN is indicated by a loud pulmonic component of S_2 and an RV lift.

Abdominal Examination

- In the setting of neck vein distention, the liver can be
  enlarged and tender to palpation.
- A pulsatile liver may indicate severe TR.
- Ascites may be present.

Peripheral Examination

- Dependent, pitting edema indicates retention of at
  least 5 liters of fluid.
- Other peripheral signs include
  Cool skin
  Pallor
  Livido reticularis
  Cyanosis

DIAGNOSTIC EVALUATION

Diagnostic tests are used to confirm clinical suspicion and
to elicit further information on underlying disorders that
may not be apparent from the history and physical
examination.

Laboratory Evaluation

In cases of mild CHF, routine tests may be within normal
limits.

Serum Electrolytes

- Hyponatremia on the basis of fluid retention and/or
  diuretic therapy is frequently present.
- Disorders of potassium and magnesium balance are
  often secondary to diuretic usage.

Hepatic Enzymes

- Elevation of total bilirubin, LDH, SGOT, and/or
  SGPT occur in the presence of significant hepatic
  congestion.

- With severe hepatic congestion and impaired synthetic function, the serum cholesterol level will be decreased and the prothrombin time increased.

Renal Function
- In the presence of advanced CHF and/or pre-renal azotemia, the serum BUN is disproportionately elevated as compared to serum creatinine.
- Measured urinary sodium and fractional excretion of sodium are low, except in cases of diuretic usage and intrinsic renal disease.

Erythrocyte Sedimentation Rate (ESR)
The ESR is usually very low in CHF.

Chest X-Ray (CXR)

The CXR is a useful screening test for determining the chronicity of underlying cardiac dysfunction and allowing evaluation of the lungs. Obtaining and comparing prior CXR examinations are mandatory.

Heart Size and Shape
Cardiomegaly is frequently present. A cardiothoracic ratio in excess of 0.55 indicates cardiomegaly.

- Straightening of the left heart border often indicates LA enlargement.
- On the lateral projection, obliteration of the anterior clear space indicates enlargement of the RV, while a posterior shadow projecting toward the spine suggests LV enlargement.
- Cardiomegaly may be secondary to increased intrapericardial fluid volume.

Pulmonary Congestion
- Pulmonary congestion is indicated by increased vascular markings with redistribution from base to apex, peribronchial cuffing, interlobar fluid, and Kerley B lines.
- With acute pulmonary edema, marked vascular redistribution in a "bat-wing-like" configuration is noted.
- Pleural effusions, more commonly right than left sided, are present in advanced cases.

Calcification

Cardiac calcification may be present in cases of organized LV thrombus, calcified LV aneurysm, chronic heart valve dysfunction, and constrictive pericardial disease.

Electrocardiography (ECG)

ECG abnormalities are primarily related to the underlying heart disease that is producing the clinical CHF. Common findings include:

- Evidence of recent and/or past MI.
- Chamber enlargement (LVH, RVH, LA enlargement) in cases of pressure and/or volume overload.
- Various cardiac arrrhythmias, such as AF, atrial flutter, VPCs, SVT.
- Conduction disturbances (LAFB, LBBB, RBBB, nonspecific IVCD).

Myocardial Imaging

Echocardiography

Echocardiography is the noninvasive test of choice to assess cardiac structure and function. This test can:

- Evaluate the regional wall motion and wall thickness.
- Semiquantify and assess the hemodynamic effects of valvar regurgitation.
- Assess the severity of valvar stenosis.
- Assess the pericardium.
- Evaluate ventricular diastolic function.

Gated Blood Pool Scanning

With gated blood pool (MUGA) scanning, the physician can:

- More precisely quantify ventricular ejection fraction.
- Qualitatively assess regional ventricular wall motion.

MRI

Cardiac MRI scanning can provide assessment of myocardial structure and function. Characterization of tissue density is possible. Assessment of pericardial thickness and characterization of cardiac mass lesions are advantages of MRI.

Assessment of Myocardial Ischemia and Viability (see Chapter 1)

Exercise or pharmacologic stress testing is indicated for the noninvasive evaluation of possible myocardial ischemia and/or myocardial viability. An ischemic response with testing indicates the need for further (often invasive) evaluation and treatment of CAD. An extensive amount of viable myocardium as detected by noninvasive testing (thallium imaging, dobutamine stress echocardiography, or PET scanning) may select CHF patients who would benefit from revascularization.

Cardiac Catheterization and Angiography

Cardiac catheterization and coronary angiography are not routinely performed in patients with CHF. Coronary angiography is required when a definitive diagnosis of CAD is required and when revascularization therapy is considered.

- Left ventriculography at the time of angiography allows determination of LV ejection fraction, semi-quantitative assessment of MR, and assessment of regional wall motion abnormalities.
- Right heart catheterization is required to measure CO, RA and RV pressures, PA pressures, PCWP, and to calculate PVR.
- The right heart catheter can be left in place for serial determinations of PA pressure and PVR in response to pharmacological interventions.
- RV biopsy is indicated if an underlying myocarditis or infiltrative process is suspected to be the primary cause of CHF.

COMPENSATORY MECHANISMS

Compensatory mechanisms are adaptations by the failing heart and circulation to preserve CO and maintain adequate peripheral organ perfusion pressure. Initially these mechanisms allow for adequate circulatory compensation, but unless the underlying pathophysiologic process is identified and reversed (if possible), these compensatory mechanisms can "overshoot" and become maladaptive, contributing in large part to the signs and symptoms seen in CHF. The major compensatory mechanisms are:

1. Neurohormonal adjustments.
2. Myocardial hypertrophy and dilatation.
3. The Frank-Starling relationship.

Neurohormonal Mechanisms

Autonomic Nervous System

The sympathetic nervous system has complex interactions with the heart, vasculature, and peripheral tissues. CHF affects the sympathetic nervous system's interrelationships:

- Myocardial norepinephrine (NE) levels are significantly diminished and myocardial β-1 receptors are downregulated.
- Peripheral catecholamine levels are elevated. The serum levels correlate with the clinical severity of CHF.
- NE acts to increase HR and myocardial contractility, increase afterload via arterial vasoconstriction to maintain systemic perfusion pressure, and increase preload via venoconstriction.

Maladaptation Long-term sympathetic nervous system overactivity is maladaptive because catecholamines are known myocardial toxins:

- They result in tachycardia and increased afterload that increase myocardial oxygen demand.
- They further downregulate β-1 receptors.
- They increase the risk of ventricular arrhythmias.

Renin-Angiotensin-Aldosterone (RAA) System

Renin release is stimulated by hypovolemia and diminished delivery of sodium to the macula densa of the juxtaglomerular apparatus. Release of renin initiates a cascade which ultimately results in the formation of angiotensin II and aldosterone.

Angiotensin II is a potent vasoconstrictor. Its actions contribute to both increased preload and afterload.

Aldosterone acts at the distal renal tubule and cortical collecting duct to stimulate salt and water retention to maintain adequate preload.

Maladaption   The actions of the RAA system become maladaptive when excessive afterload further compromises LV ejection performance and when salt and water retention lead to systemic and pulmonary venous congestion.

Arginine Vasopressin (AVP)

AVP (also known as the antidiuretic hormone) is a potent vasoconstrictor and stimulus to the retention of free water. AVP functions to maintain adequate preload and afterload early in the course of CHF.

Maladaption   The effects of AVP become maladaptive when these mechanisms overshoot, causing excessive LV afterload and venous congestion.

Atrial Natriuretic Peptide (ANP)

ANP is released by the atria and ventricles in response to atrial distention. ANP is a vasodilator peptide which enhances renal salt and water excretion. These actions, in effect, act to counterbalance the previously described neurohormonal influences.

Maladaption   Peripheral responsiveness to ANP is diminished in CHF.

Other Vasoactive Substances

Serum levels of substances such as various natriuretic peptides, endothelin-1, tumor necrosis factor, and peptide growth factors are abnormally elevated in CHF.

Hypertrophy

Ventricular hypertrophy is an increase in muscle mass without an increase in the number of myocytes.

Concentric hypertrophy (hypertrophy without significant chamber dilatation) is an adaptation to normalize wall stress. However, with increasing hypertrophy, myocardial oxygen demand increases, myocardial oxygen supply to the subendocardium diminishes, and indices of ventricular diastolic performance decline. With progressive ventricular systolic failure, eccentric hypertrophy (chamber dilatation) occurs.

Frank-Starling Relationship

According to the Frank-Starling curve, increased preload produces an increase in muscle force generation over the physiologic range. As end-diastolic volume is increased, an increase in stroke volume occurs.

With CHF, renal salt and water retention and veno-constriction lead to increased ventricular filling pressures and end-diastolic volumes in order to maintain CO. As preload reserve is exceeded, further salt and water retention leads to pulmonary and systemic venous HTN and congestion.

THERAPY OF CHF
Goal

The goal of therapy is to improve the quality and quantity of life.

Identify and Treat Underlying Etiology

Specific definition of the underlying cause of CHF yields important prognostic information, because in certain situations CHF may be totally correctable.

- Mechanical obstructions, such as AS and MS and severe regurgitant lesions of the aortic and mitral valves, may respond to valve replacement or repair. Removal of obstructing mass lesions may relieve symptoms.
- LV aneurysmectomy may relieve significant congestive symptoms if enough viable myocardium remains.
- Underlying CAD may respond to revascularization procedures with significant improvement in ventricular function.
- Endocrinopathies may respond to appropriate therapy with complete reversal of CHF.
- Proper control and therapy of HTN may significantly improve ventricular performance.
- Abstinence from alcohol and, if possible, cessation of medications with negative inotropic and sodium/water retaining effects, may lead to significantly improved ventricular function.
- Identification of diastolic dysfunction and proper therapy with CCBs and/or beta-blocking agents may have dramatic effects.

Reverse Secondary Causes

As disease processes affecting other organ systems may have significant effects on the myocardium with diminished reserve, directing therapy to those secondary causes of CHF can stabilize underlying myocardial function.

Nonpharmacologic Therapy

Reduce Cardiac Workload

Tailoring physical activity to the degree of myocardial impairment and limiting emotional and mental stress are important measures to decrease myocardial oxygen demand.

For overweight patients, a regimen designed to reduce weight should be prescribed and closely followed-up.

Dietary Modification

Dietary sodium intake should be restricted in proportion to the degree of ventricular dysfunction. Draconian restriction of sodium is not necessary in the majority of patients who respond well to diuretics. Modest sodium restriction (to <2 grams daily) is sufficient in most cases.

Fluid intake should be restricted, depending on the degree of symptoms.

Supplemental Oxygen

Oxygen therapy is indicated when arterial saturation is below 90% despite adequate medical therapy.

Mechanical Removal of Fluid

Procedures such as thoracentesis, abdominal paracentesis, and hemofiltration are indicated in the proper clinical setting and may afford great symptomatic relief.

Pharmacologic Therapy

Pharmacologic therapies are intended to counteract the mechanisms of overcompensation. Many patients require combination therapy; often, the combination therapy features a diuretic, a digitalis preparation, and a vasodilator.

Diuretic Agents

Diuretics (Table 2-2) are the agents of choice for mild to moderate CHF. The goal of therapy is to reduce ventric-

Table 2-2. Pharmacologic Therapy of CHF: Diuretic Agents

Drug	Trade Name	Site of Action	Dose Range and Route
Thiazides and Related Agents			
Bendroflumethazide	Naturetin	Distal tubule	2.5–30 mg po/d
Benzthiazide	Aquatag, Exna	Distal tubule	50–200 mg po/d
Chlorothiazide	Diuril	Distal tubule	0.5–1.0 g po/IV BID
Chlorthalidone	Hygroton, Thalitone	Distal tubule	15–120 mg po/d
Hydrochlorothiazide (HCTZ)	Esidrix, Hydrodiuril, Oretic	Distal tubule	25–200 mg po/d
Hydroflumethazide	Diucardin	Distal tubule	25–200 mg po/d
Indapamide	Lozol	Distal tubule vasodilator	2.5–5 mg po/d
Methyclothiazide	Enduron, Aquatensen	Distal tubule	2.5–10 mg po/d
Metolazone	Zaroxolyn, Diulo	Distal tubule	5–10 mg po/d
Metolazone (rapidly available formulation)	Mykrox	Distal tubule	0.5–2 mg po/d
Polythiazide	Renese	Distal tubule	2–4 mg po/d
Quinethazone	Hydromox	Distal tubule	50–200 mg po/d
Loop Diuretics			
Bumetanide	Bumex	Ascending loop	0.5–10 mg po/IV/IM daily
Ethacrynic Acid	Edecrin	Ascending loop	25–200 mg po/IV daily
Furosemide	Lasix	Ascending loop	20–600 mg po/IV daily
Torsemide	Demadex	Ascending loop	10–200 mg po/IV daily
Potassium-sparing Diuretics			
Amiloride	Midamor	Collecting duct	5–10 mg po/d
Spironolactone	Aldactone	Collecting duct	25–200 mg po/d
Triamterene	Dyrenium	Collecting duct	200–300 mg po/d

ular wall stress by decreasing cardiac volume. Many different types of diuretic agents are available, each having specific actions on a particular segment of the nephron.

Thiazides and Related Agents

Thiazide-type diuretics act at the distal cortical diluting segment to induce natriuresis. These agents are ineffective when the glomerular filtration rate is less than 30 mL/min.

Potassium-Sparing Diuretics Potassium-sparing diuretics block exchange of sodium and potassium in the distal convoluted tubule and cortical collecting duct. Potassium-sparing agents are weak diuretics when used alone; however, in combination with other classes of diuretics, they may enhance the effect of the more potent agent.

Loop Diuretics Loop agents inhibit sodium chloride absorption in the ascending limb of Henle's loop and are capable of inducing a natriuresis of up to 20% of the filtered sodium load.

- Loop diuretics are very potent and are the agents of choice in renal insufficiency, pulmonary edema, and CHF resistant to other diuretics.
- In refractory cases, the combination of a loop diuretic and a thiazide or a thiazide-like agent (such as metolazone) is required to achieve effective diuresis.

Digitalis Glycosides

Digitalis (Table 2-3) is widely used in the treatment of CHF. Mechanisms of action include a positive (albeit weak) inotropic effect, improved autonomic nervous system balance, and reduction of renin secretion.

Formerly believed useful only in patients with ventricular dysfunction and coexisting AF with rapid ventricular response, digitalis has been demonstrated to be beneficial in all patients with compromised systolic function. Symptomatic status is improved and hospitalization

Table 2-3. Pharmacologic Therapy of CHF: Cardiac Glycosides

Drug	Trade Name	GI Absorption	Excretion	Half-life	Digitalizing Dose	Daily Dose
Digoxin	Lanoxin Lanoxicaps Digoxin	60% to 80%	Renal	36–48 hr	0.75–1.5 mg	0.125–0.5 mg
Digitoxin	Crystodigin	90% to 100%	Hepatic	4–6 days	1.0–1.6 mg	0.05–0.3 mg

Table 2-4. Pharmacologic Therapy of CHF: Angiotensin-converting Enzyme Inhibitors

Drug	Trade Name	Dose Range	Frequency
Captopril	Capoten	6.25–100 mg po	TID-QID
Enalapril	Vasotec	2.5–20 mg po	BID
Enalaprilat	Vasotec IV	0.625–1.25 mg IV	QID
Fosinopril	Monopril	10–40 mg po	QD
Lisinopril	Prinivil, Zestril	5–40 mg po	QD
Quinapril	Accupril	5–40 mg po	BID
Ramipril	Altace	2.5–5 mg po	BID

for CHF is reduced. A neutral effect on mortality has been shown.

Precautions
- Recent studies have demonstrated that withdrawal of digoxin in patients with mild to moderate CHF, even in the presence of concomitant therapy with ACE-inhibitors, can lead to a decline in clinical status.
- Digoxin serum levels must be closely monitored because of the narrow therapeutic-to-toxic ratio.
- Caution should be used when digitalis is given to patients with diminished renal function, when digoxin is used in conjunction with drugs which affect potassium homeostasis, and when agents that alter free serum digoxin concentration (quinidine, verapamil, amiodarone) are concomitantly administered.

Vasodilator Agents
Vasodilator drugs (Tables 2-4 and 2-5) can have profound effects in CHF because characteristics of this condition are inappropriate vasoconstriction of the arterial and venous beds and extreme sensitivity of the heart to after-load. Some may require a combination of vasodilator agents for adequate control of symptoms.

ACE-Inhibitors   ACE-inhibitors are the afterload-reducing agents of choice in chronic CHF. These agents have beneficial effects on exercise tolerance, NYHA classification, and frequency of ventricular ectopy.

Table 2-5. Pharmacologic Therapy of CHF: Other Vasodilator Drugs

Drug	Mechanism	Dose Range	Route
Amlodipine	Calcium blocker	5–10 mg QD	po
Felodipine	Calcium blocker	5 mg BID	po
Hydralazine	Direct arteriolar vasodilator	10–100 mg QID	po
Isosorbide dinitrate	Venous ≫ Arteriolar vasodilator	10–60 mg TID	po
Isosorbide mononitrate	Venous ≫ Arteriolar vasodilator	Imdur: 30–240 mg QD	po
		Ismo, Monoket: 20 mg BID 7 hours apart	po
Nitroglycerin	Venous ≫ Arteriolar vasodilator	10–300 μg/min	IV
		5–60 mg	transdermal
Nitroprusside	Venous = Arteriolar (balanced) vasodilator	0.5–10 μg/kg/min	IV
Irbesartan	Angiotensin II receptor antagonist	150–300 mg qd	po
Losartan	Angiotensin II receptor antagonist	25–100 mg qd or BID	po
Valsartan	Angiotensin II receptor antagonist	80–320 mg qd	po

- As a class, ACE-inhibitors should be considered the cornerstone of CHF therapy due to systolic dysfunction. The use of ACE-inhibitors has been clearly shown to reduce recurrent hospitalization for CHF and all-cause mortality compared to placebo and the combination of hydralazine–isosorbide dinitrate.
- ACE-inhibitors have also been demonstrated to be clinically efficacious in patients with asymptomatic LV dysfunction (LVEF ≤35%).

- The benefit of ACE-inhibitor therapy is most apparent among patients with more severe degrees of LV dysfunction.
- When initiated as early as several hours after MI, ACE-inhibitors have shown clear clinical efficacy in reducing both mortality and morbidity due to cardiovascular disease as compared to placebo. The beneficial effects of ACE-inhibitors among the post-MI population are most likely due to favorable effects on ventricular remodeling and ventricular volume.

Precautions:
- Significant class-specific side-effects of ACE-inhibitors include renal insufficiency, hyperkalemia, cough, bone marrow suppression, hypotension, and angioedema.
- ACE-inhibitor use is contraindicated in patients with persistent hyperkalemia >5.5 mEq/L, symptomatic hypotension, or a history of intolerance or adverse reaction to therapy.
- ACE-inhibitors should not be used in the second and third trimesters of pregnancy due to the risk of injury or death to the developing fetus.

Other Vasodilator Agents

Nitrates Nitrates function primarily as venodilators, increasing venous capacitance and decreasing central venous blood volume to effect a reduction in preload. They are most effective in patients with high filling pressures and when used in combination with arterial vasodilator agents. Tolerance can quickly develop if a nitrate-free interval is not provided.

Direct-Acting Vasodilator Agents Hydralazine and minoxidil are prototype agents.

- In combination with isosorbide dinitrate, hydralazine has been demonstrated to improve LV function and decrease mortality as compared to placebo and the alpha-adrenergic blocking agent prazosin.
- Hydralazine is particularly useful in patients with renal insufficiency and in those unable to tolerate therapy with an ACE-inhibitor.

Sodium Nitroprusside Sodium nitroprusside is a potent, balanced vasodilator that requires constant IV infusion. The use of this agent is reserved for the setting of severe systolic ventricular dysfunction not responding to an oral regimen and/or when CHF is secondary to malignant HTN.

Angiotensin II Receptor-1 Blockers (ARBs) ARBs are vasodilators with a hemodynamic profile similar to ACE-inhibitors. Available data suggest that these agents are safe, well tolerated, and have efficacy to similar ACE-inhibitors in patients with chronic CHF. Results of large clinical trials employing ARBs are required before these agents can be widely recommended for treatment of CHF.

Nonglycoside Positive Inotropic Agents
Table 2-6 is a list of nonglycoside positive inotropic agents.

Catecholamines and Catecholamine-like Agents Catecholamines and catecholamine-like agents—such as dobutamine, dopamine, or epinephrine—should be used for the acute treatment of CHF only with close monitoring in an intensive care setting. These agents often lead to short-term symptomatic improvement.

- Intermittent IV administration of dobutamine to patients not fully responding to oral medications may lead to clinical stabilization and reduce hospitalization for severe episodes of CHF.
- Patients with severe, end-stage CHF may require constant infusion of dobutamine prior to anticipated surgical therapy.

Phosphodiesterase Inhibitors Phosphodiesterase inhibitors (amrinone and milrinone) act to increase intracellular cyclic AMP levels and improve short-term ventricular performance through vasodilator and positive inotropic effects.

At this time, these agents are indicated for the acute therapy of severe CHF as an alternative to dobutamine. Some investigators are administering IV milrinone intermittently on an outpatient basis to further stabilize

Table 2-6. Pharmacologic Therapy of CHF: Nonglycoside Inotropic Agents

Drug	Dose Range	Action
Amrinone	0.75 mg/kg IV bolus followed by infusion of 5–20 µg/kg/min	Phosphodiesterase inhibitor (positive inotrope and vasodilator)
Dobutamine	2–20 µg/kg/min IV	Beta-agonist (positive inotrope and chronotrope)
Dopamine	1.0–20 µg/kg/min IV	Dopaminergic effect on renal/mesenteric resistance at doses <2.0 µg/kg/min. Beta-agonist (positive inotrope) at doses of 2–6 µg/kg/min. Alpha-agonist (vasopressor) at doses >6–10 µg/kg/min.
Epinephrine	1–4 µg/min IV	Alpha- and beta-agonist (positive inotrope, chronotrope, and vasopressor)
Milrinone	50 µg/kg IV loading dose administered over 10 min slowly followed by infusion of 0.375–0.75 µg/kg/min	Phosphodiesterase inhibitor (positive inotrope and vasodilator)
Norepinephrine	2–20 µg/min IV	Alpha- > Beta-agonist

patients not fully responding to an aggressive oral CHF regimen.

Limitation: Long-term experience with oral phosphodiesterase inhibitors (milrinone and enoximone) has shown worsened prognosis compared to placebo.

Beta-Blockers

- Beta-blockers (along with CCBs) are the primary drugs of choice for CHF determined to be due to diastolic ventricular dysfunction (Table 2-7).
- Beta-blockers have also been used to treat selected patients with systolic dysfunction.

Potential mechanisms for the benefit of beta-blockers in CHF due to systolic dysfunction include:

1. Prevention of adrenergic cardiac toxicity by attenuation of prolonged sympathetic stimulation
2. Reduction of β-receptor downregulation

If beta-blockers are used to treat CHF, slow upward dose titration is indicated to minimize early hemodynamic deterioration due to withdrawal of beta-adrenergic stimulation. At present, beta-blockers should be considered

Table 2-7. Pharmacologic Therapy of CHF: Beta-Blockers

Drug	Dose Range	Action
Bisoprolol	Starting: 1.25 mg qd Maximum: 5 mg qd (<85 kg), 10 mg qd (≥85 kg)	Selective β_1-blocker
Bucindolol	Starting: 3 mg BID Maximum: 50 mg BID (<85 kg) 100 mg BID (≥85 kg)	Nonselective β-blocker and mild direct vasodilator (? cGMP-dependent)
*Carvedilol (Coreg)	Starting: 3.125 mg BID Titrate dose upward every 2 weeks Maximum: 25 mg BID (<85 kg) 50 mg BID (≥85 kg)	Nonselective β-blocker and α_1-blocker
Metoprolol (Lopressor)	Starting: 5–6.25 mg BID Maximum: 75 mg BID	Selective β_1-blocker
Nebivolol	Starting: 1 mg qd Maximum: 5 mg qd	Selective β_1-blocker and vasodilator (unknown mechanism)

*FDA-approved for treatment of CHF.
cGMP: cyclic guanosine monophosphate.

as an addition to standard therapy (ACE-inhibitors, digoxin, and diuretics) of CHF.

- Among patients with DCM, long-term treatment with beta-blockers has been shown to improve symptomatic status, LV performance, and NYHA functional class in selected patients.
- Recently, therapy with carvedilol (a nonselective beta-blocker that also blocks α-1 receptors) in addition to standard CHF therapy has been shown to reduce mortality among patients with chronic CHF. This agent is now FDA-approved for the treatment of chronic CHF due to systolic dysfunction.

Calcium Channel Blockers
In general, the use of CCBs with the most negative inotropic effects (verapamil and diltiazem) should be avoided among patients with moderate to severe systolic dysfunction.

Amlodipine   Amlodipine (5–10 mg per day) has been shown to improve exercise tolerance and symptomatic status among heart failure patients of NYHA classes II through III. In the PRAISE trial, amlodipine did not adversely affect morbidity and mortality among patients with advanced CHF. The major benefit of amlodipine was observed in the subgroup with nonischemic etiology.

Felodipine   In the V-HeFT III trial, felodipine (5 mg BID) was shown to be well tolerated but did not offer significant clinical benefit over standard CHF therapy in men in NYHA classes II and III.

Other Drugs

Morphine Sulfate   Morphine sulfate, 2–5 mg IV every 5 to 15 min, is indicated for relief of acute pulmonary congestion. Morphine has multiple actions including an increase in venous capacitance, a decrease in afterload, and a decrease in myocardial oxygen demand.

Anticoagulant Agents   Anticoagulant agents (warfarin, heparin) are indicated for patients with idiopathic DCM, certain forms of RCM, chronic AF, and large anterior-apical MIs in the presence of thrombus. For long-term therapy, warfarin is the preferred agent. A goal INR of 2.0–3.0 is optimal.

Management of Cardiac Arrhythmias

Atrial Tachyarrhythmias (see Chapter 17)

Atrial tachyarrhythmias (AF and flutter, tachycardias using bypass tracts, AV node re-entrant tachycardia, etc.) may cause acute cardiac decompensation in patients with marginal cardiac reserve or in patients dependent on adequate preload to maintain an effective forward CO.

- Acute therapy includes control of the ventricular response (beta-blockers, diltiazem, verapamil, digoxin, adenosine) in patients with relatively stable hemodynamic status; or immediate synchronized DC cardioversion in patients with severe hemodynamic compromise.
- Long-term therapy depends upon the frequency of episodes of the atrial tachyarrhythmia, the requirement for AV synchrony, and the hemodynamic response to the tachycardia. It may include antiarrhythmic drugs, radiofrequency (RF) ablation procedures, the combination of RF ablation of the AV node and permanent pacemaker implantation, or cardiac surgery (for example, the Maze procedure for AF).

Symptomatic Episodes of Bradycardia

Symptomatic episodes of bradycardia (sick sinus syndrome, sinus arrest, SA exit block, advanced AV block) may lead to episodes of CHF and decreased CO.

- Drugs that impair cardiac conduction should be discontinued if possible.
- Treatment includes temporary pacing if the condition is not expected to be long-lived, or permanent pacemaker implantation if the underlying condition is expected to persist.

Ventricular Ectopic Activity

Ventricular ectopic activity may range from a benign/asymptomatic disturbance to sustained VT and sudden cardiac death.

- Reversible causes should be investigated and corrected to the extent possible.
- Formal EP evaluation should be obtained prior to the institution of long-term therapy.

Mechanical Therapy and Surgery

CABG or PTCA should be performed in suitable candidates with documented myocardial ischemia/viable myocardium (see Chapter 1).

Mechanical Devices
Mechanical devices should be employed only in patients with severe hemodynamic compromise despite maximal medical therapy. Currently, these mechanical devices are considered as a bridge to cardiac transplantation. Available mechanical devices include:

Intra-aortic balloon counterpulsation
Left and right ventricular assist devices (VAD)
Artificial heart

Improvement in LVAD technology may allow increased patient mobility, increased potential for hospital discharge, and long-term support of the circulation as an alternative to cardiac transplantation. A randomized trial to test this hypothesis is ongoing.

Transplantation (see Chapter 20)
Transplantation is only considered in patients with severe, persistent CHF despite both aggressive medical and mechanical therapy. Cardiac transplantation offers a 1-year survival of 80% to 90% and 5-year survival approaching 75%.

Dynamic Cardiomyoplasty
Cardiomyoplasty, a surgical procedure in which a transformed fatigue-resistant skeletal muscle (usually the left latissimus dorsi muscle) is mobilized and wrapped around the heart to augment the ventricular function, has been performed in symptomatic CHF patients who are refractory to standard medical therapy.

Preliminary results indicate low operative mortality with significant improvement in NYHA functional class, exercise performance, and LV function. Measured changes in hemodynamic parameters to date have only been modest.

Batista Procedure

See Chapter 12.

Prevention

Despite rapid advances in diagnostic techniques and therapy, the incidence of CHF is increasing and an appreciable 5-year mortality still exists.

- The most cost-effective strategy in the treatment of CHF is primary prevention.

Modification of risk factors for CAD should be aggressively pursued in all patients at risk at the earliest time possible.

Equally important in preventing or delaying the onset of CHF is the attenuation of inappropriate post-MI ventricular remodeling with ACE-inhibitors. ACE-inhibitors also have a preventative role in the treatment of asymptomatic patients with LV dysfunction (ejection fraction ≤35%).

SUGGESTED READINGS

ACC/AHA Task Force on Practice Guidelines. Guidelines for the evaluation and management of heart failure. Circulation 1995;92:2764–2784.

AHA Medical/Scientific Statement. Selection and treatment of candidates for heart transplantation. Circulation 1995;92: 3593–3612.

Chiu RCJ. Dynamic cardiomyoplasty: an overview. PACE 1991;14:577–584.

Cohn JN, Archibald AD, Ziesche S, et al. Effect of vasodilator therapy on mortality in chronic congestive heart failure: results of a Veterans Administration cooperative study. N Engl J Med 1986;313:1547–1552.

Cohn JN, Johnson G, Ziesche S, et al. A comparison of enalapril with hydralazine isosorbide dinitrate in the treatment of congestive heart failure. N Engl J Med 1991;325:303–310.

Cohn JN, Ziesche S, Smith R, et al. Effect of the calcium antagonist felodipine as supplementary vasodilator therapy in patients with chronic heart failure treated with enalapril. V-HeFT III. Circulation 1997;96:856-863.

Grossman W. Diastolic dysfunction in congestive heart failure.
N Engl J Med 1991;325:1557–1564.

Ho KKL, Anderson KM, Kannel WB, et al. Survival after the
onset of congestive heart failure in Framingham Heart
Study subjects. Circulation 1993;88:107–115.

Johnson RA, Palacios I. Dilated cardiomyopathies of the
adult. N Engl J Med 1982;307:1051–1058,1119–1126.

Packer M. Vasodilator and inotropic drugs for the treatment
of chronic heart failure: distinguishing hype from hope.
J Am Coll Cardiol 1988;12:1299–1317.

Packer M, Gheorghiade M, Young JB, et al. Withdrawal of
digoxin from patients with chronic heart failure treated with
angiotensin-converting-enzyme inhibitors. N Engl J Med
1993;329:1–7.

Packer M, Bristow MR, Cohn JN, et al. The effect of carvedilol
on morbidity and mortality in patients with chronic heart
failure. N Engl J Med 1996;334:1349–1355.

Packer M, O'Connor CM, Ghali JK, et al. Effect of
amlodipine on morbidity and mortality in severe chronic
heart failure. N Engl J Med 1996;335:1107–1114.

Schocken DD, Arrieta MI, Leaveston PE, Ross EA.
Prevalence and mortality rate of congestive heart failure in
the United States. J Am Coll Cardiol 1992;20:301–306.

The CONSENSUS Trial Study Group. Effects of enalapril on
mortality in severe congestive heart failure. N Engl J Med
1987;315:1429–1435.

The SOLVD Investigators. Effects of enalapril on survival in
patients with reduced left ventricular ejection fraction and
congestive heart failure. N Engl J Med 1991;325:293–302.

The SOLVD Investigators. Effect of enalapril on mortality and
the development of heart failure in asymptomatic patients
with reduced left ventricular ejection fractions. N Engl J
Med 1992;327:685–691.

Waagstein F, Bristow MR, Swedburg K, et al. Beneficial effects
of metoprolol in idiopathic dilated cardiomyopathy. Lancet
1993;342:1441–1446.

Cardiac Arrhythmias

Edward K. Chung
Dennis A. Tighe

ANALYZING CARDIAC ARRHYTHMIAS

For a detailed ECG analysis of cardiac arrhythmias, a long rhythm strip of lead II, or sometimes leads III or aVF, is preferable, because these leads show the P wave most clearly. Occasionally, lead V_1 shows the P wave more clearly than do the above-mentioned leads.

Diagnostic Approach

A diagnostic approach to cardiac arrhythmias evaluates the following areas:

- Atrial activity
- QRS configuration
- Ashman's phenomenon
- RR cycles
- Postectopic pause
- Coupling interval
- Heart rate
- Response to vagal maneuvers

Other Tests

Ambulatory Monitoring

When suspected cardiac arrhythmias are *not* recorded by repeated 12-lead ECGs, ambulatory monitoring is indicated.

If the symptoms suggesting arrhythmia occur on a daily

basis, a Holter monitor ECG should be taken for 24 to 48 hours. If the symptoms are intermittent or infrequent an event recorder should be employed for a period of 2 to 4 weeks.

Exercise ECG and EPS

In addition to ambulatory ECG monitoring, exercise stress testing may be indicated when any cardiac arrhythmia is thought to be related to physical exercise.

In selected cases, an electrophysiologic study (EPS) may be necessary to diagnose cardiac arrhythmias more accurately, especially when dealing with tachyarrhythmias with broad QRS complexes.

Classification

Cardiac arrhythmias may be classified as follows:

1. Disturbances of impulse formation
2. Conduction disturbances
3. Combination of disturbances of impulse formation and conduction
4. Artificial pacemaker-induced rhythm

Conduction Disturbances

Conduction disturbances may be expressed as "heart blocks." The type depends on the site of the heart block. Not uncommonly, two or more sites may show conduction disturbances simultaneously.

Conduction disturbances can be summarized as follows:

- SA block
- Intra-atrial block
- AV block
- Intra-His block
- Intraventricular block: LBBB, RBBB, hemiblock, bifascicular block, trifascicular block, and nonspecific (diffuse)
- Exit block
- Combined conduction disturbances

Underlying Causes

The proper diagnostic, as well as therapeutic, approach to arrhythmias depends on the presence or absence of significant underlying heart disease or other factors, such as:

Cardiac diseases (e.g., CAD, RHD)
Noncardiac diseases (e.g., hyperthyroidism)
Electrolyte imbalances (e.g., hypokalemia,
    hyperkalemia)
Drug-induced disorders (e.g., digitalis toxicity)
Cocaine, coffee, alcohol, smoking, anxiety, etc.

Any artifacts that can cause ECG findings similar to true cardiac arrhythmias must be identified. The muscle tremors of Parkinson's disease, for example, commonly produce artifacts superficially mimicking cardiac arrhythmias (Figs 3-1 and 3-2).

Accurate Diagnosis for Proper Therapy

Rapid heart action may originate from any portion of the heart. Thus, rapid heart action can originate in the sinus or it may be ectopic. (Because sinus tachycardia can be diagnosed without difficulty in most instances, ectopic tachyarrhythmias will be a focus of discussion.) In addition, tachyarrhythmias may occur in paroxysmal and nonparoxysmal forms.

Nonparoxysmal tachyarrhythmias may originate from a
    primary or any ectopic pacemaker.
Paroxysmal tachyarrhythmias are always ectopic in
    origin.

A correct and precise diagnosis of the tachyarrhythmia is important when evaluating the total clinical picture of a given patient, because certain arrhythmias are almost pathognomonic features of certain clinical entities. For example, atrial tachycardia with varying AV block (PAT with block) and nonparoxysmal AV JT in the presence of AF during digitalization are almost pathognomonic features of digitalis intoxication.

In addition, a precise diagnosis of a given tachyarrhythmia enables one to employ the proper antiarrhythmic therapy (see Chapters 1, 17, and 18).

SUPRAVENTRICULAR VERSUS VENTRICULAR TACHYARRHYTHMIAS

The differentiation between supraventricular and ventricular tachyarrhythmias is extremely important in view of their management and prognosis; however, it is often

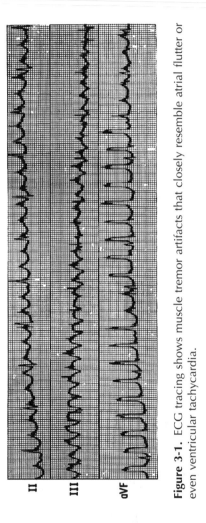

Figure 3-1. ECG tracing shows muscle tremor artifacts that closely resemble atrial flutter or even ventricular tachycardia.

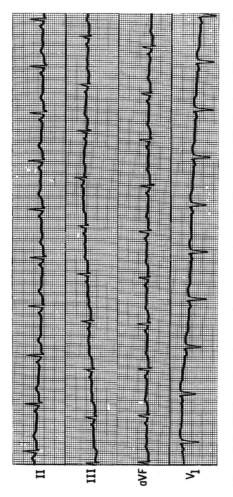

Figure 3-2. ECG tracing taken on the same patient as in Figure 3-1. Elimination of the muscle tremors reveals normal sinus rhythm without any artifact.

Table 3-1. Broad (Bizarre) QRS Complexes: Five Causes

1. Ventricular ectopy
2. Intraventricular block
3. Aberrant ventricular conduction
4. Wolff-Parkinson-White syndrome
5. Artificial pacemaker–induced ventricular beats or rhythm

Table 3-2. ECG Findings That Support (or Favor) Ventricular Ectopy

- Full compensatory pause during sinus rhythm (occasionally interpolated)—no disturbance on the sinus PP cycle.
- Significant pause after a bizarre QRS complex in atrial fibrillation or flutter.
- No premature P wave preceding a bizarre QRS complex.
- Extremely broad and bizarre QRS complex.
- No evidence of Ashman's phenomenon.
- Left bundle branch block pattern or multiformed.
- Bizarre QRS complex in elderly or cardiac patients and/or with digitalis toxicity.

difficult or at times impossible to distinguish between them. The reason for this is that supraventricular tachyarrhythmias with wide QRS complexes (regardless of the fundamental mechanism involved) may closely resemble ventricular tachyarrhythmias.

The causes of ECG findings of broad (bizarre) QRS complexes are summarized in Table 3-1; ECG findings that support (or favor) ventricular ectopy are summarized in Table 3-2.

Because of the difficulty in distinguishing these tachyarrhythmias, additional studies such as esophageal and intracardiac ECGs including EPS can be used to identify the atrial activity in relation to the His bundle potential and ventricular activity. It must be emphasized that supraventricular tachyarrhythmias may coexist with ventricular tachyarrhythmias leading to complex rhythm disturbances.

Differential Diagnosis

Several steps should be followed in distinguishing between supraventricular and ventricular tachyarrhythmias.

1. Identification of the atrial activity.
   Determination of the atrial cycles.
   Determination of the relationship between atrial and
     ventricular activities.
   Comparison between atrial and ventricular cycles.
2. Evaluation of the configuration of the QRS
   complexes during the tachyarrhythmia.
   Comparison of the QRS complexes during the
     tachyarrhythmia and isolated ectopic beats
     preceding or following the rapid heart action.
   Comparison of the QRS complex during the
     tachyarrhythmia and ventricular captured beats.
   Determination of underlying LBBB or RBBB.
   Determination of underlying Wolff-Parkinson-White
     (WPW) syndrome.
   Determination of aberrant ventricular conduction
     (AVC).
3. Evaluation of the response to carotid sinus
   stimulation (CSS).
4. Determination of the regularity of RR cycles.
5. Evaluation of the coupling intervals and the post-
   tachyarrhythmia pause.
6. Determination of the heart rate.
7. Identification of the His bundle potential in relation
   to the ventricular activity.

Identification of Atrial Activity

Identification of the atrial activity is the first step in determining the origin of a tachyarrhythmia.

Relationship between Atrial and Ventricular Activi-
ties   When the P wave is definitely present, the relationship between the P wave and the QRS complex must be
determined.

- When the ectopic P waves precede the QRS
  complexes, regardless of the configuration of the
  latter, the tachycardia is supraventricular in origin. In
  this circumstance, the tachycardia is atrial in origin if
  the axis of the ectopic P wave is similar to that of the
  sinus P wave (Fig 3-3).
- AV junctional tachycardia (JT) can be diagnosed
  when the retrograde P wave (inverted P wave in lead

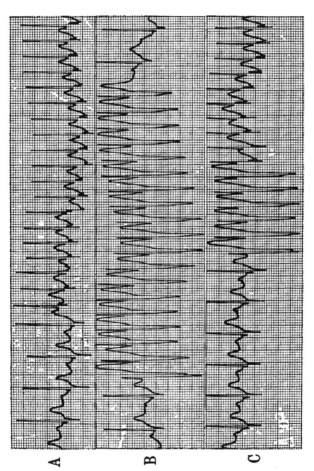

Figure 3-3. Sinus rhythm and paroxysmal AT (rate: 210–220 beats/min) with aberrant ventricular conduction of varying degree. The Holter monitor ECG rhythm strips A, B, and C are *not* continuous.

II and upright P wave in lead aVR) precedes the
QRS complex, regardless of its configuration.
- When the QRS complex is wide and/or bizarre, either
  because of preexisting or rate-dependent bundle
  branch block or because of AVC, it closely mimics VT
  even if there are P waves preceding the QRS
  complexes (see Fig 3-3). VT may be closely simulated
  even in sinus tachycardia when there is bundle branch
  block (Fig 3-4).
- When the ectopic P waves, which are conducted in a
  retrograde fashion, follow the QRS complexes, the
  origin of the ectopic impulses may be either in the
  AV junction or in the ventricles. In this circumstance,
  AV JT is probably present when the QRS complex is
  narrow. However, VT may produce retrograde P
  waves that may resemble AV JT.

Comparison between Atrial and Ventricular Cycles
Comparison between atrial and ventricular cycles is
important because the atrial to ventricular conduction
ratio may be 1:1, may be any multiple of each other, or
may show the Wenckebach phenomenon.

- In the presence of regularly occurring P waves (either
  sinus or ectopic), the QRS complexes may
  independently originate from either the AV junction
  or the ventricles, leading to complete or incomplete
  AV dissociation. Thus, the presence of AV
  dissociation does not favor or exclude the diagnosis
  of AV JT or VT.
- AV JT or VT may develop in the presence of atrial
  tachyarrhythmias including AF, flutter, and
  tachycardia, leading to AV dissociation. The
  comparison of the configuration of the QRS complex
  during the tachycardia and of a ventricular captured
  beat is often the only clue to distinguish between
  them. (This aspect of the differential diagnosis will be
  discussed later in this chapter.)
- The differential diagnosis between AV JT with a wide
  QRS complex and VT is one of the most difficult
  problems in the interpretation of cardiac arrhythmias,
  because each may closely simulate the other. The
  most common cause of a wide QRS complex in an

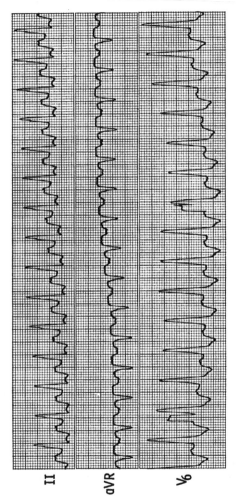

Figure 3-4. Sinus tachycardia (rate: 125 beats/min) with first-degree AV block and LBBB. Slow VT is superficially simulated.

AV JT is preexisting bundle branch block (Figs 3-5 and 3-6).

Evaluation of Configuration of QRS Complex During Tachycardia

QRS Complexes in Ectopic Beats versus Tachyarrhythmias Evaluation of the configuration of QRS complexes during the tachycardia, with comparison with isolated ectopic beats preceding or following the rapid heart action, is often the only method of identifying the exact location of the ectopic impulse formation. This is true because the same ectopic focus is believed to be capable of producing isolated ectopic beats as well as tachyarrhythmias. For example, isolated APCs often lead to atrial group beats, AT, AF, or flutter, and these atrial tachyarrhythmias are often followed by isolated APCs upon termination of the rapid heart action (see Fig 3-3).

This information is extremely valuable when the QRS complex is wide and/or bizarre during the tachyarrhythmia and isolated APCs, resulting either from preexisting or rate-dependent bundle branch block or from AVC (see Fig 3-3).

The most practical point in differential diagnosis is to compare the configuration of the QRS complex during the tachycardia with isolated VPCs before and after the tachycardia. When the configuration of the QRS complexes of the isolated VPCs and tachycardia are identical, the diagnosis of VT is certain (Fig 3-7).

QRS Complex in Ventricular Captured Beats versus Tachycardia Comparison of QRS configuration during the tachycardia and ventricular captured beats (or reciprocal beats) is another important aspect of the differential diagnosis in the presence of incomplete AV dissociation.

- When the QRS complexes of ventricular captured beats or reciprocal (echo) beats have the same configuration as that of the tachycardia, regardless of whether the QRS complex is narrow or wide, the tachycardia is AV junctional in origin.
- If the contours of the QRS complexes in the

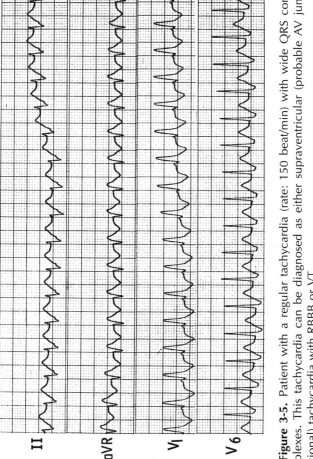

Figure 3-5. Patient with a regular tachycardia (rate: 150 beat/min) with wide QRS complexes. This tachycardia can be diagnosed as either supraventricular (probable AV junctional) tachycardia with RBBB or VT.

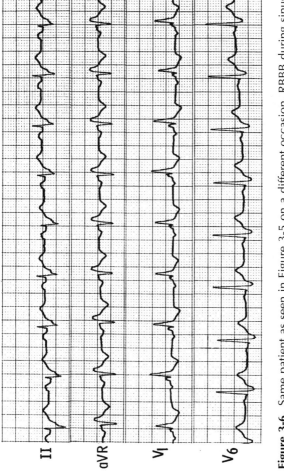

Figure 3-6. Same patient as seen in Figure 3-5 on a different occasion. RBBB during sinus rhythm (rate: 76 beats/min). Because this patient had RBBB during sinus rhythm, VT is definitely excluded.

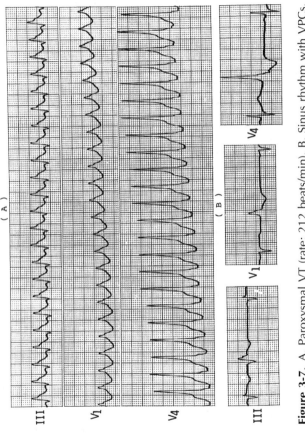

Figure 3-7. A. Paroxysmal VT (rate: 212 beats/min). B. Sinus rhythm with VPCs. Note that the configuration of an isolated VPC and VT is identical.

ventricular captured beats or reciprocal beats and the tachycardia are different, the diagnosis of VT can be made.

• The presence of fusion beats is a very important clue for the diagnosis of VT.

Underlying LBBB or RBBB Determination of pre-existing LBBB or RBBB is, at times, the only way to distinguish between supraventricular and ventricular tachyarrhythmias, particularly when the atrial activity is not discernible or is independent of the QRS complex, and the QRS complex is wide and/or bizarre.

• When the ECG taken preceding or following an episode of rapid heart action shows LBBB or RBBB and when the QRS contour is identical to that seen during the tachyarrhythmia, the diagnosis of VT is definitely excluded (see Figs 3-5 and 3-6).

• AF or flutter with preexisting or rate-dependent LBBB or RBBB also closely mimics VT (Fig 3-8). In these circumstances, grossly irregular RR cycles with identification of fibrillation or flutter waves exclude VT.

Wolff-Parkinson-White Syndrome Knowledge of underlying WPW syndrome is also very helpful for differentiating rapid heart actions. This syndrome is known to be associated with supraventricular tachyarrhythmias with wide QRS complexes due to anomalous AV conduction, closely resembling ventricular tachyarrhythmias. A detailed description of the supraventricular tachyarrhythmias associated with the WPW syndrome is found in Chapter 4.

Aberrant Ventricular Conduction Recognition of AVC in supraventricular tachyarrhythmias is extremely important for distinguishing them from ventricular tachyarrhythmias (Table 3-3). AVC is supported by the following findings:

• RBBB pattern.
• Absence of the post-tachyarrhythmia pause.
• Varying coupling intervals.
• A long cycle preceding the coupling interval (Ashman's phenomenon).

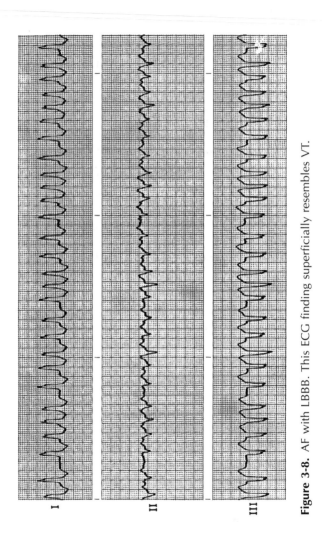

Figure 3-8. AF with LBBB. This ECG finding superficially resembles VT.

Table 3-3. Aberrant Ventricular Conduction: Three Causes

1. Ashman's phenomenon
2. Short coupling interval
3. Very rapid ventricular rate (faster than 180 beats/min)

- Identical or similar initial vectors between the abnormal beat and the normally conducted beat.

Ashman's phenomenon

The most important cause for the production of AVC is Ashman's phenomenon (Figs 3-9 and 3-10). In 1945, Ashman described the ECG finding that AVC tends to occur following a long ventricular cycle (RR interval) preceding the coupling interval (the interval from a bizarre beat to the normal beat of the basic rhythm). In other words, the longer the ventricular cycle (RR interval), the longer is the refractory period following it; the shorter the ventricular cycle, the shorter is the refractory period.

- Ashman's phenomenon may be recognized in any cardiac rhythm when AVC occurs following a long ventricular cycle (RR interval).
- The AVC is more pronounced in a ventricular complex following the longest ventricular cycle as a result of marked Ashman's phenomenon.
- Atrial or AV junctional bigeminy nearly always shows AVC in atrial or AV junctional premature beats because of Ashman's phenomenon. This is observed because atrial or AV junctional premature beats must follow a long ventricular cycle (postectopic pause) during atrial or AV junctional bigeminy (see Fig 3-10).
- Ashman's phenomenon is pronounced when the ventricular cycle becomes suddenly shortened following a long ventricular cycle, particularly in AF. As a result, AVC occurs (see Fig 3-9). It is not uncommon to observe consecutively occurring AVC once it is initiated by Ashman's phenomenon (Fig 3-11). This ECG finding closely simulates VT.
- When the ectopic beat reveals an incomplete RBBB pattern (not due to AVC), the impulse is considered

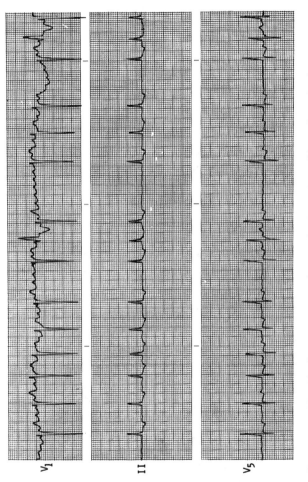

Figure 3-9. AF with aberrant ventricular conduction initiated by Ashman's phenomenon. VPC is closely simulated, but the lack of any pause following a bizarre beat excludes a possibility of a VPC.

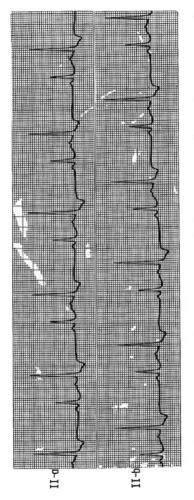

Figure 3-10. Sinus rhythm and frequent APCs with aberrant ventricular conduction as a result of Ashman's phenomenon. The rhythm strips II-a and II-b are not continuous.

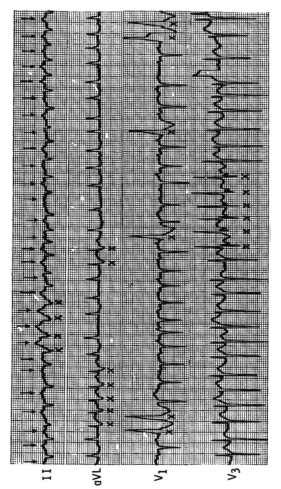

Figure 3-11. The rhythm is multifocal atrial tachycardia (MAT) with frequent aberrant ventricular conductions (X) initiated by Ashman's phenomenon. *Arrows* indicate P waves.

to be originating from one of the fascicles of the left bundle branch system (Fig 3-12).

- The PR interval of atrial or AV junctional premature beat is often long during bigeminy, again as a result of Ashman's phenomenon. For the same reason, blocked APCs are common during atrial bigeminy (blocked atrial bigeminy).

- The configuration of the QRS complex during AVC as a result of Ashman's phenomenon is commonly (in about 80% to 85% of cases) an RBBB pattern (see Figs 3-9 and 3-11); only 15% to 20% may show an LBBB pattern. Not uncommonly, aberrantly conducted beats may reveal an ECG finding of a bifascicular block (BFB) pattern consisting of an RBBB pattern and left anterior or posterior hemiblock (LAHB or LPHB) pattern. At times, AVC may show both LBBB and RBBB patterns in the same ECG tracing. The alternation of the QRS contour in AVC represents functional (*not* true) bundle branch block and/or hemiblock.

- The secondary T wave change is observed in the aberrantly conducted QRS complex. The T wave alteration in this circumstance is analogous to that of VPCs or LBBB or RBBB.

Carotid Sinus Stimulation

The response to CSS differs according to the nature and origin of the tachyarrhythmias (Table 3-4).

- **Sinus Tachycardia.** Sinus tachycardia is only transiently slowed by CSS—the original sinus rate returns soon after the procedure is over. At times, varying degrees of AV block may be produced by CSS in sinus tachycardia.

- **Atrial Tachycardia.** When CSS is applied for AT, there may be three different responses:
  1. No response at all.
  2. Restored sinus rhythm.
  3. Slowing of the ventricular rate resulting from increased AV block.

- **AV Junctional Tachycardia.** The response of AV JT to CSS is similar to that of AT: AV JT (usually

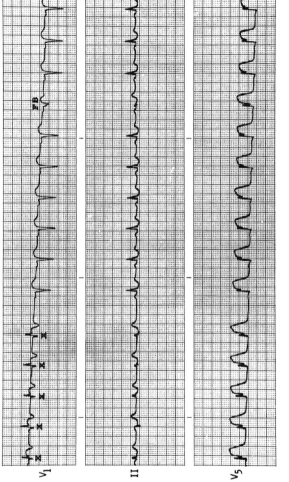

Figure 3-12. Sinus rhythm with intermittent fascicular tachycardia (*X*) and a ventricular fusion beat (*FB*).

Table 3-4. Cardiac Arrhythmias: Responses to Carotid Sinus Stimulation

Arrhythmias	Responses
Sinus tachycardia	Transient slowing of sinus (atrial) rate
	Varying degree AV block (less common)
Atrial tachycardia	Termination
	No response
	Slowing of ventricular rate due to increased AV block (less common)
	Increased atrial rate (less common)
Atrial fibrillation or flutter	Slowing of ventricular rate due to increased AV block
AV junctional tachycardia	
Paroxysmal	Termination or no response
Nonparoxysmal	No response
Ventricular tachyarrhythmias	No response (rare exceptions)
WPW syndrome	Vary
Parasystole	Vary

paroxysmal) may convert to sinus rhythm, or it may not be influenced by the procedure.

- **Reciprocating Tachycardia.** In reciprocating tachycardia, slowing of the ventricular rate may be produced as a result of increased AV block by CSS.
- **Atrial Fibrillation or Flutter.** When CSS is applied to AF or flutter, a slowing of the ventricular rate is invariably produced because of the increased AV block. Occasionally, a long ventricular standstill may result when CSS is applied to elderly patients with AF or flutter.
- **Ventricular Tachycardia.** In contrast to supraventricular tachyarrhythmias, as a rule VT does not respond to CSS. Thus, no response to the procedure does not diagnose or exclude supraventricular or VT, but VT is excluded if there is any response to CSS.

Regularity of RR Cycles

Although it has been said that VT often shows a slight irregularity of the RR cycles, it is rather uncommon to recognize any appreciable irregularity except when VT transforms to VF. Conversely, supraventricular (atrial or AV junctional) tachycardia may produce a slight irregularity of the cardiac cycle, particularly in the initial portion of the paroxysm. Thus, slight irregularity of the RR cycles is not a useful criterion for the differential diagnosis of supraventricular and VT.

- Grossly irregular RR cycles, regardless of the configuration of the QRS complex, are nearly always due to AF. Less commonly, they may be due to atrial flutter or tachycardia with varying AV response, MAT, or VF.
- VT is closely simulated when the QRS complex is wide and/or bizarre owing to preexisting or rate-dependent bundle branch block (see Fig 3-8), to AVC (see Fig 3-11), or to anomalous AV conduction in the WPW syndrome.
- When the RR cycles show a regular irregularity, the tachycardia often arises from the AV junction. The irregularity is often due to Wenckebach exit block or the periodic occurrence of reciprocal beats.

Coupling Intervals and Post-tachyarrhythmia Pause

In general, the coupling intervals are constant in VT or VPCs. Conversely, wide and/or bizarre QRS complexes due to AVC in AF always have varying coupling intervals.

In addition, VT is always followed by a post-tachycardia pause, whereas aberrantly conducted beats in AF are *not* followed by a long pause (see Fig 3-9).

Four causes of ventricular pause are found in Table 3-5.

Table 3-5. Ventricular Pause: Four Major Causes

1. Blocked (nonconducted) APC
2. Second-degree or higher AV block
3. Sinus arrest
4. SA block

Heart Rate

Although different types of tachyarrhythmias produce different rate ranges, the heart rate is not a reliable index to use for the differential diagnosis of supraventricular and ventricular tachyarrhythmias because of the overlap of the heart rates.

- A ventricular rate beyond 200 beats per minute usually favors supraventricular tachyarrhythmias.
- Ventricular rate faster than 250 beats per minute nearly always indicates AF or flutter, regardless of the width of the QRS complex.

His Bundle Potential in Relation to Ventricular Activity

EPS testing is used in many cases to locate the precise origin of the ectopic focus or conduction defect.

- When the ventricular activity is preceded by a His bundle potential, the rapid heart action is due to a supraventricular tachycardia.
- In VT the QRS complex is *not* preceded by the His bundle potential.

GUIDE TO ANTI-ARRHYTHMIC THERAPY

(see Chapters 17 and 18)

Goal

The purpose of anti-arrhythmic therapy is the prevention of untoward sequelae of the arrhythmia, including:

Fainting
Dizziness
Weakness
Palpitations
Skipped heart beats
Convulsion
Congestive heart failure (CHF)
Angina pectoris
Feeling of impending death
Cerebral ischemia
Death

Arrhythmia Diagnosis

Underlying Cause

Before any therapy is initiated, the underlying cause of unexplained arrhythmia must be identified. Some common underlying factors that may cause cardiac arrhythmias, and which should be eliminated as the first step in therapy, include:

- Use of cocaine, coffee, tea, cola drinks; cigarette smoking; emotional stress. Cocaine can be a significant contributing factor in the production of a variety of cardiac arrhythmias, especially in young individuals.
- Consumption of large quantities of alcohol. The term "holiday heart syndrome" is used to describe the sudden occurrence of tachyarrhythmias following consumption of large amounts of alcohol, as such episodes commonly follow holidays or weekends. For alcohol-induced cardiac arrhythmias, immediate discontinuation of alcohol consumption is the most important therapeutic aspect.
- Ongoing usage of an inappropriate agent. For example, the first, and most important, step in treating digitalis-induced arrhythmias is the immediate discontinuation of digitalis. Likewise, the first therapeutic approach to quinidine-induced polymorphous VT ("torsade de pointes") is the immediate discontinuation of quinidine.

Other disorders which may be common underlying causes of unexplained tachyarrhythmia include:

- Hyperthyroidism (thyrotoxicosis)
- Mitral valve prolapse (MVP) syndrome
- Wolff-Parkinson-White syndrome (see Chapter 4)

Any such direct or indirect cause of a given arrhythmia should be eliminated, if possible, before a more specific therapy is used.

Arrhythmia-Specific Therapy

Because some drugs are more effective for specific arrhythmias, the best therapeutic results are obtained when a precise diagnosis of the arrhythmia is made. Thus, arriving at the correct diagnosis of a given arrhythmia is essential. Three major categories of arrhythmias exist:

1. Tachyarrhythmias, including premature contractions (extrasystoles) of various origins.
2. Bradyarrhythmias.
3. Bradytachyarrhythmias.

EPS Studies

EPS testing can be used as a guide for initiation of specific anti-arrhythmic drug (AAD) therapy. In addition, EPS can provide a "cure" for certain refractory supraventricular tachyarrhythmias and (occasionally) for ventricular arrhythmias (see Chapters 17 and 18).

Maintenance Therapy

Prevention of the recurrence of tachyarrhythmias is another important aspect of management. For this reason, maintenance therapy with AADs (Chapter 17) is often necessary for long periods of time or even indefinitely.

Pharmacologic Therapy Precautions

Successful pharmacologic therapy of arrhythmias requires that the physician be aware of a number of factors:

- Familiarity with the recommended dosages of AADs (Chapter 17) is necessary.
- Careful consideration of indications and contraindications for various agents from EP approaches (Chapters 17 and 18) is essential.
- Prevention of side effects and toxicity of agents is essential.
- Refractory arrhythmias often require a combination of two or more anti-arrhythmic agents.
- Anti-arrhythmic agents may show synergistic or antagonistic actions. The serum digoxin level, for example, often rises excessively when digoxin and quinidine are administered together, raising the incidence of digoxin toxicity significantly.

Electrical Therapies

Anti-arrhythmic drugs are commonly used in conjunction with implanted cardioverter-defibrillators (ICDs) and artificial pacemakers when treating refractory cardiac arrhythmias (Chapters 17 and 18). Because improved artificial pacemakers and ICDs have become readily available (Chapter 18), the therapeutic approach to and results of the management of various arrhythmias have improved markedly over the past 2 decades.

SUGGESTED READINGS

Aboaf AP, Wolf PS. Paroxysmal atrial fibrillation. Arch Intern Med 1996;156:362.

ACC/AHA. Guidelines for exercise testing. J Am Coll Cardiol 1997;30:260–315.

Chakho S, Kessler KM. Recognition and management of cardiac arrhythmias. Curr Probl Cardiol 1995;20:53–120.

Chou T. Electrocardiography in clinical practice: adult and pediatric. 4th ed. Philadelphia: WB Saunders, 1996.

Chung EK. Principles of cardiac arrhythmias. 4th ed. Baltimore: Williams & Wilkins, 1989.

Chung EK. Pocket guide to ECG diagnosis. Boston: Blackwell Science, 1996.

Chung EK. Pocket guide to ECG diagnosis and self-assessment CD-ROM. Boston: Blackwell Science, 1997.

Chung EK, Tighe DA. Pocket guide to stress testing. Boston: Blackwell Science, 1997.

Dunbar SB, et al. Sudden cardiac death. Armonk, NY: Futura, 1997.

Flak RH, Podrid PJ. Atrial fibrillation: mechanisms and management. New York: Raven Press, 1992.

Golzari H, et al. Atrial fibrillation: restoration and maintenance of sinus rhythm and indications for anticoagulation therapy. Ann Intern Med 1996;125:311.

Josephson ME. Clinical cardiac electrophysiology. 2nd ed. Philadelphia: Lea & Febiger, 1993.

Kusumoto FM, Goldschlager N. Cardiac pacing. N Engl J Med 1996;334:89.

Mackstaller LL, Alpert JS. Atrial fibrillation: a review of mechanism, etiology, and therapy. Clin Cardiol 1997;20:640.

Moss AJ, Stern S. Noninvasive electrocardiology: clinical aspects of Holter monitoring. Philadelphia: WB Saunders, 1996.

Roden DM. A practical approach to torsade de pointes. Clin Cardiol 1997;20:285.

Surawicz B. Electrophysiologic basis of ECG and cardiac arrhythmias. Baltimore: Williams & Wilkins, 1995.

Waldo AL, Touboul P. Atrial flutter. Armonk, NY: Futura, 1996.

Wren C, Campbell RW. Pediatric cardiac arrhythmias. New York: Oxford University Press, 1996.

Wolff-Parkinson-White Syndrome (Ventricular Pre-excitation Syndrome)

Edward K. Chung
Dennis A. Tighe

All physicians should be fully familiar with the Wolff-Parkinson-White (WPW) syndrome because of its role in the occurrence of ectopic tachyarrhythmias. WPW syndrome is generally benign—there are no subjective manifestations or hemodynamic alterations as long as there is no ectopic tachyarrhythmia. The tachyarrhythmias may occur at any time; they may begin at birth or during infancy, childhood, or adult life.

The true incidence of the WPW syndrome is difficult to assess, but a prevalence of 0.15% to 0.2% among the general population is estimated. The syndrome occurs more frequently in men than in women. Healthy individuals without structural heart disease account for 60% to 70% of the cases of WPW syndrome. However, as WPW syndrome is a congenital cardiac anomaly, other congenital anomalies (cardiac or noncardiac) may coexist. Congenital cardiac anomalies frequently associated with the WPW syndrome include Ebstein's anomaly, atrial septal defect (ASD), IHSS, and mitral valve prolapse syndrome (MVPS).

Besides the frequent occurrence of tachyarrhythmias, WPW syndrome mimics other ECG abnormalities, including true MI, RBBB, LBBB, hemiblocks, RVH, and LVH. Ventricular tachyarrhythmias are closely simulated

146

when the WPW syndrome is associated with very rapid supraventricular tachyarrhythmias (e.g., AF) with anomalous conduction. False-positive exercise ECG test results are a very common occurrence for individuals with WPW syndrome, especially with type B.

Probably the most important clinical significance of the WPW syndrome is the danger of VT or VF following administration of digitalis or verapamil for treating supraventricular tachyarrhythmias, particularly AF. Digitalis or verapamil may enhance the conduction via an accessory pathway (bypass tract), resulting in a faster ventricular rate. The faster ventricular rate may further provoke VT or VF, even the onset of sudden death.

DIAGNOSTIC CRITERIA

WPW syndrome can be diagnosed by 12-lead ECG or by EPS.

ECG Findings

The typical ECG findings include a short PR interval and prolonged QRS interval due to a delta wave (initial slurring of the QRS complex; Fig 4-1).

- The delta wave is a primary clue to diagnosing the syndrome. In some cases of WPW syndrome, the delta wave may not be obvious.
- The PR interval may be longer than 0.12 second, whereas the QRS interval may be narrower than 0.10 second in the proven WPW syndrome.
- The actual values of the PR and the QRS intervals in the WPW syndrome are greatly influenced by the preexisting values of these intervals.

In addition to the frequent association of various supraventricular tachyarrhythmias, recognition of the WPW syndrome is extremely important because the QRS complex in WPW syndrome often resembles various other ECG findings.

- Because of the broad QRS complexes due to the delta waves in the WPW syndrome, LBBB or RBBB is closely simulated.
- At times, a pseudo-lateral MI is produced.

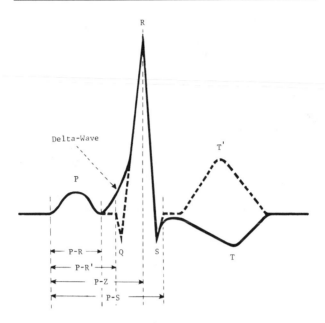

Figure 4-1. Uninterrupted line indicates anomalous conduction in Wolff-Parkinson-White syndrome; dotted line indicates normal conduction. PR and PR′ intervals are AV conduction times in Wolff-Parkinson-White syndrome and normal conduction, respectively. PR interval is shorter than PR′ interval due to delta wave. Note that PZ and PS intervals are constant during anomalous and normal conduction. T wave in Wolff-Parkinson-White syndrome is inverted because of secondary T wave change.

- When the WPW syndrome is observed intermittently, the ECG finding resembles VPCs or even short runs of VT.

Lown-Ganong-Levine Syndrome

Lown-Ganong-Levine (LGL) syndrome, a variant of WPW, is characterized by a short PR interval and narrow QRS complex without a clear-cut delta wave and associated recurrent tachyarrhythmias. Conduction through the James bundle (an AV nodal bypass tract) may be responsible for the LGL syndrome.

Concealed WPW Syndrome

Concealed bypass tract or *concealed WPW syndrome* are terms that refer to the presence of a bypass tract (accessory pathway) that is incapable of anterograde AV conduction, but the impulses can conduct retrogradely from the ventricles to the atria. In this case, 12-lead ECG fails to reveal any evidence of WPW syndrome.

During AV reciprocating tachycardia with normal QRS complexes, anterograde conduction via the AV node-His bundle pathway with retrograde conduction via an accessory pathway will occur. Under this circumstance, retrograde P waves often follow normal QRS complexes (not always visible). During ventricular pacing, ventricular premature stimulation activates the atria via an accessory pathway before retrograde activation of the His bundle. The ventricular rate tends to be faster than 200 beats per minute. Approximately 30% of all patients with supraventricular tachycardia are found to have a concealed bypass tract.

Classification

WPW syndrome has been traditionally classified into two types, A and B, depending on the direction of the delta wave. This classification is an oversimplification because many cases do not belong clearly to either type A or B. The direction of the delta wave is primarily influenced by the location of the accessory pathway (bypass tract).

Type A WPW Syndrome Superficially, type A WPW syndrome resembles RBBB, RVH, and posterior MI.

- The delta wave is directed anteriorly (commonly to the right and less commonly to the left).
- Lead V_1 shows R, RS, Rs, RSr' and Rsr' patterns, whereas leads V_5 and V_6 show Rs or R deflection (Fig 4-2). The tall R waves in leads V_{1-3} may prompt type A WPW syndrome to be misdiagnosed as true posterior MI or RVH.
- Premature activation occurs in the left ventricle.
- When the broad QRS complexes in all precordial leads are upright, type A WPW syndrome should be considered as a strong diagnostic possibility.

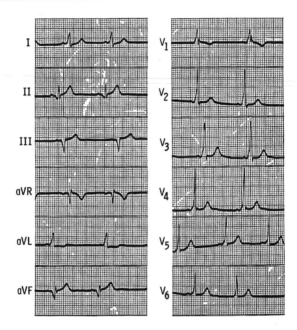

Figure 4-2. ECG of a 24-year-old man showing sinus rhythm with WPW syndrome type A. Diaphragmatic and posterior MI are superficially simulated.

Type B WPW Syndrome The ECG findings in type B WPW syndrome may closely resemble LBBB and LVH. Type B WPW syndrome may also closely resemble anterior or anteroseptal MI.

- The delta wave is directed posteriorly (commonly to the left and less commonly to the right).
- The left precordial leads (leads I, aVL, and V_{4-6}) show tall R waves with delta waves, whereas leads V_{1-2} show negative QRS complexes (QS waves) with delta waves (Fig 4-3).
- Premature activation takes place in the right ventricle.

Electrophysiologic Study

In equivocal cases of WPW syndrome, EPS may be necessary to confirm the diagnosis. The His bundle electro-

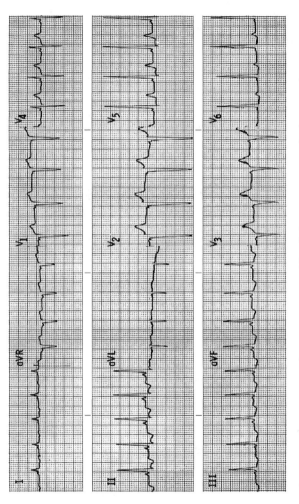

Figure 4-3. ECG tracing from an 11-year-old girl showing sinus arrhythmia with WPW syndrome type B. Anteroseptal MI is closely simulated.

Table 4-1. Indications of Electrophysiologic Study in WPW Syndrome

1. The diagnosis of WPW syndrome is equivocal in suspected individuals with tachyarrhythmias.
2. Patients have known WPW syndrome and a family history of premature sudden death.
3. Asymptomatic WPW syndrome found in a patient with a high risk occupation or activities.
4. Patients with WPW syndrome prior to cardiac surgery (for other reasons).
5. Patients with WPW syndrome associated with significant tachyarrhythmias needing proper selection of antiarrhythmic drug(s).
6. Patients considered for ablation or surgical therapy because of life-threatening or drug-resistant tachyarrhythmias.

gram shows that the HV interval is shorter than normal. The His bundle potential may occur simultaneously with the ventricular deflection, or may occur even later than the onset of the ventricular deflection. These findings occur because of premature activation of a portion of the ventricles via anomalous conduction.

EPS is performed frequently in patients with WPW syndrome for therapeutic purposes, especially in dealing with high risk patients. The indications as well as roles of EPS in WPW syndrome are summarized in Tables 4-1 and 4-2.

TACHYARRHYTHMIAS

The most significant clinical aspect of the WPW syndrome is the occurrence of supraventricular tachyarrhythmias. The frequency of tachyarrhythmias in WPW syndrome has been reported to be 10% to 40%.

Reciprocating Tachycardia

Reciprocating tachycardia (the usual rate: 140–250 beats per minute) is found in the majority of cases (75% to 80% of all tachyarrhythmias).

- The QRS complex is usually narrow (orthodromic tachycardia).

Table 4-2. Role of Electrophysiologic Study in WPW Syndrome

1. Confirm the diagnosis of WPW syndrome.
2. Localize accessory pathway(s) by mapping.
3. Determine the mechanism of tachyarrhythmias:
   - Reciprocating tachycardia (orthodromic or antidromic).
   - AF or atrial flutter.
4. Determine
   - The shortest RR interval in AF.
   - The refractory period of accessory pathways (bypass tracts).
   - The ease of AF induction and duration of AF.
5. Determine the effect of isoproterenol infusion on
   - The initiation of tachyarrhythmia(s).
   - Refractory period of accessory pathway(s).
   - Shortest RR interval during anomalous conduction.
6. Evaluate the efficacy of treatment:
   - Anti-arrhythmic agents
   - Anti-tachycardia devices
   - Catheter ablation
   - Anti-arrhythmic surgery

- A broad QRS complex due to anomalous conduction (antidromic tachycardia) is much less common.

Until recently, this type of tachycardia was called "paroxysmal atrial tachycardia." Currently, *reciprocating* or *reentrant tachycardia* is the preferred term because the tachycardia is a reentry phenomenon (Figs 4-4 and 4-5). "Circus movement" tachycardia, seen in European literature, designates the same finding.

Electrophysiologic Characteristics

Electrophysiologic and pathologic studies suggest that the WPW syndrome occurs because of a premature activation of a portion of the ventricles as a result of an anomalous AV conduction via an accessory pathway directly from the atria to the ventricles.

- The remaining portion of the ventricular activation results from varying degree fusion of transmission via both the normal AV conduction system as well as accessory pathway. In the majority of cases with WPW syndrome, the anomalous AV conduction occurs through the Kent bundle.

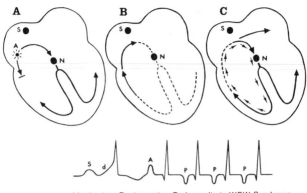

Mechanism:Reciprocating Tachycardia in WPW Syndrome
A: Normal QRS Complex

a

Figure 4-4a. A–C: Diagrams illustrating the mechanism of a reciprocating tachycardia with a normal QRS complex in the Wolff-Parkinson-White syndrome. The atrial premature impulse (*A*) is conducted to the AV node (*N*), but the atrial premature impulse is blocked in the anomalous pathway. The atrial premature impulse is then conducted to both ventricles by way of a bundle branch system. Diagram B shows the atrial premature impulse is conducted to the atria in retrograde fashion to produce an inverted P wave. Diagram C shows the impulse is conducted in a clockwise fashion producing reciprocating (reentry) cycle, and the same cycle may repeat indefinitely. Note that the QRS complex during the tachycardia is normal.

- A normal PR interval with delta wave may result from slow conduction via the Kent bundle or conduction via the Mahaim tract.

The electrophysiologic properties of both normal as well as anomalous AV pathways in the patients with WPW syndrome can be examined by the His bundle recordings and atrial stimulation.

- The P-delta interval represents the duration of the anomalous pathway conduction time, whereas the AH interval (simultaneously recorded) indicates normal AV conduction time.
- The configuration of the QRS complex in WPW

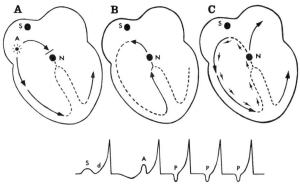

Mechanism: Reciprocating Tachycardia in WPW Syndrome
B: Abnormal QRS Complex (Anomalous A-V Conduction) b

Figure 4-4b. A–C: Diagrams illustrating a reciprocating tachycardia with anomalous conduction in the Wolff-Parkinson-White syndrome. The reentry cycle is counterclockwise, the exact reversed direction to that shown in Figure 4-4a. (*S* = sinus node; *d* = delta wave; *P* = inverted P wave.)

syndrome depends on the degree of fusion in ventricular activation between the impulse conducted via the anomalous conduction and the normal AV conduction. The QRS complex is relatively narrow when the P-delta and AH intervals are similar in duration, whereas the QRS contour is markedly bizarre when the AH interval is long and the P-delta interval is short.

Refractory periods of both normal and anomalous pathways can be determined with the extrastimulus technique. It has been demonstrated recently that supraventricular tachycardia in WPW syndrome represents reciprocating tachycardia due to a reentry phenomenon. Reentry occurs because of the marked discrepancy between the refractory periods in the normal and anomalous pathways predisposes to the initiation of the reciprocating tachycardia. Diagrammatic illustrations regarding the mechanisms of reciprocating tachycardia in this syndrome are found in Figure 4-4.

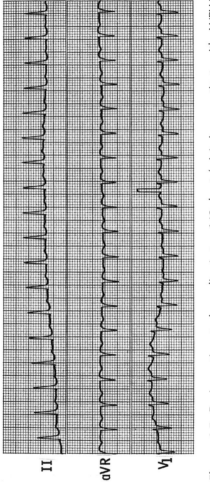

Figure 4-5. Reciprocating tachycardia (rate: 148 beats/min) in a patient with WPW syndrome.

- Once the reentry is established, the impulse may be conducted anterogradely to the ventricles via the normal pathway and retrogradely to the atria via the anomalous pathway (see Fig 4-4a). In this case, the QRS configuration during the tachycardia is normal (narrow) (Fig 4-5).
- The reentry impulse may be conducted anterogradely to the ventricles via the anomalous pathway and retrogradely to the atria via the normal pathway. In this case, the QRS complex during the tachycardia is bizarre and broad (see Fig 4-4b).
- Clinically, the majority of cases with reciprocating tachycardia in WPW syndrome show normal QRS complexes because the reentry cycle is carried out via anterograde normal AV conduction with retrograde anomalous conduction.
- The direction of the reentry cycles depends upon the availability of either the normal or the anomalous pathway, whichever is in a nonrefractory period. The premature impulse (commonly atrial and less commonly AV junctional or ventricular) will be blocked in a pathway that is refractory; it will be conducted anterogradely in another pathway that is nonrefractory. The reentry impulse then will be conducted to the atria in retrograde fashion via the pathway that was previously refractory (see Fig 4-4).
- The reentry cycles may repeat once, twice, or even indefinitely. Reciprocating tachycardia is often terminated by a properly timed atrial premature beat (either spontaneous or induced).
- Multiple accessory pathways in WPW syndrome may exist.

Atrial Fibrillation or Flutter

Atrial fibrillation (AF) and flutter occur less commonly. They constitute only 20% to 25% of all tachyarrhythmias. Of these two rhythm disorders, atrial flutter is the most rare.

AF or flutter in the WPW syndrome (Fig 4-6) may lead to VT or VF and even sudden death, especially following the administration of digitalis or verapamil.

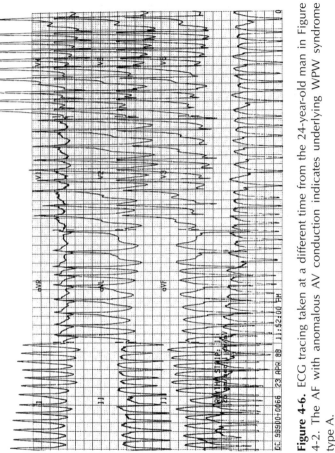

Figure 4-6. ECG tracing taken at a different time from the 24-year-old man in Figure 4-2. The AF with anomalous AV conduction indicates underlying WPW syndrome type A.

- The QRS complexes during AF or flutter in the WPW syndrome are extremely bizarre and broad in most cases.
- The broad and bizarre QRS complexes are observed with AF or flutter because of the anomalous AV conduction characteristic of WPW syndrome itself, plus AVC due to very rapid ventricular rate (ventricular rate: 250 to 300 beats).
- In WPW syndrome, atrial flutter often exhibits 1:1 AV conduction, which results in extremely rapid ventricular rate.
- According to the EPS results, when the shortest RR intervals (ventricular cycles) during AF with anomalous AV conduction range from 210 to 250 msec, these individuals belong to high-risk groups. In other words, many patients with a short RR interval during AF may develop serious symptoms (e.g., syncope or near-syncope), which may lead to life-threatening ventricular tachyarrhythmias and even sudden death. A short refractory period (<270 msec) of the bypass tract in an asymptomatic patient is shown to have a similar clinical significance.

Ventricular Tachyarrhythmias

Although the occurrence of VT has been reported in WPW syndrome, most, if not all, cases have been simply misinterpretations of AF or flutter with anomalous AV conduction. However, recently a true incidence of VF has been reported in WPW syndrome.

Sudden deaths in WPW syndrome are most likely due to VF following AF or flutter with extremely rapid ventricular response, especially after administration of digitalis or verapamil (Fig 4-7).

Other Arrhythmias

Arrhythmias such as VPCs, AV dissociation, ventricular or atrial parasystole may coexist with WPW syndrome.

PREVENTION AND TREATMENT OF TACHYARRHYTHMIAS (see Chapters 17 and 18)

No treatment is indicated when the WPW syndrome is not associated with tachyarrhythmias. Similarly, a tran-

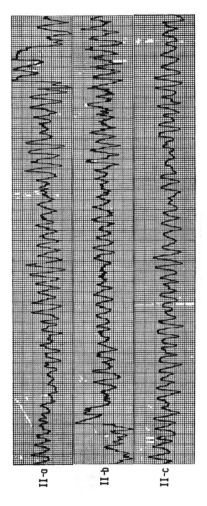

Figure 4-7. ECG tracing from a different time for the patient seen in Figure 4-2. VF is provoked following administration of digitalis in the treatment of AF with anomalous conduction in WPW syndrome (Figure 4-6). Leads II a to c are continuous.

sient arrhythmia with a short duration also requires no therapy.

- EPS is strongly recommended even in asymptomatic WPW syndrome if there is a family history of premature cardiac death or if the individual is going to participate in any type of high-risk occupations or physical activities (see Table 4-1). According to the EPS results, prophylactic drug therapy may be indicated in some cases.
- Paroxysmal reciprocating tachycardia in WPW syndrome is often terminated by vagal maneuvers such as CSS or Valsalva maneuver (see Fig 4-5) or administration of IV adenosine. Many patients with tachyarrhythmias in WPW syndrome require various AADs either acutely or as a long-term maintenance therapy.
- In urgent situations, especially in AF or flutter with extremely rapid ventricular response, DC shock may be needed. When tachyarrhythmias become refractory, nonpharmacologic therapies such as radiofrequency ablation or surgery (rare today) should be considered.

As far as the principles of AAD therapy in WPW syndrome are concerned, the therapy should be directed to change the conduction times in the normal AV and accessory pathways so that the reentry cycle becomes impossible. This can be accomplished in the following ways:

1. Equalizing the conduction times via the two pathways, either by accelerating the normal AV conduction, or by slowing the conduction in anomalous pathway; or
2. Inducing a functional or organic block in one or both pathways.

The equalization of the conduction times can be achieved with atropine or isoproterenol (Isuprel) intravenously by accelerating the normal AV conduction, but these drugs provide only transient effects. Using drugs that slow the conduction in the accessory pathway seems a more practical approach (Table 4-3).

Table 4-3. Effects of Drugs on Refractory Period in Normal and Anomalous Pathways

Drugs	AV Node	Accessory Pathway
Propranolol	⇑	0
Digitalis	⇑	⇓
Adenosine	⇑	0
Quinidine	⇓	⇑
Procainamide	0	⇑
Verapamil	⇑	⇓
Phenytoin	⇓	Variable
Amiodarone	⇑	⇑
Sotalol	⇑	⇑
Flecainide	⇑	⇑
Ajmaline	0	⇑

⇑: increase in refractory period.
⇓: decrease in refractory period.
0: no change in refractory period.

Nonpharmacologic Therapy

Pharmacologic therapy is not effective or practical in many patients for a variety of reasons:

1. Refractory to drug therapy.
2. Untoward side effects of anti-arrhythmic drug therapy.
3. Intolerance to drug therapy.
4. Poor patient compliance.
5. Patient's youth makes life-long drug therapy undesirable.
6. Short anterograde refractory period of the accessory pathway (<250 msec).

The nonpharmacologic therapies that have emerged include open heart surgical approaches, percutaneous catheter ablation methods, and anti-tachycardia pacing devices.

Surgical Methods

The objective of surgery for the WPW syndrome is to divide the accessory pathway at some point along its course thus interrupting conduction through the pathway. Two surgical approaches have been used clinically: endocardial and epicardial. A success rate of 90% to 95% with a mortality rate of less than 2% is reported in the absence of concomitant cardiac disease. With the advent of percutaneous catheter ablation, surgery for cure of the WPW syndrome is rarely required today.

Percutaneous Catheter Ablation

Despite the clinical success of surgery in curing WPW syndrome, an open heart surgical procedure predisposes the patient to the risk of perioperative death and morbidity and necessitates a relatively prolonged hospital stay. Closed-chest (percutaneous) catheter ablation, therefore, has emerged as the treatment of choice for tachyarrythmias in the WPW syndrome.

The first successful catheter ablation of an accessory pathway utilized direct current (DC) energy. Despite documented efficacy, DC energy delivery systems had several drawbacks:

- Cardiac barotrauma.
- Lack of controlled titration of electrical energy to prevent inadvertent destruction of cardiac structures.
- Inapplicability to all areas of the heart.
- The requirement for general anesthesia.

The lesions produced by DC energy were relatively large and a number of complications were observed:

Rupture of the atria or coronary sinus
Ventricular dysfunction
Coronary artery spasm
AV block
Ventricular arrhythmias

In contrast to DC, radiofrequency (RF) electrical energy is of low voltage (40 to 60 V) without resultant barotrauma and with minimal risk of rupturing thin-walled structures within the heart. Precise mapping with catheter placement is mandatory because of the comparatively small lesion size. There is no requirement for general anesthesia. RF ablation is now the method of choice to treat symptomatic and refractory WPW syndrome.

Anti-Tachycardia Pacing

A third alternative for treatment of patients with symptomatic reciprocating tachycardias is anti-tachycardia pacing.

- The majority of patients with anti-tachycardia pacing devices still require some form of long-term AAD therapy.
- Anti-tachycardia pacing is contraindicated if the anterograde refractory period of the accessory pathway is less than 300 msec.

In general, anti-tachycardia pacing seems to have a rather limited role in the management of symptomatic patients with WPW syndrome because of the high success rates reported for RF current transcatheter ablation techniques.

SUGGESTED READINGS

Chung EK. Principles of cardiac arrhythmias. 4th ed. Baltimore: Williams & Wilkins, 1989.

Chung EK. Pocket guide to ECG diagnosis. Boston: Blackwell Science, 1996.

Cox JL, Ferguson Jr, TB. Surgery for the Wolff-Parkinson-White syndrome: the endocardial approach. Semin Thorac Cardiovasc Surg 1989;1:34.

Deam AG, et al. Wide complex tachycardia due to automaticity in an accessory pathway. Pace 1995;18:2106.

Ferrer MI. Pre-excitation. Armonk, NY: Futura, 1976.

Hood MA, Smith WM, Robinson MG, et al. Operations for Wolff-Parkinson-White syndrome. J Thorac Surg 1991;101: 998.

Morillo CA, et al. The Wolff-Parkinson-White syndrome. Armonk, NY: Futura, 1996.

Oren JW, et al. A functional approach to the preexcitation syndromes. Cardiol Clin 1993;11:121–149.

Wagshal AB, et al. Use of double ventricular extrastimulation to determine the preexcitation index in AV nodal reentrant tachycardia. PACE 1995;18:2041.

Warin JF, Haissaguerre M, D'Ivernois C, et al. Catheter ablation of accessory pathways: technique and results in 248 patients. Pace 1990;13:1609.

Weber H, Schmitz L. Catheter techniques for closed-chest ablation of an accessory atrioventricular pathway. N Engl J Med 1983;308:653.

Systemic Hypertension

Dennis A. Tighe
Edward K. Chung

Hypertension (HTN) is a common clinical problem with great implications for public health. Complications of untreated HTN include ventricular hypertrophy and CHF, cerebral vascular disease and stroke, renal failure, and atherosclerotic heart disease. This chapter reviews the clinical features and treatment of HTN.

EPIDEMIOLOGY

Systemic HTN, defined as SBP ≥140 mm Hg or DBP ≥90 mm Hg (Table 5-1), affects 50 million adult Americans.

Essential HTN: Approximately 90% to 95% of HTN is "essential," which implies that a definite cause cannot be identified.

Secondary HTN: The remaining 5% to 10% have secondary HTN (Table 5-2), in which a specific cause can be identified.

• The incidence of HTN increases with age.
• The prevalence of HTN among African-Americans is twice that of whites. The complications associated with HTN are more severe among blacks.

HTN is a risk factor for the development of stroke, MI, CHF, and renal insufficiency. The degree of HTN is directly related to mortality. Treatment of HTN is associ-

Table 5-1. Classification and Follow-up of Blood Pressure in Adults Based on Initial Reading

Blood Pressure (mmHg)		Category	Follow-up
Systolic	Diastolic		
<130	<85	Normal	Recheck in 2 years
130–139	85–89	High normal	Recheck in 1 year and provide information about lifestyle modification
140–159	90–99	Mild HTN (Stage 1)	Confirm within 2 months
160–179	100–109	Moderate HTN (Stage 2)	Evaluate or refer for care within 1 month
≥180	≥110	Severe HTN (Stage 3)	Evaluate or refer for care immediately or within 1 week, depending on the clinical circumstances

Adapted from: The sixth report of the Joint National Committee on Detection, Evaluation, and Treatment of High Blood Pressure (JNC VI). Arch Intern Med 1997;157:2417–2418.

Table 5-2. Causes of Secondary Hypertension

Cause	Frequency (% all patients with HTN)	Mechanism
Renal parenchymal disease	5%	Volume expansion, hyperreninemia
Oral contraceptive use	1%	Drug-induced increase in renin causing volume expansion
Renovascular disease	0.2% to 1%	Hyperreninemia due to decreased renal blood flow
Coarctation of aorta	0.1% to 0.2%	Hyperreninemia due to decreased renal blood flow
Hyperaldosteronism	0.2%	Sodium and water retention
Cushing's syndrome	0.2%	Sodium and water retention
Pheochromocytoma	0.2%	Catecholamine-induced vasoconstriction

ated with a decreased incidence of stroke, CAD, and CHF and regression of LVH and reduced rate of progression of renal disease.

PATHOPHYSIOLOGY

Mean arterial pressure (MAP) is the product of cardiac output (CO) and total peripheral resistance (TPR).

- Regardless of etiology, HTN is related to increased TPR in almost all cases. Only infrequently is HTN caused by increased CO alone.

Renin-Angiotensin-Aldosterone (RAA) System

The secretion of renin, an enzyme released by the juxtaglomerular apparatus of the renal afferent arteriole in response to decreased sodium delivery and intravascular volume depletion, results in hepatic release of angiotensin I. Angiotensin I subsequently is transformed to angiotensin II by angiotensin-converting enzyme.

Angiotensin II functions as a potent vasoconstrictor to increase TPR and stimulate the release of aldosterone from the adrenal cortex. Absorption of salt and water is enhanced in the distal renal tubules resulting in increased intravascular volume.

- Sixty percent of patients with essential HTN have normal plasma renin levels. The significance of the action of the RAA system is unclear in this group.

Cation Metabolism

Sodium

Clinical studies and epidemiologic observations strongly support a link between HTN and dietary sodium intake.

- Especially sensitive to sodium intake are blacks, older people, and those with higher levels of BP.

Potassium

Potassium deficiency may increase BP and induce ventricular ectopic activity. High dietary potassium intake may improve BP control. Therefore, adequate potassium intake (approximately 90 mmol/d) is recommended.

Calcium

Calcium deficiency is associated with the development of HTN and may amplify the effects of high sodium intake on BP.

- The overall effect of increasing calcium intake is minimal and currently no recommendation to increase daily calcium intake in excess of the current recommended daily allowance (800–1200 mg) exists.

Magnesium

Currently, no firm data are available to suggest a causal role of magnesium deficiency in the pathogenesis of HTN.

Neurogenic Factors

Overactivity of the sympathetic nervous system can lead to increased TPR and CO.

- This factor is likely a major contributor to the pathogenesis of HTN among young people.

Endocrine Hypertension

Mineralocorticoid Excess

Mineralocorticoid excess causes HTN through sodium and water retention. It has also been suggested that mineralocorticoid excess leads to an increased cellular concentration of sodium with resultant arterial vasoconstriction and elevated TPR.

Glucocorticoid Excess

Glucocorticoid excess, as found with Cushing's disease and exogenous corticosteroid use, is believed to cause HTN by multiple effects:

A salt-retaining effect from high cortisol levels.
Increased levels of mineralocorticoids.
Increased levels of renin substrate.
Increased sensitivity of vascular wall receptors to various pressor agents.

Catecholamine Excess

Catecholamine excess causes HTN by increased arterial vasoconstriction.

Renal Parenchymal Disease

Renal disease often contributes to HTN by causing salt and water retention and activation of the RAA system.

CLINICAL MANIFESTATIONS

History and Symptoms

Symptoms

The majority of patients are asymptomatic. Symptoms of severe HTN include:

Fatigue
Lightheadedness
Blurred vision
Early morning occipital headache
Angina pectoris due to increased myocardial oxygen
   demand

History

Essential HTN A strong family history of HTN suggests that essential HTN is present.

Secondary HTN Clues suggesting a secondary cause of HTN include:

- Level of BP >180/110 mm Hg
- Onset of HTN before age 25 or after age 55 years
- Poor response or failure to respond to adequate medical therapy
- "Malignant" or accelerated phase of previously well-controlled HTN
- Paroxysmal headache, sweating, and/or palpitation while hypertensive (pheochromocytoma)
- HTN associated with unprovoked hypokalemia (primary hyperaldosteronism)
- HTN following abdominal trauma (traumatic renal artery stenosis)

Drugs A detailed history of current medications should be sought. Medications known to increase BP include:

Oral contraceptive agents
Nonsteroidal anti-inflammatory agents

Corticosteroids
Nasal decongestants
Appetite suppressants
Cyclosporin
Erythropoietin
Tricyclic antidepressants
Monoamine oxidase inhibitors

Cocaine: Illicit drug use should also be explored as cocaine use can cause HTN.

Ethanol: A detailed history of alcohol consumption is necessary. Intake of more than 2 ounces of ethanol per day can raise BP and cause resistance to antihypertensive therapy.

Obesity   Obesity predisposes to HTN by its association with hyperinsulinemia and increased intravascular volume and CO.

Cardiovascular Disease   It is important to elicit and determine the presence of other established risk factors for CAD (Chapter 1) so that an overall risk assessment can be made.

Physical Examination

The examination should focus on BP measurement, evidence of target-organ damage, and clues to a secondary cause.

Blood Pressure Measurement

1. BP should be determined with a calibrated sphygmomanometer after 5 minutes of rest and more than 30 minutes after smoking or ingestion of caffeine.
2. The rubber bladder of the sphygmomanometer should encircle at least 80% of the bared upper arm.
   - A cuff that is too small produces a falsely elevated BP measurement.
   - A cuff that is too large or loosely applied will result in a reading that is falsely low.
3. The patient should be seated with the arm horizontal at heart level.
   - Positioning the arm vertically in a dependent position results in an elevated BP reading due to changes in hydrostatic pressure.

4. Palpation is used initially to estimate the SBP.
   - The cuff is rapidly inflated until the radial pulse is extinguished.
   - The cuff is then slowly deflated and the point at which the radial pulse becomes palpable is the SBP.
5. Auscultation is then used to determine the SBP and DBP.
   - The cuff is inflated to approximately 20 mm Hg above the palpated SBP.
   - While listening with the stethoscope over the brachial artery, the highest level at which sounds are heard is the SBP.
   - The cuff is progressively deflated and the highest point at which there is complete disappearance of sound (phase V) is the DBP.
   - Initially elevated readings should be confirmed on at least 2 subsequent visits and the results averaged.
6. BP should also be measured in the opposite arm. If the determinations are not equal, then the higher measurement should be considered as the patient's BP.
7. Under certain circumstances, the BP of the leg must be determined. This is best achieved by placing a large cuff around the calf and determining the SBP by palpating the posterior tibial artery. The accuracy of DBP determination in the lower extremity is poor.

Evidence of Target-Organ Involvement

Fundoscopic Examination Fundoscopic examination may reveal retinal arteriolar narrowing, irregularity of the arterial lumen, and arteriovenous nicking indicating the presence of chronic hypertensive retinopathy. The presence of flame-shaped hemorrhages, exudates, and/or papilledema indicate accelerated or malignant HTN.

Cardiac Examination When the cardiac examination reveals evidence of LVH, chronic HTN is strongly suggested. Findings of LVH include a laterally displaced apical impulse, an LV heave, and an S_4.

Clues to a Secondary Cause

Chronic renal disease: Palpable kidneys.

Renovascular disease: Abdominal bruit, especially if heard lateral to midline and associated with a diastolic component.

Coarctation of the aorta: Upper extremity systolic HTN and strong pulses with decreased BP in the legs and delayed or absent lower extremity pulses.

Cushing's syndrome: Thin skin, muscle atrophy, central obesity.

DIAGNOSIS

In the presence of documented HTN, diagnostic tests are used to determine target-organ damage and coexisting cardiac risk factors. When secondary HTN is suspected, additional diagnostic studies are indicated (Table 5-3).

Determination of target-organ disease

Urinalysis and serum BUN and creatinine to evaluate renal function.

ECG to identify LVH.

Some experts advocate limited echocardiography to document LVH due to the low sensitivity of the ECG.

Determination of cardiac risk factors

Total, HDL, and LDL cholesterol, and triglycerides

Fasting glucose

Other laboratory studies

CBC

Serum potassium and calcium

Uric acid

GENERAL APPROACH TO THERAPY

The goal of therapy is to maintain BP at or below 140/90 mmHg (in most patients—exceptions are diabetics and those with proteinuria), thereby decreasing the incidence of HTN-related renal failure, stroke, and CHF.

Classification and suggested follow-up of adult patients with HTN based on initial BP are listed in Table 5-1.

Table 5-3. Diagnosis of Secondary Hypertension

Etiology	Clinical Features	Diagnostic Tests
Renal parenchymal disease		BUN, creatinine, renal ultrasound
Renovascular disease (fibromuscular)	Young female	Renal artery DSA, arteriogram
Renovascular disease (atherosclerotic)	Male, age >55, evidence of atherosclerosis, sudden worsening of HTN	Renal artery DSA, arteriogram
Pheochromocytoma	Paroxysmal flushing, sweating, tachycardia	Urine metanephrine, plasma catecholamines, no clonidine suppression, CT or MRI scan, ^{131}I-MIBG
Aortic coarctation	Lower extremity fatigue, blood pressure and pulses reduced in lower extremities	Chest x-ray, echocardiography, aortography, MRI
Primary hyperaldosteronism	Nondiuretic-related hypokalemia	Urinary potassium, urinary aldosterone after salt loading aldosterone suppression, CT or MRI scan

- **Essential HTN:** Therapy involves lifestyle modification (see below) alone or in combination with pharmacologic therapy, depending on the level of BP and evidence of vascular disease and target organ damage (Tables 5-4 and 5-5).
- **Secondary HTN:** The goal of therapy of secondary HTN is to identify and correct the underlying cause.

The physician should involve the patient in treatment decisions and provide positive reinforcement and education about HTN, because these measures may improve long-term compliance.

Table 5-4. Components of Cardiovascular Risk Stratification of Patients with Hypertension*

I. **Major Risk Factors**
   Smoking
   Dyslipidosis
   Diabetes mellitus
   Age >80 years
   Sex (men and postmenopausal women)
   Family history of cardiovascular disease: women, <85 years, or men <65 years

II. **Target Organ Damage/Clinical Cardiovascular Disease**
   Heart diseases
      Left ventricular hypertrophy
      Angina or prior myocardial infarction
      Prior coronary revascularization
      Heart failure
   Stroke or transient ischemic attack
   Nephropathy
   Peripheral arterial disease
   Retinopathy

* See Table 5-5.
Adapted from: The sixth report of the Joint National Committee on Detection, Evaluation, and Treatment of High Blood Pressure (JNC VI). Arch Intern Med 1997;157:2425–2426.

Table 5-5. Risk Stratification and Treatment

Blood Pressure Stages (mm Hg)	Risk Group A (no risk factors; no TOD/CCD)[a]	Risk Group B (at least 1 risk factor, not including diabetes; no TOD/CCD)	Risk Group C (TOD/CCD and/or diabetes, with or without other risk factors)
High-normal (130–139/85–89)	Lifestyle modification	Lifestyle modification[b]	Drug therapy[c]
Stage 1 (140–159/ 90–99)	Lifestyle modification (up to 12 months)	Lifestyle modification (up to 6 months)	Drug therapy
Stages 2 and 3 (≥160/≥100)	Drug therapy	Drug therapy	Drug therapy

[a] TOD/CCD indicates target organ disease/clinical cardiovascular disease (see Table 5-4).
[b] For patients with multiple risk factors, clinicians should consider drugs as initial therapy plus lifestyle modifications.
[c] For those with heart failure, renal insufficiency, or diabetes.
Adapted from: The sixth report of the Joint National Committee on Detection, Evaluation, and Treatment of High Blood Pressure (JNC VI). Arch Intern Med 1997;157:2425–2426.

TREATMENT OF ESSENTIAL HYPERTENSION
Life-style Modification

Lifestyle modification (nonpharmacologic therapy) should be considered first for all patients. These measures may occasionally lead to control of HTN, especially when DBP is less than 100 mm Hg, or may reduce the number and dosage of medications required to manage HTN. Implementation of lifestyle modifications should not delay the start of appropriate drug therapy in those at higher risk (see Table 5-5).

Weight Reduction
Weight should be maintained within 15% of ideal body weight.

- In patients who are greater than 110% to 160% of ideal body weight, evidence suggests that weight loss ≥4.5 kg (10 lb) is required to significantly lower BP.
- Overweight patients with excess fat in the upper portion of the body are especially at risk for future cardiovascular mortality.

Ethanol Intake
Excessive ethanol consumption can raise BP and cause resistance to antihypertensive therapy.

- Alcohol consumption should be limited to no more than 1 ounce (30 mL) of ethanol per day, equivalent to 2 ounces (60 mL) of 100 proof whiskey, 10 ounces (300 mL) of wine, or 24 ounces (720 mL) of beer.

Sodium Restriction
Sodium may maintain elevated BP and/or interfere with the action of antihypertensive medications.

- Moderate sodium restriction consists of limiting daily sodium intake to less than 100 mmol (<2.3 grams of sodium or 6 grams of salt).
- Although sodium restriction may not lead to decreased BP in all patients, an effort at sodium restriction should be attempted.

Exercise
Regular aerobic exercise is beneficial in reducing BP and the risk of future cardiovascular disease.

Modification of Other Cardiac Risk Factors

To the extent possible, modification of other risk factors (see Table 5-4) is strongly recommended.

Smoking. Tobacco use is associated with an increased incidence of malignant HTN as well as relative resistance to antihypertensive drug therapy. Tobacco use may cause acute HTN, but it has not been shown to cause chronic HTN.

Diet. A low-fat, low cholesterol diet should be employed among overweight patients and those with high cholesterol levels. A diet rich in fruits, vegetables, and low-fat dairy foods and with reduced saturated and total fats may significantly lower BP.

Pharmacologic Therapy

Stages 1 and 2. Pharmacologic therapy is indicated for treatment of mild HTN when 3 to 6 months of life-style modification do not result in adequate BP control.

Stage 3. In moderate or severe HTN or in the presence of target-organ damage, drug therapy is required in addition to lifestyle modification.

Institution of Antihypertensive Drug Therapy

An approach to the institution and titration of drug therapy is presented in Table 5-5 and below.

Either a diuretic or beta-blocker is recommended as initial monotherapy because controlled clinical trials have shown that these agents reduce cardiovascular morbidity and mortality.

- Other classes of antihypertensive agents have been shown to effectively reduce BP, but controlled clinical trials are not available to document their efficacy to decrease cardiovascular morbidity and mortality.
- Agents other than diuretics and beta-blockers can be used in patients with special indicators (Table 5-6) or those unable to tolerate these medications.

Titration of Therapy

Antihypertensive drug therapy should be individualized so as not to adversely impact lifestyle and to maintain

Table 5-6. Patient Characteristics Affecting Choice of Antihypertensive Therapy

Characteristic	Therapeutic Consideration
Blacks	Do not respond as well as whites to beta-blockers and possibly to ACE-inhibitors (higher doses often required), respond equally well to calcium channel blockers, and respond better than whites to diuretics (volume expansion and increased salt sensitivity)
Elderly	Respond better to diuretics or calcium channel blockers than to beta-blockers or ACE inhibitors
Obese	Diuretics often effective
Myocardial infarction	Beta-blockers (non-ISA) best initial therapy. ACE-inhibitor use favored with systolic dysfunction
Obstructive airways disease	Should not receive agents which promote bronchospasm (beta-blockers, guanethidine, guanadrel, labetolol)
Congestive heart failure	Diuretics and ACE inhibitors favored. Hydralazine/nitrates and possibly amlodipine second-line. Avoid non-dihydropyridine and calcium channel blockers with severely impaired systolic function
Coronary artery disease (angina)	Beta-blockers (preferred) or calcium channel blockers best initial therapy
Bradyarrhythmias	May worsen with beta-blockers, verapamil, diltiazem, mebifradil
Hyperlipidemia	Diuretics or beta-blockers may exacerbate
Peripheral vascular disease	Beta-blockers may worsen peripheral ischemia
Depression	May worsen with central agents or beta-blockers
Renal insufficiency	ACE-inhibitors preferred
Diabetes mellitus (type I) with proteinuria	ACE-inhibitors preferred. Non-dihydropyridine calcium channel blockers may be beneficial.

compliance while achieving optimal BP control. Initially, the lowest possible dose of medication should be selected to minimize drug-related side effects. Long-acting agents should be employed to enhance compliance, smooth HTN control, and possibly reduce cost.

Ineffective   Therapeutic   Response   Whenever   the
therapeutic response is ineffective, the physician should
investigate possible reasons, such as:

Patient noncompliance
Effects of other drugs
Inappropriate drug schedule
Inappropriate drug dosage
Volume overload
Excessive ethanol intake
Unrecognized secondary cause of HTN

Mild to Moderate HTN (Stages 1 and 2)

1. If the target BP is not achieved after 1 to 3 months
   of drug therapy, then one or more of the following is
   recommended:
   - Increase the dosage of the original medication.
   - Add an agent from another class.
   - Discontinue the original agent and substitute a
     drug from another class.
   - Consider adding a diuretic as a second agent
     because volume retention is often a cause of
     tolerance to antihypertensive therapy.
   - Assess compliance and explore potential causes of
     resistance to drug therapy.
2. If the patient remains hypertensive, a third drug
   from a different class should be added or a drug
   from another class should be substituted for the
   second drug.
3. If the BP remains uncontrolled despite therapeutic
   maneuvers, a third or fourth drug from different
   classes should be added and/or the patient should be
   evaluated for possible secondary HTN.

Severe HTN (Stage 3)   Drug selection and titration for
stage 3 HTN is similar to the recommendations for stages
1 and 2.

- Drug therapy should be initiated early in most
  cases.
- Patients usually require more than one agent for
  adequate control.
- Addition of other agents is usually required over a
  shorter time period.

Antihypertensive Agents

Table 5-7 contains information about therapy with each type of antihypertensive agent.

Diuretics

Thiazide and thiazide-like diuretics　Thiazides are the diuretics of choice. These agents initially decrease BP by reducing intravascular blood volume and CO. Chronic reduction of BP is secondary to decreased TPR.

Side Effects
- Hypokalemia—the most common side effect (up to 10% of patients). The serum potassium level should be checked at one month and, if normal, repeated at 6 months into therapy. Prophylactic potassium supplementation is not necessary when thiazides are started unless the patient is taking digitalis or has a history of organic heart disease (risk of hypokalemia-induced arrhythmia).
- Hyperglycemia.
- Hyperlipidemia—6% increase of cholesterol, 17% increase of triglycerides.
- Hyperuricemia—occasionally with provocation of acute gout.
- Hypomagnesemia.
- Hypercalcemia.

Potassium-sparing diuretics　Potassium sparing agents act at the distal nephron to inhibit the exchange of sodium for potassium.

- These agents are ineffective to control HTN when used alone.
- They are generally employed in combination with other diuretics to minimize potassium wasting and to potentiate the diuretic effect.

Side Effects
- Hyperkalemia—the most common side effect. These agents should not be used in patients with renal dysfunction. If used, they must be used with caution. They should be avoided in patients receiving potassium supplements, ACE-inhibitors, or angiotensin II receptor blockers.

Table 5-7. Antihypertensive Drugs

Drug	Trade Name	Dose Range (mg/24 hours)	Frequency
I. Diuretics			
Thiazides and related agents			
Bendroflumethazide	Naturetin	2.5–5	once daily
Benthiazide	Aquatag, Exna	12.5–50	once daily
Chlorothiazide	Diuril	125–500	twice daily
Chlorthalidone	Hygroton, Thalitone	12.5–50	once daily
Cyclothiazide	Anhydron	1–2	once daily
Hydrochlorothiazide (HCTZ)	Esidrix, Hydrodiuril, Oretic	12.5–50	once daily
Hydroflumethazide	Diucardin, Saluron	12.5–50	once daily
Indapamide	Lozol	2.5–5	once daily
Methyclothiazide	Enduron	2.5–5	once daily
Metolazone	Zaroxolyn, Diulo	0.5–10	once daily
Metolazone (rapidly available formulation)	Mykrox	0.5–1.0	once daily
Polythiazide	Renese	1–4	once daily
Quinethazone	Hydromox	25–100	once daily
Trichlormethiazide	Metahydrin, Naqua	1–4	once daily
Loop diuretics			
Bumetanide	Bumex	0.5–10	twice daily
Ethacrynic acid	Edecrin	25–100	twice daily
Furosemide	Lasix	20–480	twice daily
Torsemide	Demadex	5–10	once daily
Potassium-sparing diuretics			
Amiloride	Midamor	5–10	once or twice daily
Spironolactone	Aldactone	25–100	two or three times daily
Triamterene	Dyrenium	50–150	once or twice daily
II. Beta-Blocking Drugs			
Acebutolol[c,b]	Sectral	200–1200	once or twice/d
Atenolol[c]	Tenormin	25–100	once daily

Table 5-7. (continued)

Table 5-7. (continued) Antihypertensive Drugs

Drug	Trade Name	Dose Range (mg/24 hours)	Frequency
Betoxolol[(c)]	Kerlone	10–20	once daily
Bisoprolol[(c)]	Zebeta	2.5–20	once daily
Carteolol[(b)]	Cartrol	2.5–10	once daily
Esmolol[(c)]	Breviblock	500 µg/kg (load); 100–300 µg/kg/min (maintenance)	IV infusion
Labetolol[(a)]	Trandate, Normodyne	200–1200	twice daily
Metoprolol[(c)]	Lopressor	50–200	once or twice daily
Metoprolol, long-acting[(c)]	Toprol XL	50–200	once daily
Nadolol	Corgard	40–320	once daily
Penbutolol	Levatol	10–80	once daily
Pindolol[(b)]	Visken	10–60	twice daily
Propranolol	Inderal	40–320	twice daily
Propranolol, long acting	Inderal LA	80–320	once daily
Timolol	Blocadren	10–20	twice daily
III. Calcium Channel Blockers			
Amlodipine	Norvasc	2.5–10	once daily
Diltiazem	Cardizem	60–360	three or four times per day
Diltiazem, sustained release	Cardizem SR	60–360	twice daily
Diltiazem, continuous delivery	Cardizem CD, Dilacor XR, Tiazac	120–360	once daily
Felodipine	Plendil	5–20	once daily
Isradipine	Dynacirc	5–20	twice daily
Isradipine, long acting	Dynacirc CR	5–20	once daily
Nicardipine	Cardene	60–120	three times per day
Nicardipine, long acting	Cardene SR	60–120	twice daily
Nicardipine IV	Cardene IV	0.5–2.2 mg/hr (as substitute for po); 5–15 mg/hr to	IV infusion

Table 5-7. (continued)

Table 5-7. (continued) Antihypertensive Drugs

Drug	Trade Name	Dose Range (mg/24 hours)	Frequency
		control BP, then maintenance of 3 mg/hr (severe HTN)	
Nifedipine	Procardia, Adalat	30–120	three times daily
Nifedipine, long acting	Procardia XL, Adalat CC	30–120	once daily
Nisoldipine	Sular	20–60	once daily
Verapamil	Calan, Isoptin	120–480	two or three times daily
Verapamil, long acting	Calan SR, Isoptin SR, Verelan, Covera HS	120–480	once daily
IV. Angiotensin-Converting Enzyme Inhibitors			
Benazepril	Lotensin	10–40	once daily
Captopril	Capoten	50–300	twice daily
Enalapril	Vasotec	5–40	once or twice daily
Enalaprilat	Vasotec IV	2–5 IV	in divided doses every 6 hours
Fosinopril	Monopril	10–80	once daily
Lisinopril	Prinivil, Zestril	5–40	once daily
Moexipril	Univasc	7.5–30	once daily
Quinapril	Accupril	10–80	once daily
Ramipril	Altace	2.5–20	once daily
Trandolapril	Mavik	1–8	once daily
V. Centrally Acting Sympatholytic Agents			
Clonidine	Catapres	0.1–1.2	two or three times daily
Clonidine patch	Catapres TTS	0.1–0.3 mg	per week
Guanabenz	Wytensin	4–64	twice daily

Table 5-7. (continued)

Table 5-7. (continued) Antihypertensive Drugs

Drug	Trade Name	Dose Range (mg/24 hours)	Frequency
Guanfacine	Tenex	1–3	once or twice daily
Methyldopa	Aldomet	250–2000	two or three times daily
VI. Alpha-1 Adrenergic Blockers			
Doxazosin	Cardura	1–16	once daily
Prazosin	Minipress	1–20	twice daily
Terazosin	Hytrin	1–20	once daily
VII. Peripherally Acting Adrenergic Antagonists			
Guanadrel	Hylorel	10–100	twice daily
Guanethidine	Ismelin	10–150	once daily
Reserpine	Serpasil	0.1–0.25	once daily
VIII. Direct Acting Vasodilators			
Hydralazine	Apresoline	50–300	two or four daily
Minoxidil	Loniten	2.5–80	once or twice daily
IX. Angiotensin II Receptor Antagonists			
Losartan	Cozaar	25–100	once or twice daily
Valsartan	Diovan	80–320	once daily
Irbesartan	Avapro	150–300	once daily

[a] Alpha- and beta-blocker

[b] ISA

[c] Cardioselective

Adapted in part from: The sixth report of the Joint National Committee on Detection, Evaluation, and Treatment of High Blood Pressure (JNC VI). Arch Intern Med 1997;157:2425–2426.

Loop diuretics Loop diuretics enhance sodium and water excretion by inhibiting chloride transport in the ascending loop of Henle.

• They are less effective than thiazides for control of HTN and have a shorter duration of action.

• Loop agents should be reserved for patients with renal dysfunction who do not respond to thiazides.

Beta Adrenergic Blocking Drugs Although their exact mechanism of action in HTN is not well understood, beta-blockers reduce CO and lower plasma renin activity (PRA). A number of agents are available. All have a similar effect on BP, but each possesses unique properties that may make one agent preferable to another (see Table 5-7).

Contraindications
Beta-blockers should be used cautiously, if at all, in patients with bronchospasm, severe peripheral vascular disease, CHF, severe diabetes mellitus, or cardiac conduction abnormalities.

Calcium Channel Blockers (CCBs) CCBs reduce BP by decreasing vascular smooth muscle tone. They are equally effective in black and white patients and among the young and the old.

Side effects
• All of the available agents have some negative inotropic effects (most prominent with the non-dihydropyridine agents verapamil and diltiazem) and should be used with caution in patients with LV dysfunction, although recent evidence suggests that amlodipine may have beneficial effects in CHF.
• Verapamil and diltiazem may impair AV node conduction. These drugs should be used with caution in patients with impairment of cardiac conduction or those receiving beta-blockers and/or digitalis.
• The dihydropyridine class is associated with the most potent vasodilator effect as compared to other CCBs. CO and HR may increase with their use and potentially provoke angina in the patient with CAD.
• Other side effects include peripheral edema, headache, and constipation.

Angiotensin-Converting Enzyme (ACE) Inhibitors ACE-inhibitors reduce BP by blocking the RAA axis. Specifically these agents inhibit the conversion of angiotensin I to angiotensin II decreasing TPR.

- Certain agents within this class have effects not only on serum ACE, but also on tissue and vascular wall ACE.
- All available agents appear to have similar efficacy.
- The active metabolite of enalapril, enalaprilat, is available for IV use.

Side effects and contraindications

- Cough (incidence 4% to 16%) is a side effect unique to this class of agents that resolves upon drug discontinuation.
- Other important side effects include granulocytopenia, angioedema, renal insufficiency, taste alteration, and rash.
- ACE-inhibitors should be used with caution, if at all, in patients with a baseline serum creatinine ≥2.5 mg/dL.
- Patients who are volume deficient (and therefore angiotensin II–sensitive) may experience severe hypotension with initiation of ACE-inhibitor therapy; therefore, diuretics should be used with caution and held for several days if possible.
- Hyperkalemia is a possible side effect, due to decreased aldosterone levels. Potassium supplements as well as potassium-sparing diuretics should be avoided if possible and serum potassium levels and renal function should be periodically monitored.
- Because patients with bilateral renal artery stenosis or renal artery stenosis of a solitary kidney depend on angiotensin II to maintain renal perfusion, ACE-inhibitors should be avoided in this population.
- ACE-inhibitors are contraindicated during the second and third trimesters of pregnancy.

Centrally Acting Sympatholytic Agents These drugs act by decreasing central nervous system sympathetic output.

Side Effects: The most common side effects include fatigue, orthostatic hypotension, and depression.

Clonidine Clonidine is associated with a syndrome of rebound HTN and sympathetic overactivity when doses in excess of 1 mg per day are abruptly discontinued. A transdermal preparation, effective for up to 7 days, is available.

Side Effect: Local skin irritation is a common side effect of the transdermal preparation.

Methyldopa, guanabenz, and guanfacine Methyldopa, guanabenz, and guanfacine have similar efficacy as compared to clonidine. Methyldopa is also available in an IV preparation for patients who cannot take oral medication.

Alpha-1 Adrenergic Blockers Alpha-1 blockers cause vasodilatation by blocking vascular post-synaptic alpha adrenergic neurons. Alpha-1 adrenoreceptor blockers inhibit sympathetic stimulation of prostatic smooth muscle, thereby reducing prostatic tone. These agents may be particularly useful among male hypertensives with benign prostatic hypertrophy and urinary flow obstruction.

- Prazosin is the prototype agent of this class. Terazosin and doxazosin have a similar efficacy and side effect profile compared to prazosin, but have a longer duration of action.

Side Effect: Orthostatic hypotension, occasionally resulting in syncope, is the most unique side effect. This typically occurs 1 to 3 hours after administration of the first dose and may be avoided by giving the first dose at bedtime.

Peripherally Acting Adrenergic Antagonists

Reserpine Reserpine depletes catecholamine stores in the brain and peripheral sympathetic nervous system resulting in decreased BP and HR.

Side Effects
- Mental depression is a major side effect and therefore reserpine use should be avoided in patients with a current or past history of depression.
- Reserpine also increases gastric acid secretion and should be used with caution in those with peptic ulcer disease.

Guanethidine Guanethidine interferes with release of norepinephrine from the sympathetic nerve terminal.

Side Effects: It is rarely used due to its frequent side effect profile, which includes postural hypotension, diarrhea, and impotence.

Direct-Acting Vasodilators Hydralazine and minoxidil are the available agents. Their use is often reserved for patients refractory to other antihypertensive agents.

Side effects
- These agents are associated with reflex tachycardia and salt and water retention; therefore, they are almost always administered in conjunction with beta-blockers and/or diuretics.
- Hydralazine is associated with a lupus-like reaction when doses exceeding 200 mg per day are used.
- Minoxidil is more potent than hydralazine. It commonly causes hypertrichosis and may rarely result in pericardial effusion.

Angiotensin II (Type AT_1) Receptor Blockers (ARBs) ARBs are a new class of antihypertensive agents. The major metabolite selectively blocks the binding of angiotensin II to the AT_1 receptor, thereby inhibiting the potent vasoconstrictor and aldosterone-secreting effects of angiotensin II.

- No inhibition of the angiotensin-converting enzyme occurs.
- These drugs undergo extensive first-pass hepatic metabolism and are cleared by both the kidneys and the biliary system.
- No significant drug interactions have been reported.

Side effects
- As with other medications which act on the RAA system, these agents should be discontinued at the time of pregnancy due the risk of injury or death to the fetus.
- Caution and dosage reduction should be used in patients with intravascular volume depletion due to the risk of symptomatic hypotension.

- These agents should be used with caution in patients with renal insufficiency. Serum tests of renal function should be monitored.
- Hyperkalemia.

   Fixed-Dose Combination Agents   Most experts agree that fixed-dose combination agents should not be used as initial therapy. Rather, their role is to decrease the patient's daily pill requirements, thus promoting compliance among patients who are already taking the component drugs. However, the combinations of bisoprolol/HCTZ and captopril/HCTZ are approved for initial therapy of HTN.

SECONDARY HYPERTENSION

The causes of secondary HTN are shown in Table 5-3.

Oral Contraceptive Use

Oral contraceptive use is a common cause of secondary HTN. A small rise in BP is common among users of these agents: 5% of oral contraceptive users develop HTN, and in half of this group, HTN persists despite drug discontinuation.

   The factors associated with increased risk of HTN include:

- Age greater than 35 years
- Obesity
- Duration of use
- Excessive alcohol intake

   Treatment
Oral contraceptive use should be avoided in high-risk patients and smokers. If HTN develops, then these agents should be discontinued. In most cases, the BP will normalize within a few months.

   Among patients in whom the BP does not normalize despite drug discontinuation and among those in whom the oral contraceptive agent cannot be discontinued, lifestyle modification and antihypertensive drug therapy should be used to reduce the BP.

Renal Parenchymal Disease

Renal parenchymal disease is the cause of elevated BP in up to 5% of hypertensives and is a leading cause of secondary HTN.

- In the majority of cases (acute glomerulonephritis, acute tubular necrosis, bilateral ureteral obstruction, chronic renal insufficiency), intravascular volume overload is the cause of HTN.
- In approximately 20% of cases (chronic pyelonephritis, unilateral renal parenchymal disease), increased renin activity is the probable cause.

Treatment

- In patients with increased intravascular volume and preserved renal function, diuretics will often achieve BP control.
- For the patient with increased PRA, beta-blockers are often helpful.
- HTN due to both etiologies may respond to any class of antihypertensive agent, usually in combination. In severe cases, the addition of the vasodilator minoxidil may be required.
- In diabetic patients with proteinuria, ACE-inhibitors can control HTN, diminish proteinuria, and slow the progression of renal disease.

Renovascular Hypertension

Etiology

Renovascular HTN is the cause of HTN in 0.5% to 2.0% of the hypertensive population. It is the most common type of surgically curable secondary HTN.

Atherosclerotic renovascular disease. More than 70% of cases are secondary to atherosclerotic renovascular disease. The typical patient is a male, over age 55, with evidence of generalized atherosclerosis.

Fibromuscular dysplasia. Among the remaining cases, fibromuscular dysplasia of the renal arteries is the most common. This typically occurs in patients less than 40 years old and has a predominance among women.

Regardless of etiology, reduced renal perfusion leads to increased renin and angiotensin II production, resulting in vasoconstriction and HTN.

Diagnosis

History and Symptoms   The following features are suggestive, but not diagnostic, of renovascular HTN.

- New onset of diastolic HTN before age 30 or after age 55.
- Abrupt onset of severe HTN at any age.
- HTN that is not controlled by an appropriate triple drug regimen.
- Worsening of BP previously well controlled on an antihypertensive medical regimen.
- HTN following flank or abdominal trauma.
- New onset HTN or difficulty with antihypertensive management in the setting of carotid, coronary, or peripheral vascular disease.
- Rapid deterioration of renal function following recent initiation of ACE-inhibitors.
- Recurrent episodes of acute pulmonary edema without other explanation.

Physical Examination
- A bruit heard in the epigastrium and/or flanks with both systolic and diastolic components suggests a renovascular cause, but the sensitivity and specificity of such a finding is only 50%.
- A bruit with only a systolic component is common in the elderly and is much less specific an indicator of renal artery stenosis.
- Peripheral vascular disease is common in patients with atherosclerotic renovascular disease.
- Hypertensive retinopathy often accompanies atherosclerotic renovascular HTN.

Diagnostic Studies
In the past, rapid-sequence IV pyelography, nuclear isotopic renography, and measurement of spontaneous PRA were recommended to distinguish renovascular HTN from other forms of HTN. Because of their less-than-optimal sensitivity and specificity, these studies are no

longer recommended as part of the diagnostic evaluation. The following sections examine the currently recommended tests.

Captopril Test The captopril test is based on the principle that following administration of captopril, patients with renovascular HTN and normal renal function will have a hyperresponsive increase of PRA. A positive test in a hypertensive patient strongly suggests renovascular HTN.

Preparation In preparation for the test, the patient should maintain normal sodium intake and avoid diuretics. If possible, all antihypertensive agents should be discontinued 3 weeks prior to the test (often difficult to achieve). Acceptable sensitivity and specificity have been demonstrated when medication could not be discontinued.

Performance
1. The patient should be seated for at least 30 minutes.
2. At the conclusion of the seated period, the patient's baseline BP is recorded and a venous blood sample is obtained for measurement of baseline PRA.
3. Captopril 50 mg is then given orally.
4. BP is measured every 15 minutes thereafter for 1 hour.
5. At 1 hour after captopril administration, a venous blood sample with the patient seated is obtained for measurement of stimulated PRA.

Interpretation There are three criteria necessary for a positive test:

1. Stimulated PRA ≥12 ng/mL/hr.
2. Absolute increase in PRA of ≥10 ng/mL/hr.
3. ≥150% increase in stimulated PRA compared to baseline level; or ≥400% increase in stimulated PRA if the baseline PRA is ≤3 ng/mL/hr.

Captopril Radionuclide Scintirenography Radionuclide scintirenography (^{131}I orthoiodohippuric acid or ^{99m}Tc diethylenetriamine penta-acetic acid) in conjunction with the administration of captopril (25 mg) has a sensitivity and specificity in excess of 90% for the detection of renal artery stenosis.

Renal Artery Duplex Ultrasonography Renal ultrasound (B-mode and Doppler) to detect kidney size, renal artery peak flow velocity, and velocity waveform characteristics has a reported sensitivity to diagnose renal artery stenosis in excess of 90%.

Magnetic Resonance Angiography (MRA) MRA has the potential to visualize stenotic renal arteries in two or three dimensions. Preliminary results in comparison to conventional renal arteriography are promising.

- Advantages include its noninvasive nature and its lack of radiation exposure or contrast administration.
- Disadvantages include its cost, respiratory artifacts, difficulty in imaging tortuous vessels, and its general lack of availability.

Renal Artery Arteriography Renal arteriography is the definitive test for the diagnosis of renal artery stenosis. Visualization of a stenotic renal artery is not sufficient proof that renal vascular disease is the cause of HTN and does not predict that correction of the stenosis will result in BP control. Once renal artery stenosis is identified, an attempt to ascertain the functional significance is accomplished by comparing the renal vein renin level from the kidney presumed to be ischemic to the renal vein renin level from the contralateral kidney.

- Surgical correction of renal artery stenosis with renal vein renin ratios ≥ 2.0 usually leads to improved BP control.
- Interestingly, 50% to 60% of patients with renal vein ratios less than 1.5 will also respond to surgery.
- Renal artery stenosis with presence of poststenotic dilatation and collateral vessels in the setting of HTN of less than 5-years' duration also has a high response rate to revascularization despite renal vein renin ratios.

Digital subtraction angiography (DSA) Conventional arteriography remains widely used, but DSA has become a popular method to visualize the main renal artery.

- The main advantage of DSA is that less contrast dye is required compared with conventional arteriography (potentially resulting in less morbidity).
- The disadvantage is that DSA is somewhat less able to define the status of small renal vessels.

Treatment
The goals of treatment are to control BP and preserve renal function.

Medical Therapy The initial medical therapy is similar to that of essential HTN. Beta-blockers and ACE-inhibitors are particularly effective.

Monitoring renal function   Close monitoring of renal function is necessary during medical therapy, and medical therapy continues as long as HTN is controlled and renal function is preserved.

- Serum creatinine determinations are helpful to follow overall renal function and noninvasive isotopic renal scans provide important assessment of the status of individual kidney function.
- A reversible increase in serum creatinine may occur in patients with bilateral renal artery stenosis or renal artery stenosis of a solitary kidney during therapy with ACE-inhibitors. Renal failure may progress once the arterial stenosis exceeds 75% of vessel diameter.

Surgical Revascularization   Surgical revascularization is the most effective means to restore renal blood flow and subsequently improve BP and preserve renal function.

Indications   Surgical revascularization is recommended when:

- HTN is refractory due to a well-titrated medical regimen.
- Renal function is jeopardized.
- The patient is a suitable surgical candidate.

Percutaneous Transluminal Renal Angioplasty (PTRA)
PTRA is a nonsurgical revascularization technique that has shown favorable results.

- In renovascular HTN due to fibromuscular dysplasia, the initial success rate of PTRA is 90% and cure of HTN occurs in 60% of patients. The restenosis rate is in the range of 5%.
- PTRA is also successful in many cases of intrarenal artery stenosis and renal artery stenosis of a transplanted kidney.
- In patients with unilateral, nonostial atherosclerotic lesions the initial procedural success rate is also 90%. The rate of restenosis is 30% and only 30% of patients are cured.
- In patients with bilateral renal artery stenosis, ostial lesions, or occluded renal arteries the initial success rates are significantly lower.
- Renal artery stenting may be an effective treatment in patients with poorly controlled HTN and lesions that are difficult to treat with PTRA (ostial location, restenosis) or after a suboptimal angiographic result with PTRA alone.

In many centers PTRA is performed at the time of initial renal angiography without the use of studies to confirm the hemodynamic significance of renovascular lesions. Some centers also advocate an attempt at PTRA in all patients considered for surgical revascularization, reserving surgery for those with unsuccessful PTRA.

Coarctation of the Aorta

Pathophysiology
In adults, the narrowing of the aorta is usually congenital and typically is localized to the region immediately beyond the origin of the left subclavian artery. Aortic coarctation is a rare cause of HTN (0.1% to 0.2% of patients). The mechanism is likely related to a combination of factors that include high resistance to LV output, stimulation of the RAA system due to decreased renal perfusion, and resetting of aortic arch baroreceptors.

Diagnosis

History and Symptoms   The classic symptoms of HTN caused by aortic coarctation are:

Chronic headache
Lower extremity fatigue
Claudication (occasionally)

Physical Examination The physical examination reveals upper extremity HTN.

- BP in the arms (especially the right arm) often exceeds lower extremity BP by at least 20 mm Hg.
- The femoral pulses are delayed when compared to the right radial pulse.
- A bruit may be heard over the back due to turbulent flow across the coarctation and/or increased flow in dilated intercostal artery collateral vessels.

Diagnostic Studies

Electrocardiogram ECG usually shows evidence of LVH.

Chest X-Ray The CXR may reveal a "figure 3" sign formed by the dilated left subclavian artery, the discrete coarctation, and the poststenotic aortic dilatation.

Rib notching of the inferior margins of ribs 3–8 may be seen. This finding is secondary to bone erosion caused by increased blood flow in dilated intercostal artery collateral channels.

Echocardiography Echocardiography can examine the long axis of the aorta and its arch from the suprasternal notch position to reveal the site of coarctation and estimate the pressure gradient across it. LVH and dilated ascending aorta and arch vessels are invariably present. TEE can be used if TTE is suboptimal.

MRI MRI can localize the coarctation, precisely define the head and neck vessels, and measure the pressure gradient across the coarctation site.

Angiography Angiography is an alternative technique to identify the location of a coarctation.

Cardiac Catheterization and Coronary Angiography Cardiac catheterization can measure the pressure gradient across the coarctation, image the coarctation site and the dilated aorta and proximal head and neck vessels, and assess the status of the coronary arteries in individuals with suspected ischemic heart disease prior to surgical repair.

Treatment

Surgical correction is the treatment of choice in adult patients. In the pediatric population, surgical correction or balloon angioplasty can be used as the initial treatment.

Balloon angioplasty can be used in patients who have developed restenosis after a surgical procedure or in those with major residual gradients after surgical repair.

HTN can persist in 25% to 50% of adult patients despite relief of the coarctation, and should be treated with medical therapy as previously outlined.

Pheochromocytoma

Etiology

Pheochromocytomas are tumors which arise from chromaffin tissue and produce excessive levels of catecholamines. These tumors are the cause of HTN in less than 1% of cases. Approximately 90% arise within the adrenal medulla, 10% are bilateral, 10% are extra-abdominal, and 10% are malignant.

Diagnosis

History and Symptoms The clinical features of pheochromocytomas reflect excess catecholamine production.

The most common symptoms are:

1. Paroxysmal headache
2. Palpitations
3. Sweating

- The presence of all 3 symptoms in a hypertensive patient is 90% sensitive and 94% specific for the diagnosis of pheochromocytoma.
- In patients with paroxysmal HTN, symptoms usually last less than 1 hour. Paroxysmal symptoms may also occur in patients with persistent HTN.
- The absence of all 3 symptoms makes pheochromocytoma unlikely.

Less common symptoms are:

Fatigue
Tremor
Anxiety
Orthostasis
Weight loss

Physical Examination
HTN is the hallmark feature. It is paroxysmal 50% of the time and sustained in the remainder.

Pheochromocytoma must be considered in the following situations:

- Malignant HTN, DBP >130 mm Hg.
- HTN during abdominal palpation, anesthesia induction, or surgery.
- Worsened HTN after administration of a beta-blocker.
- HTN not responding to a well-titrated antihypertensive regimen.

Laboratory Studies
Laboratory diagnosis is based on identification of excess catecholamine production by documenting increased levels of urinary catecholamine metabolites or elevated serum catecholamines. Once catecholamine excess is documented, an imaging procedure is indicated to localize the tumor.

Metanephrine Level
A 24-hour urine collection to determine the metanephrine level is the most reliable screening test. A 24-hour urinary metanephrine level greater than 1.3 mg strongly suggests the diagnosis of pheochromocytoma.

If HTN is persistent, a single voided urine specimen to determine the ratio of metanephrine to creatinine may be obtained. A ratio of greater than 1 mg metanephrine per 1 mg creatinine strongly suggests the diagnosis.

Plasma Catecholamines
Plasma catecholamines should be measured if the urine metanephrine determination is inadequate or nondiagnostic.

The patient rests supine for 30 minutes and plasma is sampled through a previously inserted IV catheter.

Catecholamine levels greater than 2000 pg/mL are diagnostic; values less than 1000 pg/mL do not suggest pheochromocytoma.

Clonidine Suppression   Clonidine suppresses neurally mediated catecholamine release. Pheochromocytomas release catecholamine independently and therefore are not suppressed by clonidine administration.

To perform this test the patient is given clonidine 0.3 mg by mouth. Serum catecholamine levels are obtained at rest and 3 hours later.

- Normal catecholamine suppression by clonidine results in a fall of catecholamine levels to less than 500 pg/mL and a relative fall of greater than 40% compared to the resting level.
- Lack of catecholamine suppression supports the diagnosis of pheochromocytoma.

Beta-blockers interfere with hepatic clearance of catecholamines and may result in a high level of catecholamines and, therefore, a false-positive test. The test should be performed more than 48 hours after the discontinuation of beta-blockers.

Localization Studies
Localization studies are performed following documentation of elevated catecholamine levels.

- **CT or MRI** of the abdomen are the studies of choice and will identify tumors $\geq$0.5 cm in size.
- **^{131}I-metaiodobenzyl guanidine (^{131}I-MIBG)** is a norepinephrine analog that localizes in chromaffin tissue. Nuclear scanning with this agent is useful in pheochromocytoma localization if CT or MRI is negative.

If the above imaging studies are negative, abdominal angiography may be helpful to identify the tumor.

Treatment
Surgical resection of the pheochromocytoma, following medical stabilization, is the treatment of choice.

Preoperative HTN Management   Preoperatively, alpha- and beta-adrenergic blockade is achieved to blunt the effect of catecholamines released during tumor removal. Peripheral beta-adrenergic receptors mediate vasodilatation. Blockade of these receptors in the absence of alpha-blockade may result in unopposed alpha stimulation and intense vasoconstriction and HTN. Therefore, alpha-blockade is always accomplished prior to beta-blockade.

- Alpha-blockade is achieved with phenoxybenzamine (initial dose 10 mg po BID with the dose increased to achieve BP control) or prazosin (2–5 mg po BID). Effective alpha-blockade should be present at least 7 days prior to surgery.
- If the patient is experiencing tachycardia or cardiac arrhythmias, beta-blockers are added after effective alpha-blockade is achieved.

Intra-operative HTN Management HTN during surgery is best managed with IV nitroprusside.

Postoperative Management Hypotension is common after tumor removal and is secondary to vasodilatation and relative intravascular volume depletion following reversal of intense vasoconstriction. It usually responds to fluid administration.

Inoperable Pheochromocytoma In cases of inoperable pheochromocytoma, patients are treated with chronic oral alpha-adrenergic blocking agents with the addition of beta-blockers as needed.

Primary Hyperaldosteronism

Primary aldosteronism is the cause of HTN in less than 0.1% of cases. The mechanism is mineralocorticoid excess, causing sodium retention, potassium wasting, and intravascular volume expansion.

Pathology
- An adenoma of the adrenal cortex (usually unilateral) is the cause in 65% to 70% of cases (Conn's syndrome).
- Bilateral adrenal hyperplasia accounts for the majority of the remaining cases.

Diagnosis
Primary aldosteronism has no specific historical features or physical findings.

Hypokalemia may cause weakness, cramps, polyuria, or polydipsia. Patients are often discovered because of HTN associated with persistent hypokalemia or because of profound hypokalemia in diuretic-treated patients despite potassium supplementation.

Laboratory Studies

Prior to diagnostic evaluation, antihypertensive drugs should be discontinued for 2 weeks and potassium supplements should be given to hypokalemic patients. Laboratory evaluation should be performed in nondiuretic treated hypertensives who have serum potassium levels <3.6 mEq/L or in those on low-dose diuretics with serum potassium <3.0 mEq/L.

- PRA greater than 1.0 ng/mL/hr indicates that primary hyperaldosteronism is unlikely.
- A ratio of plasma aldosterone to PRA in excess of 50 is indicative of primary hyperaldosteronism.
- 24-hour urine collection should be sampled for potassium at least 2 weeks after discontinuation of diuretics with the patient receiving potassium supplementation and ingesting a normal sodium load.

If 24-hour urinary potassium is less than 30 mEq, the diagnosis of hyperaldosteronism is unlikely. If urinary potassium is more than 30 mEq/24 hour and hyperaldosteronism is suspect, then urinary aldosterone (after salt loading to suppress normal aldosterone production) should be measured. Following salt loading–aldosterone suppression, urinary aldosterone greater than 14 μg/24 hours confirms the presence of hyperaldosteronism.

Localization Studies

Localization of the aldosterone-producing tumor is performed once the laboratory diagnosis of hyperaldosteronism is confirmed.

- CT or MRI of the adrenal glands is the best imaging study to identify adrenal adenomas and adrenal hyperplasia.
- Among patients with normal or equivocal imaging studies despite biochemical evidence suggestive of primary hyperaldosteronism, and among patients with

scans indicative of adrenal hyperplasia, additional biochemical testing should be performed because a small group can be cured with unilateral adrenalectomy.

Other Diagnostic Tests

Additional diagnostic tests include:

- Postural stimulation test. Failure to augment plasma aldosterone after 2 hours of upright ambulation as compared to the overnight recumbent level.
- Plasma 18-hydroxycorticosterone level >100 ng/dL.
- Elevated urinary 18-methyl oxygenated cortisol metabolites.
- Adrenal vein sampling for aldosterone. Performed if additional biochemical studies support the diagnosis of hyperaldosteronism. Lateralization of aldosterone secretion suggests that unilateral adrenalectomy may be curative.

Treatment

Adrenal Adenoma Surgical resection of the adenoma is the treatment of choice. Only 35% are "cured" (no requirement for antihypertensive drug therapy) of HTN after adrenalectomy. The remainder require anti-hypertensive drug therapy, but HTN control is vastly improved in the majority as compared to the preoperative state.

In poor operative candidates, medical therapy with aldosterone antagonists is used.

Adrenal Hyperplasia Aldosterone antagonists (spironolactone 100–200 mg daily or amiloride 10–40 mg daily) will control HTN and correct serum potassium in patients with nonlateralizing adrenal vein aldosterone levels.

- Bilateral adrenalectomy generally is not performed because patients will require life-long steroid replacement therapy.
- In the small subgroup with suggestive biochemical studies and lateralizing adrenal vein sampling, unilateral adrenalectomy may be curative. Most patients still require medical therapy after surgery.

Miscellaneous Causes of Secondary HTN

Other secondary causes of HTN include:

Cushing's syndrome (associated with HTN in up to
  80% of cases)
Hyperthyroidism (associated with systolic HTN)
Hypothyroidism (associated with diastolic HTN)
Hyperparathyroidism
Acromegaly
Sleep apnea syndromes
Renin-producing tumors
Dysautonomia syndromes

SPECIAL PROBLEMS IN HYPERTENSION

Hypertensive Emergencies and Urgencies

General Concepts

Hypertensive emergencies are situations in which
  elevated BP is associated with target-organ damage.
  BP should be controlled within 1 hour to reduce
  morbidity and mortality.

Hypertensive urgencies are situations where BP is
  severely elevated but there is no evidence of target-
  organ damage. In this setting, BP should be
  controlled within 24 hours.

DBP generally exceeds 115 mmHg in a hypertensive
emergency, but the rate of change of BP rather than the
degree of BP elevation places the patient at risk for
target-organ damage. Thus, a patient with a hypertensive
urgency and associated chronic HTN may have a higher
BP reading than a patient with acute HTN and an associated hypertensive emergency.

Hypertensive Emergencies

The most common examples of hypertensive emergencies are severe HTN associated with the following
conditions:

Encephalopathy (papilledema, abnormal mental status,
  focal neurologic findings, seizures)
Intracranial hemorrhage
Acute LV failure

Aortic dissection
Eclampsia or severe HTN associated with pregnancy
Head trauma
Extensive burns
Unstable angina
Acute MI

Treatment The therapeutic goal is to decrease BP to a safer level—usually no more than a 25% to 30% decrease in MAP or to a DBP of 100 to 110mmHg. BP should remain at this level for several days before decreasing it to "normal" levels. With severe HTN, autoregulation of cerebral, coronary, and renal blood flow is shifted to accommodate the increased pressure and maintain vital organ perfusion. Too rapid a diminution in BP may result in ischemia to these vital organ beds.

Antihypertensive agents Initially, the vast majority of patients should be treated in an ICU setting with parenteral antihypertensive drugs (Table 5-8) and intra-arterial BP monitoring.

- **Nitroprusside.** Nitroprusside is the drug of choice for the patient with hypertensive encephalopathy, acute LV failure, or acute renal failure. Nitroprusside is also recommended for acute aortic dissection; however, beta-blocking agents must be used in conjunction to decrease the force of cardiac contraction and aortic shearing forces that are augmented with the use of nitroprusside alone.
- **Trimethaphan.** Trimethaphan is also useful in the setting of aortic dissection as a monotherapy because it decreases both BP and the rate of pressure rise in the aorta.
- **IV nitroglycerin.** NTG is the drug of choice for severe HTN associated with myocardial ischemia.
- **Labetolol, diazoxide, enalaprilat.** These agents require less intense monitoring, but do not offer as precise control of BP.

Most patients with hypertensive emergencies are volume depleted as a result of diuresis induced by the elevated BP. For this reason diuretics do not play a role in

Table 5-8. Parenteral Therapy of Hypertensive Emergencies

Drug	IV Dose	Onset	Comment
Vasodilators			
Nitroprusside	0.25–10 µg/kg/ min infusion	Immediate	Requires exact monitoring. Thiocyanate toxicity a risk if infused >48 hrs. Drug of choice for aortic dissection and HTN encephalopathy.
Nitroglycerin	5–300 µg/min infusion	2–5 minutes	Requires exact monitoring. Preferred drug when angina present.
Diazoxide	50–150 mg bolus	1–5 minutes	Reflex tachycardia common, and may provoke angina if coronary artery disease is present.
Enalaprilat	0.625–1.25 mg bolus every 6 hours	15 minutes	
Nicardipine	5–15 mg/hr to control BP, then maintenance of 3 mg/hr (severe HTN)	5–10 minutes	Reflex tachycardia, flushing.
Hydralazine	10–40 mg IV, 10–50 mg IM	10–30 minutes	Reflex tachycardia, flushing, worsened angina.
Adrenergic Inhibitors			
Propranolol	5–10 mg over 10 min up to 0.15 mg/kg	Immediate	Use to treat tachycardia or decrease aortic shearing force when vasodilators used for aortic dissection.
Labetolol	20 mg initial bolus, then 20–80 mg bolus every	1–5 minutes	

Table 5-8. (continued)

Table 5-8. (continued) Parenteral Therapy of Hypertensive Emergencies

Drug	IV Dose	Onset	Comment
	10 min up to dose of 300 mg; or 2 mg/min IV infusion		
Trimethaphan	1–4 mg/min infusion	1–5 minutes	Useful as monotherapy in aortic dissection.
Esmolol	500 µg/kg (load); 100–300 µg/ kg/min (maintenance)	1–2 minutes	
Phentolamine	5–15 mg IV	2 minutes	Useful for pheochromocytoma. Tachycardia and arrhythmias are adverse effects.

initial therapy and are reserved for the patient with evident intravascular volume overload.

Hypertensive Urgencies

In this circumstance, too rapid a decline in BP may lead to greater patient morbidity than the risk of HTN itself. Therefore, the goal of therapy should be to reduce the DBP to 100 to 110 mm Hg over a 24-hour period.

Treatment Drug therapy is similar to that for essential HTN and is almost always achieved with the use of oral medications in the outpatient setting.

Clonidine. Initial dose of 0.1–0.2 mg followed by 0.1 mg/hour by mouth up to a total of 0.6 mg or until DBP <110 mm Hg.

Nifedipine. 10–20 mg by mouth, repeated after 30 minutes and then every 6 hours.

Captopril. 25 mg by mouth, repeated as required.

Labetolol. 200–400 mg by mouth, repeated every 2 to 3 hours.

In many instances patients stop taking their medications or their supply runs out with a resultant loss of BP control. If the previous regimen was adequate, then reinstitution of this regimen is usually sufficient.

Hypertension in the Elderly

Epidemiology

The prevalence of both systolic and diastolic HTN increases with age.

- Age-related DBP increase peaks at 55 years of age, while increases in SBP continue as the patient ages.
- Systolic HTN is the strongest cardiac risk factor in the elderly other than advanced age itself.

Pathophysiology

Increased TPR secondary to atherosclerosis as well as decreased vessel elasticity is the major cause of HTN. Renin levels are normal or decreased.

Diagnosis

Measurement of BP in the elderly is the same as that for other patient groups.

Pseudohypertension Pseudohypertension is a cause for overestimation of SBP in the elderly. This phenomenon occurs when the brachial artery is excessively rigid due to calcification so that it cannot be compressed with a sphygmomanometer.

To screen for this possibility, the BP cuff is inflated above SBP and an attempt is made to palpate the pulseless brachial and radial arteries (Osler's sign). If the arterial pulsation is palpable, pseudohypertension may exist. In this situation, intra-arterial BP measurement is the most accurate means to determine BP.

Treatment

Proven benefit exists for the treatment of both diastolic and systolic HTN in the elderly. It is recommended that DBP be reduced to less than 90 mm Hg and that SBP be reduced to less than 140 mm Hg.

Lifestyle Modification Lifestyle modification should be used initially for 3 to 6 months for patients with DBP of 90 to 100 mm Hg and SBP of 140 to 160 mm Hg.

Antihypertensive Drug Therapy Antihypertensive drug therapy should be utilized when DBP is ≥110 mm Hg, DBP is ≥100 mm Hg despite an adequate trial of lifestyle modification, or when SBP is ≥160 to 180 mm Hg.

Drug therapy precautions
- The elderly are sensitive to volume depletion, hypotension, sympathetic inhibition, and the sedative effects of antihypertensive therapy.
- They are also prone to hypokalemia, hyponatremia, and hypomagnesemia.

For these reasons, pharmacologic therapy should be initiated at approximately *one-half* the dose of that recommended for the younger patient.

Agents that produce severe orthostatic hypotension (alpha-1 blockers, guanadrel, guanethidine, and labetolol) should be avoided.

Drug therapy options
Low-dose thiazide diuretics. Low-dose thiazide diuretics are the initial drugs of choice. Chlorthalidone has been demonstrated to significantly reduce the risk of both stroke and MI in elderly patients with isolated systolic HTN.

Calcium channel blockers and ACE-inhibitors. Calcium channel blockers and ACE-inhibitors have also been found to be effective.

Other drugs. Beta-blockers, methyldopa, or clonidine may be added to a diuretic if diuretic monotherapy is ineffective. However, use of these medications may be associated with CNS depression.

Hypertension in Pregnancy

HTN complicates 10% of pregnancies and is associated with increased fetal and maternal complications:

- Increased fetal morbidity and mortality is due to prematurity, intrauterine growth retardation, and abruptio placentae.
- Increased maternal morbidity and mortality is due to eclampsia, cerebral hemorrhage, multiorgan failure, HELLP (hemolysis, elevated liver function tests, low platelets) syndrome, and death.

Types of Pregnancy Hypertension

HTN in pregnancy may be classified as:

Chronic HTN. BP $\geq$140/90 mm Hg that is present before pregnancy or that is diagnosed prior to the 20th week of gestation.

Preeclampsia and eclampsia. HTN that develops after the 20th week of gestation, associated with edema and proteinuria (>300 mg/24 hr).

Chronic HTN with superimposed preeclampsia. Development of proteinuria after the 20th week of gestation in the setting of preexisting HTN.

Transient HTN. Elevated BP during pregnancy without proteinuria. BP usually returns to normal levels within days to a few weeks postpartum.

The criteria for diagnosing HTN in pregnancy include:

1. Increase in SBP $\geq$30 mm Hg.
2. Increase in DBP $\geq$15 mm Hg.
3. BP $\geq$140/90 mm Hg if prior BP unknown.

Evaluation of HTN in Pregnancy

Patients with chronic HTN should be monitored closely. A secondary cause of HTN should be considered. These patients are at risk of superimposed preeclampsia.

Patients with HTN after the 20th week of gestation require close evaluation. Transient and uncomplicated chronic HTN are often benign disorders, whereas preeclampsia and chronic HTN with superimposed preeclampsia can represent serious conditions. Significant abnormalities on these laboratory tests may identify preeclampsia:

CBC, platelet count, and blood smear
Serum BUN and creatinine
Liver function tests
Urinalysis

Treatment of HTN in Pregnancy

Chronic HTN　Antihypertensive medications should be reviewed.

- ACE-inhibitors and AT_1-receptor blockers should be discontinued and another medication substituted.

- If HTN is mild, stopping medication should be considered because BP usually declines during the second trimester (physiologic vasodilatation of pregnancy). In this situation, the increased risk of developing preeclampsia means close follow-up is indicated. If medications are continued, the goal of therapy should be DBP <105 mm Hg.

Preeclampsia Therapy of preeclampsia includes hospitalization, bed rest, seizure prophylaxis if eclampsia is impending, and control of BP.

No general agreement exists at which BP level antihypertensive drug therapy should be initiated. A reasonable goal is to stabilize the BP around 160 to 170/100 to 105 mm Hg. Excessive lowering of BP may compromise uteroplacental blood flow.

- The most widely used antihypertensive agent is methyldopa because of its well-documented efficacy and safety.
- Short-term (4 to 6 weeks) use of beta-blockers is safe in pregnancy. Long-term treatment is associated with low birth weight and increased fetal distress.
- Labetolol has been documented to be safe and effective in pregnancy, but reduced birth weight may occur as a side effect.
- CCBs have been documented to be safe and effective in the short-term treatment of HTN.
- IV hydralazine is the agent of choice to control acute HTN.

Transient HTN Transient HTN is usually a benign condition. It responds well to antihypertensive therapy; the same criteria for initiation of therapy for preeclampsia are suggested for transient HTN.

Hypertension in Diabetics

HTN is common in patients with diabetes. Most diabetics with HTN have essential HTN. The goal of antihypertensive therapy should be a BP ≤130/85 mm Hg.

The antihypertensive medications recommended by the JNC as first-line agents (diuretics, beta-blockers) may not be suitable for diabetic patients:

- Diuretics inhibit insulin secretion and raise blood lipid levels.
- Beta-blockers can increase lipid levels, inhibit insulin secretion, and mask the adrenergic symptoms of hypoglycemia.

Recommended Treatments

ACE-Inhibitors ACE-inhibitors have been convincingly shown to retard the progression of renal disease in patients with insulin-requiring diabetes mellitus if microalbuminuria is present. It is not known if AT_1-receptor blockers have similar efficacy.

Calcium Channel Blockers Like ACE-inhibitors, non-dihydropyridine CCBs (diltiazem, verapamil) have been shown to decrease microalbuminuria.

- These agents can be used when ACE-inhibitor therapy is contraindicated or when side effects of therapy occur.
- CCBs can be added to ACE-inhibitor therapy when HTN control with the single agent is inadequate. A synergistic effect of these agents on microalbuminuria has yet to be demonstrated.

SUGGESTED READINGS

Appel LJ, Moore TH, Obarzane K, et al. for the DASH Collaborative Research Group. A clinical trial of the effects of dietary patterns on blood pressure. N Engl J Med 1997;336:1117–1124.

Blumenfeld JD, Sealey JE, Schlussel Y, et al. Diagnosis and treatment of primary aldosteronism. Ann Intern Med 1994;121:877–885.

Bravo EL, Gifford RW, Jr. Pheochromocytoma: diagnosis, localization, and management. N Engl J Med 1986;311: 1298–1303.

Calhoun D, Oparil S. Treatment of hypertensive crisis. N Engl J Med 1990;323:1177–1183.

Fatourechi V, Kennedy FP, Rizza RA, Hogan MJ. A practical guideline for management of hypertension in patients with diabetes. Mayo Clin Proc 1996;71:53–58.

Frolich ED, Grim C, Labarthe DR, et al. Recommendations for human blood pressure determination by sphygmomanometers. Report of a special task force appointed by the steering committee, American Heart Association. Circulation 1988;77:502A–514A.

Henriksen T. Hypertension in pregnancy: Use of antihypertensive drugs. Acta Obstet Gynecol Scand 1997;76:96–106.

Houston MC. Pathophysiology, clinical aspects, and treatment of hypertensive crises. Prog Cardiovasc Dis 1989;32:99–148.

Houston MC. New insights and new approaches for the treatment of essential hypertension: selection of therapy based on coronary heart disease risk factor analysis, hemodynamic profiles, quality of life, and subsets of hypertension. Am Heart J 1989;117:911–951.

Izzo JL, Black HR. Hypertension primer. Dallas, TX: American Heart Association, 1993.

Kaplan MN. Clinical hypertension. 6th ed. Baltimore: Williams & Wilkins, 1994.

Muller FB, Sealey JE, Case DB, et al. The captopril test for identifying renovascular disease in hypertensive patients. Am J Med 1986;80:633–644.

National High Blood Pressure Education Program Working Group. 1995 update of the working group reports on chronic renal failure and renovascular hypertension. Arch Intern Med 1996;156:1938–1947.

Saige A, Larson MG, Levy D. The natural history of borderline isolated systolic hypertension. N Engl J Med 1993;329:1912–1917.

Saunders E. Hypertension in minorities: blacks. Am J Hypertens 1995;8:115S–119S.

SHEP Cooperative Research Group. Prevention of stroke by antihypertensive drug treatment in older persons with isolated systolic hypertension. JAMA 1991;265:3255–3264.

Staesen JA, Fagard R, Thijs L, et al. Randomised double-blind comparison of placebo and active treatment for older patients with isolated systolic hypertension. Lancet 1997; 350:757–764.

The sixth report of the Joint National Committee on Detection, Evaluation, and Treatment of High Blood Pressure (JNC VI). Arch Intern Med 1997;157:2413–2446.

Valvular Heart Disease

Dennis A. Tighe
Edward K. Chung

Valvular heart disease is a common clinical problem. This chapter reviews the epidemiology, diagnosis, and treatment of valvular heart disease. A discussion of prosthetic heart valves is provided.

SPECIFIC VALVE LESIONS

Aortic Stenosis (AS)

Etiology

All acquired AS and 70% of congenital AS are valvular in location. Subvalvular or supravalvular obstruction to LV outflow is present in the remaining 30% of cases of congenital AS.

Valvular AS The prevalence of rheumatic AS has significantly declined over the past 30 years. Isolated valvular AS occurs more commonly in men and is usually congenital or degenerative in origin.

Congenital valvular AS Congenital deformity of the aortic valve may be unicuspid, bicuspid, tricuspid, or quadricuspid in nature.

- *Unicuspid valves* most often present as CHF secondary to severe outflow obstruction during infancy.
- *Bicuspid valves* may be stenotic at birth, but much more frequently become stenotic several decades

later. This is the most common cause of AS in adults less than 70 years old.

- *Tricuspid valves*, having cusps of unequal size and possible commissural fusion, also may be stenotic at birth, but more commonly become narrowed later in life.
- *Quadricuspid deformity* is rare.

Degenerative valvular AS Degenerative (senile) AS of a previously normal trileaflet aortic valve is due to calcium deposition on the valve leaflets with secondary thickening and restriction of motion. This is the most common cause of AS in those older than 70 years.

Less common causes of AS

Rheumatic fever. Rheumatic fever rarely results in isolated valvular AS (less than 5% of cases). Most commonly, AS occurs in association with rheumatic MV disease. Concomitant AR is very common. Rheumatic involvement is characterized by commissural fusion, leaflet retraction and scarring, and deposition of calcium nodules on the valve leaflet surface.

Rheumatoid arthritis. Nodular thickening of the valve leaflets.

External beam radiation therapy.

Nonvalvular AS

Congenital abnormalities of the LV outflow tract and aorta may result in subvalvular or supravalvular AS.

- Subvalvular stenosis is the result of a fibromuscular ring or membranous obstruction below the aortic valve.
- Obstructive HCM is the most common cause of subvalvular LV outflow tract obstruction in adults.
- Supravalvular AS, characterized by localized or diffuse narrowing of the ascending aorta, is rare. It is often associated with craniofacial abnormalities and mental retardation (Williams' syndrome).

Coarctation of the aorta can mimic many of the features of AS (see Chapter 9).

Pathophysiology

The pathophysiologic features of AS are the result of obstruction to LV outflow.

Left Ventricular Hypertrophy (LVH) With progressive aortic valve narrowing, LV pressure must rise to maintain normal aortic perfusion pressure. Concentric LVH (increase in muscle mass without significant chamber dilation) is the initial adaptation to increased afterload.

Decreased Left Ventricular Compliance LVH causes a decrease in LV compliance and increased LV end-diastolic pressure (LVEDP). As ventricular stiffness increases, the LA hypertrophies and serves as a "booster pump" to maintain adequate LV filling without a significant rise in LA pressure. Loss of appropriately timed atrial contraction often results in elevation of LA pressure and diminished CO.

Decreased Cardiac Output As AS becomes severe, CO fails to augment appropriately with exercise or stress. The LV dilates (eccentric hypertrophy) and may fail, resulting in reduced CO and transvalvular pressure gradient. Concomitant elevation of the LA, PCW, PA, and right heart pressures (late finding) occurs.

Myocardial Ischemia With severe AS and LVH, the subendocardium may experience inadequate perfusion in the absence of epicardial CAD. The mechanism of myocardial ischemia with normal epicardial coronary arteries is not completely known, but it may be due to decreased coronary perfusion gradient resulting from increased LVEDP, compression of the coronary arteries by the hypertrophied myocardium, or increased myocardial oxygen consumption in the setting of inadequate coronary flow reserve.

Presentation and Natural History

Valvular AS is characterized by a long latent period of gradually increasing LV pressure overload without symptoms. In most cases a murmur has been "known about" for many years.

Although 5% of patients with hemodynamically severe AS are truly asymptomatic, the classic symptom triad of aortic stenosis is angina, syncope, and dyspnea. When symptoms occur, the degree of valvular obstruction is usually severe.

Exertional Angina Angina occurs in 66% of patients with critical AS. There may be multiple causes of the angina, including:

Increased myocardial oxygen demand
Decreased subendocardial perfusion
Significant epicardial CAD
Calcium embolization to the coronary vascular tree
(rare)

Fifty to sixty percent of patients with angina have significant CAD. In contrast, significant stenosis of at least one major coronary artery is present in 33% of AS patients without exertional angina.

Syncope Syncope occurs in 15% to 30% of patients with severe AS. There may be multiple causes of syncope:

- A rise in LV pressure during exertion may stimulate a baroreceptor reflex resulting in peripheral vasodilatation and cerebral hypoperfusion.
- Less commonly, syncope is caused by transient arrhythmia or AV block as a result of calcium encroachment into the conduction system.

Dyspnea Fatigue and exertional dyspnea are indicators of LV systolic dysfunction. These symptoms result from a decrease in CO and a progressive increase in LVEDP and PCWP.

Physical Examination

Arterial Pulsations Decreased carotid pulse amplitude with delayed pulse upstroke (pulsus parvus et tardus) are classic findings.

- These findings may not be seen in the elderly or those with chronic HTN, due to the decreased elasticity and compliance of the vascular tree.

Heart Examination
- The cardiac apical impulse is sustained. Late in the disease it is inferolaterally displaced.
- A double apical impulse is often palpable. The first

component is secondary to ventricular distention
during atrial contraction (palpable S_4) and the second
impulse is due to sustained ventricular systolic
contraction.

• A systolic thrill is often palpable in the right and left
second intercostal spaces.

Auscultation

First heart sound. S_1 is usually normal in isolated AS.

• An *ejection sound* may be audible in cases of
congenital AS, due to the halting upward
movement of a pliable but stenotic valve. This
sound occurs 0.06 seconds after S_1 and disappears
as the severity of stenosis increases. An ejection
sound is rarely heard in degenerative AS.

Second heart sound. S_2 may be single due to an
inaudible A2 as a result of severe valve calcification
and immobility. Prolongation of LV systole may delay
aortic valve closure, resulting in either a single S_2 due
to synchronous closure of the aortic and pulmonic
valves or (in the absence of LBBB) paradoxical
splitting of S_2 when aortic valve closure follows
pulmonic valve (PV) closure.

Third heart sound. Audible S_3 usually implies LV
systolic dysfunction.

Fourth heart sound. S_4 is usually prominent.

Systolic murmur. A harsh systolic crescendo-
decrescendo murmur heard best at the second right
intercostal space and along the left sternal border is
characteristic of AS. This murmur classically radiates
to the carotid arteries and is not transmitted to the
axilla. As the degree of AS becomes more severe,
duration of the murmur increases and it peaks later
in systole.

• In very severe cases murmur intensity can be
markedly diminished.

• The intensity of the murmur can fluctuate from
beat to beat with variation in diastolic filling time.
This variability is prominent during AF and with
VPCs. Murmur intensity increases after a prolonged
diastolic interval.

• The murmur of AS may be confused with that of

HCM. Dynamic auscultation can allow differentiation. The murmur of valvular AS diminishes in intensity during the Valsalva strain, while that of HCM intensifies.

Diastolic murmur. A diastolic decrescendo murmur may be heard in patients with concomitant AR.

Holosystolic apical murmur. A holosystolic apical murmur of MR is commonly present.

Diagnostic Evaluation

Electrocardiography (ECG) A normal ECG should lead to a reassessment of the diagnosis of hemodynamically severe AS. The vast majority of patients with severe AS (up to 98.9%) have associated ECG changes. The most common ECG manifestations include:

LVH
LA abnormality
Nonspecific ST segment and T wave changes
Conduction defects (LBBB, LAFB, LPHB, AV block)

Chest X-Ray
- In early compensated AS, the cardiac silhouette is usually normal in size despite concentric LVH. Subtle rounding of the inferior left heart border is usually present.
- Cardiac enlargement is present in late (decompensated) disease as LV dilatation occurs. LV enlargement often is accompanied by LA enlargement and evidence of pulmonary vascular congestion.
- Aortic valve calcification is almost always found on fluoroscopic examination of adult patients with severe AS. The absence of valve calcification in a patient over 35 years old makes the diagnosis of severe AS very unlikely.
- Post-stenotic dilatation of the ascending aorta is commonly present on the lateral projection.

Echocardiography Echocardiography is the most important test to evaluate suspected AS.

Two-Dimensional (2D) echocardiography 2D imaging shows thickened and calcified valve leaflets with diminished (restricted) mobility. The number of valve cusps can be accurately assessed.

- Secondary signs include LVH and LA enlargement.
- Planimetry of a short-axis view of the aortic valve by TEE is an accurate means to measure valve surface area when TTE is inadequate.

Doppler echocardiography Doppler allows localization of the site of stenosis and measurement of the peak and mean gradients across the valve. The mean aortic valve gradient determined by Doppler correlates well with the mean gradient found at invasive catheterization.

- The severity of AS may be underestimated by Doppler when CO is reduced, a large angle of incidence (greater than 20°) exists between the ultrasound beam and the stenotic jet, and if all available windows are not interrogated.
- In the presence of relatively normal LV function, a peak Doppler velocity in excess of 4.5 m/sec implies severe AS and a peak velocity of less than 2.5 m/sec correlates with mild AS. A mean gradient in excess of 50 mm Hg implies severe AS.

Aortic valve orifice area may be more directly determined by application of the continuity equation (conservation of mass and energy theory).

In cases where CO is severely depressed, the peak velocity and mean gradient may be low in spite of a critically narrowed valve. In this situation, administration of dobutamine may increase contractility and valve gradient, thus unmasking the true hemodynamic severity.

Cardiac Catheterization and Coronary Angiography
Cardiac catheterization remains the "gold standard" in some institutions for measuring the pressure gradient and flow across the aortic valve, thereby allowing calculation of the valve orifice area by the Gorlin hydraulic formula (see below). Well-performed and complete echocardiography can accurately determine the severity of AS and obviate the need to determine valve area invasively.

- Cardiac catheterization is required for hemodynamic evaluation of AS when clinical suspicion for significant AS is high and confirmation is not provided by echocardiography.

- Coronary arteriography should be performed in patients with critical AS who present with angina, young patients with significant risk factors for CAD, and in males over 35 years old and females over 40 years old to evaluate for the possibility of coexisting CAD.

Gorlin hydraulic formula for calculation of aortic valve area The catheterization-derived peak-to-peak pressure gradient between the LV and the aorta estimates the severity of AS if the CO is normal. Critical AS is present once the peak-to-peak pressure gradient exceeds 50 mm Hg.

The Gorlin formula is considered the gold standard method for estimating the hemodynamic severity of valvular stenosis (Fig 6-1).

Clinically, significant AS occurs when the valve orifice area is reduced to ≤30% of normal. Since the normal aortic surface area in the adult is 3.0 to 4.0 cm^2, a decrease

$$\text{Valve orifice area} = \frac{\text{CO}/(\text{SEP or DFP})(\text{HR})}{44.3\text{C}\sqrt{\text{Mean pressure gradient}}}$$

Where:

CO = Cardiac output in mL/min.
SEP = Systolic ejection period in sec/beat (used to calculate aortic valve area).
DFP = Diastolic filling period in sec/beat (used to calculate mitral valve area).
HR = Heart rate in beat/min.
C   = Constant.
C   = 1 for the aortic, tricuspid, and pulmonic valves.
C   = 0.85 for the mitral valve.

Normal aortic valve orifice area is 3.0 to 4.0 cm^2.

- Critical AS is present when valve area ≤0.7 cm^2 or ≤0.5 cm^2/m^2 body surface area.

Normal mitral valve orifice area is 4.0 to 6.0 cm^2.

- Critical MS is present when valve area ≤1.0 cm^2.

Figure 6-1. Calculation of stenotic valve orifice area (Gorlin hydraulic formula).

in the valve area by 70% to approximately $1.0\,cm^2$ results in hemodynamically significant AS. Valve orifice area less than $0.7\,cm^2$ or less than $0.5\,cm^2/m^2$ of body surface area represents severe or critical AS.

Natural History

AS is characterized by an asymptomatic period of many years. The rate at which stenosis progresses is variable and difficult to predict. Progression is most rapid in the elderly with senile calcification and slower in younger patients with rheumatic valve disease. In some patients there is no or only mild progression over many years.

When symptoms occur, the risk for sudden cardiac death is significantly increased and the prognosis is poor for patients who are not surgically treated. The average survival after symptom onset is 2 to 3 years once angina or syncope occur and 1 to 1.5 years after the onset of CHF.

Sudden death as the first manifestation of AS is very unusual. Therefore, valve replacement should be offered only to symptomatic patients.

Treatment

Surgery

Symptomatic patients   All symptomatic patients with critical AS are potential surgical candidates. Since AS represents mechanical obstruction to LV outflow, the treatment of choice is replacement of the stenotic valve. Significant CAD should be bypassed at the time of valve surgery.

- For the patient younger than age 80, the operative risk ranges from less than 5% among those with preserved LV function to 15% or greater in the patient with severe LV dysfunction. Operative risk is significantly increased in patients >80 years old and in the presence of cachexia, NYHA Class IV symptoms, previous MI, or need for emergency surgery.
- Among patients with LV dysfunction, relief of obstruction usually results in considerable improvement in or normalization of systolic function.

Regression of LVH and significant improvement in diastolic function are additional long-term benefits.

Asymptomatic patients   Controversy exists surrounding surgical therapy for asymptomatic patients with severe AS.

- Surgery is probably beneficial for the rare asymptomatic patient with severe AS and evidence of declining LV function.
- For patients with severe AS and normal LV function, advocates of surgery argue that given a 1% to 5% incidence of sudden death, surgery should be performed prophylactically to avoid this risk.
- Other studies acknowledge the risk of sudden death, but note that it rarely occurs without symptoms and that the risk of surgery is higher than the risk of sudden death in asymptomatic patients.

Our recommendation is that the truly asymptomatic patient should be followed carefully with history and physical examination every 3 to 6 months and echocardiography every 6 to 12 months.

Medical Therapy   Avoidance of vigorous physical activity is essential for patients with critical AS, whether or not they have symptoms.

Antibiotics. Prophylaxis for IE is recommended in the appropriate clinical settings (see Chapter 7).

Diuretics. Diuretics may be helpful if fluid retention occurs, but these agents must be used with caution and in low doses as hypovolemia may result in hypotension and decreased CO. For similar reasons, nitrates and other vasodilators should be used with caution.

Percutaneous Balloon Aortic Valvuloplasty (BAV)
BAV has proven to be an effective technique to acutely reduce LV outflow obstruction in the patient with critical AS who is at too high a risk to undergo valve replacement surgery.

Although short-term hemodynamic benefits along with significant relief of symptoms have been reported, a nearly 50% rate of restenosis occurs within 1 year in adult patients undergoing this procedure. Due to this poor long-term success rate, BAV is used only in very limited situations:

- For cardiogenic shock due to severe LV outflow obstruction.
- As a bridge to emergent noncardiac surgery in symptomatic patients.
- To relieve symptoms in patients with critical AS and severe concomitant medical problems that preclude aortic valve replacement.
- For symptomatic patients who refuse surgery.

AORTIC REGURGITATION (AR)

AR may be acute or chronic. Clinical features relate to the severity of regurgitation as well as to the degree of hemodynamic compensation.

Etiology

Acute AR
Causes include aortic dissection, IE, or traumatic avulsion of an aortic valve cusp.

Chronic AR
The most common causes are an incompetent bicuspid aortic valve, rheumatic disease, idiopathic degeneration of the aortic valve, and aortic root dilatation.

Pathophysiology

Acute AR
The effect of a sudden, severe increase in diastolic volume on a previously normal LV is a significant increase in LVEDP. Increased LA and PCWP often result in acute pulmonary edema.

Chronic AR
A gradual increase of LV end-diastolic volume (LVEDV) results in LV dilatation and increased ventricular compliance so that the increased LVEDV does not result in increased LVEDP. LA pressure and PCWP remain normal. The LV hypertrophies to normalize systolic wall stress (Law of Laplace). Widened pulse pressure is characteristic of chronic severe AR.

In late stages of the disease, the LV can no longer accommodate the increased LVEDV, and as LV volume increases, so does LVEDP. This increase in LVEDP may be associated with decreased stroke volume and lead to signs and symptoms of LV failure.

Myocardial ischemia may occur as a result of decreased coronary blood flow due to a decrease in the diastolic aortic-myocardial perfusion gradient, compression of the LV subendocardium, and the greatly increased LV mass invariably associated with chronic AR.

Diagnosis

History and Symptoms

Acute AR   Patients with acute AR present with symptoms of sudden left heart failure:

Acute dyspnea at rest or with minimal exertion
Orthopnea
Fatigue
Weakness

Chronic AR   Patients with chronic AR are usually asymptomatic for many years.

Due to the great increase in LV stroke volume, an awareness of the heartbeat is often experienced. As AR progresses and LV failure occurs, the chronic AR symptoms develop:

Dyspnea
Orthopnea
Paroxysmal nocturnal dyspnea
Fatigue

Physical Examination

Acute AR

The findings with acute AR reflect sudden and severe LV volume overload:

- Patients may appear acutely ill and manifest signs of LV failure such as pulmonary congestion, tachycardia, and ventricular gallop sounds.
- Signs of increased stroke volume and increased diastolic runoff rarely occur.

Chronic AR   The findings for chronic AR reflect compensated LV volume overload, increased stroke volume, and increased diastolic runoff:

- Widened pulse pressure is present with significant AR. If DBP is greater than 70 mm Hg or the pulse pressure does not exceed 50% of the peak SBP, then severe AR is unlikely.
- Pulse contour is quick in onset with rapid collapse (water hammer or Corrigan's pulse).
- Capillary pulsations are visible as intermittent flushing of the skin at the base of the nail beds as pressure is applied to the nail tip (Quincke's pulse).
- A "pistol shot" sound may be heard over the femoral arteries (Traube's sign) and a biphasic bruit may be heard with mild stethoscope pressure (Duroziez's sign).
- The apical impulse is inferolaterally displaced if LV dilatation is present.

Auscultation

First and second heart sounds. S_1 and S_2 are usually normal. With acute severe AR, S_1 may be soft due to early (premature) closure of the MV.

Third heart sound. S_3 may be present in severe AR and implies significant LV dysfunction.

Diastolic murmur. A high-frequency diastolic decrescendo murmur is characteristic.

- The murmur is best heard at the lower left sternal border as the patient leans forward, holding the breath in forced expiration.
- In the presence of aortic root dilatation, the murmur may be best heard along the right sternal border.
- Murmur intensity is increased by maneuvers such as handgrip, which increases SVR and therefore regurgitant volume.

Systolic ejection murmur. A systolic ejection murmur is often heard along the left sternal border. It is a manifestation of increased stroke volume.

Diastolic murmur. A rumbling, low-pitched diastolic murmur (Austin-Flint murmur) may be heard at the apex. This murmur is believed to be secondary to partial diastolic closure of the anterior mitral leaflet by the AR.

Diagnostic Studies

Chest X-Ray
- With acute severe AR, interstitial pulmonary edema is usually present. Heart size is normal.
- With chronic moderate to severe AR, the LV is generally dilated.
- When AR is secondary to an abnormality of the aortic root, aortic dilatation is often present.

Electrocardiography (ECG)
- In acute AR and mild to moderate chronic AR, the QRS complexes are usually normal and LVH is absent. Sinus tachycardia often accompanies acute severe AR.
- In chronic severe AR, typical ECG findings reflect LVH and dilatation: initially increased QRS amplitude alone (diastolic overload pattern) with later development of secondary ST segment and T wave changes in the lateral leads (strain).

Echocardiography

M-mode echocardiography
Acute AR: premature closure of the MV before end-diastole, high-frequency vibration (fluttering) of the anterior mitral leaflet, and vigorous LV contraction.

Chronic AR: LV dilatation, enhanced (hyperdynamic) cardiac wall motion if LV failure has not occurred, and high-frequency diastolic fluttering of the anterior mitral leaflet and/or the proximal interventricular septum.

Two-dimensional (2D) echocardiography 2D echo-cardiography of the aortic valve and aortic root is less helpful to assess the degree of regurgitation, but is invaluable to assess the causes of the condition.

Specific findings with AR include:

Valve deformity: bicuspid, rheumatic, degenerative
Valvar vegetations
Flail aortic valve cusp

Aortic root dilatation
Aortic dissection flap

Echocardiography can be used to serially follow LV size in patients with chronic moderate to severe AR. A progressive increase in LV dimensions over time and/or an end-systolic dimension in excess of 55 mm correlates with a decline in LV systolic function and is an indication for surgical intervention.

Doppler echocardiography Doppler is the most sensitive noninvasive technique to detect and semi-quantitate the severity of AR.

Radionuclide Studies Radionuclide angiography to assess LV function at rest and/or during exercise may be helpful to detect LV dysfunction before the onset of symptoms.

• A decline in resting LV ejection fraction with serial studies to <50% implies the onset of LV dysfunction.
• Failure to increase ejection fraction ≥5% with exercise also implies impaired LV reserve capacity.

Cardiac Catheterization
Aortography. Aortography can estimate the degree of AR. The extent of LV opacification and its rate of clearance correlates with severity of AR.

Coronary arteriography. Coronary arteriography should be performed in patients older than 40 years and in younger patients if risk factors for CAD or symptoms suggesting CAD are present. In patients with chronic severe AR, 58% of those with angina and 19% without angina have significant CAD at angiography.

Natural History

Acute AR
Acute severe AR is associated with a 1-year mortality in excess of 90% in medically treated patients. Perioperative mortality of 6% or less has been reported if urgent valve replacement is undertaken within 24 hours of the diagnosis.

Chronic AR
Chronic AR is characterized by a relatively long, asymptomatic period of gradually increasing LV volume over-

load. Symptoms usually come to clinical attention after significant LV dysfunction has occurred. When symptoms occur, clinical deterioration is often progressive. Medical or surgical intervention is indicated at this time.

Treatment

Acute Severe AR
Aortic valve replacement (AVR) should be performed as soon as possible.

Medications Medical therapy should be initiated in an attempt to stabilize hemodynamics while awaiting surgical intervention.

Antibiotics. Empiric antibiotic therapy should be initiated if IE is suspected (see Chapter 7). Appropriate culture material should be obtained.

Vasodilators. Vasodilators (IV nitroprusside) to decrease afterload and positive inotropic agents (dobutamine or dopamine) are often required.

Chronic AR
AVR is the treatment of choice in the presence of symptoms or when a decline in LV function is documented with noninvasive testing (Fig 6-2). The operative risk correlates with the degree of LV dysfunction.

Medical therapy should also be employed in the symptomatic patient with severe AR who refuses therapy or who is no longer a surgical candidate due to severe LV dysfunction (severely dilated ventricle with ejection fraction <20–25%) or significant comorbid conditions:

- All patients with AR should receive antibiotic prophylaxis to minimize the risk of developing IE in appropriate clinical situations (see Chapter 7).
- For symptomatic patients awaiting surgery (see Chapter 2), medical therapy with vasodilators, digitalis, and diuretics is indicated.

Because AVR may not restore normal ventricular function, the following general guidelines are suggested.

- *Severe symptomatic AR without severe LV systolic impairment.* All patients in this condition are candidates for AVR.

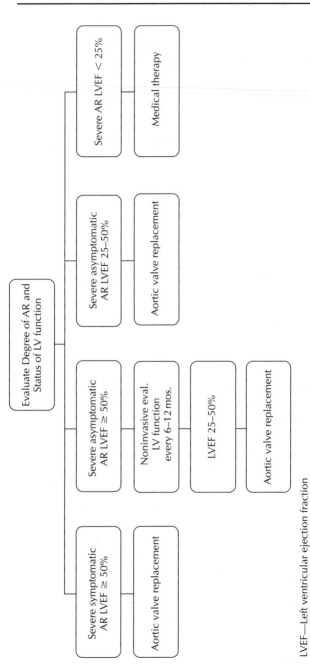

LVEF—Left ventricular ejection fraction

Figure 6-2. Treatment of severe chronic aortic regurgitation.

- *Severe asymptomatic AR with impaired LV function* (resting ejection fraction <50%, end-systolic volume >60 mL/m^2, LV systolic dimension >55 mm, or a decrease in exercise ejection fraction). Patients should be considered for AVR. If surgery is postponed, further deterioration of LV function and symptoms may occur, leading to increased surgical risk.
- *Severe asymptomatic AR and normal LV function.* Patients so classified should be closely followed. Noninvasive evaluation of LV function should be performed every 6 to 12 months and AVR performed at the time of symptom onset or with evidence of LV dysfunction. Recent data suggest that nifedipine reduces or delays the need for AVR in these patients. Similar benefits for other vasodilators are yet to be documented.
- *Moderately severe symptomatic AR.* The degree of AR should be documented by noninvasive testing. Patients should receive medical therapy and undergo further evaluation including cardiac catheterization to evaluate the coronary arteries and for the possibility of angiographically severe AR. Further therapy is guided by the results of the heart catheterization. Valve surgery may be indicated.
- *Moderately severe asymptomatic AR.* Patients should be reevaluated every 6 to 12 months with physical examination and noninvasive testing to monitor for the onset of symptoms and/or LV dysfunction.
- *Mild asymptomatic AR.* Medical therapy has not been shown to alter the clinical course in asymptomatic patients with a mild degree of AR.

MITRAL STENOSIS (MS)

Etiology

MS results in obstruction to LV filling. It must be differentiated from other (rare) conditions that impede left heart filling such as LA tumors, thrombus, and cor triatriatum, and pulmonary vein stenosis.

Rheumatic fever. The most common cause of MS is rheumatic fever, which ultimately leads to retraction, scarring, thickening, calcification, and immobility of the valve leaflets and subvalvular apparatus. Two-thirds of cases of rheumatic MS occur in women.

Other conditions. Rare causes of MS include:

Mitral annulus calcification (elderly)
Malignant carcinoid syndrome
Systemic lupus erythematosus
Rheumatoid arthritis

Congenital Causes

In infants and children, MS may occur as a result of congenital deformity of the mitral valve, obstructing membranes, or abnormalities of the MV apparatus.

Pathophysiology

MS results in obstruction to LV filling with a corresponding increase in LA pressure. With advanced MS, PA pressure rises and CO decreases.

With progressive LV inflow obstruction, LA pressure rises in an attempt to maintain adequate LV filling. At an orifice area of approximately $1\,cm^2$, LA pressure is generally in the range of 20 to 25 mm Hg. At this level of LA pressure, pulmonary interstitial edema and reactive changes in the pulmonary circulation occur. These hemodynamic effects result in increased pulmonary vascular resistance (PVR), elevation of PA pressures, and reduction in pulmonary compliance.

LV contractile function is usually well preserved in patients with pure MS. However, in patients with critical MS, CO may be normal or even subnormal at rest and exhibit an insufficient increase or a decline with any hemodynamic stress.

- Without mechanical relief of MS, further progression leads to more severe and possibly fixed pulmonary HTN with irreversible changes in the architecture of the pulmonary vascular bed ("the second stenosis" of MS).
- Clinical situations that demand increased flow across the MV (fever, pregnancy, severe anemia) or that reduce LV diastolic filling time (tachycardia) will increase LA pressure. Transvalvular pressure gradient

is a function of the square of the flow rate. Therefore, if flow rate doubles, transvalvular pressure gradient will increase fourfold.

- Long-standing elevation of LA pressure as well as rheumatic atrial scarring often results in left atrial dilatation and AF.
- Severe, long-standing MS can result in severe right heart dilatation and dysfunction, peripheral edema, and ascites.

Diagnosis

History
Only 50% to 60% of patients may remember having had an attack of ARF.

Symptoms

Pulmonary Symptoms
Dyspnea. Dyspnea is the most common symptom.
- With moderate MS, dyspnea occurs in settings that require increased CO (fever, anemia, pregnancy, exercise).
- As MS progresses, dyspnea occurs with minimal exertion and eventually at rest.
- Dyspnea often accompanies the onset of AF with rapid ventricular response. Elevated pulmonary pressure is caused by the decreased diastolic filling period as well as loss of effective (synchronous) atrial contraction necessary to propel blood across the stenotic mitral orifice.

Hemoptysis. Hemoptysis is caused by rupture of thin-walled bronchial veins due to an acute rise in pulmonary venous pressure. Hemoptysis may be massive and life-threatening. Other causes of hemoptysis include pulmonary edema and chronic bronchitis.

Hoarseness. Hoarseness due to compression of the left recurrent laryngeal nerve by a dilated LA or PA (Ortner's syndrome) is a rare symptom.

Cardiac Symptoms
Fatigue. Fatigue is secondary to diminished CO.

Palpitation. Palpitation is commonly the result of atrial arrhythmias.

Chest pain. Chest pains occur in 10% to 15% of patients. Possible causes include pulmonary HTN, underlying CAD, or embolism to the coronary vascular bed.

Systemic embolism. Systemic embolic phenomena occur as a result of LA body or appendage thrombus formation due to AF, stagnant LA blood flow, decreased CO, and LA dilatation. Patients with rheumatic MS and AF have an 18-fold greater risk of suffering a systemic embolic event than do patients with a normal MV in sinus rhythm.

Physical Examination

General Signs

- Patients with a low CO have pink patches on the cheeks (mitral facies).
- Signs of systemic venous HTN occur when RV failure is present. These signs include:

  Jugular venous distention (a prominent V wave suggests associated TR)

  Peripheral edema

  Hepatomegaly

  Ascites
- An RV lift is palpable along the left sternal border when significant pulmonary HTN is present.
- Sinus tachycardia or AF (more common) is present in advanced cases.

Auscultation

First heart sound. S_1 is usually accentuated ("loud"). S_1 intensity may be decreased in advanced cases where heavily thickened valve leaflets have severely reduced mobility.

Second heart sound. P_2 is accentuated when moderate pulmonary HTN is present. As pulmonary HTN becomes more severe, S_2 narrows and eventually becomes single.

Fourth heart sound. An RV S_4 is heard along the left sternal border in patients with moderate to severe MS who remain in sinus rhythm.

Opening snap. An opening snap (OS) is a classic finding in moderate to severe MS. The OS is the result of sudden excursion and tensing of the mitral valve leaflets in early to mid-diastole. This sound, which occurs 0.03 to 0.14 second after S_2, is high pitched and best appreciated with the diaphragm of the stethoscope at the apex. The higher the LA pressure, the shorter the A_2–OS interval will be.

Diastolic apical murmur. An apical diastolic rumbling murmur is the classic auscultatory finding associated with MS.

- The murmur is low pitched and therefore best heard with the bell of the stethoscope. The patient should be placed in the left lateral decubitus position. The murmur begins immediately after the OS, often does not persist throughout diastole, and frequently has a late diastolic crescendo component caused by atrial contraction.
- Murmur length, rather than intensity, correlates best with the hemodynamic severity of MS. Murmur intensity decreases if marked valve rigidity exists or CO is significantly diminished.

Diagnostic Studies

ECG

- LA enlargement (if the patient is in sinus rhythm) and AF are common in patients with moderate or severe MS.
- Evidence of RVH is found in association with pulmonary HTN.

Chest X-Ray

LA enlargement results in straightening of the left heart border and a double cardiac density along the right heart border.

Increased pulmonary venous pressure causes redistribution of pulmonary blood flow to the lung apices.

- Pulmonary interstitial edema is common when PCWP exceeds 25 mm Hg. Kerley B lines, short horizontal lines perpendicular to the pleura, are commonly seen when PCWP is elevated.
- Chronic pulmonary HTN is associated with RV

enlargement and prominence of the central pulmonary vasculature.
- Severe, long-standing MS may cause pulmonary parenchymal ossification and Kerley A lines.

Echocardiography

M-mode echocardiography M-mode signs of MS include:

Mitral leaflet thickening
Diminished leaflet excursion
Loss of antiparallel motion of the anterior and
   posterior mitral leaflets in diastole
Diminished E-F slope

Two-dimensional echocardiography In pure MS the LV size and function is preserved. The echocardiographic appearance of the valve alone is not sufficient to determine the severity of MS.

2D signs of MS include:

- LA dilatation.
- Thickening, calcification, and restricted motion (diastolic doming) of the mitral leaflets.
- Involvement of the subvalvular apparatus (thickening, calcification, and retraction of the chords) by the rheumatic process.
- Right heart dilatation (if pulmonary HTN exists).
- The parasternal short axis view can be used to planimeter the mitral orifice area.

Often TEE is required to evaluate the LA for thrombus. Echocardiography should also be used to evaluate for coexisting valve lesions such as AS and TS.

Doppler echocardiography
- **Mitral oriface area.** Doppler echocardiography is used to approximate mitral orifice area. The most commonly used technique is the pressure half-time ($T_{1/2}$) determination. The $T_{1/2}$ is the time required for the initial diastolic pressure gradient across the MV to decay to one-half its initial value.

   Mitral orifice area (in cm^2) is estimated by:

$$MVA \left(in\ cm^2\right) = 220/T_{1/2}$$

Severe, or critical, MS is present when the mitral valve orifice area is less than $1\,cm^2$ (the normal orifice area is 4 to $6\,cm^2$).

• **Flow convergence method.** Isovelocity surface area measurements can also be used to estimate mitral orifice area.

• **Pulmonary artery pressure.** Doppler can be used to estimate PA pressure. Estimates of the PA systolic and diastolic pressures may be made by application of the modified Bernoulli equation to the peak velocity of TR and the end-diastolic velocity of PR, respectively. When a reliable estimate of the central venous pressure (CVP) is available, addition of these Doppler-derived values to the CVP yields reliable estimates of the PA systolic and diastolic pressures.

Cardiac Catheterization Simultaneous right and left heart catheterization allows measurement of PCWP (estimate of LA pressure) and LV diastolic pressure so that the gradient across the MV can be determined. In combination with the measured CO, MV area may be calculated using the Gorlin formula (see Fig 6-1).

Catheterization also allows accurate measurement of the PA systolic and diastolic pressures as well as estimation of the PVR and its response to vasodilators.

Natural History

Symptoms of MS usually first appear in the fourth decade.

• In developed countries, the clinical features of MS manifest approximately 20 years following the acute episode of rheumatic valvulitis.
• In subtropical countries, the disease has a much more rapid progression (<5 years) for reasons that are not completely understood.
• Symptoms may occur earlier if the patient undergoes any stress requiring a large increase in CO (such as pregnancy).
• If MS is untreated, death occurs in the majority of patients within 10 years of symptom onset.
• Fifty percent of patients have AF by age 40. The incidence of thromboembolic complications with MS

and AF is high: as many as 40% of patients sustain an event at some point.

Treatment

Medical Therapy

Antibiotics

Rheumatic fever. Rheumatic fever antibiotic prophylaxis should follow recommended guidelines (see Chapter 8).

Infective endocarditis. Antibiotic prophylaxis for IE is necessary for all patients (see Chapter 7).

Diuretics and Sodium Restriction
Diuretic therapy and dietary sodium restriction are indicated when pulmonary vascular congestion is present.

Treatment of Atrial Fibrillation

Digitalis Digitalis (loading dose of 1.0 mg IV or orally given over 16 to 24 hours, followed by an IV or oral maintenance dose of 0.125–0.25 mg daily) is used to decrease the ventricular response to AF.

Beta-blockers and Calcium Channel Blockers Beta-blockers and CCBs (verapamil, diltiazem) are alternative agents that can be administered in oral or IV form to slow the ventricular response to AF.

Warfarin Long-term warfarin therapy sufficient to prolong the INR to 2.0 to 3.0 is recommended for patients with MS and chronic or paroxysmal AF to decrease the risk of thromboembolic events.

- Patients with prior systemic embolic events should also receive warfarin therapy sufficient to maintain an INR of 2.0 to 3.0.
- If recurrent systemic embolism occurs despite adequate documentation of proper low-dose warfarin therapy, the warfarin dose can be increased to maintain the INR at 3.0 to 4.0.
- If embolization still occurs despite the higher intensity of warfarin therapy, 80 mg per day of ASA or 400 mg per day of dipyridamole can be added.

Cardioversion Cardioversion (electrical or medical) should be considered for new onset AF of less than 48 hours' duration if there are no contraindications. With hemodynamic instability or severe pulmonary congestion, emergency cardioversion is indicated.

In the presence of chronic (>48 hours' duration) AF, anticoagulation (INR 2.0 to 3.0) for 3 weeks prior to cardioversion is indicated to decrease the risk of thromboembolic events.

- The use of TEE to exclude LA appendage and body thrombus may allow immediate cardioversion if thrombus is not detected.

Therapeutic anticoagulation (usually with heparin followed by warfarin) should be administered at the time of cardioversion and for up to 4 weeks after cardioversion because the risk for thromboembolism remains high during this period.

Intervention Therapy

Intervention therapy is indicated for the patient with moderate to severe symptomatic MS despite medical therapy (NYHA class III and IV with mitral valve area $<1.0\,cm^2/m^2$).

Open Mitral Commissurotomy Open mitral commissurotomy, performed with direct vision on cardiopulmonary bypass, is indicated in the symptomatic patient with moderate to severe MS whose valve is flexible and free of significant calcification or regurgitation.

- At surgery, the fused commissures are separated, atrial thrombus is removed, and separation of fused chordae or papillary muscles is performed.
- This procedure is preferable to prosthetic mitral valve replacement (MVR) because of lower perioperative mortality, lower long-term morbidity, and lack of requirement for long-term anticoagulation if sinus rhythm is maintained.

Approximately 50% of patients require repeat surgery (commissurotomy or MVR) within 10 years. After 10 years, the incidence of restenosis increases dramatically, requiring repeat operation.

Percutaneous Balloon Mitral Valvuloplasty (PBMV)
PBMV is an alternative to surgical commissurotomy. This procedure is available to patients with a pliable, relatively noncalcified valve. PBMV offers similar and sustained reductions in transmitral valve gradient, PCWP, and PA pressure. The rate of restenosis at three years is 12%.

PBMV complications and contraindications LA thrombus and significant baseline MR are contraindications to the procedure.

Procedure-related complications include death, stroke, residual ASD (up to 10% of patients), severe MR (up to 5% risk), and cardiac perforation with resultant hemopericardium and cardiac tamponade.

Prosthetic Valve Replacement MVR is indicated in symptomatic, severe MS when the valve is not amenable to open commissurotomy or PBMV.

- MVR is associated with greater perioperative mortality and long-term morbidity compared to other mitral procedures.
- In most cases, MVR requires life-long anticoagulation.

MITRAL REGURGITATION (MR)
Etiology

MR occurs when a defect of the MV apparatus (valve leaflets, annulus, chordae tendineae, papillary muscles, LV myocardium) leads to failure of normal systolic coaptation. MR may be an acute or chronic process.

Valve Leaflet Abnormalities
Valve leaflet abnormalities may result from:

Myxomatous degeneration and prolapse (the most common cause of MR)
IE
Rheumatic valvular disease
Collagen vascular disease
Connective tissue disease (Marfan's syndrome)
HCM

Congenital valve deformities (such as cleft anterior
   leaflet)
Trauma (rare)

Annular Disease

Annular diseases, such as calcification of the annulus or
dilatation due to LV cavity enlargement, can disrupt the
valve apparatus causing incomplete systolic closure.

Chordae Tendineae Rupture

Rupture of chordae tendineae—usually idiopathic or
   due to IE

Papillary Muscle Ischemia

Transient papillary muscle ischemia may lead to intermittent dysfunction with sometimes severe MR. The
posterior-medial papillary muscle is most frequently
involved because of its single blood supply from the
posterior descending coronary artery. Transient ischemia
and rupture of the anterolateral papillary muscle are far
less common because it receives a dual blood supply.

Papillary Muscle Rupture

Rupture of a papillary muscle belly or tip may result from
acute MI, trauma, or IE.

Left Ventricular Wall Dysfunction

LV wall dysfunction—from DCM or MI—results in MR
by altering the geometry (spatial orientation) of the papillary muscles and annular base.

Pathophysiology

MR Characteristics

Acute MR   Acute MR is characterized by:

1. Sudden, severe regurgitation into a normal sized,
   noncompliant LA.
2. LVEDV rises and LV end-systolic volume decreases
   while forward stroke volume decreases markedly.
3. LA pressure and PCWP rise precipitously.

Chronic MR   Chronic MR is characterized by:

1. Gradual LA and LV volume overload.
2. The LV is filled by blood that had regurgitated into

the LA during the previous systole plus the blood volume entering it from the pulmonary veins, resulting in increased LVEDV. The LV and LA dilate to accommodate this additional volume; therefore, chamber compliance increases.

3. Increased LVEDV is initially maintained without a significant increase in LVEDP, LA, or pulmonary venous pressures.

4. As long as ventricular contractility is preserved, LV ejection fraction remains supernormal (>65%) because increased ventricular volume (preload) results in enhanced ventricular contraction, and afterload is decreased as the ventricle ejects into the low pressure LA as well as into the systemic circulation.

5. As MR becomes increasingly severe, the LA pressure rises, the LV dilates further, and ventricular function declines. Ejection fraction decreases to "normal" (55% to 60%) and finally subnormal values. The presence of an abnormal ejection fraction (<55%) in patients with isolated, chronic severe MR usually indicates severe LV dysfunction.

Diagnosis

History and Symptoms

Acute MR   Acute MR is characterized by symptoms associated with sudden elevation of pulmonary pressures such as:

Severe dyspnea
Orthopnea
Paroxysmal nocturnal dyspnea

Chronic MR   Chronic MR is associated with slow progression of symptoms of diminished CO such as fatigue and weakness. Pulmonary symptoms do not occur until the onset of advanced LV dysfunction because the dilated and compliant LA characteristic of chronic MR serves to prevent acute elevations of LA pressure and PCWP.

Physical Examination

Acute MR

General signs The general signs reflect acute elevation of PA pressure.

- LV function generally well preserved.
- Patients often appear acutely ill.
- Tachycardia is present.
- Cardiac apex is hyperdynamic.
- Systolic thrill is often present.

Auscultation
First heart sound. S_1 is normal.
Second heart sound. S_2 may be widely split due to early closure of the aortic valve.
Fourth heart sound. S_4 is common.
Systolic murmur. A harsh systolic murmur is heard at the precordium, axilla, and back. The murmur may be soft or absent because of a small pressure gradient between the LV and LA.

Chronic MR

General signs General signs reflect long-standing volume overload of the LA and LV.

- AF is common as the LA dilates.
- The cardiac apex is hyperdynamic in the early stages, but as the disease progresses and the LV dilates, the apical impulse becomes sustained and inferolaterally displaced.

Auscultation
First heart sound. S_1 is normal but may be soft in advanced cases.
Second heart sound. S_2 is widely split. A_2 occurs early because only a portion of the LV volume is ejected across the aortic valve. P_2 is loud if pulmonary HTN is present.
Third heart sound. S_3 is present in advanced cases.
Fourth heart sound. S_4 is unusual.
Holosystolic murmur. A harsh holosystolic murmur is heard at the apex which radiates to the precordium, axilla, and back.

- Maneuvers that increase PVR (squatting, handgrip) will increase murmur intensity while those decreasing PVR (exercise) will decrease murmur intensity.

Early diastolic murmur. An early diastolic murmur may be heard at the apex if the regurgitant volume is large.

- When MR becomes so severe that the LV is unable to generate a significant LV-LA pressure gradient, murmur intensity and duration will decrease and may even disappear.

Diagnostic Studies

Chest X-Ray

Acute MR   Acute severe MR is associated with normal heart size and evidence of pulmonary vascular congestion.

Chronic MR   Chronic MR is most often accompanied by LA and LV enlargement. Pulmonary congestion is seen with advanced cases.

ECG

Acute MR
- Sinus tachycardia is usually present.
- Evidence of acute MI or ischemia, particularly of the inferior or posterior walls, is present when coronary insufficiency is the cause of acute MR.

Chronic MR
- LA abnormality and LVH are usually present.
- Atrial and ventricular arrhythmias are common.
- Sustained AF is a late finding.

Echocardiography   Echocardiography may identify specific causes of MR such as ruptured papillary muscle, ruptured chordae tendineae, MVP, vegetations, segmental wall motion abnormalities with functional MR (as occurs with ischemic heart disease), or annular dilatation secondary to LV cavity enlargement.

Echocardiography is ideally suited for noninvasive

assessment and follow-up of LV function in a serial fashion.

- **Transesophageal echocardiography.** TEE is superior to TTE when detailed evaluation of the mitral valve and its apparatus is required.
- **Doppler echocardiography.** Doppler echocardiography provides a semi-quantitative estimation of the severity of MR. Doppler parameters used to estimate MR severity include:
  The area of regurgitant color-flow jet in the LA.
  The spectral profile of the systolic phase of the pulmonary venous inflow pattern.
  The regurgitant jet morphology (eccentricity).
  The maximal radius of the proximal flow convergence region.
  The regurgitant jet width measured at its origin (vena contracta).

Acute MR Acute MR is characterized by normal chamber sizes and hyperdynamic LV function.

Chronic MR In chronic compensated MR, the left heart chambers may be mildly dilated with normal to dynamic LV systolic function.
Chronic decompensated MR is characterized by dilated left heart chambers, diminished MV excursion, and depressed LV contractile function.

Cardiac Catheterization Left and right heart catheterization can assess the hemodynamic severity of MR and its effect on LV function. Coronary angiography should also be performed.

Presence of V waves in the pulmonary artery or left atrial tracing The presence of a V wave suggests MR only when it is at least twice the mean LA or PCWP. In chronic MR, V waves are often not prominent because the dilated and compliant LA can accept the regurgitant volume without a significant rise in LA pressure.

Opacification of the left atrium during left ventriculography The degree of MR can be qualitatively estimated by observing the degree of opacification of the LA due to regurgitation through the incompetent mitral valve.

Natural History

The clinical course depends on the cause of the MR and the status of the LV function. (See the section "Therapy.")

- Acute MR with pulmonary edema is associated with a mortality as high as 80%.
- Chronic slowly progressive MR may be associated with an asymptomatic period of as long as 20 years.

Therapy

Figure 6-3 traces the course of therapy for MR.

- **Mild to moderate asymptomatic MR.** Patients should be followed on a regular basis to identify progression of the MR. No specific medical therapy, other than IE prophylaxis, is indicated.
- **Severe asymptomatic MR with normal LV function.** Controversy exists as to the treatment of these patients. Because decline of LV dysfunction is usually irreversible in this situation, it is prudent to closely follow these patients with serial determinations of LV function and recommend valve repair or MVR once LV dysfunction is identified.

1. If LV function is normal, the ejection fraction should be more than 60% to 70% and the LV should not be dilated (end-systolic dimension <40 mm). The presence of a "normal" LV ejection fraction (50% to 60%) and/or LV dilation (ESD > 45 mm) suggests the presence of LV dysfunction.
2. If the LV ejection fraction is ≥60% and the LV is not dilated, the patient should be followed with repeat study in approximately 3 to 6 months. Exercise testing for functional capacity may be very helpful in this situation to uncover LV dysfunction.
3. If evidence of decreased LV function (ESD > 45 mm) is present, surgical intervention is recommended. Once the ejection fraction decreases to ≤55% to 60%, significant impairment of LV function may already be present and surgery should be recommended.

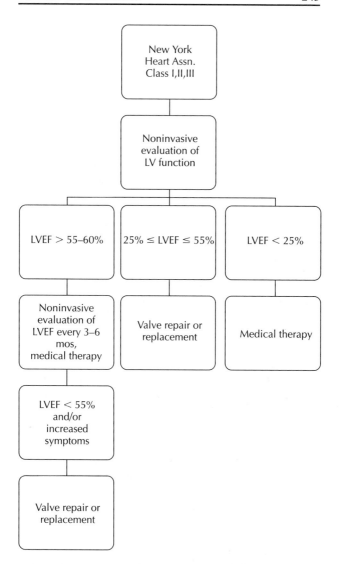

New York
Heart Assn.
Class I,II,III

Noninvasive
evaluation of
LV function

LVEF > 55–60%

25% ≤ LVEF ≤ 55%

LVEF < 25%

Noninvasive
evaluation of
LVEF every 3–6
mos,
medical therapy

Valve repair or
replacement

Medical therapy

LVEF < 55%
and/or
increased
symptoms

Valve repair or
replacement

LVEF—Left ventricular ejection fraction

Figure 6-3. Treatment of severe chronic mitral regurgitation.

Patients with severe MR and "flail" leaflets may represent a special group in whom early surgery offers a mortality advantage over medical therapy.

• **NYHA Class II and III symptomatic MR with preserved LV function** (ejection fraction >55% to 60%). Patients should receive medical therapy to diminish pulmonary congestion and decrease afterload. The etiology of the MR should be determined and surgery should be recommended.

• **Symptomatic MR and/or reduced LV function** (ejection fraction <55%). Patients should receive medical therapy and be considered for early surgery.

Medical Therapy

Antibiotics. Antibiotic prophylaxis against IE is recommended.

Diuretics and sodium restriction. Low-salt diet and diuretics are helpful for volume retention.

ACE-inhibitors. Afterload reducing agents (ACE-inhibitors or hydralazine-nitrates) may improve forward CO and diminish regurgitant volume.

Digoxin. Digoxin is helpful to control the ventricular response to AF.

Anticoagulation drugs. Anticoagulation is indicated to reduce the risk of thromboembolic phenomena in the presence of chronic AF. There is evidence that MR is somewhat protective against the risk of forming LA thrombus in the setting of chronic AF.

Nitroprusside: In the patient with acute severe MR, afterload reduction with IV nitroprusside (0.5–10 µg/kg/min) and/or insertion of an IABP often contributes to clinical stabilization in patients awaiting cardiac catheterization and surgery.

Surgical Therapy

Surgery does not improve LV function and may even lead to a decline in function. Surgery is best timed to occur just before the onset of irreversible LV dysfunction. Often this timing is difficult to determine on the basis of symptoms and physical signs alone, so periodic noninvasive evaluation as outlined above is of paramount importance. Due to the risk of decreased postoperative ventricular performance, surgery is relatively contraindicated when severe LV dysfunction (ejection fraction <20%) is present.

Mitral Valve Repair Mitral valve repair is being performed with increasing frequency (up to 70% of patients may be eligible) and is the first surgical option in many institutions. It is preferable to MVR because annular geometry is relatively well preserved, surgical mortality is lower (3%), and anticoagulation can be avoided.

Repair is an effective option in the patient with a pliable, noncalcified valve often found in association with MVP, ruptured chordae tendineae, annular dilatation, rheumatic disease without calcification, and in some cases of IE.

- **Complications:** Major complications of valve repair surgery include aortic outflow obstruction and persistent MR (greater than mild to moderate). These complications may require an immediate attempt at re-repair or MVR.

Prosthetic mitral valve replacement MVR is indicated when valve repair cannot be performed or when attempted repair fails.

- Current surgical technique spares resection of the subvalvular apparatus, which helps to maintain ventricular geometry and more adequately preserve LV function.
- Overall surgical mortality is 5% to 10%, but may approach 25% in the high-risk patient with LV dysfunction and concomitant severe CAD.

MITRAL VALVE PROLAPSE SYNDROME (MVP)

MVP is characterized by abnormal systolic displacement of the mitral valve leaflet(s) beyond the annular plane into the LA cavity.

Epidemiology and Etiology

MVP is the most common congenital valvular abnormality among adults:

- The prevalence is 3% to 4% (range 2% to 20%) in unselected populations.
- The prevalence in women is twice that in men. An increased familial incidence is noted.
- MVP is present in 20% of patients with ostium secundum ASD.
- MVP is the most common cause of isolated severe MR in North America.

MVP is most often the result of myxomatous degeneration of the MV apparatus (leaflets, annulus, and chordae tendineae).

Primary (idiopathic) MVP occurs as an isolated finding. The posterior leaflet is more frequently affected.

Secondary MVP may result from heritable disorders of collagen structure (Marfan's syndrome, Ehlers-Danlos syndrome types I and II, osteogenesis imperfecta, pseudoxanthoma elasticum), cardiomyopathy, anorexia nervosa, ischemic heart disease, or ARF.

Pathophysiology

MVP is characterized by redundant, thickened valve apparatus and leaflet tissue that billows into the LA during systole.

Patients with MVP are usually stable from a hemodynamic standpoint, but in a minority of cases acute severe MR may occur. The usual causes of acute MR include ruptured chordae tendineae and IE.

Diagnosis

The diagnostic features of MVP are outlined Table 6-1.

History and Symptoms
- The vast majority of patients are asymptomatic.
- A minority experience atypical chest pain, palpitation, anxiety symptoms, or rarely syncope.
- Panic attacks have been associated with MVP.

Physical Examination

General Signs Asthenic body habitus and thoracic cage bony abnormalities, such as pectus excavatum and "straight back" syndrome, are common.

Table 6-1. Diagnostic Features of Mitral Valve Prolapse

Auscultation	Mid- to late systolic click(s) and a late systolic murmur at the cardiac apex.
	Mobile mid- to late systolic apical clicks.
	Late systolic apical murmur in the young patient.
Auscultation plus echocardiography	Apical holosystolic murmur of MR plus echocardiographic criteria (see below).
Two-dimensional/Doppler echocardiography	Marked systolic displacement of mitral leaflets with coaptation point at or on the left atrial side of the annulus.
	Moderate systolic displacement of the mitral leaflets with at least moderate MR, chordal rupture, and annular dilatation.
M-mode echocardiography	Marked (≥3 mm) late systolic buckling posterior to the C–D line.

Adapted from: Perloff JK, Child JS. Clinical and epidemiologic issues in mitral valve prolapse: overview and perspective. Am Heart J 1987;113:1330.

Auscultation Presence of an apical midsystolic click and late systolic murmur has high diagnostic correlation with MVP. On a single auscultatory examination, these sounds are present less than 25% of the time and variability between examinations is frequent.

- The click and murmur occur earlier in systole with maneuvers that decrease ventricular size (sitting, standing, Valsalva maneuver).
- Maneuvers that increase ventricular size (squatting) shift the occurrence of the click and murmur to later in systole.
- An isolated apical midsystolic click has moderately high diagnostic accuracy. The timing of the click can be shifted in systole with maneuvers. Other causes of midsystolic clicks include tricuspid valve clicks, noncardiac effects, and mobile interatrial septal aneurysms.
- A late systolic murmur alone has moderate diagnostic accuracy. This murmur may be due to causes of MR other than MVP such as mitral annular calcification or papillary muscle dysfunction.

With dysfunction of the posterior leaflet, the MR jet is directed anteriorly and the murmur may be best heard in the aortic area. Conversely, with anterior leaflet prolapse, the MR jet is directed posteriorly and the murmur may be best heard over the back.

Diagnostic Studies

ECG   Nonspecific abnormalities include inversion of the T waves in the inferior or lateral leads. ST segment depression during exercise may occur in the absence of CAD.

Chest X-Ray   No CXR findings are unique to or diagnostic of MVP.

Echocardiography   Echocardiography is the most sensitive and specific test to confirm the diagnosis of MVP.

Two-dimensional echocardiography   2D echocardiography exhibits systolic displacement of the mitral leaflet(s) across the plane of the mitral valve annulus.

- This diagnosis should be made from the parasternal long-axis plane. False-positive diagnosis of MVP is common if only the apical four-chamber plane is used for assessment because the MV annulus is saddle-shaped.
- This technique assesses leaflet thickening and redundancy. Patients with thickened (>5 mm) and redundant leaflets are at increased risk for infectious and hemodynamic complications of MVP.
- Associated tricuspid and/or aortic valve prolapse may also be identified.

M-mode echocardiography   M-mode echocardiography reveals mid- to late systolic (most frequently) or pansystolic ("hammocking") posterior displacement of the mitral leaflet(s).

Doppler echocardiography   Doppler echocardiography may reveal the presence of MR in mid- to late systole. Anterior leaflet prolapse is associated with a posteriorly directed jet, while in posterior leaflet prolapse, an anteriorly directed jet is noted.

Cardiac Catheterization Left ventriculography in the right anterior oblique projection displays systolic bulging of the mitral leaflets toward the LA as well as the presence of MR.

Because the diagnosis is usually apparent on physical examination and confirmed with echocardiography, cardiac catheterization is almost never necessary to make the diagnosis of MVP. Catheterization is used to define the coronary anatomy when chest pain suggesting CAD or risk factors for CAD are present and to measure hemodynamics in anticipation of surgery.

Natural History

Atypical chest pain and palpitation due to atrial or ventricular arrhythmias may occur; however, the majority of patients with MVP are asymptomatic. MVP is often an incidental finding on routine physical examination or echocardiography.

Patients at higher risk for complications include:

Males
Age >45 years
Concomitant MR
Thickened and redundant leaflets

MVP Complications
• **Severe MR requiring valve repair or replacement.** The mechanism most often responsible is spontaneous rupture of chordae tendineae.
• **Infective endocarditis.** The risk of IE is increased if more than trivial MR is present. This complication is estimated to occur in 1 out of 2000 patients per year. Endocarditis prophylaxis is recommended in this group of patients. The risk of IE among patients with MVP but without auscultatory or echocardiographic evidence of MR does not differ from that of the general population.
• **Transient ischemic attacks and stroke.** Ischemic neurologic events may occur in patients with MVP. They are probably due to fibrin-platelet emboli from the abnormal valve. Recent data indicate that MVP is an infrequent cause of neurologic events.
• **Atrial and ventricular arrhythmias.** The risk of significant arrhythmia is increased with significant MR. AF is

common with chronic severe MR and atrial dilatation. Patients with MVP, LV dysfunction, MR, and complex ventricular ectopy have an increased risk of sudden cardiac death. Patients with MVP and no or minimal MR have a frequency of arrhythmia similar to that of the general population.

Treatment

Management strategies should be directed toward the anticipated risk level for infectious and hemodynamic complications based upon clinical findings and noninvasive testing.

- The majority of patients require no specific treatment.
- A minority of patients require therapy for disabling symptoms and/or complications.
- IE prophylaxis is indicated for the patient with mild or greater MR.

Management of Chest Pain

Chest pain is often secondary to anxiety and is usually alleviated by reassurance from the physician. If pain persists, administration of a beta-blocker will usually result in symptom relief.

Management of Arrhythmias

Arrhythmias usually have a benign prognosis, except when severe LV dysfunction is present. Treatment in most cases is indicated for the relief of symptoms.

- For patients with preserved LV function and symptomatic ectopy manifesting only as palpitation, beta-blockers are the agents of choice.
- Patients with little or no MR, normal LV function, and complex ventricular ectopy manifesting only as palpitation who do not respond to beta-blockers are best left untreated. These patients are not at increased risk of sudden death and the use of empiric anti-arrhythmic drugs may lead to a worsening of arrhythmia (proarrhythmia).
- Patients with syncope and frequent ectopy should have formal EP evaluation to guide therapy.
- Patients with MR and poor LV function who

experience sustained VT or cardiac arrest should have a formal EP evaluation.

Management of Cerebrovascular Complications

Patients with cerebral infarction and echocardiographic MVP usually have other identifiable mechanisms for stroke other than embolism due to MVP. Antithrombotic therapy is indicated for the patient who has experienced a cerebrovascular event with no other detectable cause for the cerebral ischemia.

TRICUSPID REGURGITATION (TR)

Etiology

TR is most often secondary to tricuspid annular dilatation as a result of increased RV afterload. Less frequently, primary disease of the TV causes TR.

- **Secondary (functional) causes of TR:**
  Pulmonary HTN of any etiology
  RVMI (RV dilatation)
  RV papillary muscle rupture
- **Primary causes of TR:**
  IE (most common primary cause often due to IVDA)
  Thoracic trauma
  Tricuspid valve prolapse (present in one-third of
    patients with MVP)
  Carcinoid syndrome
  Rheumatic valve disease
  Ebstein's anomaly
  Connective tissue disorders
  Papillary muscle dysfunction
  DCM
  Radiation injury
  Cardiac tumors (RA myxoma)
  Iatrogenic injury
  Idiopathic TR

Pathophysiology

The presence and degree of pulmonary HTN is the major determinant of the hemodynamic consequences of TR.

- When pulmonary pressures are normal, the compliant RA and RV are able to accommodate the volume overload associated with TR, and the degree of regurgitation and systemic vascular congestion is modest.
- Pulmonary HTN intensifies the degree of TR, resulting in elevated systemic venous pressure and congestion. In this setting, RVH and decreased ventricular compliance further contribute to the elevation of venous pressure.
- With chronic severe TR, RV volume overload, dilatation, and ultimately failure occur.

Diagnosis

History and Symptoms

Trivial TR is common on routine echocardiography. In the absence of pulmonary HTN, TR is usually well tolerated.

- When TR is secondary to LV failure, dyspnea and orthopnea are common complaints.
- The symptoms of pulmonary congestion may resolve when RV failure ensues because of the inability of the RV to maintain adequate CO in the presence of elevated pulmonary pressures.
- With severe TR and right heart failure, symptoms of decreased CO (weakness, fatigue, malaise, anorexia) occur.

Physical Examination

General Signs

- Cachexia is common when TR is severe and long-standing.
- Jaundice may accompany significant hepatic congestion.
- AF occurs in the presence of RA dilation due to RV failure and/or pulmonary HTN.
- With mild TR, the systolic X-descent is attenuated.
- With moderate to severe TR, jugular venous distention occurs and a prominent systolic pulse wave (V wave) replaces the normal systolic X-descent. The RA Y-descent becomes prominent due to rapid early RV diastolic filling.

- Systolic pulsation of the liver, peripheral edema, and ascites result from elevation of systemic venous pressure.

Auscultation

First heart sound. S_1 is normal and generally unaffected in TR.

Second heart sound. P_2 is accentuated in the presence of pulmonary HTN.

Third heart sound. RV S_3 is audible at the left sternal border in the presence of RV failure.

Fourth heart sound. A right-sided S_4 may be heard with acute onset of TR.

Holosystolic murmur. A blowing holosystolic murmur is audible along the left sternal border at the 4th to 5th intercostal space. The murmur is seldom greater than grade III intensity. Murmur intensity can be increased with inspiration (Carvallo's sign) when right heart venous return is augmented and diminished with expiration.

Diagnostic Studies

ECG   ECG findings are nonspecific and reflect the primary cardiac process responsible for the TR.

- Up to 90% of patients with severe rheumatic TR are in AF.
- ECG evidence of RVH is common when TR is secondary to severe pulmonary HTN.
- Incomplete RBBB is present in 50% of patients with primary TR.
- Ebstein's anomaly is associated with giant P waves, prolonged PR interval, RBBB, and ventricular pre-excitation.

Chest X-Ray

- The RA is prominent in moderate to severe TR.
- RV dilatation is often seen when TR is secondary to pulmonary HTN.

Echocardiography

Two-dimensional echocardiography   2D echocardiography allows:

Accurate measurement of right heart chamber sizes
Determination of RV wall thickness
Overall assessment of RV systolic performance
Inspection of the tricuspid valve apparatus
Assessment of the degree of tricuspid annular dilatation

- Secondary signs of pulmonary HTN—such as RV
  dilatation, thickening of the RV free wall, paradoxical
  interventricular septal motion, and septal flattening—
  may be present.
- Elevated RA pressure is suggested by persistent
  bowing of the interatrial septum to the left and by
  "plethora" of the IVC with no or minimal change in
  its size with inspiration.

TR may be detected by rapid agitated-saline contrast
injection into an arm vein. Severe TR is present if contrast (reflectile microbubbles) is observed to reflux into
the IVC or hepatic veins with systole.

Doppler echocardiography   Doppler echocardiography is used to semiquantitatively estimate TR severity by
delineating the extent of regurgitation into the RA and
hepatic veins.

- PA systolic pressure can be estimated from addition
  of the pressure obtained from the peak velocity of
  the TR by application of the Bernoulli principle to
  the estimated CVP.

Cardiac Catheterization   Cardiac catheterization is
rarely required to diagnose TR. The hemodynamic features of TR are often identified when cardiac catheterization is performed to investigate a coexisting cardiac
abnormality.

Hemodynamics   RA   pressure   is   elevated   and
increases with inspiration in contrast to the normal inspiratory decrease of RA pressure.

- RV and RA diastolic pressures are elevated.
- The normal X-descent is replaced by a systolic
  regurgitant V wave in the presence of moderate to
  severe TR.
- The Y-descent is prominent in moderate to severe
  TR.

PA pressure is elevated in most cases of severe TR. PA systolic pressure less than 40 mm Hg favors that primary TR is present, whereas a pressure greater than 60 mm Hg suggests a secondary etiology.

Right ventriculography   Contrast opacification of the RV is of limited diagnostic utility to document the degree of TR. Artifactual TR may be caused by the angiographic catheter itself.

Natural History

The clinical course of TR usually depends on the nature of the underlying disease.

- In the absence of pulmonary HTN and with normal RV systolic pressure, TR does not usually lead to clinically significant sequelae.
- With the development of systemic venous congestion and symptoms of diminished CO, investigation of the etiology of TR and its treatment is indicated.

Treatment

Treatment strategies depend on the etiology of TR, presence or absence of pulmonary HTN, and symptoms.

Mild to moderate primary or secondary TR in the presence of normal PA pressure. These patients require no specific treatment. In the presence of peripheral edema, low-dose diuretic therapy may be indicated.

Secondary TR due to elevated PA pressure caused by left heart failure. This condition often responds to therapy directed at the cause of the left heart failure (see Chapter 2).

Severe, symptomatic TR associated with pulmonary HTN.
- Moderate to severe, symptomatic secondary TR associated with pulmonary HTN that does not respond to medical therapy will often respond to TV annuloplasty (decreases annular circumference and regurgitant orifice area).
- Prosthetic TV replacement is indicated for patients with diseased or severely deformed valves who are

not candidates for annuloplasty. The low-flow characteristics of the right heart favor implantation of a bioprosthetic valve over a mechanical prosthesis.

Primary TR due to IE in the intravenous drug user.

- Antibiotics are the first line of therapy (see Chapter 7).
- Surgical excision of the valve (valvectomy) is indicated if antibiotic therapy is unsuccessful. Valvectomy is often hemodynamically well tolerated for a long period of time if RV systolic pressure is normal or only mildly elevated.
- Diuretic therapy is indicated if systemic venous congestion is present.
- Prosthetic valve replacement is indicated when medical therapy of right heart failure (diuretics plus digitalis) is unsuccessful.

TRICUSPID STENOSIS (TS)

Etiology

The predominant cause of TS is rheumatic heart disease.

- Rheumatic TS is almost always associated with rheumatic involvement of the MV. At autopsy, approximately 15% of patients with rheumatic MS have evidence of TS, but clinically important TS occurs in less than 5% of cases.
- Carcinoid syndrome can also cause TS, but more frequently causes TR.
- Congenital tricuspid atresia is another potential cause of TS.

Other forms of RV inflow obstruction such as atrial tumor, thrombus, large TV vegetation(s), pericardial constriction, and extra-cardiac mass lesions may mimic TS.

Pathophysiology

Obstruction to RV inflow results in elevation of RA pressure and a diastolic pressure gradient between the RA and RV. A mean pressure gradient ≥5 mm Hg is present with hemodynamically significant TS, and usually results in systemic venous congestion. Obstruction to RV filling eventually leads to decreased CO.

Diagnosis

TS should be suspected in the setting of MS and prominent jugular venous A waves, peripheral edema, absence of pulmonary HTN, and clear lung fields.

History and Symptoms

1. Early in the course of TS, symptoms of associated MS predominate:
   Exertional dyspnea
   Orthopnea
   Paroxysmal nocturnal dyspnea
   Hemoptysis
2. As severity of TS increases, RV output decreases resulting in a decreased left heart filling pressures and CO. These hemodynamic alterations lead to a diminution of the pulmonary congestive symptoms that accompany MS.
   - Absence of pulmonary congestive symptoms in a patient with rheumatic MS should suggest coexistent significant TS.
3. Common presenting complaints with severe TS are:
   Fatigue
   Edema
   Abdominal fullness

Physical Examination

General Signs

- Jugular venous distention is common. A prominent presystolic venous A wave indicates obstruction to RV filling during RA systole; a slow and diminished venous Y-descent is characteristic of delayed early diastolic RV filling.
- Ascites, peripheral edema, and anasarca reflect systemic venous HTN.
- Lung fields usually are clear.
- An RV lift is absent despite signs of systemic venous HTN.

Auscultation   The auscultatory features of MS usually obscure the more subtle findings of TS.

Opening snap. An OS may be audible at the lower left sternal border.

Diastolic murmur. The diastolic rumble of TS is best heard at the left lower sternal border.

- It is often higher pitched, softer, and of shorter duration compared to the murmur of MS.
- The murmur can be augmented by inspiration and reduced during expiration or Valsalva strain.

Diagnostic Studies

ECG

- Two-thirds of patients are in sinus rhythm; the remainder are in AF.
- Evidence of biatrial enlargement is common. If the sinus rhythm is present, TS is suggested by the presence of RA enlargement out of proportion to the degree of RVH.

Chest X-Ray

- RA enlargement, characterized by prominence of the right heart border, is universally present.
- Pulmonary congestion is often absent; however, LA enlargement is often prominent.

Echocardiography

Two-dimensional echocardiography   Two-dimensional study reveals:

Calcified and thickened tricuspid leaflets.
Reduced leaflet motion with diastolic doming.
Reduction of the valve orifice area. RA dilatation and congested systemic veins are present.
Findings of MS (see above) are common.

Doppler echocardiography   Doppler examination displays an increased diastolic transvalvular filling velocity and prolonged slope (increased pressure half-time) of diastolic filling.

Cardiac Catheterization

- RA pressure is elevated and the A wave approaches 10 to 15 mm Hg.

- The transtricuspid valve gradient is elevated. A mean diastolic pressure gradient $\geq 5\,mm\,Hg$ is present in moderate to severe TS, although a mean gradient $>2\,mm\,Hg$ is sufficient to establish the diagnosis.
- TV area is calculated in a manner similar to that for other valves. An orifice area $\leq 1.5\,cm^2$ indicates severe TS.

Treatment

Medical Therapy

In most cases, sodium restriction and diuretics are used to treat systemic venous HTN. This therapy may significantly diminish hepatic congestion and improve symptomatic status and biochemical markers of hepatic dysfunction.

Surgical Therapy

Surgery is indicated for severe TS and for failure of medical therapy.

- Because TS almost always occurs in conjunction with MS, TV surgery is performed at the time of mitral valve surgery.
- Open tricuspid commissurotomy may be performed if the valve is not heavily calcified and the leaflets are pliable. Worsening of TR is a potential complication.
- Prosthetic valve replacement is indicated if commissurotomy is not technically feasible or does not restore adequate valve function. A bioprosthesis is preferred over a mechanical valve because the low-pressure–low-flow characteristics of the right heart increase the risk of valve thrombosis.
- Percutaneous balloon valvuloplasty may be an option in selected patients.

PULMONIC REGURGITATION (PR)

Etiology

PR is almost always secondary to pulmonic ring dilatation caused by pulmonary HTN or dilatation of PA.

Primary valve defects are rare causes of PR:

Congenital leaflet abnormality
IE
Iatrogenic injury produced by a flow-directed PA
    catheter
Injury produced at the time of repair of congenital
    cardiac lesions
Chest trauma
Carcinoid syndrome

Pathophysiology

- In the absence of pulmonary HTN, PR is rarely of
  hemodynamic consequence.
- In the presence of pulmonary HTN, PR will further
  contribute to RV diastolic volume overload.

Diagnosis

History and Symptoms
Isolated PR is usually asymptomatic, so the symptoms of
PR are related to the primary cardiac disorder.

Physical Examination

Palpation   In the setting of pulmonary HTN, a hyperdynamic RV impulse is palpable along the lower left
sternal border.

- Palpable systolic pulsations at the second left
  intercostal space are the result of an enlarged PA.
- A tap indicative of PV closure may be felt at the
  second left intercostal space.

Auscultation
Second heart sound. P_2 is accentuated when pulmonary
    HTN is present.
Pulmonic ejection sound. A pulmonic ejection sound,
    caused by sudden expansion of the PA by an
    increased RV stroke volume, is commonly heard at
    the second left intercostal space.
Diastolic murmur. The character of the diastolic
    murmur of PR is directly related to the PA pressure.
- In the presence of pulmonary HTN (PA systolic
    pressure ≥60 mm Hg), the Graham-Steel murmur is
    characteristically heard. The murmur, which

commences immediately following P_2, is high-pitched and blowing and best heard in the second left intercostal space. Murmur intensity increases with inspiration and decreases during the Valsalva maneuver. It may resemble the murmur of AR.

- If the PA systolic pressure is less than 60 mm Hg, then the PR murmur has a brief, crescendo-decrescendo configuration, and is low-pitched.

Diagnostic Studies

ECG

- In the presence of pulmonary HTN, the ECG usually shows evidence of RVH.
- If the PA pressure is normal or minimally elevated but RV diastolic overload is present, findings of incomplete or complete RBBB are seen.

Chest X-Ray CXR findings are nonspecific. When pulmonary HTN is present, findings of RV enlargement and dilatation of the central PAs are noted.

Echocardiography In cases of severe long-standing PR, echocardiography reveals evidence of RV diastolic overload (RV dilatation, paradoxical motion of the interventricular septum).

Visualization of the PV may reveal the etiology of PR in cases of primary valve dysfunction.

Doppler echocardiography Doppler can semiquantitatively assess the degree of PR by detecting the turbulent diastolic regurgitant flow in the RV outflow tract. Color mapping can add to this assessment, but no formal grading system has been devised.

Treatment

Specific therapy is directed at the primary etiologic disorder.

- Diuretic agents and digitalis are indicated in cases of right heart failure.
- IE prophylaxis is recommended in cases of a deformed pulmonic valve.

PULMONIC STENOSIS (PS)

PS may occur at the level of the valve, infundibulum, or peripherally in the proximal PA or its more distal branches.

- Most cases of PS are congenital in origin.
- Rare causes of acquired PS include:
  Carcinoid heart disease
  Rheumatic heart disease
  Extrinsic compression (sinus of Valsalva aneurysm, tumor, abscesses)

A complete discussion of PS may be found in Chapter 9.

PROSTHETIC CARDIAC VALVES

Although replacement of dysfunctional native heart valves with valvular prostheses has been routinely performed for more than 30 years, the ideal prosthesis has yet to be devised. Characteristics would include durability, lack of thrombogenicity, excellent hemodynamic features, and resistance to infection.

Currently available prosthetic valves are either mechanical or bioprosthetic (tissue) devices. Homograft or autograft replacement of the aortic valve are alternative strategies in selected patients. Each prosthetic device has specific advantages and disadvantages that must be considered.

Mechanical Valves

The major types of mechanical prosthetic valves include caged-ball, tilting disc, and bileaflet valves. The mechanical valves have excellent durability, but require chronic anticoagulation to avoid valve thrombosis and thromboembolic complications.

Caged-Ball Valves

Caged-ball valves were the first mechanical prostheses available. These prostheses are composed of a sewing ring attached to a metal cage containing a ball. The Starr-Edwards, the most frequently used prosthesis of this class, has a superior durability record.

- The relatively large size of the valve makes it unsuitable for use in the aortic position of patients with a small aortic root. When used in the mitral position in a patient with a small heart, LV outflow obstruction may occur.
- The incidence of hemolysis (especially if a periprosthetic leak is present) is greater than that of any other type of prosthetic valve.
- The incidence of systemic embolism is 2% to 3% per year despite anticoagulation.
- Caged-ball valves are also associated with greater transvalvular pressure gradients than tilting disc, bileaflet, or bioprosthetic valves of similar size.

Tilting Disc Valves

Tilting disc valves are composed of a disc attached to a strut that tilts open allowing for passage of blood. These valves include the Lillehei-Kaster, Medtronic-Hall, Bjork-Shiley, and Omniscience valves. They are constructed to be of low profile, making them less obstructive and less thrombogenic than caged-ball prostheses.

Bjork-Shiley 60° Convexo-concave Valve   The Bjork-Shiley 60° convexo-concave valve was withdrawn from the market in 1986 due to the risk of outlet strut fracture with distal embolization and sudden, massive regurgitation (fatal in 67% of cases). The risk of fracture is highest among larger size valves (>29 mm) manufactured from 1981 to 1982 (up to 10.5% at 10 years). High-resolution cineradiographic imaging may be used to screen for and detect early signs of strut fracture. Early elective valve removal, prior to possible sudden valve failure, should be considered if characteristic findings are detected.

Bileaflet Valves

Bileaflet valves, such as the St. Jude Medical and Carbomedics prosthetic heart valves, are variants of the tilting disc type. These valves consist of two semicircular leaflets that tilt nearly perpendicular to the annulus when the valve opens. They are currently the most commonly implanted type of mechanical prosthesis.

- Bileaflet valves have superior hemodynamics compared to other mechanical valves and durability is excellent.
- Bileaflet prostheses are less thrombogenic than other mechanical valves.

Bioprosthetic (Tissue) Valves

Currently available bioprosthetic valves include the excised porcine aortic valve tanned in glutaraldehyde (Hancock and Carpentier-Edwards valves) and the pericardial xenograft (Ionescu-Shiley) valve. The Ionescu-Shiley valve is no longer widely used due to its high failure rate.

- Bioprosthetic valves are less thrombogenic than mechanical valves.
- Their primary advantage over mechanical valves is that chronic anticoagulation is not necessary if sinus rhythm is present.

Durability

The main disadvantage of tissue valves is durability. Valve survival averages 7 to 10 years. Degeneration appears in the form of valve stenosis and/or valve leaflet perforation. Valve failure is rarely sudden, and repeat operation can usually be performed on an elective basis.

- Valve durability is good among older patients, making selection of a bioprosthesis an acceptable alternative to a mechanical one.
- The relatively large size of the sewing ring sometimes makes this prosthesis type unsuitable for the patient with a small heart or aortic root.

The incidence of thromboembolic complications is greatest in the first 3 months following implantation until sewing ring and leaflet endothelialization occurs. Full dose anticoagulation should be administered for a 3-month period after implantation, especially if the prosthesis is placed in the mitral position.

Homograft and Autograft Replacement of the Aortic Valve

Homograft Valves

Homograft valves are procured from donors satisfying requirements for organ donation. The homograft valve is obtained under sterile conditions, preserved, and frozen until usage.

The ideal candidate to receive a homograft replacement is a relatively young patient without marked distortion of the aortic root in whom long-term anticoagulation is undesirable. A homograft is frequently used when IE involving the aortic root is present.

Pulmonary Autograft Replacement

Pulmonary autograft replacement of the aortic root for aortic valve disease with the patient's own main PA and valve with coronary artery reimplantation (a cryopreserved pulmonary allograft is implanted into the pulmonary position) has been used in selected children and young adults as an alternative to prosthetic AVR. The procedure is more complex than standard AVR. Intermediate-term results are good. Long-term follow-up is required before this procedure is considered the optimal substitute for AVR in children and young adults.

Choice of a Prosthetic Valve

Because few hemodynamic differences exist between bioprosthetic and mechanical valve prostheses, the choice of a prosthetic valve depends upon

1. Durability.
2. Expected patient longevity.
3. Risk of long-term anticoagulation.

Mechanical Valves

Because of their excellent durability, mechanical valves should be implanted in younger patients without a contraindication to long-term anticoagulation.

The possible exception is the woman of child-bearing age planning pregnancy. A bioprosthetic valve may be favored in this situation because the requirement for chronic warfarin anticoagulation, which is known to be teratogenic, is eliminated. An alternative is to implant a mechanical prosthesis and use subcutaneous heparin in the risk period of warfarin teratogenesis.

Bioprosthetic Valves

Bioprosthetic valves should be used when difficulty with anticoagulation is anticipated, a contraindication to chronic anticoagulation exists, or the patient is not expected to comply with an anticoagulation regimen.

- When a bioprosthetic valve is implanted, possible replacement of the prosthesis within 10 years should be anticipated.
- Recent data indicate that bioprosthetic valve failure is inversely related to patient age at implantation. Bioprosthetic valves tend to have greater longevity in the elderly who are most prone to complications associated with chronic anticoagulation.

Clinical Features

After prosthetic valve implantation, close follow-up is required to assess hemodynamics, proper valve function, and for potential complications. Close monitoring of anticoagulation therapy is required.

Implant Follow-up
Following hospital discharge, clinical follow-up with physical examination and echocardiography is required on a regular basis.

Physical Examination Physical examination should focus on auscultatory features associated with prosthesis type and implantation site. A change in prosthetic valve sounds or a new regurgitant murmur may indicate valve dysfunction and should prompt further investigation.

Echocardiogram The echocardiographic guidelines for follow-up are shown in Table 6-2.

Anticoagulation

Anticoagulation is administered to all patients without a contraindication. Close monitoring and follow-up are required for all patients receiving oral anticoagulants.

Bioprosthetic Valves
For patients with bioprosthetic valves in normal sinus rhythm, anticoagulation with warfarin to an INR of 2.0 to 3.0 is recommended for a period of 3 months until adequate tissue endothelialization has occurred.

Table 6-2. Guidelines for Echocardiographic Follow-up of Prosthetic Heart Valves

Patient Characteristics	Recommended Follow-Up
1. Early postoperative	
Biologic or mechanical valves	Baseline in all patients
2. Long-term follow-up	
Bioprosthetic valves	Every 2 years for the first 6 years and then every year
Mechanical valves	Every 2 years
3. Clinical suspicion of prosthetic valve dysfunction	
Mitral position	Both transthoracic and transesophageal echocardiography
Aortic position	Transthoracic first; if results are suboptimal then proceed to transesophageal echocardiography.

Adapted with permission from: Zabalgoitia M. Echocardiographic assessment of prosthetic heart valves. Curr Prob Cardiol 1992;17:312.

Mechanical Valves

Mechanical prosthetic valves require life-long anticoagulation.

Tilting Disc and Bileaflet Valves   Current recommendations suggest that moderate intensity anticoagulation (INR of 2.5 to 3.5) is as effective as more intensive therapy (INR 3.0 to 4.5) for tilting disc and bileaflet valves with a significantly lower risk of bleeding.

Caged-Ball Valves   Patients with caged-ball valves may require the more intensive anticoagulation regimen.

Complications

When a prosthetic valve is implanted, the expected complications of chronic uncorrected native valve disease are exchanged for those associated with prosthetic devices. Complications include:

1. IE
2. Structural failure
3. Obstruction

4. Thromboembolism
5. Bleeding due to anticoagulant therapy
6. Hemolysis

Infective Endocarditis

Patients with prosthetic valves are at high risk for infection of the valve.

Antibiotic prophylaxis for IE is indicated for any procedure likely to produce significant bacteremia. The microbial spectrum and therapy of prosthetic valve endocarditis is discussed in Chapter 7.

Structural Failure

Mechanical Valves   Structural failure is rare with the clinically available mechanical prosthetic valves.

Bioprosthetic Valves   Structural failure is more common with bioprosthetic valves. Within 10 years after implantation, approximately 30% of tissue valves will have failed and the risk appears to increase exponentially with longer follow-up. In general, bioprosthetic valve structural failure is gradual in onset, but acute, severe failure can occur.

- **Calcification** and subsequent valve leaflet stenosis and/or regurgitation is the major limitation to the use of tissue prostheses.
- **Cuspal tears or perforation** leading to valve regurgitation also account for many cases of bioprosthetic failure.

Obstruction

Obstruction is a serious problem that primarily occurs with mechanical prostheses. Reported mortality ranges from 0% to 44% depending upon hemodynamic status at the time of presentation. Causes of obstruction include:

Thrombosis (usually due to inadequate anticoagulation)
Ingrowth of tissue (pannus)
Large vegetations

Clinical presentation varies from an insidious onset of very mild congestive symptoms to severe hemodynamic instability if the obstruction is large and occurs abruptly.

Diagnosis Echocardiography is the most important diagnostic test to evaluate for suspected prosthetic valve obstruction. TEE is especially valuable in this clinical situation.

Treatment Treatment options for thrombotic obstruction include:

IV thrombolytic therapy
Surgical valve declotting
Surgical removal and replacement of the thrombosed valve

Obstruction due to chronic pannus formation and IE requires surgical removal and replacement of the involved valve. In selected cases, pannus excision is possible.

Thromboembolism
Thromboembolism is a major complication associated with mechanical prostheses and bioprosthetic valves within the first 3 months of implantation.

- Among the mechanical valves, the risk of thromboembolism is highest with caged-ball valves and lowest with bileaflet valves. Systemic embolism is more common with prosthetic valves in the mitral position.
- Other factors increasing the risk of embolization include age older than 70 years, AF, and LV dysfunction.
- Most thromboembolic events are related to inadequate anticoagulation. Despite adequate INR levels, the risk of thromboembolism averages 1% to 2% per year.

Anticoagulation
- **Mechanical valves.** For patients with mechanical valves who suffer systemic embolism despite therapeutic INR levels (see above), options include increasing the warfarin dosage to achieve an INR of 3.5 to 4.5; adding dipyridamole 400 mg per day to warfarin; or adding ASA 100–160 mg per day to warfarin.
- **Bioprosthetic valves.** Systemic embolization in the presence of a tissue valve is treated with long-term war-

farin therapy to maintain an INR of 2.0 to 3.0. Repeated embolization despite increasing the intensity of anticoagulant therapy may require valve replacement with a different type of prosthesis.

Hemorrhage

Hemorrhage is an ever-present risk among patients receiving anticoagulant therapy. The risk is increased among patients older than 65 years, those with a history of stroke or GI bleeding, those receiving high intensity anticoagulation, and those with hepatic insufficiency.

Warfarin. The effects of concomitant medications and diet on warfarin metabolism cannot be ignored. Medications that affect platelet function may also increase the risk of bleeding in warfarin-treated patients. The risk of major bleeding in patients with prosthetic heart valves treated with coumarin derivatives ranges from 0.7 to 6.3 episodes per 100 patient-years.

Treatment   Treatment of hemorrhagic complications of warfarin therapy depends upon the seriousness of the clinical event:

- Minor bleeding can be treated by withholding warfarin. In this situation, the INR gradually returns to normal levels over a 2 to 4 day period.
- More serious bleeding is treated with discontinuation of warfarin and administration of vitamin K_1 (2.5–10 mg subcutaneously for 3 days or repeated doses of 0.5–1.0 mg IV by slow infusion).
- Severe (life-threatening) bleeding is treated by administration of fresh-frozen plasma (2 to 4 units IV).

Hemolysis

Hemolysis occurs with normally functioning mechanical valves and is frequently of little clinical consequence. With prosthetic valve dysfunction and perivalvular leakage, hemolysis may become clinically significant. Signs of hemolysis include:

1. Anemia and reticulocytosis in the presence of no clinically obvious bleeding.
2. An increased serum LDH.
3. Severely decreased serum haptoglobin level.
4. Increased plasma hemoglobin.
5. Urinary hemosiderin.
6. Schistocytes and other red blood cell fragments on the peripheral smear.

Treatment

- Medical management consists of administering oral folic acid and iron, and possibly a blood transfusion.
- If severe symptomatic anemia persists despite medical therapy, valve replacement or repair may be necessary.

Pregnancy and Mechanical Valve Prostheses

A woman with a mechanical valve who becomes pregnant is at particularly high risk for thromboembolic complications.

1. **First trimester.** During the first trimester, subcutaneous heparin anticoagulation (10,000 to 20,000 units every 12 hours) is used to avoid the harmful effects of warfarin on fetal development.
2. **Second trimester.** Warfarin can safely be administered during the second trimester. Warfarin therapy is continued until the 37th week, at which time it is stopped and heparin is again initiated in anticipation of labor.
3. **Labor and delivery.** With the onset of labor, heparin is discontinued and anticoagulation is resumed as soon as possible in the postpartum period. Antibiotic prophylaxis for IE is recommended around the time of delivery.

SUGGESTED READINGS

Bloomfield P, Wheatley DJ, Prescott RJ, Miller HG. Twelve-year comparison of a Bjork-Shiley mechanical heart valve with porcine bioprosthesis. N Engl J Med 1991;324:573–579.

Bonow RO, Lakatos E, Maron BJ, Epstein SE. Serial long-term assessment of the natural history of asymptomatic patients with chronic aortic regurgitation and normal left ventricular systolic function. Circulation 1991;84:1625–1635.

Carabello BA, Crawford FA Jr. Valvular heart disease. N Engl J Med 1997;337:32–41.

Devereux RB, Kramer-Fox R, Kligfield P. Mitral valve prolapse: causes, clinical manifestations, and management. Ann Intern Med 1989;111:305–317.

Devri E, Sareli P, Wisenbaugh T, Cronje SL. Obstruction of mechanical heart valve prostheses: clinical aspects and surgical management. J Am Coll Cardiol 1991;17:646–650.

Dzavik V, Cohen G, Chan KL. Role of transesophageal echocardiography in the diagnosis and management of prosthetic valve thrombosis. J Am Coll Cardiol 1991;18:1829–1833.

Fenoglio JJ, McAllister HA, DeCastro CM, et al. Congenital bicuspid aortic valve after age 20. Am J Cardiol 1977;39:164–169.

Fenster MS, Feldman MD. Mitral regurgitation: an overview. Curr Prob Cardiol 1995;20:193–280.

Hammermeister KE, Sethi GK, Henderson WG, et al. A comparison of outcomes in men 11 years after heart-valve replacement with a mechanical valve or bioprosthesis. N Engl J Med 1993;328:1289–1296.

Hiratzka LF, Kouchoukos NT, Grunkemeier GL, et al. Outlet strut fracture of the Bjork-Shiley 60 convexo-concave valve: current information and recommendations for patient care. J Am Coll Cardiol 1988;11:1130–1137.

Hirsh J. Oral anticoagulant drugs. N Engl J Med 1991;324:1865–1875.

Houck AJ, Freeman DP, Ackerman DM, et al. Surgical pathology of the tricuspid valve: a study of 363 cases spanning 25 years. Mayo Clin Proc 1988;63:851–863.

Kirklin JK, Kirklin JW, Pacifico AD. Homograft replacement of the aortic valve. Cardiol Clin 1985;3:329–341.

Kouchoukos NT, Davila-Roman VG, Spray TL, et al. Replacement of the aortic root with a pulmonary autograft in children and young adults with aortic valve disease. N Engl J Med 1994;330:1–6.

Lombard JT, Selzer A. Valvular aortic stenosis: a clinical and hemodynamic profile of patients. Ann Intern Med 1987;106:292–298.

Markus AR, Choong CY, Sanfilippo AJ, et al. Identification of high-risk and low-risk subgroups of patients with mitral-valve prolapse. N Engl J Med 1989;320:1031–1036.

NHLBI Balloon Valvuloplasty Registry Participants. Percutaneous balloon aortic valvuloplasty: acute and 30-day follow-up results in 674 patients from the NHLBI valvuloplasty registry. Circulation 1991;84:2383–2397.

O'Neill WW, Chandler JG, Gordon RE, et al. Radiographic detection of strut separations in Bjork-Shiley convexo-concave mitral valves. N Engl J Med 1995;333:414–419.

Otto CM, Pearlman AS, Gardner CL. Hemodynamic progression of aortic stenosis in adults assessed by Doppler echocardiography. J Am Coll Cardiol 1989;13:545–550.

Pellikka PA, Tajik AJ, Khandheria BK, et al. Carcinoid heart disease: clinical and echocardiographic spectrum in 74 patients. Circulation 1993;87:1188–1196.

Reyes VP, Raju BS, Wynne J, et al. Percutaneous balloon valvuloplasty compared with open surgical commissurotomy for mitral stenosis. N Engl J Med 1994;331:961–967.

Roberts WC. Morphologic aspects of cardiac valve dysfunction. Am Heart J 1992;123:1610–1631.

Rozich JD, Carabello BA, Usher BW, et al. Mitral valve replacement with and without chordal preservation in patients with chronic mitral regurgitation: mechanisms for differences in postoperative ejection performance. Circulation 1992;86:1718–1726.

Safian RD, Berman AD, Diver DJ, et al. Balloon aortic valvuloplasty in 170 consecutive patients. N Engl J Med 1988;319:125–130.

Scognamiglio R, Rahimtoola SH, Fasoli G, et al. Nifedipine in asymptomatic patients with severe aortic regurgitation and normal left ventricular function. N Engl J Med 1994;331:689–694.

Silber H, Khan SS, Matloff JM, et al. The St. Jude valve: thrombolysis as the first line of therapy for cardiac valve thrombosis. Circulation 1993;87:30–37.

Stein PD, Alpert JS, Copeland J, et al. Antithrombotic therapy in patients with mechanical and biological prosthetic heart valves. Chest 1995;108:371S–379S.

Turpie AGG, Gent M, Laupacis A, et al. A comparison of aspirin with placebo in patients treated with warfarin after heart-valve replacement. N Engl J Med 1993;329:524–529.

Vongpatanasin W, Hillis LD, Lange RA. Prosthetic heart valves. N Engl J Med 1996;335:407–416.

Wilkins GT, Weyman AE, Abascal VM, et al. Percutaneous mitral valvotomy: an analysis of echocardiographic variables related to outcome and mechanism of dilatation. Br Heart J 1988;60:299–308.

Zabalgoitia M. Echocardiographic assessment of prosthetic heart valves. Curr Prob Cardiol 1992;17:267–325.

Infective Endocarditis

Dennis A. Tighe
Edward K. Chung

Infective endocarditis (IE) is an infection of the native heart valve, mural endocardium, endothelium near congenital anatomic defects, or prosthetic heart valve. The microbiology and clinical course of IE has changed markedly over the past 30 years due to advances in medical care. In spite of these advances, a significant mortality is associated with IE. This chapter reviews the clinical spectrum of IE and its current therapy.

PATHOGENESIS

The characteristic lesion of IE, the vegetation, is a platelet and fibrin mass in which infective organisms and inflammatory cells are intermixed.

The risk of endothelial injury is greatest at sites of turbulence in the vascular system:

- High-velocity jet impacting against an endothelial surface.
- Flow from a high- to a low-pressure chamber.
- Flow across a comparatively narrow orifice creating a relatively large pressure gradient.

These hemodynamic factors explain the distribution of infected vegetations in the heart:

- Ventricular surface of the incompetent aortic valve or PV

- Atrial surface of the incompetent MV or TV
- Structure opposite the jet lesions of small VSDs, PDA, AR, or MR

CLINICAL CLASSIFICATION

Endocarditis can be classified based on:

1. The tempo of its clinical presentation.
2. Whether prosthetic material is involved.
3. Susceptibility of the underlying host.

Acute Bacterial Endocarditis (ABE)

ABE is caused by virulent, invasive organisms that commonly infect previously normal cardiac structures. It typically presents in a fulminant fashion. Affected patients often appear critically ill, and evidence of metastatic infection is common.

Subacute Bacterial Endocarditis (SBE)

SBE is caused by organisms of low virulence that infect the following structures:

Structurally abnormal native valves
Prosthetic valves
Congenital cardiac defects
Surgically created conduits

SBE usually evolves in an indolent fashion over a period of weeks to months.

Native Valve Endocarditis (NVE)

NVE is infection of a native heart valve or other cardiac structure, whether or not it was previously normal or damaged by acquired or congenital disease.

Prosthetic Valve Endocarditis (PVE)

PVE is infection of a prosthetic (artificial) heart valve. PVE is subclassified into early and late forms.

IE in Intravenous Drug Abusers (IVDA)

The bacteriologic spectrum and location of vegetations among patients who use injection drugs is different than among patients without this risk factor.

Nosocomial Endocarditis

Hospital-acquired (nosocomial) IE is becoming increasingly common. Iatrogenic endothelial injury caused by surgery, indwelling venous catheters, and more aggressive therapy of seriously ill patients likely contributes to this increased incidence.

Microorganisms Causing IE

The microbiology of IE has changed markedly over the past 30 years. Major factors in this change are:

- Widespread use of antibiotics.
- Increased implantation of prosthetic heart valves and other prosthetic devices.
- Nosocomial bacteremia.
- Decline in the incidence of rheumatic heart disease.
- Aging of the population.
- Increased incidence of IVDA.

Streptococcus Species

Streptococci (excluding enterococci) account for 50% to 70% of all cases of endocarditis involving native valves in non-IVDA patients.

Viridans Streptococci

Viridans streptococci are responsible for more than half of all streptococcal infections. Common species include *S. sanguis*, *S. mitior*, *S. mutans*, *S. salivarius*, and *S. anginosus*. These organisms are normal oral cavity flora, relatively noninvasive, and cause IE by infecting previously deformed cardiac valves.

Most organisms are highly susceptible to penicillin. Nutritionally variant streptococci (*S. defectivus* and *S. adjacens*) are more resistant to penicillin.

Streptococcus bovis

Streptococcus bovis (Group D non-enterococcal streptococcus) is a component of the normal GI flora. *S. bovis* IE presents in a subacute fashion, occurs primarily in the elderly, and is associated with the presence of colonic polyps or malignancy. *S. bovis* is penicillin susceptible.

Streptococcus pneumoniae

Streptococcus pneumoniae IE is now relatively uncommon (1% to 3% of cases of IE). Risk factors for infection include advanced age, alcoholism, and diabetes.

S. pneumoniae has a predilection for the aortic valve and usually presents in an acute, fulminant manner with abscess formation and valvar destruction. Concomitant pneumonia or meningitis is common. Most strains are highly susceptible to penicillin, but resistant strains have been identified.

Enterococci

Enterococci (formerly group D streptococcus) account for 10% of cases of IE. Enterococci are normal flora of the lower GI tract and female genitourinary (GU) tract, and are a common cause of urinary tract infection in older men with prostatic obstruction. GI and GU tract instrumentation and surgery resulting in bacteremia are common sources of infection. *E. faecalis* and *E. faecium* are the most common species causing IE.

All enterococci are resistant to cephalosporins. Almost all are resistant to penicillin used as monotherapy. Combination with an aminoglycoside is required to achieve a bactericidal effect. Vancomycin-resistant strains have been isolated.

Staphylococci

Staphylococcus aureus

Staphylococcus aureus (coagulase positive) is a rapidly invasive and destructive organism which accounts for 25% of cases of IE.

Risk factors for infection include skin and soft tissue infections, indwelling catheters, and IVDA. A mortality rate approaching 40% to 50% is reported.

Almost all isolates are resistant to penicillin G. Nosocomially acquired infection is frequently resistant to methicillin.

Staphylococcus epidermidis

Staphylococcus epidermidis (coagulase negative) is a common skin organism. Endocarditis involving native valves usually follows an indolent course. Risk factors for infection include indwelling vascular catheters, IVDA, and prosthetic heart valves. Community acquired isolates are usually sensitive to methicillin while nosocomial infection is generally methicillin resistant.

Gram-Negative Organisms

Gram negative organisms account for 5% to 10% of endocarditis involving native valves, 20% of PVE, and 10% of isolates among injection drug users.

Gram-Negative Bacilli
Pseudomonas aeruginosa is the most common infecting organism. Other organisms, such as *Serratia* sp., *Klebsiella* sp., *Salmonella* sp., *Neisseria gonorrhoeae*, and *Haemophilus* sp., infrequently cause IE.

Gram-negative rod endocarditis may present in an acute or subacute manner. IE due to enteric organisms, such as *Escherichia coli*, is rare due to poor adherence of these organisms to valve structures.

HACEK Organisms
HACEK organisms (*Haemophilus, Actinobacillus, Cardiobacterium, Eikenella, and Kingella* spp.) are fastidious, slow-growing, Gram-negative organisms.

Other Organisms

Other types of organisms account for up to 10% of cases of IE. The clinical course may be indolent or acute, depending on the particular organism involved.

Fungi
Candida sp. (most common), *Aspergillus* sp., and *Torulopsis* sp. are the usual pathogens. Fungal endocarditis is more common among certain groups:

- Intravenous drug users.
- Immunosuppressed patients.
- Patients who have undergone cardiac surgery (*Aspergillus* sp.).
- Patients undergoing prolonged antibiotic therapy.
- Patients receiving parenteral hyperalimentation.
- Patients with chronic indwelling venous catheters.

Fungal endocarditis usually follows a subacute course, but is associated with large vegetations with a high risk of peripheral embolization. Treatment usually requires surgery, but in some cases medical therapy alone may be curative.

Bartonella *sp.*

Bartonella sp. are fastidious gram-negative organisms.

- *B. quintana*, the etiologic agent of trench fever, has been identified as an important pathogen causing IE among the homeless and alcoholics.
- *B. henselae* and *B. elizabethae* also can cause IE among humans.

Diagnosis requires special culture techniques, serologic studies, or polymerase chain reaction methods.

Rare Organisms

Legionella sp., *Brucella* sp., *Listeria monocytogenes*, *Corynebacterium JK*, *Chlamydia* sp., *Coxiella burnetti*, diphtheroids, and spirochetes rarely cause IE.

Culture-Negative Endocarditis

The incidence of culture-negative endocarditis is reported to be 5% to 10%. The most common cause is prior antibiotic therapy.

Among patients without prior antibiotic therapy, causative organisms include fungi, anaerobes, fastidious organisms (e.g., the HACEK group), nutritionally deficient streptococci, rickettsia species, and the other miscellaneous organisms listed above. Special culture methods are required. Specimens should be held for up to 3 to 4 weeks in order to make the diagnosis.

- Empiric therapy while awaiting culture results and therapy for patients with negative cultures despite special techniques should include penicillin or ampicillin in combination with an aminoglycoside.
- In the presence of continuing toxicity, hemodynamic deterioration, or peripheral embolization, surgical therapy is indicated for cure and diagnosis.

PREDISPOSING FACTORS TO IE

Preexisting Cardiac Disease

Any lesion disrupting normal endocardium or valvular structures can predispose to IE.

• Acquired valvular dysfunction such as senile degeneration and rheumatic heart disease is associated with up to 40% to 50% of cases of IE.
• Congenital cardiac lesions and surgically created shunts account for up to 20% of cases of IE. Specific lesions include:
    Bicuspid aortic valve
    Ostium primum and sinus venosus ASDs
    VSD
    PDA
    Ebstein's anomaly
    Coarctation of the aorta
    Tetralogy of Fallot
Ostium secundum ASD in isolation is not associated with an increased risk of IE.
• MVP with MR leads to a 5 to 8 times increased risk for endocarditis compared to the risk among patients in whom MR is not present.
    The presence of thickened (≥ 5 mm) and/or
        redundant valve leaflets, especially among men
        greater than 45 years old, is associated with high
        risk of IE.
• Obstructive HCM predisposes to aortic valve or MV endocarditis.
    Aortic valve infection usually results from injury to
        the valve caused by a "jet stream" of blood flow
        induced by septal hypertrophy.
    MV infection is secondary to repeated trauma to the
        anterior leaflet as it strikes the hypertrophied
        interventricular septum.

Intravenous Drug Use

Intravenous drugs predispose users to IE via bacteremia and possibly valvular injury induced by injected particulate matter. The skin at the site of needle puncture is the most common source of infection. Contaminated drug paraphernalia is also a source.

Compared to NVE, IE caused by IVDA is associated with more right heart involvement and a different microbiologic spectrum.

- The TV is involved in greater than 50% of cases. Septic pulmonary emboli and pneumonia occur in greater than 70% cases of TV endocarditis.
- The aortic valve is involved in 25% of cases.
- The MV is involved in 20% of cases.
- The PV is involved in 1%.
- Multivalve infection occurs in approximately 6%.

Microbiologic Spectrum
- *Staphylococcus aureus* accounts for 60% to 80% of cases.
- Streptococci cause 20% of cases. The majority of cases occur among patients with preexisting valvular heart disease.
- Gram-negative organisms (usually *Pseudomonas* or *Serratia* sp.) cause 15% to 20% of cases. Approximately 30% of IV drug abusers with gram-negative endocarditis have polymicrobial infection.
- Polymicrobial infection occurs in approximately 5% of patients.
- Fungi (usually *Candida* sp.) cause 5% of cases. Fungal infection rarely involves the TV and usually infects a previously damaged aortic or mitral valve.

Prosthetic Heart Valves

The risk of IE among patients with prosthetic heart valves is up to 0.5%/year. PVE is divided into two categories in relation to the prosthesis implantation:

- "Early PVE" occurs within 60 days of prosthesis implantation.
- "Late PVE" occurs more than 60 days following valve surgery.

Early PVE
Early PVE occurs as a result of perioperative contamination of the valve and is associated with a 40% to

80% mortality rate. The most common infecting organisms are:

Staphylococcus epidermidis, 25% to 30%
S. aureus, 20% to 25%
Gram-negative organisms, 20%
Fungi (especially *Candida* sp.), 10 to 12%
Diphtheroids, 5% to 10%
Enterococci, 5% to 10%
Legionella sp., *Coxiella* sp., and atypical mycobacteria (rare)

Late PVE

Late PVE is caused by transient bacteremia and has a microbiologic spectrum similar to that of NVE. An associated mortality rate of 19% to 50% is reported. The most common infecting organisms are:

Streptococci, 25% to 30%
S. epidermidis, 20%
S. aureus, 10%
Gram-negative bacilli, 10%
Enterococci, 5% to 10%

Other IE Risk Factors

Processes that inhibit the immune system increase the risk of endocarditis:

Diabetes mellitus
Collagen vascular disease
Immunosuppressive drugs
Chronic alcoholism

CLINICAL MANIFESTATIONS

Clinical presentation depends on the infecting organism and whether the course is acute or subacute.

ABE: The predominant signs and symptoms reflect fulminant valve infection with valve destruction, hemodynamic impairment, and possible metastatic infection.

SBE: More indolent presentation dominated by fever, constitutional symptoms, and immunologic phenomena.

Fever

Fever is the dominant clinical feature.

- Fever occurs in 95% of cases at some point during the clinical course.
- Approximately 15% of patients are initially afebrile.
- Fever may be absent in elderly or debilitated patients and in those with CHF, uremia, or subarachnoid hemorrhage.

Constitutional Symptoms

Constitutional symptoms are common:

- Malaise
- Anorexia
- Weight loss

Heart Murmurs

Heart murmurs are a key manifestation, but their presence is variable.

- A new onset murmur of valvar insufficiency in a febrile patient is suggestive of IE.
- A change in intensity of a preexisting murmur may be due to IE, but many other causes are recognized (fever, sepsis, anemia). A change in a preexisting murmur occurs in only 17% of patients with SBE.
- A heart murmur may be initially absent in up to 33% to 60% of cases of left-sided IE, and in the majority of those with TV endocarditis.

Renal Involvement

Up to 50% of patients exhibit proteinuria and/or microscopic hematuria on routine urinalysis. The most common renal lesions are infarction secondary to embolic events and immunologic phenomena such as diffuse membranoproliferative glomerulonephritis and focal glomerulonephritis.

Renal insufficiency may also occur as a complication of antibiotic therapy.

Musculoskeletal Manifestations

Musculoskeletal manifestations are usually immunologic and resolve with antimicrobial therapy.

- Myalgias, arthralgias, and arthritis occur in up to 45% of patients.
- Lower back pain occurs in 33% of patients with IE. Five percent have a lumbar disc infection or spinal abscess.

Splenomegaly

Splenomegaly occurs in up to 40% of cases of SBE and 22% of cases of ABE. Splenic infarction is reported to occur in up to 44% of autopsy cases.

Embolic Phenomena

Peripheral embolization of vegetation material may be the event that brings the patient to clinical attention. Most often, however, emboli are clinically silent.

- Embolization occurs in up to 30% of cases of SBE and 50% of cases of ABE. The middle cerebral artery is the most commonly involved peripheral vessel.
- Septic pulmonary emboli with infarction may present as pneumonia among patients with right-sided endocarditis.
- Fungal endocarditis is associated with large peripheral emboli, often to the lower extremities.
- Large (>10mm diameter), mobile vegetations involving the MV are associated with increased risk of embolization.

Cutaneous Manifestations

Cutaneous manifestations of IE are less commonly encountered today.

Petechiae
Petechiae, the most common cutaneous manifestation, occur in 20% to 40% of cases. Common locations include the conjunctivae, dorsum of the hands and feet, and the oropharynx.

Subungual Splinter Hemorrhages

Nail bed splinter hemorrhages are found in many cases. However, splinter hemorrhages are a nonspecific finding because they are often associated with local trauma and other processes (such as trichinosis).

Osler Nodes

Osler nodes are small, tender, subcutaneous erythematous nodules found on the palms, soles, and pulp spaces of the terminal phalanges of the hands and feet.

Janeway Lesions

Janeway lesions are small, nontender macular lesions that occur on the palms and soles.

Roth Spots

Roth spots are oval retinal lesions which occur near the optic disc. They are characterized by a pale center with surrounding hemorrhage.

- Roth spots occur in ≤5% of cases of IE and strongly support the diagnosis if other clinical manifestations are present.
- Roth spots are not specific for IE. They may also be found in association with hematologic disorders and collagen vascular diseases.

Congestive Heart Failure

CHF suggests hemodynamically significant involvement with destruction of valvular structures and possible extension of infection.

Mycotic Cerebral Aneurysms

Aneurysms of the cerebral circulation occur in up to 25% of patients. Most are asymptomatic, but focal headache may be a presenting complaint.

DIAGNOSIS

A high degree of suspicion must be maintained as many other conditions can present with a similar clinical picture. Diagnosis rests primarily on the isolation and identification of the responsible pathogen.

Other laboratory studies and imaging techniques can

support the diagnosis. Criteria for a diagnosis of IE based on microbiologic, echocardiographic, and clinical findings have been proposed (Table 7-1).

Blood Cultures

Blood cultures are the most important diagnostic test. Because bacteremia is continuous, isolation of the causative organism is achieved from one of the first three sets of blood cultures obtained in 95% to 98% of cases if antibiotics have not been administered in the preceding 2 weeks.

Presumed SBE
Three sets of venous blood cultures should be obtained over a 24-hour period. If the cultures remain negative after 24 to 48 hours or if the patient has received antibiotics during the preceding 2 weeks, additional blood cultures should be obtained and the laboratory should be notified to suspect fastidious organisms.

Presumed ABE
Three to five sets of venous blood cultures should be obtained from separate sites over a 1 to 2 hour period prior to the initiation of empiric antibiotic therapy.

Fungal Endocarditis
Fungal endocarditis is usually associated with negative blood cultures. Because embolic events are common, embolic material should be surgically removed, if possible, and both cultured and histologically examined.

Serologic Studies

Specific assays for organisms such as *Coxiella burnetii*, *Chlamydia psittaci*, *Bartonella* sp., and *Legionella* may be helpful in cases where the blood cultures are negative and infection with one of these organisms is highly suspected.

Nonspecific Laboratory Abnormalities

- Normochromic, normocytic anemia is present in up to 80% of patients.
- Elevated ESR is present in nearly all patients.
- Elevated rheumatoid factor is present in 50% of patients with IE.

Table 7-1. Proposed Diagnostic Criteria for IE

Definite IE

Pathologic criteria

- **Microorganisms.** Demonstrated by culture or histology in a vegetation, *or* in a vegetation that has embolized, *or* in an intracardiac abscess, *or*
- **Pathologic lesions.** Vegetation or intracardiac abscess present, confirmed by histology showing active IE.

Clinical criteria. Using specific definitions listed below:
- 2 major criteria, *or*
- 1 major and 3 minor criteria, *or*
- 5 minor criteria

Possible IE

Findings consistent with IE that fall short of "Definite IE" but not "Rejected."

Rejected

- Firm alternate diagnosis for manifestations of IE, *or*
- Resolution of manifestations of IE with antibiotic therapy for 4 days or less, *or*
- No pathologic evidence of IE at surgery or autopsy after antibiotic therapy for 4 days or less.

Clinical Criteria for Diagnosis of IE

Major criteria

Positive blood culture for IE

Typical microorganism for IE from 2 separate blood cultures:
- Viridans streptococci, *Streptococcus bovis,* HACEK group, *or*
- Community-acquired *Staphylococcus aureus* or enterococci, in the absence of a primary focus, *or*

Persistently positive blood culture, defined as recovery of a microorganism consistent with IE from:
- Blood cultures drawn more than 12 hours apart, *or*
- All of 3 or a majority of 4 or more separate blood cultures, with first and last drawn at least 1 hour apart.

Evidence of endocardial involvement:
- Positive echocardiogram for IE.
  Oscillating intracardiac mass on valve or supporting structure, *or* in the path of regurgitant jets, *or* on implanted material, in the absence of an alternative anatomical explanation, *or*
  Abscess, *or*
  New partial dehiscence of prosthetic valve, *or*
- New valvular regurgitation (increase or change in preexisting murmur not sufficient).

Table 7-1. (continued)

Table 7-1. (continued) Proposed Diagnostic Criteria for IE

Minor criteria

Predisposition
Predisposing heart condition *or*
Intravenous drug use

Fever
≥38.0°C (100.4°F)

Vascular Phenomena
Major arterial emboli
Septic pulmonary infarcts
Mycotic aneurysm
Intracranial hemorrhage
Conjunctival hemorrhages
Janeway lesions

Immunologic Phenomena
Glomerulonephritis
Osler's nodes
Roth spots
Rheumatoid factor

Microbiologic Evidence
Positive blood culture but not meeting major criteria as noted
    previously *or*
Serologic evidence of active infection with organism consistent with IE

Echocardiogram
Consistent with IE but not meeting major criteria as noted previously

Adapted with permission from: Durack DT, Lukes AS, Bright DK, and the Duke Endocarditis Service. New criteria for diagnosis of infective endocarditis: utilization of specific echocardiographic findings. Am J Med 1994;96:200–209.

Echocardiography

Transthoracic Echocardiography (TTE)
TTE is a sensitive technique to identify valvular vegetations that are at least 3 to 5mm in size, structurally damaged valves, and valvular regurgitation.

- TTE is insensitive to diagnose myocardial or aortic root abscesses and infection of prosthetic valves.
- Valvular thickening, calcification, mass lesions, and thrombi may mimic the echocardiographic appearance of infectious vegetations.

A "negative" echocardiographic examination does not exclude a diagnosis of IE. Serial echocardiograms performed over an interval of several days to 1 week may show changes in the size of a vegetation favoring a diagnosis of IE.

Transesophageal Echocardiography (TEE)

Due to its enhanced spatial resolution and image quality, TEE has a sensitivity approaching 100% for vegetations as small as 2 mm.

- TEE can detect complications of endocarditis (fistulous tracts, perforation, abscess formation) in 90% to 95% of cases.
- TEE is superior to TTE for PVE.

TREATMENT OF INFECTIVE ENDOCARDITIS

Antibiotic Therapy

High doses of bactericidal parenteral antibiotics are required because infecting organisms exist in very high density within a vegetation and complete sterilization is required for cure.

The causative organism's sensitivity to antibiotics and its susceptibility—minimal inhibitory concentration (MIC), minimal bactericidal concentration (MBC), and serum bactericidal titer—should be obtained as soon as the organism is isolated. The serum concentration of antimicrobial agent should exceed the MBC. A peak bactericidal titer of at least 1:8 is considered satisfactory.

Antimicrobial therapy is guided by the sensitivity of the infecting organism as well as determination of the serum antibacterial activity (Table 7-2). The duration of antibacterial therapy depends on the infecting organism, the valve involved, host factors, and the organism's bacterial susceptibility.

Empiric Antibiotic Therapy

Patients with Acute Endocarditis or Hemodynamic Instability Among patients with ABE or hemodynamic instability, empiric broad-spectrum antibiotics effective against enterococcus and *S. aureus* (semisynthetic

Table 7-2. Recommended Treatment Regimens for IE

Antibiotic	Dose and Route	Duration
A. Treatment of Staphylococcal Endocarditis without Presence of Prosthetic Material		
1. Methicillin sensitive, no penicillin allergy		
Nafcillin or oxacillin	2 gm IV every 4 hr	4–6 weeks
plus optional		
Gentamycin*	1 mg/kg IV/IM (not to exceed 80 mg) every 8 hr	3–5 days
2. Methicillin sensitive with penicillin allergy		
Cefazolin (or equivalent first-generation cephalosporin)	2 gm IV every 8 hr	4–6 weeks
plus optional		
Gentamycin*	1 mg/kg IV/IM (not to exceed 80 mg) every 8 hr	3–5 days
or		
Vancomycin*	Up to 2 gm/24 hr IV in divided doses every 6–12 hr	4–6 weeks
3. Methicillin resistant		
Vancomycin	Up to 2 gm/24 hr IV in divided doses every 6–12 hr	4–6 weeks
B. Treatment of Staphylococcal Endocarditis in Presence of Prosthetic Material		
1. Methicillin resistant		
Vancomycin*	Up to 2 gm/24 hr IV in divided doses every 6–12 hr	6 weeks
plus		
Gentamycin*	1 mg/kg IV/IM (not to exceed 80 mg) every 8 hr	2 weeks
plus		
Rifampin	300 mg oral every 8 hr	6 weeks
2. Methicillin sensitive		
Nafcillin or oxacillin	2 gm IV every 4 hr	6 weeks
plus		
Gentamycin*	1 mg/kg IV/IM (not to exceed 80 mg) every 8 hr	2 weeks
plus		
Rifampin	300 mg oral every 8 hr	6 weeks

Table 7-2. (continued)

Table 7-2. (continued) Recommended Treatment Regimens for IE

Antibiotic	Dose and Route	Duration
C. Treatment of Penicillin-Susceptible Viridans streptococci and *Streptococcus bovis* Native Valve Endocarditis (MIC < 0.1 μg/mL)		
1. No penicillin allergy Aqueous penicillin G	10–20 million U/24 hr IV in 6 divided doses	4 weeks
or Ceftriaxone	2 gm IV or IM daily	4 weeks
or Aqueous penicillin G	10–20 million U/24 hr IV in 6 divided doses	2 weeks
plus Gentamycin*	1 mg/kg IV/IM (not to exceed 80 mg) every 8 hr	2 weeks
2. Penicillin allergy Vancomycin*	Up to 2 gm/24 hr IV in divided doses every 6–12 hr	4 weeks
D. Treatment of Viridans Streptococci and *Streptococcus bovis* Native Valve Endocarditis Relatively Resistant to Penicillin G (MIC > 0.1 and < 0.5 μg/mL)		
Aqueous penicillin G	20 million U/24 hr IV in 6 divided doses	4 weeks
plus Gentamycin*	1 mg/kg IV/IM (not to exceed 80 mg) every 8 hr	2 weeks
E. Treatment of Endocarditis Caused by Enterococci, Viridans Streptococci with MIC > 0.5 μg/mL, Nutritionally Variant Streptococci, and Prosthetic Valve Endocarditis Caused by Viridans Streptococci or *Streptococcus bovis*		
1. No penicillin allergy Aqueous penicillin G	18–30 million U IV/24 hr in 6 divided doses	4–6 weeks
plus Gentamycin*	1 mg/kg IV/IM (not to exceed 80 mg) every 8 hr	4–6 weeks
or Ampicillin	2 gm IV every 4 hours	4–6 weeks
plus Gentamycin*	1 mg/kg IV/IM (not to exceed 80 mg) every 8 hr	4–6 weeks

Table 7-2. (continued)

Table 7-2. (continued) Recommended Treatment Regimens for IE

Antibiotic	Dose and Route	Duration
2. Penicillin allergy		
Vancomycin*	Up to 2 gm/24 hr IV in divided doses every 6–12 hr	4–6 weeks
plus		
Gentamycin*	1 mg/kg IV/IM (not to exceed 80 mg) every 8 hr	4–6 weeks
F. Therapy for Endocarditis Due to HACEK Microorganisms		
Ceftriaxone	2 gm IV or IM daily	4 weeks
or		
Ampicillin	2 gm IV every 4 hr	4 weeks
plus		
Gentamycin*	1 mg/kg IV/IM (not to exceed 80 mg) every 8 hr	4 weeks
G. Treatment of Endocarditis Caused by Other Organisms		
1. Gram-negative rods (excluding *Pseudomonas* sp.)		
Cefotaxime (or equivalent third-generation cephalosporin)	2 gm IV every 6 hr	4–6 weeks
or		
Imipenem	2–4 gm/24 hr IV in 4 divided doses	4–6 weeks
or		
Aztreonam	2 gm IV every 6 hr	4–6 weeks
plus		
Gentamycin*	1 mg/kg IV/IM (not to exceed 80 mg) every 8 hr	4–6 weeks
2. *Pseudomonas* sp.		
Piperacillin	3 gm IV every 4 hr	6 weeks
or		
Mezlocillin	3 gm IV every 4 hr	6 weeks
or		
Ceftazidime	2 gm IV every 8 hr	6 weeks
or		
Imipenem	2–4 gm/24 hr IV in 4 divided doses	6 weeks

Table 7-2. (continued)

Table 7-2. (continued) Recommended Treatment Regimens for IE

Antibiotic	Dose and Route	Duration
or		
Aztreonam	2 gm IV every 6 hr	6 weeks
plus		
Gentamycin*	1 mg/kg IV/IM (not to exceed 80 mg) every 8 hr	6 weeks
or		
Tobramycin*	1.7 mg/kg every 8 hr	6 weeks
3. Fungi		
Amphotericin B	1 mg/kg/24 hr IV	6–8 weeks
plus		
Flucytosine	150 mg/kg/24 hr orally in 4 divided doses	6–8 weeks

* Gentamycin, Tobramycin, and Vancomycin serum peak and trough levels should be followed to monitor for therapeutic efficacy and to avoid toxicity. Adapted with permission from: Wilson WR, et al. Antibiotic treatment of adults with infective endocarditis due to streptococci, enterococci, staphylococci, and HACEK microorganisms. JAMA 1995;274:1706–1713.

penicillin or vancomycin plus an aminoglycoside) should be given while awaiting culture results.

Patients with Native Valve Endocarditis For most cases of NVE in non-IV drug abusers, empiric therapy should be directed against enterococci and viridans streptococci.

The most effective regimen is a combination of penicillin or ampicillin and gentamycin. In penicillin-allergic patients, vancomycin can be substituted.

Patients with Prosthetic Cardiac Material In patients with prosthetic cardiac material initial empiric therapy should be directed at *S. aureus, S. epidermidis*, and gram-negative rods.

The most effective regimens include vancomycin if methicillin resistance is suspected, or nafcillin and gentamycin. If coagulase negative staphylococcal infection is confirmed, rifampin (300 mg orally every 8 hours) should be added.

Intravenous Drug Users   In the IV drug user, initial empiric therapy should be directed against *S. aureus*.

Nafcillin or oxacillin or a first-generation cephalosporin plus or minus gentamycin is an effective regimen when methicillin resistance is not present. In cases of suspected methicillin resistance, vancomycin is recommended.

Surgery

Indications for Cardiac Surgery

The indications for cardiac surgery are:

- Refractory CHF as a result of structural valve damage.
- Repeated (two or more) episodes of systemic embolization or one episode in the presence of a large vegetation (≥ 10 mm).
- Perivalvular or myocardial abscess.
- Persistent infection despite adequate antibiotic therapy.
- Fungal endocarditis (majority of cases).

The indications for replacement of an infected prosthetic valve are similar to those listed above. Because relapse rates are high and hemodynamic complications common, PVE frequently necessitates valve replacement.

COMPLICATIONS OF INFECTIVE ENDOCARDITIS

Congestive Heart Failure

CHF is a life-threatening complication of IE which often results from valvular damage causing hemodynamically significant regurgitation.

CHF is more common with aortic valve endocarditis than IE involving the MV. In rare cases, large, friable vegetations may cause inflow obstruction producing CHF. Other causes of CHF include:

Coronary artery embolization with MI.
Myocarditis.
Pericardial effusion.
Myocardial abscess/fistula formation.

Hemodynamically significant CHF not responsive to medical therapy is an indication for surgery. In certain instances, where valve tissue is relatively intact, vegetation resection and valve repair can be performed.

With clinically mild CHF, the decision to replace the damaged valve is made on an individual basis, taking into account the patient's hemodynamic status and response to antibiotics and heart failure therapy (see Chapter 2).

Myocardial or Perivalvular Abscess

Abscess formation occurs in up to 20% of patients with IE. Typical locations include the

Aortic valve annulus.
Posterior mitral valve annulus.
Mitral-aortic intervalvular fibrosa.

- Characteristic clinical features of an intracardiac abscess include the presence of pericarditis, new onset AV block, and rapid progression of hemodynamic deterioration.
- The development of LBBB with IE strongly suggests the presence of an abscess involving the lower interventricular septum.
- Among patients with aortic valve endocarditis, serial ECGs should be monitored early in the course of therapy to detect new-onset AV block.

Pericarditis

Pericarditis may complicate both ABE and SBE.

ABE. Pericarditis is caused by organisms directly involving the pericardium or due to rupture of an abscess into the pericardial space.
SBE. Pericarditis is usually secondary to immune complex deposition.

Other Complications

Other complications include embolic stroke, mycotic aneurysm formation, splenic infarction or abscess formation, and renal insufficiency.

PROPHYLAXIS OF IE

Prophylactic antibiotics are indicated for use in patients who have a higher risk for developing IE than the general population (Table 7-3) when a procedure associated with transient bacteremia is performed.

Procedures for which IE prophylaxis is recommended include:

- Dental procedures that induce gingival bleeding or mucosal bleeding (including routine cleaning)

Table 7-3. Endocarditis Prophylaxis for Various Cardiac Conditions

Endocarditis prophylaxis recommended
  High-risk category
    Prosthetic cardiac valves, including bioprosthetic and homograft valves
    Previous bacterial endocarditis
    Complex cyanotic congenital heart disease (e.g., single ventricle states, transposition of the great arteries, tetralogy of Fallot)
    Surgically constructed systemic pulmonary shunts or conduits
  Moderate-risk category
    Most other congenital cardiac malformations (other than above and below)
    Acquired valvar dysfunction (e.g., rheumatic heart disease)
    Hypertrophic cardiomyopathy
    Mitral valve prolapse with valvar regurgitation and/or thickened leaflets*

Endocarditis prophylaxis not recommended
  Negligible-risk category (no greater risk than the general population)
    Isolated secundum atrial septal defect
    Surgical repair of atrial septal defect, ventricular septal defect, or patent ductus arteriosus (without residua beyond 6 mo)
    Previous coronary artery bypass graft surgery
    Mitral valve prolapse without valvar regurgitation*
    Physiologic, functional, or innocent heart murmurs*
    Previous Kawasaki disease without valvar dysfunction
    Previous rheumatic fever without valvar dysfunction
    Cardiac pacemakers (intravascular and epicardial) and implanted defibrillators

*See text for further details.
Adapted with permission from: Dajani AS, et al. Prevention of bacterial endocarditis. Recommendations by the American Heart Association. *Circulation* 1997;96:359.

- Tonsillectomy and/or adenoidectomy
- Surgical operations involving intestinal or respiratory mucosa
- Bronchoscopy with a rigid bronchoscope
- Sclerotherapy of esophageal varices
- Endoscopic retrograde cholangiography with biliary obstruction
- Esophageal stricture dilatation
- Biliary tract surgery

Table 7-4. Prophylactic Regimens for Dental, Oral, Respiratory Tract, or Esophageal Procedures

Situation	Agent*	Regimen[†]
Standard general prophylaxis	Amoxicillin	Adults: 2.0 g; children: 50 mg/kg orally 1 h before procedure
Unable to take oral medications	Ampicillin	Adults: 2.0 g IM or IV: children: 50 mg/kg IM or IV within 30 min before procedure
Allergic to penicillin	Clindamycin or Cephalexin or cefadroxil or Azithromycin or clarithromycin	Adults: 600 mg; children: 20 mg/kg orally 1 h before procedure Adults: 2.0 g; children: 50 mg/kg orally 1 h before procedure Adults: 500 mg; children: 15 mg/kg orally 1 h before procedure
Allergic to penicillin and unable to take oral medications	Clindamycin or Cefazolin	Adults: 600 mg; children: 20 mg/kg IV within 30 min before procedure Adults: 1.0 g; children: 25 mg/kg IM or IV within 30 min before procedure

IM indicates intramuscularly, and IV, intravenously.

*Total children's dose should not exceed adult dose.

[†] Cephalosporins should not be used in individuals with immediate-type hypersensitivity reaction (urticaria, angioedema, or anaphylaxis) to penicillins.

Reproduced with permission from: Dajani AS, et al. Prevention of bacterial endocarditis. Recommendations by the American Heart Association. Circulation 1997;96:363.

Table 7-5. Prophylactic Regimens for Genitourinary/
Gastrointestinal (Excluding Esophageal) Procedures

Situation	Agents*	Regimen†
High risk patients	Ampicillin plus gentamicin	Adults: ampicillin 2.0 g IM or IV plus gentamicin 1.5 mg/kg (not to exceed 120 mg) within 30 min of starting procedure; 6 h later, ampicillin 1 g IM/IV or amoxicillin 1 g orally
		Children: ampicillin 50 mg/kg IM or IV (not to exceed 2.0 g) plus gentamicin 1.5 mg/kg within 30 min of starting the procedure; 6 h later, ampicillin 25 mg/kg IM/IV or amoxicillin 25 mg/kg orally
High risk patients allergic to ampicillin/ amoxicillin	Vancomycin plus gentamicin	Adults: vancomycin 1.0 g IV over 1–2 h plus gentamicin 1.5 mg/kg IV/IM (not to exceed 120 mg); complete injection/infusion within 30 min of starting procedure
		Children: vancomycin 20 mg/kg IV over 1–2 h plus gentamicin 1.5 mg/kg IV/IM; complete injection/infusion within 30 min of starting procedure
Moderate risk patients	Amoxicillin or ampicillin	Adults: amoxicillin 2.0 g orally 1 h before procedure, or ampicillin 2.0 g IM/IV within 30 min of starting procedure
		Children: amoxicillin 50 mg/kg orally 1 h before procedure, or ampicillin 50 mg/kg IM/IV within 30 min of starting procedure

Table 7-5. (continued)

Table 7-5. (continued) Prophylactic Regimens for Genitourinary/Gastrointestinal (Excluding Esophageal) Procedures

Situation	Agents*	Regimen†
Moderate risk patients allergic to ampicillin/ amoxicillin	Vancomycin	Adults: vancomycin 1.0 g IV over 1–2 h complete infusion within 30 min of starting procedure
		Children: vancomycin 20 mg/kg IV over 1–2 h; complete infusion within 30 min of starting procedure

IM indicates intramuscularly, and IV, intravenously.
* Total children's dose should not exceed adult dose.
† No second dose of vancomycin or gentamicin is recommended.
Reproduced with permission from: Dajani AS, et al. Prevention of bacterial endocarditis. Recommendations by the American Heart Association. Circulation 1997;96:364.

- Cystoscopy
- Urethral dilatation
- Urethral catheterization or urinary tract surgery if urinary tract infection is present
- Prostatic surgery
- Incision and drainage of infected tissue
- Vaginal hysterectomy (in high risk patients)
- Vaginal delivery in the presence of infection

Prophylactic Antibiotic Recommendations

Antibiotics are administered 0.5 to 2 hours prior to the procedure and in some cases are repeated following the procedure. Both oral or parenteral regimens are available. Recommendations are based on patient characteristics and procedure type. See Tables 7-4 and 7-5.

SUGGESTED READINGS

Ali AS, Trivedi V, Lesch M. Culture-negative endocarditis—a historical review and 1990s update. Prog Cardiovasc Dis 1994;37:149–160.
Dajani AS, Taubert KA, Wilson W, et al. Prevention of

bacterial endocarditis. Recommendations by the American Heart Association. JAMA 1997;277:1794–1801.

Daniel WG, Mugge A, Martin RP, et al. Improvement in the diagnosis of abscesses associated with endocarditis by transesophageal echocardiography. N Engl J Med 1991;324: 795–800.

Durack DT. Prevention of infective endocarditis. N Engl J Med 1995;332:38–44.

Durack DT, Lukes AS, Bright DK, Duke Endocarditis Service. New criteria for diagnosis of infective endocarditis: utilization of specific echocardiographic findings. Am J Med 1994;96:200–209.

Dinubile MJ. Surgery in active endocarditis. Ann Intern Med 1982;96:650–659.

Hermans PE. The clinical manifestations of infective endocarditis. Mayo Clin Proc 1982;57:15–21.

Joffe II, Jacobs LE, Owen AN, et al. Noninfective valvular masses: review of the literature with emphasis on imaging techniques and management. Am Heart J 1996;131:1175–1183.

Karalis DG, Bansal RC, Hauck AJ, et al. Transesophageal echocardiographic recognition of subaortic complications in aortic valve endocarditis. Circulation 1992;86:353–362.

Karchmer AW. Infective endocarditis. In: Braunwald E, ed. Heart disease: a textbook of cardiovascular medicine. 5th ed. Philadelphia: WB Saunders, 1996:1077–1104.

Linder JR, Case RA, Dent JM, et al. Diagnostic value of echocardiography in suspected endocarditis. An evaluation based on the pretest probability of disease. Circulation 1996;93:730–736.

Mansur AJ, Grinberg M, Da Luz PL, Bellotti G. The complications of infective endocarditis. A reappraisal of the 1980s. Arch Intern Med 1992;152:2428–2432.

Middlemost S, Wisenbaugh T, Meyerowitz C, et al. A case for early surgery in native left-sided endocarditis complicated by heart failure: results in 203 patients. J Am Coll Cardiol 1991;18:663–667.

Raoult D, Fournier PE, Drancourt M, et al. Diagnosis of 22 new cases of *Bartonella* endocarditis. Ann Intern Med 1996;126:646–652.

Washington JA II. The role of the microbiology laboratory in the diagnosis and antimicrobial treatment of infective endocarditis. Mayo Clin Proc 1982;57:22–32.

Wilson WR, Giuliani ER, Danielson GK, Geraci JE. General considerations in the diagnosis and treatment of infective endocarditis. Mayo Clin Proc 1982;57:81–85.

Wilson WR, Karchmer AW, Dajani AS, et al. Antibiotic treatment of adults with infective endocarditis due to streptococci, enterococci, staphylococci, and HACEK microrganisms. JAMA 1995;274:1706–1713.

Acute Rheumatic Fever

Dennis A. Tighe
Edward K. Chung

Acute rheumatic fever (ARF) is the most common cause of acquired heart disease among children worldwide. Although a decline in the incidence of ARF has been experienced in developed nations, it remains a major public health problem for developing countries. This chapter reviews the epidemiology, diagnosis, treatment, and prevention of ARF.

EPIDEMIOLOGY OF ARF

ARF is an unusual complication of group A streptococcal (GAS) infection of the upper respiratory tract (tonsillopharyngitis).

- ARF does not occur as a complication of streptococcal skin infections (impetigo or pyoderma).
- Attack rates are highly variable. During epidemics, as many as 3% of untreated GAS throat infections may be followed by ARF. Attack rates are much lower (0.3% to 1.0%) in endemic conditions.
- In developed countries, the incidence of ARF has steadily declined, accompanied by a reduced prevalence of rheumatic heart disease. This decline was observed to begin prior to the introduction of penicillin.
- In developing nations, the incidence of ARF remains high. As a consequence, the prevalence of rheumatic

heart disease is great (up to 7 to 20 per 1000 children).

- Initial attacks of ARF occur most often between the ages of 5 and 15 years. The occurrence of ARF prior to 5 years of age is rare. Recent outbreaks in the United States emphasize, however, that an initial attack of ARF may occur in adults.
- Attacks of ARF show a marked seasonal variation. ARF tends to occur more often in winter and spring.

PATHOPHYSIOLOGY

A number of factors may be associated with increased risk of developing ARF following GAS throat infection.

Environmental

Overcrowding, poor hygiene, and poor nutrition are believed to be factors that promote the spread of GAS infection.

- The incidence of ARF has been observed to be higher among people with lower socioeconomic status.
- A higher incidence of ARF among military recruits and school-aged children exemplifies the increased risk of ARF in overcrowded situations.

The Etiologic Agent: Group A *Streptococcus*

Untreated GAS tonsillopharyngitis is the event that precipitates an attack of ARF. The clinical manifestations of ARF (see below) follow streptococcal infection after a 2- to 4-week latency period. The variation in attack rates implies that certain GAS strains are more "rheumatogenic" than others.

- GAS strains with the M (mucoid) cell wall protein moiety have been associated with ARF. Strains possessing cell wall protein types T and R have not been associated with ARF.
- Approximately 80 M serotypes are present among GAS. Among these 80 M serotypes, only a few have been associated with outbreaks of ARF.

- Cross reactivity between purified M proteins and human cardiac proteins has been demonstrated.

The Host

The degree of host immune response has been correlated with the risk of developing ARF.

- Patients with a greater immunologic response to GAS infection are more likely to develop ARF as compared to those with a lesser response.
- Patients with a previous episode of ARF are at significantly higher risk of developing a new attack following untreated GAS infection than are patients without prior ARF.

A genetic susceptibility to ARF may be present.

- Familial aggregation of ARF has been observed.
- A B-cell alloantigen, identified by a monoclonal antibody (D 8/17), has been shown to be present in 99% of patients with rheumatic carditis as compared to 14% of healthy controls.
- HLA haplotypes associated with increased susceptibility have been identified among various ethnic groups.

DIAGNOSIS OF ARF

ARF is characterized by an inflammatory reaction that primarily involves the heart, joints, basal ganglia, skin, and subcutaneous tissues.

No specific clinical or laboratory test can firmly establish the diagnosis of ARF. The Modified Jones Criteria (Table 8-1) aids in the diagnosis. The presence of two major or one major and two minor manifestations, in the presence of evidence of preceding GAS infection, indicates a high probability of ARF.

Evidence of GAS Infection

A number of important points must be considered in regards to the presence of supporting evidence of antecedent GAS infection:

- The lack of serologic response to streptococcal antibodies along with the lack of microbiologic

Table 8-1. Jones Criteria: Guidelines for the Diagnosis of Initial Attack of Rheumatic Fever (1992 Update)

Major Manifestations
Carditis
Polyarthritis
Chorea
Erythema marginatum
Subcutaneous nodules

Minor Manifestations
Clinical findings
Arthralgia
Fever
Laboratory findings
Elevated acute phase reactants
• ESR
• C-reactive protein
Prolonged PR interval

Supporting Evidence of Antecedent GAS Infection
Positive throat culture or rapid streptococcal antigen test
Elevated or rising streptococcal antibody titer

If supported by evidence of preceding GAS infection, the presence of 2 major manifestations or of 1 major and 2 minor manifestations indicates a high probability of ARF.

Adapted with permission from: Special Writing Group of the Committee on Rheumatic Fever, Endocarditis, and Kawasaki Disease of the Council on Cardiovascular Disease in the Young of the American Heart Association. Guidelines for the diagnosis of rheumatic fever. Jones Criteria, 1992 Update. JAMA 1992;268:2070. Copyrighted 1992, American Medical Association.

evidence of GAS infection makes the diagnosis of ARF unlikely. Exceptions to this rule are the presence of indolent carditis and Syndenham's chorea.

• A throat culture or results of a single rapid antigen test positive for GAS does not separate chronic pharyngeal carriage with superimposed viral infection from recent GAS infection.

• Rapid GAS antigen detection tests are very specific but rather insensitive for diagnosis of GAS pharyngitis. A negative result does not exclude GAS pharyngitis and a throat culture should be obtained for confirmation.

Antibody Titers

At the time of diagnosis of ARF, only 11% to 25% of patients have positive throat cultures for GAS. If ARF is suspected, elevated or rising antistreptococcal antibody titers provide more reliable evidence of recent GAS pharyngeal infection.

- The antistreptolysin O (ASO) titer is the most widely used antibody test. Other tests include anti-DNase B and antistreptokinase.
  The ASO titer is elevated in approximately 80% of patients with (suspected) ARF.
  If ASO is not elevated, then the anti-DNase test should be performed.
- To document a recent streptococcal infection by rising antibody titers, acute and convalescent serum samples should be obtained at 2- to 4-week intervals. The samples should be tested simultaneously.
- Patients, especially children, with disease processes other than ARF may have elevated streptococcal antibody titers.

Clinical Features

Major Manifestations

Carditis   Carditis is the most specific clinical feature of ARF. ARF is a pancarditis—involving heart valves, endocardium, myocardium, and pericardium. This feature distinguishes ARF from other rheumatologic disorders that involve the heart.

- Isolated involvement of the myocardium or pericardium in the absence of valvulitis (suggested by a heart murmur) should prompt reconsideration of the diagnosis of ARF.

Valvulitis   The MV is most frequently involved, followed by involvement of both the mitral and aortic valves, and less commonly the aortic valve in isolation. TV and PV involvement is rare.

- The holosystolic murmur of MR is the hallmark of ARF. MR due to MVP, congenital MR, and HCM, in addition to innocent murmurs must be excluded.

- Echocardiography reveals that MR related to ARF is due to ventricular dilatation and/or restriction of leaflet mobility.
- The high-pitched, decrescendo murmur of AR may also be noted. Differentiation from AR caused by a congenital bicuspid aortic valve must be made.

Myocarditis Myocarditis may lead to severe CHF and death, but most commonly has no symptoms of its own. Tachycardia, dyspnea, cough, and cardiomegaly may be clinical manifestations.

- Endomyocardial biopsy in patients with acute rheumatic carditis shows myocyte degeneration without lymphocytic infiltration and often without Aschoff bodies.
- Biopsy does not provide further diagnostic information in situations where clinical consensus is certain about the diagnosis of ARF.

Pericarditis Pericardial effusion, friction rub, and chest pain are clinical manifestations of rheumatic pericarditis. Large pericardial effusions are rare.

Arthritis Polyarthritis, the most common clinical manifestation of ARF, is also the least specific finding. Arthritis is characteristically asymmetric, migratory, and involves the larger joints (knees, elbows, ankles, wrists).

- Untreated, arthritis may last for up to 2 to 4 weeks.
- Permanent joint damage rarely, if ever, occurs.

A characteristic feature of the arthritis due to ARF is its dramatic response to salicylate therapy. If the arthritis does not respond to adequate salicylate therapy (a serum salicylate level may be necessary) within 48 hours, then the diagnosis of ARF should be reconsidered.

Chorea (Syndenham's Chorea, Saint Vitus Dance) Chorea, characterized by purposeless, rapid involuntary movements with associated muscular weakness and emotional lability, is a late manifestation of ARF. Chorea is a sign of involvement of the caudate nuclei and basal ganglia in the rheumatic process.

- Chorea typically manifests 1 to 6 months after the antecedent GAS pharyngeal infection.

- Chorea may be the only clinically apparent manifestation of ARF.
- Chorea is a benign, self-limited manifestation without permanent neurological sequelae.

Erythema Marginatum Erythema marginatum is a distinctive, evanescent, nonpruritic rash occurring mainly on the trunk and proximal extremities. It appears as a pink ring that spreads serpiginously with faded central portion and sharply demarcated outer edge.

- The rash may be induced by application of heat.
- Erythema marginatum is the least common clinical manifestation of ARF. It occurs in ≤5% of cases.
- Similar to other clinical manifestations of ARF, erythema marginatum is benign and self-limited.

Subcutaneous Nodules Small (usually 0.5 to 2.0 cm in diameter), painless, movable nodules which are primarily located over bony prominences of the spinal column or surrounding joints occur in up to 20% of cases.

- Subcutaneous nodules most often are found in patients with rheumatic carditis.
- Nodules rarely persist more than 3 to 4 weeks.

Minor Manifestations
These clinical findings should be used to support a diagnosis of ARF when only a single major manifestation is present. Nonspecific findings that occur frequently with ARF and a variety of other diseases are:

Arthralgia—pain in one or more joints without evidence of inflammation
Fever—usually 38.4 to 40°C (101.2 to 104°F)

Laboratory Findings Objective, but nonspecific, indicators of an inflammatory process are:

Leukocytosis
Anemia
Elevated acute phase reactants
- The ESR and C-reactive protein are nearly always elevated with carditis or arthritis, but most often are normal when chorea is the sole major manifestation.

- The ESR may be normal in the presence of CHF; however C-reactive protein is usually elevated.

Prolonged PR Interval A prolonged PR interval for age and rate is a common, but nonspecific, finding. It is not a predictor of chronic rheumatic heart disease.

DIFFERENTIAL DIAGNOSIS OF ARF

A number of disease processes may share similar clinical features with ARF (Table 8-2), so a careful history and physical examination are required. The diagnosis of ARF should be reserved for those cases which clearly fulfill the diagnostic criteria listed above. Premature administration of salicylates or corticosteroids should be avoided until signs and symptoms of ARF become clear.

Exceptions to the Jones Criteria must be recognized:

- Chorea most commonly presents late and may be the only clinically apparent manifestation of ARF.
- Indolent carditis may be the only manifestation among patients who present many months after the onset of ARF.
- A recurrent attack of ARF may present in a patient with prior rheumatic fever or rheumatic heart disease.

Table 8-2. Differential Diagnosis of ARF

Juvenile rheumatoid arthritis
Systemic lupus erythematosus
Takayasu's arteritis
Primary antiphospholipid syndrome
Infective endocarditis
Viral infections (esp. coxsackievirus or parvovirus)
Lyme disease
Poststreptococcal reactive arthritis
Sepsis
Rubella
Drug allergy
Serum sickness
Sickle cell disease
Leukemia
Tuberculosis

TREATMENT

For the acute attack of ARF, hospital admission for bedrest and observation is indicated. CHF is treated in standard fashion (see Chapter 2).

The duration of therapy is 1 to 3 months depending upon disease severity and response to treatment.

- A 10-day course of penicillin is indicated for all patients with ARF. Penicillin-allergic patients should receive erythromycin.
- Salicylates and steroids should be withheld until a firm diagnosis is established.

   Salicylates. Patients without carditis or with only mild carditis usually respond to salicylates (ASA 50–100 mg/kg/day) given 4 to 5 times per day. A salicylate level of 20 mg percent is optimal.

   Steroids. Among patients with significant carditis, steroids (prednisone, 40–60 mg/day, or its equivalent) should be used.

PREVENTION OF ARF

ARF can be prevented if GAS pharyngeal infection is identified in a timely fashion and properly treated.

Up to one-third of patients deny a preceding episode of symptomatic pharyngitis. In this situation, a regimen which offers secondary prevention against recurrent attacks of ARF should be the goal.

Prevention Strategies

Public health measures designed to reduce overcrowding, malnutrition, and poor sanitation decrease exposure to GAS. Measures designed to improve living standards, though effective, are not always able to be achieved in developing nations due to economic considerations.

Prevention of Initial Attacks (Primary Prevention)

Primary prevention requires case identification and confirmation of GAS infection. Appropriate and timely antibiotic therapy can prevent ARF in most cases. Prevention of ARF requires eradication of GAS from the throat. Treatment regimens are presented in Table 8-3.

Table 8-3. Primary Prevention of Rheumatic Fever

Agent	Dose	Mode	Duration
Benzathine Penicillin G	600,000 U for patients ≤27 kg; 1,200,000 U for patients >27 kg	Intramuscular	Once
or			
Penicillin V	Children: 250 mg, 2 to 3 times daily. Adolescents and adults: 500 mg, 2 to 3 times daily.	Oral	10 days
For penicillin-allergic individuals			
Erythromycin estolate	20–40 mg/kg/day, 2 to 4 times daily (maximum 1 gram/day)	Oral	10 days
or			
Erythromycin ethylsuccinate	40 mg/kg/day, 2 to 4 times daily (maximum 1 gram/day)	Oral	10 days

Reproduced by permission of Pediatrics. From: Dajani A, et al. Treatment of acute streptococcal pharyngitis and prevention of rheumatic fever: a statement for health professionals. Pediatrics 1995;96:760.

- IM or oral penicillin regimens are equally effective; however, IM penicillin should be administered if compliance with an oral regimen is anticipated to be problematic.
- For penicillin-allergic patients, oral erythromycin is an acceptable alternative.
- Oral cephalosporins and other macrolide-type antibiotics are also acceptable alternatives for penicillin-allergic patients, but their higher cost may be a consideration.

Implementation of primary prevention measures may be difficult in developing countries. A vaccine against GAS would be the most effective form of primary prevention, but such a vaccine does not currently exist.

Prevention of Recurrent Attacks of ARF (Secondary Prevention)

In the setting of a previous attack of ARF, current GAS pharyngeal infection places the patient at high risk of a recurrent episode of ARF. Rheumatic fever can recur even if GAS infection is optimally treated. Therefore, continuous antibiotic prophylaxis, rather than symptomatic treatment of GAS pharyngitis, is recommended. Regimens for secondary prevention of rheumatic fever are presented in Table 8-4.

The duration of the antibiotic prophylaxis depends upon the number of previous attacks, the time lapsed since the last attack, the severity of infection, and risk for recurrent disease. Recommendations of an expert panel are presented in Table 8-5.

- Compliance with prophylaxis regimens is as low as 50%. Careful education and diligent patient follow-up are important aspects of therapy.
- Secondary prevention programs may be the most beneficial and cost-effective means for developing countries to prevent and control rheumatic heart disease.

Table 8-4. Secondary Prevention of Rheumatic Fever

Agent	Dose	Mode
Benzathine penicillin G	1,200,000 U every 4 weeks*	Intramuscular
or		
Penicillin V	250 mg twice daily	Oral
or		
Sulfadiazine	0.5 g once daily for patients ≤27 kg; 1.0 g once daily for patients >27 kg	Oral
For patients allergic to penicillin or sulfadiazine		
Erythromycin	250 mg twice daily	Oral

* In high-risk situations, administration every 3 weeks is justified and recommended.

Reproduced by permission of Pediatrics. From: Dajani A, et al. Treatment of acute streptococcal pharyngitis and prevention of rheumatic fever: a statement for health professionals. Pediatrics 1995;96:762.

Table 8-5. Duration of Secondary Rheumatic Fever Prophylaxis

Category	Duration
Rheumatic fever with carditis and residual heart disease (persistent valvar disease*)	At least 10 years since last episode (and until at least 40 years old), lifelong prophylaxis.
Rheumatic fever with carditis but no residual heart disease (no valvar disease*)	10 years or well into adulthood, whichever is longer.
Rheumatic fever without carditis	5 years or until age 21, whichever is longer.

* Clinical or echocardiographic evidence.
Reproduced by permission of Pediatrics. From: Dajani A, et al. Treatment of acute streptococcal pharyngitis and prevention of rheumatic fever: a statement for health professionals. Pediatrics 1995;96:762.

SUGGESTED READINGS

Albert DA, Harel L, Karrison T. The treatment of rheumatic carditis: a review and meta-analysis. Medicine 1995;74:1–12.

Amigo MC, Martinez-Lavin M, Reyes PA. Acute rheumatic fever. Rheum Dis Clin North Am 1993;19(2):333–350.

Burge DJ, DeHoratius RJ. Acute rheumatic fever. In: Frankl WS, Brest AN, eds. Valvular heart disease: comprehensive evaluation and treatment, Cardiovascular Clinics. Philadelphia: FA Davis, 1993:3–23.

Dajani A, Taubert K, Ferrier P, et al. Treatment of acute streptococcal pharyngitis and prevention of rheumatic fever: a statement for health professionals. Pediatrics 1995;96:758–764.

Dajani AS. Rheumatic fever. In: Braunwald E, ed. Heart disease: a textbook of cardiovascular medicine. 5th ed. Philadelphia: WB Saunders, 1996:1769–1775.

Eisenberg MJ. Rheumatic heart disease in the developing world: prevalence, prevention, and control. Eur Heart J 1993;14:122–128.

Marcus RH, Sareli P, Pocock WA, Barlow JB. The spectrum of severe rheumatic mitral valve disease in a developing country. Ann Intern Med 1994;120:177–183.

Narula J, Chopra P, Talwar KK, et al. Does endomyocardial biopsy aid in the diagnosis of active rheumatic carditis? Circulation 1993;88(I):2198–2205.

Vasan RS, Shrivastava S, Vijayakumar M, et al. Echocardiographic evaluation of patients with acute rheumatic fever and rheumatic carditis. Circulation 1996;94:73–82.

Special Writing Group of the Committee on Rheumatic Fever, Endocarditis, and Kawasaki Disease of the Council on Cardiovascular Disease in the Young of the American Heart Association. Guidelines for the diagnosis of rheumatic fever. Jones Criteria, 1992 Update. JAMA 1992;268:2069–2073.

9

Congenital Heart Disease in the Adult

Yvonne M. Paris
Dennis A. Tighe

The past 40 years have witnessed a revolution in the evaluation and management of congenital heart disease. Advances in medical therapy have improved the longevity of patients. The development of technology enabling precise anatomic diagnosis and hemodynamic evaluation has led to a better understanding of particular lesions and has resulted in new therapeutic interventions. This chapter reviews the more common congenital cardiac defects that may be encountered in the adult.

ATRIAL SEPTAL DEFECT (ASD)

ASD is the most common shunt lesion in adults. It often remains undetected until adulthood because patients are often asymptomatic. Survival into adulthood is expected, but with premature mortality if the defect is not corrected.

Morbidity is related to several factors:

- Development of supraventricular tachyarrhythmias (particularly atrial flutter). Repair of the ASD does not generally alleviate this problem.
- Systemic HTN and CAD. These common diseases in the adult ASD patient can result in diminished LV compliance and potentially increase left-to-right shunting.

- RV dysfunction. Rarely, pulmonary vascular obstructive disease (PVOD) can result from the presence of a large ASD.
- Paradoxical embolism.
- Progressive MR.

Anatomy

Ostium Secundum ASD
Ostium secundum ASD, the most common type (70% of patients), results from a defect in the region of the fossa ovalis. MVP coexists in 20% of cases.

Ostium Primum ASD
An ostium primum defect (partial AV canal defect) accounts for 15% of all ASDs. An increased incidence is observed among patients with Down's syndrome. This type of ASD results from absence of septum primum, and is associated with a cleft anterior mitral leaflet in over two-thirds of cases.

Sinus Venosus ASD
A sinus venosus defect accounts for 10% to 15% of all ASDs. It is often associated with anomalous pulmonary venous drainage.

Unroofed Coronary Sinus ASD
Unroofed coronary sinus ASD is the least common type. It results from a defect in the membrane separating the coronary sinus from the LA. A persistent left SVC commonly coexists.

Physiology

ASD represents a left-to-right shunt with resultant right heart volume overload. The direction of shunting is determined by the relative compliance of the RV and LV.

History and Physical Exam

- The ASD patient is usually asymptomatic and often comes to clinical attention because of a heart murmur or abnormal ECG.
- Symptomatic patients come to clinical attention because of dyspnea, fatigue, CHF, and arrhythmias.
- In rare cases, paradoxical embolization may lead to

clinical recognition of an ASD. PVOD occurs in less than 10% of cases.

Auscultation

The cardiac impulse is hyperactive.

- The S_1 is accentuated.
- Fixed splitting of S_2 is present.
- A systolic murmur, due to increased flow across the PV and ejection into a dilated pulmonary trunk, is present at the left upper sternal border.
- A diastolic rumble may be heard at the base.

Diagnostic Tests

ECG

Most patients are in sinus rhythm at the time of diagnosis. Atrial arrhythmias may bring the patient to clinical attention.

- An incomplete RBBB pattern is often present. Rarely, RVH may be present (may indicate the presence of PVOD).
- Primum defects are associated with left axis deviation.
- Sinus venosus defects may be associated with an ectopic atrial rhythm.
- Notching on the R wave in the inferior leads ("Crochetage" pattern) is reported to be frequently present with ostium secundum ASD and may correlate with larger defect size and greater shunting.

Chest X-Ray

Cardiomegaly, in proportion to the amount of shunting, and increased pulmonary vascular markings are noted.

Echocardiography

Echocardiography is the mainstay of diagnosis. Echocardiography can:

1. Identify the type of defect.
2. Demonstrate the pulmonary venous drainage.
3. Exclude associated defects.
4. Assess the MV.
5. Assess the size of the RA and RV.
6. Estimate the pulmonary artery (PA) pressure

utilizing the TR jet (modified Bernoulli equation, see Chapter 6).

ASDs are best evaluated from the subcostal position.

- The most common finding is volume overload of the right heart and paradoxical motion of the interventricular septum.

In the adult, it is often necessary to perform TEE to fully evaluate the ASD (especially those of the sinus venosus type) and to assess the status of the pulmonary veins and their drainage.

Cardiac Catheterization

Cardiac catheterization is not indicated unless there is a suspicion of PVOD or CAD.

Treatment

Treatment of ASD is surgical rather than medical. If the patient is operated on at less than 24 years of age, then normal survival is expected. Surgery is not indicated when the Qp:Qs ratio is less than 1.5:1.

Postoperative complications include:

- Conduction abnormalities—sinus node dysfunction, mild prolongation of AV node conduction, significant atrial tachyarrhythmias
- Postpericardiotomy syndrome

Percutaneous device closure is available in some centers on an investigational basis.

Endocarditis Prophylaxis

Not recommended. Prophylaxis is not recommended in uncomplicated and unrepaired ostium secundum ASD.

Recommended. Prophylaxis is recommended only for first 6 months following surgical repair, provided no surgically created conduits or other residua are present.

VENTRICULAR SEPTAL DEFECT (VSD)

VSD is one of the most prevalent congenital heart lesions in children, but is rarely a presenting lesion in the adult. This is because either the defect has closed spontaneously, decreased in size as to be hemodynamically insignificant, or has been surgically closed in childhood. Rarely, an adult with an undetected nonrestrictive VSD may present with cyanosis secondary to PVOD (Eisenmenger's syndrome).

Anatomy

Five types types of congenital VSD are recognized:

1. **Muscular.** Most common type of VSD in infants and children.
2. **Perimembranous** (conoventricular, subaortic VSD). Most common type observed in adults.
3. **Conoseptal** (supracristal, doubly committed subarterial VSD).
4. **Malalignment** (tetralogy of Fallot, double outlet RV).
5. **Endocardial cushion defect** (AV canal defect).

Physiology

VSD results in a left-to-right shunt and a volume load placed on the left heart.

Restrictive VSD. The magnitude of the shunt is determined by the size of the defect.

Nonrestrictive VSD. The shunt is determined by the relative resistance between the pulmonary vascular bed and the systemic vascular bed.

History and Physical Exam

Small Defect

The patient is usually asymptomatic. The only finding may be a murmur.

Auscultation

- A loud systolic ejection murmur that peaks in midsystole is characteristic. It is generally localized to the left lower sternal border.
- The murmur may be accompanied by a thrill and be loud enough to obscure S_2.

Moderate and Large Defects

Moderate and large VSDs are usually discovered in infancy, with symptoms appearing when the newborn's PVR begins to fall between 2 and 6 weeks of age.

- Symptoms consist of tachypnea, tachycardia, and failure to thrive.

Diagnostic Tests

ECG

Small defect: Generally normal ECG.

Moderate defect: Biventricular hypertrophy with prominent mid-precordial voltages.

Large defect: Prominent left-sided voltages.

Large defect with Eisenmenger's physiology: RVH with right axis deviation.

Chest X-Ray

Small defect: Essentially normal with a slight increase in pulmonary vascularity.

Moderate to large defect: Cardiomegaly, with a dilated LA and LV. Large pulmonary trunk with dilated central PAs.

Eisenmenger's complex: Slight increase in the heart size. A large pulmonary trunk with gross enlargement of central PAs and decreased pulmonary vascular markings in the periphery.

Echocardiography

Echocardiography is the mainstay of diagnosis. Its goals are to:

1. Delineate the anatomic location of the VSD and ascertain its type.
2. Estimate the size of the defect.
3. Determine the number of defects.
4. Estimate the LA and LV size.
5. Calculate the gradient across the VSD, and hence estimate the RV systolic pressure if systemic SBP is known.
6. Estimate PA pressure.
7. Exclude other associated congenital anomalies.

Echocardiography is also important in the postoperative patient to assess LV function and integrity of the repair.

Cardiac Catheterization

Cardiac catheterization is not required if the echocardiogram is complete and repair takes place at less than 1 year of age. The goals of cardiac catheterization are to:

1. Define the anatomy in detail.
2. Quantitate the shunt.
3. Determine PVR.

Treatment

In asymptomatic patients with small defects and normal heart size, no surgery is required, but IE prophylaxis is indicated.

Surgery

Patients with Eisenmenger's syndrome are not candidates for VSD repair. Otherwise, indications for VSD surgery are:

- A Qp:Qs ratio greater than 2:1.
- PA pressures greater than half systemic pressure.
- Recurrent endocarditis.
- Progressive AR from prolapse of the aortic valve.

Postoperative Complications

- RBBB (often without sequelae) is frequent.
- Bifasicular block may be seen occasionally and is believed to be associated with an increased incidence of sudden death. Complete AV block is rare.
- Residual VSD may not be well tolerated postoperatively if the Qp:Qs ratio is greater than 1.5:1. Reoperation in this situation is often necessary.

Endocarditis Prophylaxis

Recommended. Prophylaxis is indicated in the presence of a VSD.

Not recommended. Prophylaxis is not indicated more than 6 months after surgical repair as long as a residual VSD is not present.

PATENT DUCTUS ARTERIOSUS (PDA)

PDA is most often diagnosed in childhood.

- By the third decade, undetected PDA presents with symptoms of CHF if a sizable left-to-right shunt is present.
- If the shunt is small the patient will be asymptomatic, but the risk of endocarditis is significant.

Adult patients with an unrestrictive PDA reach adulthood because they have developed pulmonary vascular
disease that results in a reversal of the shunt, thus relieving the LV volume overload.

Anatomy

The ductus arteriosus is derived from the distal portion
of the embryonic left sixth aortic arch. In the fetus it con-
nects the main PA to the aorta, thereby permitting ejection of 2/3 of the RV output into the descending aorta
(bypassing the lungs). The ductus is located just distal to
the left subclavian artery. Spontaneous closure usually
occurs in the first 24 hours of life.

Physiology

Persistent ductal patency results in a left-to-right shunt
and subsequent left heart volume overload. Determinants of shunt magnitude include:

- Diameter and length of the ductus (which govern the
  resistance to flow)
- Pressure gradient between the aorta and the PA
- Ratio of the PVR to SVR in an unrestrictive PDA

Small PDA
A small PDA will have little effect on the pulmonary
circulation.

Large PDA
A large PDA will decrease aortic diastolic pressure and
increase LVEDP, resulting in decreased coronary blood
flow and increased myocardial pressure. This can potentially cause a decrease in the myocardial perfusion.

Pulmonary Vascular Obstructive Disease
A large PDA results in equalization of the PA and systemic pressures, thus resulting in PVOD and reversal in
the left-to-right shunt.

History and Physical Examination
Small PDA
The patient is asymptomatic and has minimal physical
findings.

Auscultation Physical exam reveals only a continuous murmur with late accentuation in systole and extension into diastole.

Moderate to Large PDA

The patient may have symptoms of LV failure—tachycardia, tachypnea, bounding pulses.

Auscultation The following are usually present:

- A loud continuous ("machinery") murmur
- Thrill at the left upper sternal border
- S_3 gallop
- Diastolic rumble at the apex

Pulmonary Vascular Obstructive Disease

Auscultation

- No continuous murmur is present.
- S_2 is loud and single.
- A diastolic murmur of PR is commonly present.

Diagnostic Tests

Small PDA

- Little or no change on the ECG or CXR.
- Echocardiography is diagnostic.
- Catheterization is only necessary if the patient is to undergo transcatheter closure of the PDA.

Moderate to Large PDA

ECG

- LVH, with deep Q waves and large R waves in the inferior leads.
- RVH (signifies PVOD).

Chest X-Ray

- Cardiomegaly with a prominent LA and LV.
- Increased pulmonary vascular markings.

Cardiac Catheterization

The purpose of catheterization is to:

1. Define the communication.
2. Determine the reactivity of the pulmonary vascular bed if pulmonary HTN is present.
3. Exclude other lesions.

Only right heart catheterization is necessary. The catheter course is main PA to ductus to aorta. Common findings include:

Increased PA pressures.
Decreased systemic pressure.
Elevated RA and LA mean pressures.
Increased LVEDP.

Angiography in the LAO or lateral projections can demonstrate the PDA well.

Treatment

Closure

Closure represents definitive cure. Closure is always indicated secondary to the risk of IE in the presence of a small ductus and the development of PVOD in the presence of a large ductus.

- Transcatheter embolization with Gianturco coils is the most commonly performed procedure.
- Thorascopic clipping of the PDA is performed in some centers.
- Surgical closure via a thoracotomy for isolated PDA is rarely performed today.

Endocarditis Prophylaxis

Recommended. Prophylaxis is indicated in the presence of a PDA.

Not recommended. Prophylaxis is not indicated following closure.

PULMONARY VALVE STENOSIS (PS)

Patients with untreated valvular PS usually survive into adult life.

Mild PS. Because patients with mild obstruction (peak gradient <30 mm Hg) are asymptomatic and rarely progress, treatment is not indicated.

Moderate to severe PS. Patients with moderate or severe PS will eventually develop RV failure and will require treatment.

Anatomy

Three forms of valvar PS are recognized:

1. Fusion of valve leaflets (the most common form in children)
2. Bicuspid PV (generally associated with tetralogy of Fallot)
3. Dysplastic leaflets (associated with Noonan's syndrome)

PS results in secondary changes:

RVH
Infundibular hypertrophy
Thickening of the TV
Dilated RA. A patent foramen ovale (PFO) is usually present in moderate to severe cases.
Post-stenotic dilatation of the pulmonary trunk

Physiology

Valvar PS causes obstruction to RV outflow resulting in high RV pressure, which in turn causes an increase in RV muscle mass. If RV failure occurs, there is a decrease in pulmonary blood flow. With exercise, the patient may no longer be able to meet tissue oxygen requirements and will develop peripheral cyanosis.

Clinical Presentation

Mild PS. Mild stenosis is asymptomatic.
Moderate to severe PS. Moderate to severe stenosis may be asymptomatic, but the most common complaint is dyspnea or fatigue with exertion. Strenuous exercise may provoke syncope and even sudden death in patients with a severe degree of obstruction (peak gradient >50 mm Hg).

Physical Examination

Auscultation

- A pulmonary ejection click occurs when the PV domes. The click varies in intensity (it is louder with expiration). The earlier the click, the more severe the obstruction.
- A systolic ejection murmur is best heard at the left upper sternal border. Loudness is not an index of severity. The more severe the obstruction, the longer the duration of the murmur.

- A coexisting blowing holosystolic murmur heard at the base may indicate the presence of TR.

Diagnostic Tests

ECG

Mild PS. A slight rightward shift of axis is characteristic of mild stenosis.

Moderate PS. Moderate stenosis shows a right axis deviation, R/S ratio in V_1 greater than $2:1$.

Severe PS. In severe stenosis, the axis is greater than $110°$, with a dominant R wave in aVR with increased right-sided voltages.

Chest X-Ray

PS appears as prominent main PA segment with normal pulmonary vascular markings. Severe PS results in cardiomegaly with a decrease in pulmonary vascular markings (secondary to right-to-left shunting at the atrial level).

Echocardiogram

The echocardiogram is used to:

1. Localize the anatomic level of obstruction.
2. Assess the severity of obstruction.
3. Measure the pulmonary valve annulus size.
4. Determine the RV ejection period.
5. Assess for the presence of RVH.
6. Determine the presence of an atrial level shunt.

Cardiac Catheterization

The goals of catheterization include:

1. Demonstrate the severity of the stenosis.
   - If two gradients are encountered, then infundibular stenosis likely coexists.
   - If the RV pressure is less than 50 mm Hg, then no intervention is necessary.
2. Exclude other diagnoses.
3. Provide definitive therapy.

Treatment

- Percutaneous balloon valvuloplasty is the procedure of choice.

- The dysplastic PV characteristic of Noonan's syndrome is not usually amenable to balloon valvuloplasty. This type of PS usually requires surgical intervention.

Endocarditis Prophylaxis

Recommended. Prophylaxis is recommended for any indicated procedure before and after valvotomy.

AORTIC STENOSIS (AS) AND LEFT VENTRICULAR OUTFLOW TRACT (LVOT) OBSTRUCTION

A congenital bicuspid aortic valve, present in 1% to 2% of the population, is one of the most common congenital heart defects. It may not become stenotic through the entire lifespan, but, more commonly, valvar AS develops due to progressive fibrocalcific thickening of the valve leaflets.

- Because of the high incidence of a bicuspid aortic valve and its tendency to become stenotic, LVOT obstruction is a common problem in the adult with congenital heart disease.
- Other etiologies of LVOT obstruction are less common, though the physiology and the indications for surgery are similar.
- The patient with LVOT obstruction is also prone to the development of AR, complicating the clinical progression of this disease.

In general, the natural history of LVOT obstruction depends on the severity of the obstruction at the time of diagnosis. Once symptoms appear, the 5-year mortality approaches 90% without intervention.

Anatomy

Three types of AS are recognized: valvar, subvalvar, and supravalvar.

Valvar Aortic Stenosis

Bicuspid aortic valve is the most common type of AS. It is caused by commissural fusion of the aortic valve leaflets.

Subvalvar Aortic Stenosis

Discrete Fibromuscular Stenosis A fibrous diaphragm encircles the LVOT below the aortic valve, creating obstruction. Discrete fibromuscular stenosis may often be associated with the development of AR because of the valve leaflet distortion from the turbulence produced by the stenotic jet.

Tunnel-Type Stenosis The tunnel-type stenosis is similar to the fibromuscular ring, except that a greater length of narrowing is present. This form is less common than the discrete form.

Hypertrophic Cardiomyopathy Asymmetric hypertrophy of the interventricular septum will often cause obstruction of the LVOT from systolic anterior motion of the mitral valve.

Supravalvar Aortic Stenosis

Supravalvar AS is a congenital narrowing of the ascending aorta above the sinuses of Valsalva. The length of the narrowing may vary greatly, from a discrete "napkin ring" lesion to involving the entire length of the ascending aorta. This form of LVOT obstruction is very rare. Often it is associated with neonatal hypercalcemia and Williams syndrome.

History and Physical Examination

Most patients are asymptomatic and present only with a murmur. Those with symptoms may complain of angina or exertional dyspnea, indicating a moderate to severe degree of stenosis. Symptomatic patients are at greater risk for arrhythmias and sudden death.

Auscultation
- A thrill is usually present with transmission to the suprasternal notch.
- With a bicuspid valve, a click is heard. The click does not vary with respiration, thus differentiating it from MVP.
- Single S_2 can result secondary to a delay in closure of the aortic valve. This finding indicates severe AS.

- The presence of S_4 indicates an increased force of atrial contraction.
- A systolic crescendo/decrescendo murmur heard at the base and radiating to the carotid arteries is the classic auscultatory finding.

Diagnostic Tests

ECG

The ECG may be normal without significant stenosis. As AS progresses and becomes severe, LVH, LAE, and repolarization abnormalities are often present.

Chest X-Ray

The classic finding is a normal heart size with concentric rounding of the LV apex. LA enlargement indicates that the obstruction is severe.

Echocardiography

The goals of echocardiography in the evaluation of AS are:

1. Determine the exact location of the LVOT obstruction.
2. Determine if LVH is present.
3. Determine the peak instantaneous and mean gradients across the obstruction.

Cardiac Catheterization

Cardiac catheterization is generally reserved for patients who are candidates for intervention with balloon valvotomy and those in whom CAD is suspected.

- Patients with supravalvar AS should undergo catheterization to accurately determine the gradient above the aortic valve and to assess the coronary vasculature for the presence of CAD.

Treatment

Generally, the treatment for AS is surgical rather than medical. Indications for intervention are:

- Mean gradient by echocardiogram of greater than 50 mm Hg
- Calculated valve orifice area of less than $0.5\,cm^2/m^2$

- Presence of symptoms with ECG changes indicating LVH and strain.

Valvar Aortic Stenosis

Balloon valvotomy has been shown to be as effective as surgical valvotomy in the young patient with AS who does not have AR or fibrocalcific thickening of the valve. It is a palliative technique with the possibility of restenosis or progression of AR.

The majority of adult patients with valvar AS have fibrocalcific thickening and are therefore not candidates for balloon valvotomy. AVR is the procedure of choice.

Subvalvar Aortic Stenosis

Discrete stenosis is repaired by excision of the membrane. The development and progression of AR is an additional indication. Tunnel-like stenosis has a higher incidence of recurrence after surgery.

Supravalvar Aortic Stenosis

Patch enlargement of the affected ascending aorta is the procedure of choice for supravalvar AS. The long-term postoperative outcome is affected adversely by the presence of Williams syndrome and/or CAD.

Endocarditis Prophylaxis

Recommended for any indicated procedures.

COARCTATION OF THE AORTA

Coarctation of the aorta is a common defect, representing 6% of cases of congenital heart disease. Up to 20% of patients are diagnosed in adolescence or adulthood. In infancy, coarctation may present as CHF; later in life it presents in asymptomatic patients as upper extremity HTN or a murmur.

Mortality and Morbidity

Unrepaired Coarctation

The longevity of patients with unrepaired coarctation is related to the coexistence of associated congenital heart malformations, of which bicuspid aortic valve is the most common. The mortality rate for patients with unrepaired coarctation is 25% by age 20 and >50% by age 30.

Age at the time of repair is the best predictor of morbidity and mortality. The best survival rates are among those repaired before the age of 9. Patients whose defects are repaired before 14 years of age have an actuarial survival of 91% at 20 years after repair, as compared to 79% among those repaired later in life.

Repaired Coarctation

Despite a low risk of sudden death, repaired coarctation patients remain at risk for late HTN, premature CAD, and complications related to associated malformations. In order of importance, the risk of mortality is related to:

CAD
Sudden cardiac death
CHF
Cerebral vascular accident from ruptured aneurysm of
   the circle of Willis
Aortic aneurysm rupture

Repaired coarctation patients require long-term medical follow-up, which must include assessment of residual gradient and BP.

- Late HTN, 25 years or more after repair, has been documented in 75% of patients.
- IE prophylaxis should be given to patients with an associated bicuspid aortic valve, and these patients should be monitored for the subsequent development of AS or AR.
- Evaluation of the aorta by serial MRI or CT scanning at 12 month intervals is indicated to evaluate for the presence of aneurysm formation and recoarctation.

Anatomy

- **Discrete coarctation.** Coarctation most commonly involves the upper thoracic aorta near the ductus arteriosus ("juxtaductal" or discrete). Histologically, the discrete coarctation consists of a thickened intimal and medial ridge that protrudes posteriorly into the lumen of the aorta at the area where the ductus inserts anteriorly.

Note: Coarctation may be due to a long-segment hypoplasia involving the transverse aortic arch and isthmus.

- **Complex coarctation.** "Complex coarctation" is said to be present when an associated congenital malformation exists.
- **Collateral circulation.** Collateral circulation often develops in the adult with a moderate or severe degree of stenosis.
    Anteriorly, these collaterals develop from the internal mammary to the external iliac system.
    Posteriorly, they develop from the thyrocervical and intercostal arteries to the descending thoracic aorta.

Physiology

Coarctation causes an increased impedance to flow from the LV, thus increasing the systolic pressure in the LV and ascending aorta. To compensate, myocardial hypertrophy occurs in an attempt to decrease wall stress and ventricular afterload.

History and Physical Examination

Most patients are asymptomatic and generally present with systolic HTN in the upper extremities and a murmur. A gradient in the SBP of greater than 20 mm Hg is noted between the upper and the lower extremities. A radial-femoral delay in the timing of the pulse is a classic finding.

Palpation
- On palpation of the chest, a prominent heaving LV impulse may be present due to the pressure-overloaded LV.
- If a collateral system exists, there may be prominent pulses palpated in the intercostal areas.
- A systolic thrill may be felt in the suprasternal notch.

Auscultation
- S_1 and S_2 are normal.
- If a bicuspid aortic valve is present, then a click may be heard.
- A grade 2 to 3/6 systolic murmur is best heard at the right upper sternal border and between the scapulae.
- Continuous murmurs may be heard throughout the chest due to collateral circulation.

Diagnostic Tests

ECG
LVH and left axis deviation are commonly observed.

Chest X-Ray
- Rib notching, caused by prominent intercostal collateral channels eroding the lower margin of the ribs, is commonly seen in adults.
- A "figure-of-3" sign may be seen in the AP projection.

Echocardiography
The suprasternal long axis view may demonstrate the posterior shelf of the discrete coarctation and localize the site of narrowing. This view can also be utilized to measure the transverse arch and isthmus to rule out hypoplasia.

Secondary signs of coarctation include:

LVH
Dilated ascending aorta and arch
Dilated great vessels

Doppler localizes the site of the coarctation and can estimate the pressure gradient across it.

Aortography
Aortography using the AP view will demonstrate the anatomy of the aorta, the brachiocephalic vessels, and the coarctation.

Cardiac Catheterization
Cardiac catheterization is generally not indicated for coarctation unless the anatomy is not clearly defined by echocardiography, CAD is suspected, or balloon aorto-plasty is planned. The goals of cardiac catheterization include:

1. Define the anatomy and the severity of the coarctation.
2. Define the ductus arteriosus (if present).
3. Define the presence or the extent of the collateral circulation.
4. Document the severity of associated lesions.
5. Assess LV function.

6. Assess PA pressure and PVR.
7. Exclude significant CAD.

Treatment

Surgical

Sugical procedures include resection with anastomosis or aortoplasty. They are performed through a left thoracotomy unless repair of an intracardiac lesion is planned.

Surgical morbidity is related to:

Postoperative paradoxical HTN
Spinal cord ischemia
Recurrent laryngeal nerve injury
Phrenic nerve injury
Chylothorax
Bleeding
Infection

Percutaneous Balloon Aortoplasty

Although percutaneous balloon aortoplasty has been widely accepted as a treatment of recurrent coarctation, its use as a treatment of native coarctation is more controversial.

- Most common complication is femoral artery injury or thrombosis.
- Potential for aneurysm formation is under study.
- Restenosis rate may potentially be higher in those treated for native coarctation.

EBSTEIN'S ANOMALY OF THE TRICUSPID VALVE

Ebstein's anomaly occurs in 1/20,000 live births. Equal frequency in males and females is observed. Maternal exposure to lithium carbonate in the first trimester is associated with increased risk of developing Ebstein's anomaly. Occasional cases may first present in the adult years.

- Survival and symptomatic status are related to the function and condition of the TV, degree of RV impairment, and the presence of ectopic atrial arrhythmias.

- Patients with little cardiac impairment may have asymptomatic survival into adulthood, but most will exhibit symptoms and some degree of functional impairment.

Anatomy

In the normal adult, the attachment of the base of the septal leaflet of the TV is apically displaced in relation to the MV by no more than 15 to 20 mm. Ebstein's anomaly is characterized by apical displacement of the septal and posterior TV leaflets by more than 20 mm. In addition, these leaflets exhibit impaired mobility. The anterior TV leaflet is not apically displaced, but it is elongated, redundant, and highly mobile ("sail-like") in most cases. Due to this anatomic derangement, TR occurs.

As a consequence of the apical TV displacement, the proximal portion of the RV is said to be "atrialized." This atrialized RV is thin walled and often dilated. The portion of the RV distal to the TV is termed the "functional" portion. The functional RV is characterized by a decreased number of myocytes.

- A PFO or ostium secundum ASD are present in over 50% of cases.
- Right-sided accessory pathways (may be multiple) are frequently present.

Physiology

The deformed TV is most often regurgitant and in some cases stenotic. TR may be substantial in utero due to the high PVR and may lessen greatly after birth as the PVR diminishes. In addition, this high vascular resistance imposed upon the functional RV may lead to right-to-left shunting at the atrial level in the presence of a PFO or ASD.

If the infant survives, the RA dilates and its compliance increases, thus enabling the RA to accept a large regurgitant volume with little or no increase in mean pressure. Later in life, PVR may rise again due to a variety of processes, and right-to-left shunting and cyanosis may result.

Clinical Presentation

- Severe Ebstein's anomaly presents in utero or infancy as CHF, cyanosis, and death.
- Many patients experience transient neonatal cyanosis that may recur many years to decades later.
- Among older patients, dyspnea, palpitation, fatigue, and cyanosis are common presentations.
- In more than 25% to 30% of patients, SVT, atrial flutter, AF, or tachycardias associated with accessory pathway conduction are present.
- Uncommon presentations include chest pain, paradoxical embolization, and brain abscess.

Physical Examination

Cyanosis (variable degrees) may be present in 50% to 80% of patients. The arterial and jugular pulses are usually normal.

Auscultation

- The S_1 and S_2 are widely split.
- An S_3 and S_4 are commonly present.
- A systolic murmur of TR is present. The murmur is infrequently greater than grade III intensity. The murmur does not increase with inspiration and classically is decrescendo.

Diagnostic Studies

ECG

Normal sinus rhythm is present in the majority of patients. An atrial arrhythmia may be present in 25% to 30%.

- Preexcitation (usually type B pattern) is manifest in 5% to 25% of patients.
- The P waves are characteristically tall and peaked ("Himalayan").
- The PR interval is usually prolonged; however, it may be shortened if a delta wave is present.
- An RBBB-type conduction defect is present in more than 75% of cases.
- Q waves are present in lead V_1 in over 50% of cases

and may extend out to V_4. Deep Q waves may also be present in the inferior leads.

Chest X-Ray
- Pulmonary vascular markings are normal or diminished. The vascularity is never increased.
- The pulmonary trunk and aortic size are usually small.
- The RA border is usually conspicuous and convexity of the infundibulum often forms a prominent shoulder.

Echocardiography
The echocardiogram is diagnostic.

- The RA is enlarged.
- The septal leaflet of the TV is apically displaced in relation to the MV by greater than 15 to 20 mm.
- The anterior TV leaflet is elongated and redundant.
- Paradoxical septal motion is often present.
- Significant TR is present. The gradient between the functional RV and RA can be measured by Doppler.
- In some cases, a PFO or ASD can be demonstrated.

Treatment

In symptomatic adult patients (or asymptomatic ones with increasing heart size), surgical reconstruction of the TV—with closure of any interatrial communication, plication of the RV free wall, and reduction of RA size—is the procedure of choice.

For significant arrhythmias involving conduction over an accessory pathway, division at the time of surgery or percutaneous catheter ablation is indicated.

CONGENITALLY CORRECTED TRANSPOSITION OF THE GREAT ARTERIES

Corrected transposition of the great arteries occurs in 1/13,000 live births. Males are affected in a 1.5:1 to 2.0:1 ratio as compared to females.

Survival and symptomatic status are most closely related to the exposure of the morphologic RV to the systemic circulation and the presence of left-sided AV valve regurgitation. Beyond infancy, the mortality is 1% to 2% per year. In the absence of significant associated lesions, patients may survive to adulthood.

Anatomy

In congenitally corrected transposition of the great arteries, the atrial and ventricular morphological structures and those of the ventricles and great arteries arising from them are discordant.

- The morphologic RV—defined by crescent shape, presence of a moderator band, coarse trabeculations, more apical insertion of the AV valve, and discontinuity between the AV valve and the great artery—is on the left side and is followed by the anatomic TV.
- The morphologic LV—defined by ovoid/ellipsoid shape, fine apical trabeculations, and fibrous continuity between the AV valve and the great artery—is on the right side and is followed by the anatomic MV.
- The anatomic RA—receiving systemic venous blood—is in continuity with the morphologic LV from which the pulmonary trunk arises.
- The anatomic LA—receiving pulmonary venous blood—is in continuity with the morphologic RV from which the aorta arises.

The aorta is located anterior and leftward in relation to the pulmonary trunk. The aorta and PA are parallel to each other and do not cross as in the normal heart.

Associated Defects
Associated defects are common:

- A nonrestrictive perimembranous VSD is present in over 70% of cases.
- PS or obstruction to pulmonary outflow at other levels is present in 50% of cases.
- Dysplasia of the TV is often present.
- Ebstein's anomaly of the left-sided (tricuspid) AV valve occurs in 25% of cases.
- The AV conduction system is structurally and functionally abnormal. The His bundle is elongated

and relatively nonbranching. Progressive fibrosis of the conduction system occurs with age.

Physiology

The transposition of the circulation is "corrected" because systemic venous blood returns to a morphologic RA, traverses an MV and morphologic LV to reach the pulmonary circulation, while pulmonary venous blood returns to a morphologic LA, traverses a TV, and reaches the aorta via a morphologic RV. The morphologic RV must hypertrophy to maintain an adequate systemic CO.

The physiologic consequences of congenitally corrected transposition depend heavily on the hemodynamic effects of the coexisting lesions (described above).

Clinical Presentation

The clinical manifestations are varied and depend upon the nature of coexisting lesions.

- Patients with isolated corrected transposition may be asymptomatic for many years.
- Often, the typical clinical consequences of one of the coexisting lesions may bring the patient to clinical attention (see above individual lesions).
- The risk of developing complete AV block is 2%/year. Clinical consequences of advanced AV block (bradycardia, fatigue, syncope, sudden death) may be presenting complaints.

Physical Examination

Findings on physical examination are often those of associated lesions (see above).

The physical appearance is normal unless PS or high PVR and right-to-left shunting causes clubbing and cyanosis.

Findings unique to corrected transposition include:

- Bradycardia (in the presence of AV block).
- A loud, often single S_2 at the second left intercostal space due to closure of the anteriorly located aortic valve.

Diagnostic Studies

ECG

P Waves

- In uncomplicated corrected transposition, P wave morphology and axis is normal.
- With pulmonary HTN, tall, peaked P waves occur.
- In the presence of a significant left-to-right shunt or left-sided AV-valve regurgitation, broad and notched P waves occur.

AV Conduction AV conduction abnormalities are common. These may range from first-degree AV block to complete AV block. When second-degree AV block is present, a 2:1 conduction ratio is usually observed.

Q Waves Because the left and right bundle branches are inverted (follow their morphologic ventricle), septal activation occurs from right to left. In this situation, Q waves are conspicuously absent in leads V_{5-6}, I, and aVL and common in the right precordial leads. The presence of Q waves in leads III and aVF and left axis deviation are also common findings. Positive concordance of the precordial T waves is observed in 80% of cases.

Chest X-Ray

Heart size and pulmonary vascular markings depend upon the presence of coexisting lesions. Because the ascending aorta has anterior and leftward displacement, the left superior cardiac border is often straightened or convex on the PA projection.

Echocardiography

1. The morphologic RV with its TV, the morphologic LV with its MV, and the relationship of the great arteries to the ventricles are readily identified.
2. The parasternal short-axis image shows "double circles" which represent the anterior and leftwardly displaced aorta and posteromedial pulmonary trunk in cross-section.

3. The apical long-axis projection shows the aorta and pulmonary trunk rising in parallel to one another.
4. Associated lesions can be identified.

Treatment

- Artificial pacing should be instituted for patients with symptomatic AV block.
- Associated lesions are managed as described above for each individual lesion.

SUGGESTED READINGS

Baum VC. The adult patient with congenital heart disease. J Cardiothorac Vasc Anesth 1996;10:261–282.

Chen CR, Cheng TO, Huang T, et al. Percutaneous balloon valvuloplasty for pulmonic stenosis in adolescents and adults. N Engl J Med 1996;335:21–25.

Connelly MS, Liu PP, Williams WG, et al. Congenitally corrected transposition of the great arteries in the adult: functional status and complications. J Am Coll Cardiol 1996;27:1238–1243.

Dhar PK, Fyfe DA, Sharma S. Multiplane transesophageal echocardiographic evaluation of defects of the atrioventricular septum: the crux of the matter. Echocardiography 1996;13:663–676.

Foster E. Congenital heart disease in adults. West J Med 1995;163:492–498.

Heller J, Hagege AA, Besse B, et al. "Crochetage" (notch) on R wave in inferior limb leads: a new independent electrocardiographic sign of atrial septal defect. J Am Coll Cardiol 1996;27:877–882.

Moss AJ, Adams FH. Heart disease in infants, children, and adolescents. 5th ed. Baltimore: Williams & Wilkins, 1995.

Perloff JK. The clinical recognition of congenital heart disease. 4th ed. Philadelphia: WB Saunders, 1994.

Perloff JK. Congenital heart disease and pregnancy. Clin Cardiol 1994;17:579–587.

Perloff JK, Child JS. Congenital heart disease in adults. Philadelphia: WB Saunders, 1991.

Diseases of the Aorta

Dennis A. Tighe
Howard H. Weitz
Edward K. Chung

The aorta is composed of three layers: the thin inner lining (intima), the elastic media, and the outer adventitia. The aorta has great tensile strength, but is also elastic and distensible. Anatomically it is divided into its abdominal and thoracic portions. A number of disease processes can affect this most important blood vessel. This chapter reviews these disease processes, their diagnosis, and management.

ABDOMINAL AORTIC ANEURYSM (AAA)

Etiology and Pathology

Disruption of the medial elastic component of the aorta, causing weakness of the vessel wall and subsequent aortic dilatation, is almost always the cause of aneurysms of the abdominal aorta.

Atherosclerosis is the most common etiology. Aortic trauma, congenital disorders of connective tissue, and aortitis are less common etiologies. Smoking and HTN increase the risk of AAA formation.

Seventy-five percent of all aortic aneurysms occur in the abdominal aorta. Greater than 90% of these are confined to the region inferior to the origin of the renal arteries. AAAs often extend to the aortic bifurcation and may involve the iliac arteries.

- Aneurysms are usually fusiform (rarely saccular).
- With increasing size and wall tension, the aneurysm may rupture.
- Associated thrombus formation adjacent to the internal wall is common.

Diagnosis

History

Men are three to four times more likely to have an AAA than are women. The typical patient is an elderly man with associated atherosclerotic vascular disease.

- Most patients are asymptomatic.
- Awareness of a pulsating abdominal mass or abdominal fullness suggests a large aneurysm.
- Back, abdominal, flank, or leg pain may indicate aneurysm expansion and impending rupture.
- Sudden abdominal or back pain followed by hypotension strongly suggests aneurysm rupture.

Physical Examination

A palpable, pulsatile, periumbilical mass to the left of midline is characteristic. *Caution:* Excessive palpation of a rapidly expanding aneurysm may cause rupture.

- An abdominal bruit may be heard.
- The femoral pulses may be diminished or absent due to vascular compromise from the aneurysm and/or preexisting peripheral vascular disease.

Rupture Aneurysm rupture is usually associated with evidence of hemorrhagic shock.

- Rupture into the retroperitoneum may be accompanied by flank ecchymosis.
- If rupture occurs into the abdominal cavity, abdominal distention may be present.
- Rupture may rarely occur into the duodenum, resulting in massive GI bleeding.

Diagnostic Studies

Abdominal X-Ray Abdominal x-ray (cross-table lateral view) may demonstrate the configuration of the aneurysm when its wall is calcified (eggshell pattern).

Ultrasound Ultrasound is the most convenient and cost-effective noninvasive technique to document the presence of an aneurysm. It is the study of choice for serial evaluation.

Computed Tomography (CT) CT is an excellent technique for demonstrating AAA size, location, and relationship to surrounding structures.

Magnetic Resonance Imaging (MRI) MRI has similar accuracy to ultrasound and CT in quantification of aneurysm size, but is much more accurate in determining the presence of associated vascular disease. MRI is usually capable of providing the necessary preoperative information for AAA repair.

Aortography Aortography is used to detect and evaluate coexisting vascular disease that may affect the surgical repair. Aortography is currently performed in most centers as a routine study prior to surgery.

- Aortography is less accurate than noninvasive imaging techniques in determining aneurysm size because the presence of intraluminal thrombus may make the aneurysm diameter appear smaller.

As availability and experience with MRI and high-resolution CT scanning increase, the use of preoperative aortography will likely decrease.

Natural History

AAAs enlarge, on average, by 0.2 to 0.5 cm per year. The rate of expansion for an individual patient is highly variable and difficult to predict.

The risk of rupture is directly related to aneurysm diameter. When the aneurysm diameter exceeds 5 cm, the risk of rupture is significantly increased. When the aneurysm becomes symptomatic, mortality significantly increases.

Treatment

Figure 10-1 charts the treatment options for AAAs.

Nonsurgical Treatment

For AAAs less than 4.5–5 cm diameter, noninvasive evaluation of aneurysm size every 6 months is indicated.

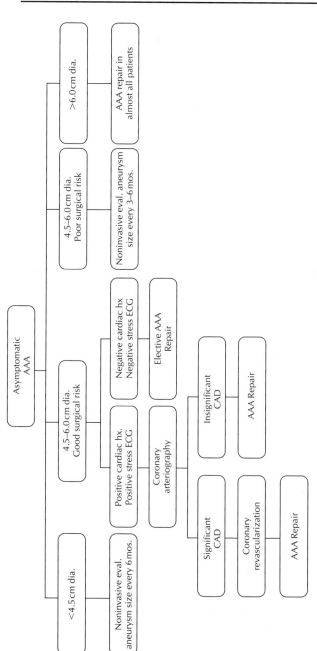

Figure 10-1. Treatment of Asymptomatic Abdominal Aortic Aneurysms

Control of HTN (see Chapter 5) and modification of other cardiac risk factors should be implemented.

Surgical Treatment

Elective Repair   Elective aneurysm repair is indicated among patients with aneurysms ≥5cm diameter if they are otherwise healthy and the risk of surgery is estimated to be low. Operative mortality of elective surgery is 4% to 6%.

If the patient has coexisting medical problems that increase the risk of surgery, noninvasive imaging of the AAA should be performed at least every 6 months—surgery is performed when there is evidence of aneurysm expansion.

Coexisting CAD   Approximately 60% of patients considered for AAA repair have coexisting significant CAD. MI is the leading cause of perioperative death. Appropriate pre-operative evaluation as detailed in Chapter 16 is suggested prior to surgery.

Surgical Complications   Potential complications early after elective aneurysm repair include:

Myocardial ischemia
CHF
Arrhythmias
Renal failure
Bleeding
Pulmonary insufficiency
Distal vascular ischemia/embolism
Wound infection

Late complications of surgical aneurysm repair include:

Graft occlusion
Infection
False aneurysm formation
Enteric fistula formation

A possible alternative to surgery for infrarenal AAA is the endoluminal stent-graft prosthesis. At present, clinical trials of this system are ongoing. Long-term follow-up data are lacking as is a randomized, controlled trial comparing this treatment to surgical repair.

Emergency Repair Ruptured abdominal aneurysms are surgical emergencies which require immediate repair. Ruptured AAA is associated with a 50% perioperative mortality.

THORACIC AORTIC ANEURYSM (TAA)

Pathology and Etiology

Thoracic aortic aneurysms (TAA) are much less common than AAAs.

Descending aorta. The descending thoracic aorta is the most common location.
- Atherosclerosis is the most common etiology.
- Trauma is a much less frequent etiology.

Ascending aorta. The ascending aorta is the next most common site.
- Cystic medial necrosis (due to Marfan's syndrome, other connective tissue diseases, or idiopathic) is the most frequent etiology.
- Less common causes include syphilis, infectious aortitis, and giant cell arteritis.

Diagnosis

History

Approximately 40% to 50% of patients are asymptomatic. Symptoms are usually a result of compression of adjacent structures by the expanding aneurysm. Symptoms due to local compression depend on the site of aortic involvement:

- Ascending aorta: chest pain, SVC syndrome
- Aortic arch or descending aorta: dysphagia (esophageal compression), hoarseness (recurrent laryngeal nerve compression), cough or dyspnea (trachea or lung compression)

Aneurysm enlargement may cause erosion of adjacent ribs, the sternum, or vertebral column, producing chest and/or back pain. Acute, severe pain is often a premonitory symptom of aneurysm rupture.

Physical Examination

Physical findings depend upon the location of the aneurysm and its size:

- Aneurysms of the ascending aorta may extend to the aortic root and result in AR.
- Aneurysms of the aortic arch may exhibit pulsations above the suprasternal notch.
- Aneurysms confined to the descending aorta often have no characteristic physical findings.

Diagnostic Studies

Chest X-Ray Although smaller-sized aneurysms may not be evident, CXR can identify thoracic aortic dilatation and calcification. Mediastinal widening and enlargement of the aortic knob may indicate the presence of an aneurysm.

CT and MRI CT scanning with IV contrast material and MRI are effective techniques for:

- Demonstrating aneurysm size.
- Finding intraluminal thrombus.
- Documenting compression and/or erosion of adjacent structures.

MRI (with angiography) may be preferred because it:

1. Does not require administration of contrast dye.
2. Has better sensitivity.
3. Can study the great vessels and assess AR.

Echocardiography

Transthoracic (TTE) TTE is reliable only for aneurysms involving the most proximal portion (aortic sinuses and adjacent tubular portion) of the ascending aorta. It is a superior technique to evaluate for AR.

Transesophageal (TEE) TEE is a more reliable method to evaluate the thoracic aorta. TEE is useful in the diagnosis of aneurysms involving the ascending aorta, distal aortic arch, and descending thoracic aorta.

Angiography Angiography remains the gold standard in some centers for evaluation prior to surgical repair primarily because of its ability to define the status of associated vascular structures.

Natural History

The natural history of TAAs is poorly defined.

- Aneurysms ≥ 6.0 to 7 cm diameter, as well as those that are symptomatic, are most likely to rupture.
- Patients with asymptomatic TAA have been shown to have a 58%, 5-year survival rate compared to 27% in patients with symptoms (approximately one-third of deaths are due to aneurysm rupture).

Recent data in patients with mild to moderate aortic root dilatation due to Marfan's syndrome indicate that prophylactic therapy with beta-blockers can slow the progression of aortic dilatation and aortic complications.

Treatment

Surgery

Surgical resection and replacement with a prosthetic graft is the treatment of choice for symptomatic aneurysms of the ascending or descending thoracic aorta of any size or those ≥ 5.5 cm diameter if asymptomatic. Surgery has a 90% survival rate when performed on an elective basis. Repair of aneurysms involving the aortic arch is associated with greater surgical risk because reimplantation of the great vessels is also required.

- Some experts recommend surgery for patients with Marfan's syndrome when the aneurysm reaches 5.0 cm diameter.
- When proximal aortic aneurysms extend to the aortic annulus and result in AR, a composite graft with prosthetic aortic valve is usually implanted.

Complications Complications associated with thoracic aneurysmectomy include:

Paraplegia due to anterior spinal artery ischemia (up to 5% incidence)
MI
Stroke
Renal insufficiency

Surgical Alternatives

An alternative to surgical repair of descending TAA is transluminal placement of an endovascular stent-graft.

As with endovascular stent-graft placement in the abdominal aorta, clinical experience is limited and long-term follow-up data are not available.

Long-Term Treatment

Long-term treatment includes close clinical follow-up for aneurysm recurrence (including serial imaging studies every 12 months) and treatment with beta-blockers to reduce aortic shearing forces.

AORTIC DISSECTION

Aortic dissection is characterized by a tear in the intimal lining of the aorta with disruption of the media by a hematoma. The dissecting hematoma may remain confined to the media, reenter the aortic lumen through a separate intimal tear, or rupture the adventitia.

Classification of aortic dissection is based upon location of the intimal tear and extent of dissection (Table 10-1).

Etiology

Degenerative changes of the aortic media are associated with most cases of aortic dissection. Predisposing factors for dissection include:

Table 10-1. Classification of Aortic Dissection

DeBakey Classification	
Type I (proximal)	Dissection originates in and extends beyond the ascending aorta.
Type II (proximal)	Dissection originates in and is confined to the ascending aorta.
Type IIIA (distal)	Dissection limited to the descending thoracic aorta.
Type IIIB (distal)	Dissection originates in the descending thoracic aorta and extends below the diaphragm.
Dailey (Stanford) Classification	
Type A (proximal)	Dissection involves the ascending aorta and/or arch regardless of site of intimal tear. May or may not extend to involve the descending thoracic aorta.
Type B (distal)	Dissection limited to descending thoracic aorta.

HTN (70% to 90% of cases)

Collagen vascular diseases (associated with proximal dissection)

Marfan's syndrome

Cystic medial necrosis

Coarctation of the aorta

Bicuspid aortic valve

Third trimester pregnancy

Chest trauma

An increasing incidence of aortic dissection following aortic instrumentation or the manipulation of cardiac surgery is being reported.

Pathophysiology

Dissection is presumed to be initiated by either an intimal disruption followed by propagation of blood into the media or an initial spontaneous hemorrhage into an abnormal media. A false channel is created between the intima and adventitia, which may extend, reenter the intima through another tear, or rupture through the adventitia (usually into the pericardium or left pleural space).

- Propagation of dissection may compress vessels that arise from the aorta or great veins or may extend in a retrograde direction to the aortic root and annulus leading to AR and cardiac tamponade.
- Rupture into the pericardial space can cause cardiac tamponade and rupture into the left pleural space can lead to hemorrhagic shock.
- Increased systemic BP contributes to propagation of dissection.

Diagnosis

History

Pain Acute, severe pain, which is maximum at its onset, is present in >90% of patients.

- With proximal dissection, pain is usually localized to the anterior chest.
- With more distal dissection pain may be migratory, felt in the back and interscapular area.

- If progressive, dissection pain may extend to the abdomen, legs, and flank.

Neurologic Symptoms Neurologic symptoms are common.

- Stroke may occur if the aortic arch and great vessels are involved.
- Paraplegia may result if intercostal or spinal arteries are compromised.

Cardiac Symptoms The diagnosis of aortic dissection should be strongly suspected in any patient with chest discomfort, especially with a history of HTN, in whom the ECG is normal and the chest pain is not responding to standard therapy for cardiac ischemia.

- Syncope is rare.
- Symptoms of CHF may be present if acute AR develops.

Differential Diagnoses The differential diagnosis of abrupt onset chest or back pain suggesting acute aortic dissection should include penetrating aortic ulcer and intramural hematoma of the thoracic aorta. Both conditions are most common in an older, hypertensive population. Therapy and follow-up of these patients are similar to those employed for aortic dissection (see below).

- **Penetrating aortic ulcer.** Penetrating aortic ulcer is characterized by atherosclerotic ulceration penetrating into the wall of the descending thoracic aorta (most common), which can remain stable or lead to medial disruption, hematoma formation, adventitial rupture, and dissection.
- **Intramural hematoma.** Intramural hematoma of the thoracic aorta is characterized by spontaneous and localized hemorrhage into the wall of the aorta without evidence of an intimal tear or penetrating aortic ulcer.

Physical Examination
Patients typically appear acutely ill.

- BP may be normal, elevated from stress or involvement of the renal vessels, or decreased from aortic rupture or cardiac tamponade. In 50% of cases involving the proximal aorta, BP is decreased in one (usually the right) or both arms, and pulse deficits occur due to compromise of the innominate or subclavian arteries. Inequality of carotid and peripheral pulses may be observed.

- AR is present in 50% of proximal dissections. Left pleural effusion may occur with aortic rupture.
- Signs of an acute abdomen occur when distal dissection compromises splanchnic blood flow causing bowel ischemia.
- Jugular venous distention and paradoxical pulse may occur when dissection leads to cardiac tamponade. Isolated jugular venous distention may be present if compression of the SVC occurs.
- Horner's syndrome, due to compression of the superior cervical sympathetic ganglion, or vocal chord paralysis secondary to left recurrent laryngeal nerve compression, may occur with proximal dissection.

Diagnostic Tests

ECG ECG is usually unremarkable; therefore, acute dissection must be highly suspected in the setting of severe, sudden chest pain and a normal ECG. Rarely, proximal dissection may involve the right coronary artery with ECG findings of an inferior MI.

Chest X-Ray Comparison with a previous CXR, if available, can be crucial because subtle changes may be present. CXR reveals widening of the thoracic aorta in 90% of patients, but the CXR may be normal or minimally abnormal in up to 18% of cases.

- The aortic contour may appear irregular or a discrepancy in the sizes of the ascending and descending thoracic aorta may be present.
- If the aortic knob is calcified, separation of the inner aortic margin from the outer edge of the aortic shadow by more than 1 cm strongly suggests dissection.
- A left pleural effusion suggests rupture into this space.

Aortography Aortography was formerly considered the gold standard for diagnosis of dissection. Because its accuracy is 90%, it is still performed in many centers when dissection is suspected.

Aortography advantages It furnishes anatomical information that is crucial in planning therapy, including:

Extent of dissection
Site of intimal tear
Quantification of AR
Status of vasculature that arises from the aorta

Aortography disadvantages False-negative angio-grams may occur in these situations:

Complete thrombosis of the false lumen
Equal and simultaneous opacification of the true and
    false lumens
Intramural hematoma
Inadequate testing technique

Echocardiography

TTE TTE has a diagnostic accuracy of approximately 80% for proximal dissection, but its sensitivity is limited in the diagnosis of distal dissection.

TEE TEE has become the procedure of choice for the diagnosis of acute aortic dissection in many institutions. It has a sensitivity of 98% to 100% and a specificity exceeding 90%.

TEE Advantages
1. The primary advantage of TEE is that it is portable and can be performed safely within 15 minutes in this critically ill patient group.
2. TEE can accurately identify the dissection "flap," site of entry, and the true and false lumens.
3. TEE can quantitate AR.
4. TEE can evaluate for pericardial effusion and proximal coronary artery involvement.

TEE Disadvantages
1. TEE is limited by the "blind spot" created by the air-filled left mainstem bronchus which overlies and obscures a portion of the distal ascending aorta.

2. TEE cannot consistently image the arch vessels.
3. TEE is subject to reverberation artifacts.
4. TEE requires esophageal intubation and sedation.

Computed Tomography (CT) CT with contrast enhancement has a sensitivity of 83% to 90% and a specificity of 87%.

CT advantages

1. In many smaller centers, CT is the most readily available and accurate diagnostic test to evaluate for suspected aortic dissection.
2. CT is very useful in the long-term follow-up of treated patients.

CT disadvantages

1. CT cannot evaluate for the presence and severity of AR.
2. CT cannot determine the extent of peripheral arterial involvement.
3. CT cannot define the site of intimal tear.

Magnetic Resonance Imaging (MRI) MRI is the most sensitive (99% to 100%) and specific (97% to 99%) technique. It is an excellent test to diagnose dissection in hemodynamically stable patients.

MRI advantages

1. MRI can assess for pericardial effusion and AR.
2. MRI can identify abnormalities of the aortic arterial branches and the site of intimal tear.
3. MRI is an excellent study for long-term follow-up of patients with treated, as well as chronic, dissection.

MRI disadvantages

1. Critically ill patients need to be transported to the MRI scanner.
2. MRI has a relatively long imaging sequence (up to 45 minutes).
3. MRI is expensive.
4. MRI has only limited availability.

A summary of the diagnostic performance of the major imaging modalities for the diagnosis of suspected aortic dissection is presented in Table 10-2.

Table 10-2. Summary of the Diagnostic Performance of the Major Imaging Techniques for the Evaluation of Suspected Aortic Dissection

Variable	Aortography	CT	MRI	TEE
Sensitivity	++	++	+++	+++
Specificity	+++	+++	+++	++/+++
Site of intimal tear	++	+	+++	++
Presence of thrombus	+++	++	+++	+
Presence of aortic insufficiency	+++	−	+	+++
Pericardial effusion	−	++	+++	+++
Branch vessel involvement	+++	+	++	+
Coronary artery involvement	++	−	−	++

TEE denotes transesophageal echocardiography; +++ denotes excellent results; ++ denotes good results; + denotes fair results; − is not detected. Reproduced with permission from: Cigarroa JE, Isselbacher EM, DeSanctis RW, Eagle KA. Diagnostic imaging in the evaluation of suspected aortic dissection. N Engl J Med 1993;328:42. Copyright 1993 Massachusetts Medical Society. All rights reserved.

Natural History

Untreated Aortic Dissection

Untreated aortic dissection has a mortality rate following onset of:

25% by 24 hours
50% within 1 week
75% within 3 months

The 10-year survival of patients treated both medically and surgically is approximately 40%.

Treatment

Treatment (Fig 10-2) consists of three phases:

1. Initial emergency care
2. Definitive therapy
3. Long-term care and follow-up

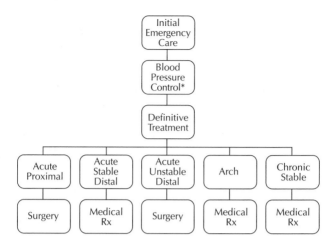

*Systolic blood pressure should be lowered to 100–120 mm Hg or to the lowest level possible to maintain vital organ perfusion. See text for details.

Figure 10-2. Treatment of Aortic Dissection

Emergency Care

Initial care is the same for all dissections regardless of location. Therapy is directed toward acutely reducing the factors that serve to propagate the dissection: systemic BP and the rate of rise of velocity (dV/dt) of LV ejection.

Ideally, SBP should be lowered to 100 to 120 mm Hg or to the lowest level compatible with vital organ perfusion if the patient has chronic HTN.

Sodium Nitroprusside Sodium nitroprusside infusion, starting at a dosage of 0.5 μg/kg/min and titrated to BP and adequate vital organ perfusion, is the initial treatment of choice.

• **Beta-blockade:** Because nitroprusside is a potent vasodilator and leads to an increase in dV/dt, simultaneous administration of beta-blockers is required (goal: resting HR of 60 to 80 beats per minute). Propranolol, or an equivalent IV beta-blocker, at an initial dose of 0.5–1.0 mg IV, is administered every 5 minutes (maximum dose 0.15 mg/kg) until adequate beta-blockade is achieved; and then 1.0–4.0 mg IV or 20–60 mg by mouth every 6 hours is given to maintain effective beta-blockade. Other effective beta-blockers include metoprolol, labetolol, and esmolol.

Trimethaphan If nitroprusside is ineffective or contraindications to the use of beta-blockers exist, trimethaphan (Arfonad), infused at a rate of 1 mg/min and titrated to maintain SBP at 100 to 120 mm Hg, may be used. Trimethaphan acts by decreasing both BP and dV/dt, making coadministration of beta-blockers unnecessary.

Side effects: Severe orthostasis, somnolence, ileus, urinary retention, and rapid tachyphylaxis.

Reserpine Reserpine (rarely used today) is a third choice to decrease BP and dV/dt. The dosage is 1.0–2.0 mg IM every 4 to 6 hours.

Definitive Treatment
Definitive therapy depends upon the location of the dissection and its chronicity.

Patients presenting within 2 weeks of symptom onset are considered to have acute dissection.
Patients presenting after 2 weeks are considered to have a chronic dissection.

• **Acute proximal dissection.** Acute proximal dissection is best treated with surgery. Surgical repair includes resection of the intimal tear, obliteration of the false lumen, and repair of the aorta often with the use of a synthetic vascular graft. When the aortic root or aortic valve annulus is involved, replacement of the root and valve is accomplished with insertion of a composite conduit (prosthetic aortic valve and synthetic aortic root) and reimplantation of the coronary arteries.
• **Stable acute distal dissection.** Stable and uncomplicated acute distal dissection is best treated with long-term medical therapy designed to reduce SBP and dV/dt.
• **Unstable acute distal dissection.** Unstable or complicated acute distal dissection (aortic leakage, rupture, continued pain despite adequate BP control, extension, compromise of vital organ perfusion, or in the presence

of Marfan syndrome) is an indication for surgical therapy.

• **Stable isolated arch dissection.** A stable isolated arch dissection should be treated with medicine to control BP and dV/dt because of the high risk associated with surgery.

• **Stable chronic aortic dissection.** Stable, uncomplicated, chronic aortic dissection at any level of the aorta should be treated medically.

Long-Term Care and Follow-Up

Follow-up is directed toward optimization of medical therapy and identification of late complications such as AR, aneurysm formation, and redissection.

Pharmacologic Therapy

Chronic medical therapy with beta-blockers to decrease aortic shearing forces and with additional antihypertensive therapy as necessary to maintain SBP less than 130 mm Hg is mandatory for all patients, including those who have undergone surgical repair.

If antihypertensive drugs that increase CO and dV/dt are used (hydralazine, minoxidil), then aggressive beta-blockade is indicated.

Follow-Up Imaging Studies

• CXR every 3 months for 1 year, then twice yearly thereafter.
• CT or MRI scanning is indicated if a late complication is suspected. CT or MRI should be performed as part of routine follow-up at a frequency of 2 times during the first year, and then 1 to 2 times per year thereafter.

AORTIC ATHEROMATOUS DISEASE

As many as 40% of cases of cerebral infarction are reported to have an undetermined cause. Among autopsy specimens of patients with ischemic stroke—and especially among those with cerebral infarction of unknown cause—are found a high incidence of ulcerated plaques involving the aortic arch. These plaques are predominantly found in patients older than 60 years.

Emboli from these plaques may be of three types: cholesterol emboli, atheromatous emboli, and thrombus.

Atheromatous Plaque Risks

Atheromatous plaques may be disturbed during invasive aortic procedures (cardiac catheterization, aortography, balloon pumping) or may spontaneously dislodge with anticoagulation or thrombolytic therapy to cause embolization to distal vascular beds and ischemic symptoms.

- With the widespread use of TEE, atheromatous debris in the aortic arch has become increasingly recognized as a risk factor for ischemic stroke and possible source of cerebral (and peripheral) emboli.
- The risk association is strongest among patients with plaque thickness ≥ 4 mm (which may contain superimposed thrombotic material).
- Mobile and protruding elements appear to carry increased risk as well.

Detection

For detecting atherosclerosis of the ascending aorta and its arch, TEE is the procedure of choice. At the time of heart surgery, epiaortic ultrasound and TEE are superior (and complementary) methods, as compared to manual palpation by the surgeon.

Treatment

The precise management of protruding aortic atheromata is not certain for all patients.

- Patients with thrombi or mobile elements (likely to contain thrombus) may benefit from long-term anticoagulation to reduce future embolic risk. This recommendation is based on observations of a small number of patients in whom repeat TEE documented a reduction in size or disappearance of atheromata without further (clinically apparent) embolic events while the patients were on warfarin.
- The value of antiplatelet agents in this situation is not known.

- Treatment to decrease lipid levels may be prudent, but this remains unproved in this situation.
- Aortic endarterectomy and graft replacement of the ascending aorta has been performed in highly selected cases.

TRAUMATIC AORTIC INJURY

See Chapter 15.

AORTIC ARTERITIS SYNDROMES

Takayasu's Arteritis (Pulseless Disease)

Pathophysiology

Takayasu's arteritis most often involves the aortic arch and its major branches. It is characterized by marked intimal proliferation and fibrotic scarring. Vascular involvement may be segmental, with areas of normal appearing artery separating affected sites. Three types of Takayasu's arteritis are recognized:

Type 1. Characterized by involvement of the aortic arch and its branches.

Type 2. Arteritis involving the thoracoabdominal aorta with sparing of the aortic arch.

Type 3. Characterized by involvement of both the aortic arch and the thoracoabdominal aorta.

Clinical Features

Most reported clinical series of Takayasu's arteritis are from Asia. The disease is eight times more common in women as compared to men. Onset is frequently in the teenage years, and nearly all cases occur in patients less than 40 years old.

- Systemic complaints of fever, fatigue, anorexia, weight loss, and pleuritic-type pain are present in ≥50% of patients.
- Diminished or absent pulses, vascular bruits, and decreased BP in the upper extremities associated with normal BP and pulse contour in the lower extremities ("reversed coarctation") occur in >90% of patients with disease types 1 and 3.

- HTN (due to involvement of the renal arteries),
  abdominal angina, and claudication occur in patients
  with type 2 disease. HTN may also occur secondary
  to acquired aortic coarctation.
- CHF may occur and is usually a consequence of long-
  standing, severe HTN. Angina pectoris or MI may
  occur with coronary artery involvement.

Diagnosis

Clinical diagnosis is based on patient age (≤40 years old
is an obligatory criterion) and the presence of either 2
major criteria; 1 major and 2 minor criteria; or 4 minor
criteria (Table 10-3).

- The ESR is elevated.
- Mild leukocytosis and anemia of chronic disease are
  common.

Table 10-3. Proposed Criteria for the Clinical Diagnosis of
Takayasu's Disease

Obligatory criterion
  Age ≤40 years
Two major criteria
  1. Left mid-subclavian artery lesion by angiography
  2. Right mid-subclavian artery lesion by angiography
Nine minor criteria
  1. High ESR (≥20 mm/hr with Westergren method)
  2. Carotid artery tenderness
  3. HTN (persistent brachial blood pressure ≥140/90 mm Hg or a
     history of HTN prior to age 40)
  4. AR or annuloaortic ectasia
  5. Pulmonary artery lesion by angiography or scintigraphy
  6. Left mid common carotid lesion by angiography
  7. Distal brachiocephalic trunk lesion by angiography
  8. Descending thoracic aorta lesion by angiography
  9. Abdominal aorta lesion by angiography
In addition to the obligatory criterion, the presence of
  2 major criteria,
  1 major and ≥2 minor criteria, or
  4 or more minor criteria
highly suggests the diagnosis of Takayasu's disease.

Adapted with permission from the American College of Cardiology. From:
Ishikawa K. Diagnostic approach and proposed criteria for the clinical
diagnosis of Takayasu's arteriopathy. J Am Coll Cardiol 1988;12:964–972.

- CXR may show aortic or arterial calcification.
- Aortography reveals a narrowed thoracic aorta with characteristic "rat-tail" appearance, saccular aneurysms, vessel stenosis or occlusion, and poststenotic vessel dilatation.

Therapy

Corticosteroids relieve constitutional symptoms and may halt disease progression.

- Cyclophosphamide is often added to steroid therapy in cases of documented disease progression.
- Medical therapy of HTN is important to prevent CHF and strokes.

Surgery (including bypass, aneurysm resection, or endarterectomy) may be required in some cases to maintain adequate perfusion.

Giant Cell (Temporal) Arteritis

Pathophysiology

Giant cell arteritis is characterized by granulomatous inflammation of the media of small and medium-sized arteries of the head and neck.

- The aorta and its major branches can be involved in 15% of cases.
- Aneurysms of the thoracic aorta may occur in up to 15% of cases.
- Symptomatic AR or aortic dissection may also occur.

Clinical Features

Giant cell arteritis is most common in women older than 50 years of age. It presents with classic constitutional symptoms (anorexia, weight loss), headache, fever, and malaise.

- Jaw claudication with chewing occurs in up to 70% of patients.
- Visual symptoms, which may progress to irreversible blindness, occur in 25% to 50% of patients.
- Multiple rheumatologic complaints (polymyalgia rheumatica) occur in 40% of patients.
- Aortic involvement is suggested by claudication,

coronary ischemia, and transient ischemic attacks. The renal arteries are almost never involved.

Diagnosis

A high index of clinical suspicion is required.

- Very elevated ESR is invariably present.
- Normochromic, normocytic anemia is common.
- Temporal artery biopsy is diagnostic. In 15% of cases, a second biopsy is required to make the diagnosis.

Therapy

High-dose corticosteroid therapy (prednisone, 60–80 mg per day) is recommended in all patients.

- The ESR is followed closely as a marker of disease activity and adequacy of therapy. The steroid dose can be gradually tapered, depending upon clinical disease activity and the ESR.
- Methotrexate may be required in steroid-resistant cases.
- Surgery may be required for patients developing TAA.

CARDIOVASCULAR SYPHILIS

Epidemiology and Natural History

Cardiovascular syphilis is now considered a rare entity. Earlier in the 20th century, the prevalence of syphilis was much higher and evidence of cardiovascular involvement at autopsy ranged from 0.76% to 6.9%.

Aortitis

Aortitis is the most common manifestation, occurring in 70% to 80% of patients with untreated syphilis. Aortitis and its complications (AR, aortic aneurysm, ostial coronary artery stenoses) usually manifest 10 to 25 years after primary infection.

Pathology

With aortitis spirochetal organisms disseminate hematogenously and lodge within the vasa vasorum of the aortic adventitia. Inflammatory changes occur initially; over time, damage occurs:

Obliterative endarteritis
Adventitial scarring
Medical necrosis with destruction of elastic fibers

These changes cause progressive weakening and calcification ("eggshell") of the aortic wall. The predilection for proximal involvement is explained by the larger number of vasa vasora in the ascending aorta and arch.

Clinical Manifestations

Asymptomatic Aortitis

Asymptomatic dilatation of the aortic root and proximal aorta is the most common manifestation of aortitis.

- Linear calcification of the ascending aorta detected on CXR involves the anterolateral wall in 20% of patients and is a useful diagnostic sign.
- The VDRL test is reactive in only 40% of cases, but specific treponemal tests (FTA-ABS and MHA-TP) are 94% to 100% sensitive.

Aortic Regurgitation

AR as a result of aortic root dilatation occurs in 20% to 30% of cases.

- Approximately 20% of patients have associated ostial coronary stenosis.
- The diastolic blowing murmur of syphilitic AR is best heard along the right sternal border.
- Medical and/or surgical therapy should be employed as indicated in other patients with AR (see Chapter 6).

Aortic Aneurysm

Syphilitic aneurysm is the least common complication of aortitis. The aneurysms are usually saccular. The wall of the aneurysm is characteristically thick and fibrotic and frequently contains laminated thrombus. Aortic dissection is unusual because of the intense fibrosis.

Ostial Coronary Stenosis

Coronary ostial stenosis occurs in 20% of patients with syphilitic aortitis.

- Angina pectoris is the most common clinical manifestation.

- MI is rare.
- Approximately 87% of patients have associated AR.

Therapy

All patients should receive penicillin unless an allergy exists.

Pharmacologic Therapy

The optimal antibiotic regimen has not been determined, but the current recommendation is three weekly IM injections of 2.4 million U of benzathine penicillin G.

Penicillin-allergic patients should receive a 30-day treatment of oral tetracycline, 500 mg four times per day, or doxycycline, 100 mg twice per day.

Surgical Therapy

- Indications for surgical treatment of luetic aneurysm depends on the aneurysm size and symptoms; surgery is similar to that recommended for TAA of any etiology.
- Medical and/or surgical treatment of AR is guided by severity and hemodynamic consequences.
- CABG is the treatment of choice for symptomatic ischemia due to coronary ostial stenosis.

SUGGESTED READINGS

Amarenco P, Cohen A, Tzourio C, et al. Atherosclerotic disease of the aortic arch and the risk of ischemic stroke. N Engl J Med 1994;331:1474–1479.

Applebe AF, Walker PG, Yeoh JK, et al. Clinical significance and origin of artifacts in transesophageal echocardiography of the thoracic aorta. J Am Coll Cardiol 1993;21:754–760.

Blum U, Voshage G, Lammer J, et al. Endoluminal stent-grafts for infrarenal abdominal aortic aneurysms. N Engl J Med 1997;336:13–20.

Cigarroa JE, Isselbacher EM, DeSanctis RW, Eagle KA. Diagnostic imaging in the evaluation of suspected aortic dissection. Old standards and new directions. N Engl J Med 1993;328:35–43.

Cooke JP, Kazmier FJ, Orszulak TA. The penetrating aortic ulcer: pathologic manifestations, diagnosis, and management. Mayo Clin Proc 1988;63:718–725.

Crawford ES. The diagnosis and management of aortic dissection. JAMA 1990;264:2537–2541.

Dake MD, Miller DC, Semba CP, et al. Transluminal placement of endovascular stent-grafts for the treatment of descending thoracic aortic aneurysms. N Engl J Med 1994;331:1729–1734.

Eagle KA, Coney CM, Newall JB, et al. Combining clinical and thallium data optimize preoperative assessment of cardiac risk before major vascular surgery. Ann Intern Med 1989;110:859–866.

Ernst CB. Abdominal aortic aneurysm. N Engl J Med 1993;328:1167–1172.

Ishikawa K. Diagnostic approach and proposed criteria for the clinical diagnosis of Takayasu's arteriopathy. J Am Coll Cardiol 1988;12:964–972.

Jackman JD Jr, Radolf JD. Cardiovascular syphilis. Am J Med 1989;87:425–433.

Kouchoukos NT, Dougenis D. Surgery of the thoracic aorta. N Engl J Med 1997;336:1876–1888.

Kronzon I, Tunick PA. Atheromatous disease of the thoracic aorta: pathologic and clinical implications. Ann Intern Med 1997;126:629–637.

Neinaber CA, Kodolitsch Y, Nicolas V, et al. The diagnosis of thoracic aortic dissection by noninvasive imaging procedures. N Engl J Med 1993;328:1–9.

Nevitt MP, Ballard DJ, Hallett JW Jr. Prognosis of abdominal aortic aneurysms. A population-based study. N Engl J Med 1989;321:1009–1014.

Robbins RC, McManus RP, Mitchell RS, et al. Management of patients with intramural hematoma of the thoracic aorta. Circulation 1993;88 (II):1–10.

Spittel PC, Spittel JA Jr, Joyce JW, et al. Clinical features and differential diagnosis of aortic dissection: experience with 236 cases (1980 through 1990). Mayo Clin Proc 1993;68:642–651.

Peripheral Vascular Disease

Dennis A. Tighe
Howard H. Weitz
Edward K. Chung

Peripheral vascular disease is commonly encountered in patients with cardiac disease. A complete assessment of the peripheral arteries and veins should be part of the comprehensive cardiovascular evaluation. Disease involving the peripheral arteries is oftentimes a marker of underlying CAD. Deep venous thrombosis and its complications are common disease processes associated with significant morbidity and mortality. This chapter provides an overview of common disease processes involving the peripheral arteries and veins.

CHRONIC LOWER EXTREMITY OCCLUSIVE ARTERIAL DISEASE

Epidemiology and Etiology

Atherosclerotic vascular disease of the arteries of the lower extremities is the most common form of peripheral vascular disease. The true prevalence of disease is unknown because it may remain subclinical or minimally symptomatic or its presence may be obscured by the clinical manifestations of CAD or cerebrovascular disease.

It is estimated that 5% of men and 2.5% of women over age 60 years have intermittent claudication. The disease prevalence is estimated to be threefold higher if an ankle-brachial index (see below) less than or equal to

0.9 is considered a marker of disease. Associated risk factors include:

1. Cigarette smoking. The clinical presentation of arterial disease often precedes that in nonsmokers by one decade.
2. Diabetes mellitus.
3. HTN and hyperlipidemia.
4. Age and male gender. The prevalence of arterial disease of the lower extremities increases with age. Its predominance in males diminishes after 70 years of age.

Pathology

The major cause of chronic occlusive arterial disease is atherosclerosis.

- Atherosclerosis primarily affects the large and medium-sized arteries in a segmental fashion. Sites of bifurcation and branch points are most commonly involved. Disease may be present at multiple arterial levels.
- Occlusive disease of the superficial femoral artery (SFA) is the most common symptomatic lesion.
- Tibioperoneal disease affects approximately 40% of patients and is especially common among diabetics.

Natural History

Depending on the disease's severity and the extent of the collateral circulation, chronic lower extremity arterial disease may present as:

Asymptomatic arterial insufficiency
Intermittent claudication
Rest pain or ischemic ulceration

Asymptomatic Arterial Disease
Asymptomatic arterial disease is a marker of atherosclerosis involving other beds, especially the coronary and cerebral circulations.

Intermittent Claudication
Intermittent claudication indicates that blood flow and oxygen delivery to the extremity is sufficient at rest, but

the demand for increased oxygen delivery cannot be met during exertion.

- Among nondiabetics, over 80% to 90% will have stable or improved clinical status over the ensuing 5 years, and less than 5% will require a major amputation.
- Among diabetics, the amputation rate is significantly higher because the arterial disease is more often distal and diffuse.

The major morbidity and mortality of intermittent claudication is that associated with CAD.

Rest Pain or Ischemic Ulceration

Rest pain or ischemic ulceration indicates a more advanced stage in which arterial flow is inadequate to meet the resting metabolic demands of tissues. The risk of amputation is several times higher in this situation.

Clinical Presentation

Intermittent Claudication

Intermittent claudication is typically described as pain in the affected limb during exertion that resolves in a few minutes with rest. Some patients describe aching, fatigue, or heaviness rather than pain.

The site of arterial occlusion may be identified by determining which muscle group(s) is affected because discomfort always occurs distal to the involved artery:

- Disease involving the SFA manifests as calf pain.
- Disease involving the aortoiliac system manifests as thigh, hip, buttocks, and calf pain.
- Disease involving the tibioperoneal vessels manifests as foot and ankle discomfort.
- Diffuse disease involving multiple levels of the vascular tree usually presents as claudication involving the most distal significant lesion or the area with the least well-developed collateral circulation.

Conditions that may be confused with intermittent claudication include:

Musculoskeletal disorders: pseudoclaudication (due to spinal stenosis or lumbosacral radiculopathy) and arthritis of the hip and knee joints.

Nonatherosclerotic causes of leg pain: arterial
embolism, arterial compression by cysts or due to
muscle entrapment, and arteritis.

Ischemic Rest Pain/Ulceration

Ischemic rest pain 1) always involves the foot, 2) is worse
at night, and 3) often is diminished by placing the affected
extremity in a dependent position.

- Gangrene or nonhealing ischemic ulceration may be
  present.
- Diabetic patients with advanced neuropathy may
  have gangrene or ulcerations with minimal pain.

Physical Examination

Limb Appearance

In the absence of rest ischemia, the affected limb of the
patient with intermittent claudication appears healthy
and well perfused at rest.

- Trophic changes, such as dry cool skin, loss of hair,
  and poor nail growth imply significant ischemia.
- Gangrene and cutaneous ulceration (often involving
  the heel and tips of the toes) are observed with
  severe ischemia.

Elevation and dependency of the limb should be used to
estimate pedal perfusion.

1. With the patient supine, the extremity is elevated to
   60° from the horizontal position.
   - No pallor within 60 seconds of elevation implies
     normal perfusion.
   - Pallor that occurs within 60 seconds implies that
     significant arterial occlusive disease is present.
   - Pallor on level is indicative of severe occlusive
     disease.
2. With the limb dependent after elevation, the time for
   color to return and the time for venous refilling are
   measured.
   - If color returns in less than 10 seconds and venous
     refilling occurs within 15 seconds, then ischemia is
     not present.
   - If the time to color return and venous refilling is in
     excess of 40 to 60 seconds, this implies the
     presence of significant limb ischemia.

Peripheral Pulses

Diminished or absent peripheral pulses are key findings. The femoral, popliteal, posterior tibial, and dorsalis pedis pulses should be routinely examined. The dorsalis pedis pulse is normally absent in 10% to 15% of patients, but the posterior tibial pulse is never normally absent.

Bruits

The presence of vascular bruits in the abdomen and over the femoral arteries should be sought.

- The presence of bruits implies upstream limitation to arterial flow.
- Bruits most often occur during systole; however, the presence of a bruit that extends into diastole implies a stenosis approaching 80% of luminal diameter.
- Bruits may be absent when a severely stenotic lesion is present.

Diagnostic Testing

Noninvasive Evaluation

Noninvasive testing is used to obtain objective confirmation of the findings observed during the physical examination.

Ankle-Brachial Index (ABI)
A standard BP cuff and hand-held continuous wave Doppler device are used to measure brachial and ankle SBPs in the supine position. The normal ABI exceeds 1.0 because the ankle pressure is normally higher than the brachial pressure.

- The ABI can be used to grade the severity of arterial insufficiency.
- The ABI can used as a baseline for follow-up purposes.
- Calcification of the tibial and peroneal arteries makes the ABI an unreliable index among diabetics.

Grade	ABI
Normal	≥ 0.95
Mild insufficiency	0.7–0.9
Moderate insufficiency	0.5–0.7
Severe insufficiency	<0.5

Exercise Testing Measurement of supine ankle BP before and following treadmill exercise (2 mph at 12% grade for 5 minutes) can assess the dynamics of intermittent claudication.

- The normal response is an increase or no change in ankle systolic pressure.
- Among patients with intermittent claudication, a fall in ankle systolic pressure of ≥20% compared to baseline requiring ≥3 minutes for recovery is considered abnormal.

Toe Systolic Pressure Index (TSPI) Because medial calcinosis of the tibial system, common in diabetics, does not extend into the digital arteries, it is possible to assess perfusion by measuring the toe systolic pressure. This is accomplished by using either a strain gauge sensor or a photoplethysmograph.

The TSPI is expressed as the ratio of systolic pressure from the toe to that of the arm.

- The normal TSPI is >0.60.
- If the absolute toe systolic pressure is <30 mm Hg, then healing is unlikely to occur without intervention.

Segmental Pressure Measurement The location of arterial disease can be obtained by placing a pneumatic BP cuff at various levels along the limb (ankle, calf, above the knee, upper thigh) to determine systolic pressure. Obstruction is generally present proximal to the level at which pressure drops.

Pulse Volume Recording Pulse volume recordings are often obtained at the time of segmental pressure recordings. Plethysmography is used to evaluate changes in leg volume with each pulse.

- The normal recording is composed of a systolic upstroke with a sharp peak and prominent dicrotic wave on the downslope.
- As the degree of arterial insufficiency worsens, the appearance of the recording becomes increasingly abnormal.

Flow Velocity Determination The presence of a normal appearing triphasic Doppler velocity pattern excludes a hemodynamically significant lesion proximal to the recording site. When the Doppler probe is placed distal to a flow-limiting lesion, the normal triphasic velocity pattern is altered.

Ultrasound Duplex Scanning Duplex scanning, the combination of pulsed Doppler (including color flow) with imaging methods, can identify the site of arterial narrowing and its hemodynamic significance.

Magnetic Resonance Angiography (MRA) In selected centers, MRA appears to be an acceptable alternative to invasive angiography for preoperative assessment of infrainguinal vascular disease.

Contrast Angiography
Angiography is indicated to define the extent and location of arterial disease prior to planned revascularization.

Therapy

The natural history of the disease process should be taken into account when planning therapy. The management depends on the degree of limb ischemia, associated functional impairment, and any comorbid conditions.

Medical therapy is indicated for all patients with disease in whom severe, threatened ischemic limb compromise is not present. The goals of therapy include limiting disease progression, increasing exercise tolerance, protecting ischemic tissue, and improving blood flow.

Exercise Therapy
Regular walking (30 to 60 minutes a day, 5 times a week) can significantly increase pain-free exercise time and distance in patients with claudication. The mechanism accounting for this response is not known.

Smoking Cessation
Smoking is the most significant independent risk factor for development of lower extremity arterial disease.

- Continued smoking after the onset of claudication is associated with accelerated progression of disease and increased frequency of complications (life-threatening ischemia and amputation).

- Continued smoking after arterial reconstructive surgery adversely impacts on the patency of bypass grafts.

Local Measures

Local measures that reduce the likelihood of skin breakdown and infection are indicated in all patients. Foot care is essential:

- The feet should be kept clean and dry.
- Fissuring should be prevented by using moisturizing cream.
- Meticulous care should be afforded to in-grown toenails and calluses.
- Well-fitted shoes should be worn to reduce the risk of pressure necrosis.

Drug Therapy

Vasodilators Vasodilators have not been shown to effectively increase blood flow or alleviate symptoms. This lack of effect is likely secondary to the fact that large vessel diameters are fixed by the atherosclerotic process while resistance vessels are already maximally vasodilated to maintain distal perfusion.

Rheologic Agents

Pentoxifylline Pentoxifylline (400 mg, three times a day) is the only agent approved for the treatment of intermittent claudication. Pentoxifylline is reported to:

- Improve abnormal erythrocyte deformability.
- Reduce hyperviscosity.
- Diminish platelet hyperreactivity and plasma hypercoagulability.

Despite reports showing that pentoxifylline increases walking distance, the results compared to placebo may not be clinically important. Suitable criteria to identify which particular patient may benefit from pentoxifylline are not available.

Antithrombotic Agents

Aspirin ASA (75–325 mg/day) may delay the progression of established disease and decrease the need for revascularization.

- Peripheral arterial disease is a marker of CAD and cerebrovascular disease. Administration of ASA to patients with peripheral vascular disease has been shown to decrease vascular mortality as well as nonfatal stroke and MI.
- Neither warfarin nor other antiplatelet agents have been shown to delay or prevent progression of atherosclerotic vascular disease.

Lipid-Lowering Agents Aggressive treatment of lipids is indicated for any patient with symptomatic vascular disease to reduce cardiovascular mortality. To date, no evidence clearly shows that lowering lipids will prevent or delay the complications of peripheral vascular disease.

Revascularization Therapy

Restoration of pulsatile flow is indicated in the setting of disabling or limiting claudication, ischemic rest pain, or ischemic ulceration.

- Prior to revascularization, an arteriogram should be performed. MRA in some centers is an alternative.
- Underlying CAD is very common among patients with lower extremity ischemia referred for revascularization. Appropriate preoperative cardiac evaluation is required prior to surgery (see Chapter 16).

Revascularization options include percutaneous angioplasty and surgery.

Percutaneous Transluminal Angioplasty (PTA) PTA is an alternative to surgery in appropriate candidates. The ideal lesion amenable to PTA is less than 10 cm in length and proximal (aortoiliac) in location.

When considering PTA, three regions of interest can be defined:

1. **Aortoiliac.** Aortoiliac disease is associated with the highest success rate and the lowest restenosis rate.
2. **Femoropopliteal.** Femoropopliteal disease is

associated with a similar high success rate, but a significantly lower long-term patency rate compared to aortoiliac PTA.

3. **Inferopopliteal.** Inferopopliteal disease is infrequently amenable to PTA (20% to 30% of cases). Data are limited, but restenosis rates are high.

Surgical Revascularization   Surgery is indicated when rest pain, ischemic ulceration, or gangrene and anatomy suitable for revascularization are present.

Aortoiliac disease   Aortoiliac disease is most commonly treated with endarterectomy or implantation of a synthetic bypass graft. Long-term patency and relief of symptoms may exceed 80% at 10 years.

For the patient unable to tolerate the risk of aortoiliac surgery, extra-anatomic bypass procedures such as axillofemoral bypass and femorofemoral bypass may be performed.

Femoropopliteal disease   Femoropopliteal disease is most commonly treated using reversed autologous saphenous vein as the bypass conduit. The vein is anastomosed proximally to the common femoral artery and distally to the popliteal artery. Patency rates decline proportionately as the anastomosis is performed more distal to the knee. Graft patency rates average 60% to 70% at 5 years and 38% at 10 years.

Tibioperoneal disease   Tibioperoneal disease often responds poorly to bypass surgery. In terms of patency at 2 years, vein grafts have proven superior to grafts made of prosthetic material.

Amputation

Amputation is used as a last resort in the patient with ischemic gangrene and intolerable pain or serious infection.

ACUTE PERIPHERAL ARTERIAL OCCLUSIVE DISEASE

Etiology

The major causes of acute arterial occlusion are embolism, trauma, and in situ thrombosis. In rare cases, aortic dissection or ergot toxicity may present as acute limb ischemia.

Embolism
Arterial embolism arises from the heart in 80% of cases.

- Common etiologies include AF and ventricular mural thrombus.
- Other etiologies include IE, paradoxic embolism, cardiac tumors, mural thrombi within arterial aneurysms, and ulcerating atherosclerotic lesions.

Trauma
Traumatic arterial occlusion often occurs in association with external compression, laceration, or transection of the vessel.

In Situ Thrombosis
In situ arterial thrombosis is associated with systemic hypercoagulable disorders (antiphospholipid antibody syndrome, neoplasia, myeloproliferative disorders, heparin-induced thrombocytopenia, and other hereditary coagulation disorders).

Pathophysiology

Most cardioemboli lodge at bifurcations of larger vessels (>5 mm diameter). The bifurcation of the common femoral artery is involved 50% of the time. Microemboli tend to obstruct smaller vessels (<5 mm diameter).

In many cases, preexisting atherosclerotic lesions are present where emboli lodge or in situ thrombosis occurs. Spasm of the vessel distal to the site of obstruction occurs. Due to insufficient collateral development, acute occlusion of a lower extremity vessel often leads to limb ischemia.

Clinical Presentation

Acute peripheral arterial occlusion can be abrupt and dramatic. The "Five Ps"—pain, paresthesias, pallor, pulselessness, and/or paralysis—may be presenting complaints. Acute occlusion may also present in a more subtle fashion, manifesting as sudden shortening of the previous claudication distance.

- With large occlusive thrombi, peripheral pulses are absent distal to the site of occlusion and the affected area is cool and pale.
- If insufficient collateral supply to the ischemic area is present, then tissue necrosis (indicated by paresthesias, paralysis, blotchy cyanosis that does not blanch with pressure) will occur within 6 to 8 hours. Reperfusion of the ischemic extremity within 4 to 6 hours will preserve limb function in most cases.
- When the acute process is secondary to a shower of microemboli, the involved area is usually peripheral and large arterial pulses remain intact.

Diagnosis and Treatment

1. Full-dose IV heparin anticoagulation should be started immediately (and continued for several days) in all patients to prevent distal clot propagation.
2. Arteriography should be performed as soon as possible to localize the area of ischemia in patients in whom the diagnosis is unclear.
3. If the patient presents within 4 to 6 hours and limb viability is in question, then an embolectomy, surgical revascularization, or administration of an intra-arterial thrombolytic agent is indicated to restore antegrade flow.
   - Revascularization beyond 8 to 12 hours of ischemia offers no additional limb salvage beyond that obtained with anticoagulation.
4. A search for the source of embolism should follow the acute therapy of limb ischemia. Patients with documented or strongly suspected cardioembolism should receive long-term anticoagulation. If the origin of the embolus is a proximal arterial aneurysm, then surgical repair of the aneurysm is indicated.

DEEP VENOUS THROMBOSIS (DVT)

DVT is a common disorder that may lead to significant morbidity and mortality if not recognized and appropriately treated. DVT most commonly involves the veins of the lower extremities.

- Thrombosis of the deep veins proximal to the knee is associated with pulmonary embolism (PE) in up to 50% of patients (the majority of whom are clinically silent) and with postphlebitic syndrome.
- Calf vein thrombosis (which remains confined to the calf) significantly less often results in PE or postphlebitic syndrome.

Etiology

DVT occurs in association with many common medical conditions and as a complication of surgical procedures.

Acquired Risk Factors

Acquired risk factors for DVT include:

Malignancy
Immobilization (especially after certain surgical
   procedures)
Age >40 years
High-dose estrogen therapy
Sepsis
Stroke
Obesity
Prior thromboembolism
Pregnancy
CHF
Trauma
Nephrotic syndrome
Indwelling venous catheters
Heparin therapy
MI
Inflammatory bowel disease
Intravenous drug abuse
Varicose veins

Inherited Risk Factors

Inherited risk factors for DVT include:

Antithrombin III deficiency
Protein C deficiency
Protein S deficiency
Dysfibrinogenemias
Disorders of plasminogen and plasminogen activation

Antiphospholipid antibody syndrome
Mutation in coagulation factor V (factor V Leiden)

Surgical Risk Factors (Table 11-1)
The risk of DVT as a result of surgery is related to age of the patient; location, duration, and extent of surgery; and degree of postoperative immobilization.

General Surgery Patients of advanced age and with malignancy have a greater risk of DVT and PE.

• The average incidence of DVT is 16% to 30% for patients older than 40 years.
• DVT extends proximally in 6% to 10%.
• Clinically significant PE occurs in 1.6%.
• Fatal PE occurs in 0.8%.

Orthopedic Surgery All patients having lower extremity surgery are at risk.

Table 11-1. Risk Categories for Venous Thromboembolism with Surgery

Thrombotic Event	Low Risk Category 1	Moderate Risk Category 2	High Risk Category 3
	Age <40 years. Uncomplicated surgery. Duration of surgery <60 min. Minimal immobility.	General surgery in patient >40 years old. Duration of surgery >60 min. Acute MI. Chronic illness. Leg fracture in patient <40 years old.	Major surgery in patient >40 years old with risk factors for DVT. Hip and major knee surgery. Surgery for extensive malignancy. Multiple trauma. Stroke.
Calf vein thrombosis	≈2%	10% to 20%	40% to 70%
Proximal vein thrombosis	≈0.4%	2% to 4%	10% to 20%
Fatal PE	<0.02%	0.2% to 0.5%	1% to 5%

Adapted with permission from: Hirsh J, Hoak J. Management of deep venous thrombosis and pulmonary embolism. Circulation 1996;93:2216.

- For hip and knee surgery, the incidence of DVT is 45% to 70%.
- Clinically significant PE occurs in up to 20% of patients having hip surgery.
- The incidence of fatal PE is 1% to 3% of patients having hip surgery.

Urologic Surgery The incidence of DVT/PE in urologic surgery is similar to that of general surgery. Many patients having urologic surgery are older, and therefore are at increased risk.

Gynecologic and Obstetric Surgery
- The incidence of DVT in gynecologic surgery ranges from 7% to 45%. Fatal PE occurs in ≤1%. The risk is increased for patients having extensive pelvic or abdominal surgery for malignancy.
- The risk of DVT/PE among pregnant women is up to fivefold higher than among nonpregnant women of similar age. Purported etiologic factors include venous stasis and alterations of the coagulation and fibrinolytic systems.

Neurologic Surgery
- The incidence of DVT in neurologic surgery ranges from 9% to 50%.
- Fatal PE occurs in 1.5% to 3.0%.
- Among patients with stroke, the risk of DVT in the paralyzed leg is as high as 75%. The risk of DVT in the nonparalyzed leg is less than 10%.

Trauma
- Following major trauma, the incidence of venographically confirmed DVT is 58%.
- Proximal DVT occurs in 18%.

Pathophysiology/Natural History

Virchow's triad of venous stasis, hypercoagulability, and endothelial trauma are purported risk factors for intravascular coagulation. A genetic predisposition to thrombosis may also be operative.

- Approximately 90% of PEs originate in the deep veins of the lower extremities. Most DVTs that originate in the calf veins remain clinically silent; however, 20% to 30% may extend into the larger, more proximal veins.

- It is estimated that PE will occur in 50% of patients with proximal DVT. The majority (70% to 80%) of these PEs will be clinically silent.
- Most episodes of DVT resolve spontaneously without specific treatment. Long-term sequelae of DVT include recurrent thrombosis (20% to 24%), PE, and postphlebitic syndrome (up to 25% to 30%).
- Postphlebitic syndrome is caused by venous HTN from scarred and incompetent venous valves (most common) or persistent outflow obstruction of large veins (less common). Increased venous flow and pressure is transmitted from the deep veins to the superficial system leading to edema, subcutaneous tissue injury, and, if severe, skin ulceration.
- After a diagnosis of unexplained DVT, a previously occult cancer may be discovered, especially if venous thromboembolism recurs.

Clinical Presentation

Clinical findings are often insensitive and nonspecific. Up to two-thirds of DVTs are clinically silent. DVT is only present 50% of the time when it is clinically suspected. PE may be the condition which brings DVT to clinical attention.

Pain
Pain is the most common symptom.

- Pain localized to the thigh or buttocks may suggest proximal DVT.
- Localized calf pain may suggest calf vein thrombosis. Nonthrombotic causes of calf pain (such as muscle strain/tear, arthritis, ruptured Baker's cyst) must be considered in the differential diagnosis.
- Homans' sign (calf pain upon forced dorsiflexion of the foot) is present in less than 40% of patients with DVT. It is present in ≥50% of symptomatic patients in whom DVT is clinically suggested but proven to be absent.

Swelling

Unilateral limb swelling or edema is the most common sign of DVT.

Other conditions such as lymphedema, cellulitis, or iliac vein compression may produce unilateral leg edema.

Fever

Low-grade fever without evidence of infection is common.

Postphlebitic Syndrome

A dull ache or pressure sensation in the lower leg (accompanied by swelling) that worsens with standing and improves with elevation is a common presenting complaint of the postphlebitic syndrome.

- Increased leg circumference, edema, varicose veins, and brown ankle discoloration (brawny induration) are common physical findings.

Diagnostic Studies

Clinically suspected DVT must be confirmed by objective diagnostic tests because patients with minimal symptoms may have extensive venous thrombosis, whereas symptomatic patients will have DVT only one-third to one-half of the time.

Contrast Venography

Venography is the gold standard test for diagnosis of DVT. Venography can detect both proximal and calf vein thrombosis with great accuracy.

Procedure: Venography is performed by injecting radio-opaque contrast material into a superficial vein on the dorsum of the foot. The most reliable finding is the presence of an intraluminal filling defect.

Disadvantages: Disadvantages of venography include its invasive nature, limited usefulness for serial study, and side effects which include superficial phlebitis (1% to 3%), allergic reaction to contrast material, and dye-induced renal dysfunction.

Impedance Plethysmography (IPG)

IPG is sensitive and specific for proximal DVT in symptomatic patients, but is insensitive to calf vein thrombosis and nonocclusive proximal DVT.

Procedure: IPG is performed by placing two sets of electrodes around the calf and a pneumatic blood pressure cuff around the thigh. The electrical impedance between the two calf electrodes is measured. Proximal DVT lowers impedance as the cuff is inflated and the leg veins are engorged and delays the characteristic rise in calf impedance when the cuff is deflated.

- A positive unilateral IPG is highly predictive of proximal DVT.
- Among patients with serial negative IPGs over a 10- to 14-day period, it is safe to withhold anticoagulation as the risk of proximal DVT or extension of calf vein DVT to the proximal veins is very low.

Disadvantages: False-positive IPGs may occur with CHF, pregnancy, and external compression of the proximal veins.

Ultrasound

Venous imaging with real-time B-mode ultrasound is the standard technique in many institutions to evaluate clinically suspected DVT. The sensitivity and specificity of ultrasound exceeds 95% for detection of symptomatic proximal DVT. The most sensitive finding is failure of the vein to collapse under gentle external pressure.

Similar to IPG, serial testing with ultrasound over a several-day period while withholding anticoagulants can exclude proximal DVT or extension of calf vein DVT.

Disadvantages: Venous imaging is insensitive for calf vein thrombosis. In addition, as with IPG, ultrasound is insensitive for diagnosis of asymptomatic DVT.

D-Dimer

The plasma concentration of D-dimer, a product of degradation of cross-linked fibrin, is increased in patients with DVT and PE. The sensitivity of D-dimer for DVT/PE exceeds 95%.

- An elevated D-dimer concentration suggests but does not confirm the presence of DVT. An imaging test is required for confirmation.
- Venous thrombosis is unlikely if the D-dimer concentration is normal.

Treatment

The goals of therapy are to prevent PE and postphlebitic syndrome by restoring venous patency and valvular function.

Standard therapy for most patients includes the use of a heparin and warfarin. In certain cases, thrombolytic therapy or surgical therapy is indicated.

Anticoagulants

- In spite of adequate anticoagulation, asymptomatic extension of DVT to the proximal veins or PE occurs in 8% and symptomatic PE occurs in 0.5%.

Intravenous Heparin

The heparin infusion should be continued for a minimum of 5 days and should not be stopped until the INR is in the therapeutic range for 2 days.

- Heparin is often administered as a 5000 U bolus followed by a continuous infusion adjusted to keep the aPTT at 1.5 to 2.5 times control.
- Alternatively, weight-based intravenous heparin dosing can be used. An 80 U/kg bolus is followed by an infusion of 18 U/kg/hr adjusted to keep the aPTT at 1.5 to 2.5 times control.

The risk of heparin-induced thrombocytopenia mandates that the platelet count be obtained at least every other day while heparin is administered.

Subcutaneous Heparin Administration of subcutaneous heparin twice daily is an effective alternative to continuous IV infusion. Subcutaneous heparin must be used in adequate doses to achieve therapeutic anticoagulation.

- Following a 5000 U bolus of IV heparin, a minimum subcutaneous dose of 12,500 U twice a day should be administered.
- The aPTT should be drawn 6 hours after the morning dose and the dose should be adjusted to maintain the aPTT at 1.5 to 2.5 times control.
- Warfarin is administered as described below.

Low Molecular Weight Heparins (LMWHs) LMWH fractions have a longer half-life than unfractionated heparin, making twice daily subcutaneous injection regimens possible. LMWHs have been demonstrated to be as efficacious and safe as continuous IV infusion of heparin for treatment of DVT.

- The incidence of heparin-induced thrombocytopenia is lower with LMWHs.
- Recent studies have shown that LMWHs can be used safely and effectively for the outpatient treatment of uncomplicated proximal DVT. In some studies, fixed dose LMWH was administered without monitoring of the aPTT.
- As with IV and subcutaneous heparin, it is recommended that warfarin be started early, and LMWH therapy be continued for a minimum of 5 days and at least 2 days after the INR is therapeutic.

Oral Warfarin Oral warfarin can be started at 24 hours. A goal INR of 2.0 to 3.0 is recommended.

- Oral anticoagulation should be continued for at least 3 to 6 months.
- A more prolonged course of anticoagulation should be prescribed for patients with ongoing DVT risk factors.
- Indefinite oral anticoagulation with warfarin should be administered to patients with recurrent venous thromboembolism.

Thrombolytic Therapy
The role of thrombolytic therapy in the treatment of DVT remains poorly defined. The vast majority of patients should be treated with a heparin-based regimen followed by oral anticoagulation.

- Thrombolytic therapy appears to significantly decrease the incidence of postphlebitic syndrome in patients with acute DVT through more complete clot lysis and less loss of venous valves.
- Thrombolytic therapy may be indicated for selected patients with extensive proximal DVT.

- Thrombolytic agents should also be considered for DVT complicated by massive PE causing hemodynamic compromise.

Caval Interruption

IVC interruption should be considered when there is a contraindication to or complication of anticoagulant therapy for high-risk proximal DVT to prevent PE. Other less frequent indications include:

- Prevention of PE when failure of adequate anticoagulation occurs.
- Prophylaxis against PE in patients deemed at high risk of death despite anticoagulation.
- Treatment when "large, free-floating" thrombi are noted on venography.

Postphlebitic Syndrome

Conservative measures for treating postphlebitic syndrome include:

- Avoiding prolonged sitting or standing.
- Wearing graded compression stockings and elevating the leg.
- Enlarging and maintaining collateral channels through walking and gentle exercise.

Skin ulceration is treated with intensified efforts to enhance venous return and local measures, such as:

Careful hygiene
Protective dressings
Topical antibiotics
Wet to dry dressings
Unna's paste boot (if necessary)

If conservative measures are not effective, then surgical approaches may be required, such as:

Interruption of incompetent communicating veins
Valvular reconstruction
Bypass of venous occlusions

Prophylaxis of DVT

DVT and PE are often clinically silent events, and the history and physical examination are often unreliable.

Because many patients who succumb to clinically recognized PE do so before effective therapy can be started, a strategy to prevent DVT and its complications is preferable for patients at increased risk.

Prophylaxis is achieved by either modulating activation of blood coagulation or preventing venous stasis. Prophylactic measures include:

- Low-dose subcutaneous heparin (5000 U 2 hours prior to surgery and then 5000 U every 8 to 12 hours)
- Intermittent pneumatic compression (IPC) of the legs
- Low-dose oral anticoagulation (INR 2.0 to 3.0)
- Graded elastic stockings (GES)
- Adjusted dose subcutaneous heparin
- Low molecular weight heparin (LMWH)

Application of effective prophylaxis depends upon the presence of clinical risk factors for the development of DVT and the type and extent of planned surgery (see Table 11-1).

General Surgery
- Low risk patients who are younger than 40 years of age without other risk factors for DVT: Early ambulation.
- Moderate risk patients: GES, low dose subcutaneous heparin, or IPC.
- Higher risk patients: Low dose subcutaneous heparin or LMWH.
- Very high risk patients: Low dose subcutaneous heparin or LMWH plus IPC.

Orthopedic Surgery

Hip surgery LMWH, low dose oral anticoagulation, or adjusted dose subcutaneous heparin can be used. An advantage of LMWH use is that laboratory monitoring is not required. Most orthopedic surgeons in the United States use low intensity oral anticoagulation started the night prior to surgery and continued postoperatively to raise the INR to 2.0 to 3.0.

Major knee surgery
- LMWH and IPC are effective.
- Low intensity warfarin is ineffective.

- The prophylaxis for major knee surgery should continue for a minimum of 7 to 10 days after surgery.

Acute Spinal Cord Trauma Inadequate data exist to give a firm recommendation on prophylaxis for acute spinal cord trauma. Prophylaxis should probably continue for 3 months after the acute injury.

- The most promising strategy appears to be LMWH.
- Low dose subcutaneous heparin, GES, and IPC provide less than optimal protection when used alone.

Neurosurgery and Genitourinary Surgery For neurosurgery and genitourinary surgery,

- IPC (with or without GES) is the method of choice.
- Low-dose subcutaneous heparin appears to be an effective alternative.

Major Trauma Prophylactic methods are problematic for major trauma victims because of the risk of intracranial bleeding and the inability to perform IPC in many patients. Only one randomized trial has been performed in major trauma victims, so no official recommendations currently exist.

The results of the single trial indicated that LMWH (enoxaparin) was more effective than low-dose heparin in preventing DVT. The study's authors recommended that enoxaparin be given to all patients with multiple trauma (with one exception: frank intracranial bleeding) and that prophylaxis should continue at least until hospital discharge.

SUGGESTED READINGS

Becker DM, Philbrick JT, Selby JB. Inferior vena cava filters. Indications, safety, effectiveness. Arch Intern Med 1992;152: 1985–1994.

Brewster DC. Current controversies in the management of aortoiliac occlusive disease. J Vasc Surg 1997;25:365–379.

Cambria RP, Kaufman JA, L'Italien GJ, et al. Magnetic resonance angiography in the management of lower extremity arterial occlusive disease: a prospective study. J Vasc Surg 1997;25:380–389.

Clagett GP, Anderson FA Jr, Heit J, et al. Prevention of venous thromboembolism. Chest 1995;108:312S–334S.

Geerts WH, Jay RM, Code KI, et al. A comparison of low-dose heparin with low-molecular-weight heparin as prophylaxis against venous thromboembolism after major trauma. N Engl J Med 1996;335:701–707.

Hirsh J, Hoak J. Management of deep venous thrombosis and pulmonary embolism. Circulation 1996;93:2212–2245.

Hyers TM, Hull RD, Weg JG. Antithrombotic therapy for venous thromboembolic disease. Chest 1995;108:335S–351S.

Levine M, Gent M, Hirsh J, et al. A comparison of low-molecular weight heparin administered primarily at home with unfractionated heparin administered in the hospital for proximal deep venous thrombosis. N Engl J Med 1996;334: 677–681.

Loscalzo J, Creager MA, Dzau VJ. Vascular medicine: a textbook of vascular biology and diseases. 2nd ed. Boston: Little, Brown, 1996.

Pineo GF, Hull RD. Low-molecular-weight heparin: prophylaxis and treatment of venous thromboembolism. Annu Rev Med 1997;48:79–91.

Prandoni P, Lensing AWA, Cogo A, et al. The long-term clinical course of acute deep venous thrombosis. Ann Intern Med 1996;125:1–7.

Radack K, Wyderski RJ. Conservative management of intermittent claudication. Ann Intern Med 1990;113:135–146.

Schulman S, Granquist S, Holmstrom M, et al. The duration of oral anticoagulant therapy after a second episode of venous thromboembolism. N Engl J Med 1997;336:393–398.

Spittell JA Jr. Peripheral arterial disease. Dis Month 1994;40: 643–700.

Weinmann EE, Salzman EW. Deep-vein thrombosis. N Engl J Med 1994;331:1630–1641.

Weitz JI, Byrne J, Clagett GP, et al. Diagnosis and treatment of chronic arterial insufficiency of the lower extremities: a critical review. Circulation 1996;94:3026–3049.

Weitz JI. Low-molecular-weight heparins. N Engl J Med 1997;337:688–698.

The Cardiomyopathies and Myocarditis

Dennis A. Tighe
Edward K. Chung

The cardiomyopathies and myocarditis are characterized by their involvement of heart muscle.

Four distinct categories of cardiomyopathy are recognized on the basis of morphology and clinical presentation.

1. Dilated (congestive) cardiomyopathy (DCM).
2. Hypertrophic cardiomyopathy (HCM).
3. Restrictive cardiomyopathy (RCM).
4. Arrhythmogenic right ventricular dysplasia/cardiomyopathy (ARVD).

Myocarditis is an inflammatory process that involves the heart. It is most often caused by an infectious agent.

CARDIOMYOPATHIES

DILATED CARDIOMYOPATHY (DCM)

DCM is characterized by ventricular dilatation and primary systolic dysfunction.

Pathology

- Dilatation of the cardiac chambers, especially the LV, is characteristic.
- Myocardial mass is always elevated. Average heart weight approximates 600 grams (average normal

values for men: 325 ± 75 grams; average normal values for women: 275 ± 75 grams).

- Intracardiac thrombi, most often found at the apex of the LV, are present in 75% of autopsy cases.
- The epicardial and intramuscular coronary arteries are without significant atherosclerotic disease except in "ischemic" cardiomyopathy.
- Valve leaflets are normal, except in long-standing AV valve regurgitation in which minor degrees of focal thickening may be present.
- Histology reveals myofiber hypertrophy and atrophy along with areas of interstitial myocardial fibrosis. In general, inflammatory cells are absent and viral agents are not identified by electron microscopy.

Etiology

A wide variety of disease states and/or insults to the myocardium may cause DCM.

- The leading causes of DCM include:
  1. Chronic ethanol abuse
  2. Pregnancy and the puerperium
  3. Immunologic dysfunction
  4. Chemotherapeutic and other toxic agents
  5. Infectious agents
  6. Metabolic disorders
- Familial DCM is being recognized with increasing frequency. Up to 20% of idiopathic DCM patients have a first-degree relative with cardiomegaly and reduced ejection fraction.
- Other causes of DCM have been identified (Table 12-1).
- Those cases in which an etiologic process cannot be identified are termed "idiopathic" DCM.

CAD, HTN, and valvular heart disease can commonly cause ventricular dilatation and systolic dysfunction, but these entities are not referred to as primary DCM per se.

Alcohol Abuse

Ethanol abuse is the leading cause of nonischemic DCM in developed countries. Alcoholic cardiomyopathy occurs primarily among middle-aged men with a history of

Table 12-1. Rare Causes of Dilated Cardiomyopathy

Acromegaly
Acute leukemia
Acute rheumatic fever
Amphetamines
Argemone mexicana toxicity
Cobalt poisoning
Combination antituberculous drugs
Dermatomyositis
Duchenne's muscular dystrophy
Endocardial fibroelastosis
Erb's limb-girdle muscular dystrophy
Fabry's disease
Fibrocystic disease
Glycogen storage disease
Henoch-Schönlein purpura
Heroin
High-dose combination chemotherapy
Hypertaurinuria
Irradiation
Lead poisoning
Mucopolysaccharidoses
Myotonic dystrophy
Osteogenesis imperfecta
Phosphorus (elemental poisoning)
Rheumatoid arthritis
Roussy-Lévy polyneuropathy
Sandhoff's disease
Scleroderma
Selenium deficiency
Sulfonamides
Systemic carnitine deficiency
Systemic lupus erythematosus
Tuberculosis
Wegener's granulomatosis

Adapted with permission from: Johnson PA, Palacios I. Dilated cardiomyopathies of the adult. N Engl J Med 1982;307:1122.

heavy alcohol consumption of greater than 10 years' duration.

- The exact mechanism of myocardial injury in alcoholic cardiomyopathy is unknown. Potential mechanisms include:
  Direct toxic effect of ethanol or its metabolites
  Potentiation of other cardiac risk factors

Nutritional imbalance (particularly thiamine
    deficiency)
- Most importantly, alcoholic cardiomyopathy is
  potentially reversible with abstinence. The prognosis
  for those who continue to consume alcohol is
  poor.

Peripartum Cardiomyopathy

Peripartum cardiomyopathy usually occurs during the
last trimester of pregnancy or within 6 months after
delivery. The peak incidence is 1 to 3 months post partum.
It is estimated to occur in 1 in 4000 to 1 in 15,000
deliveries.

Risk factors for developing peripartum cardiomyopathy include:

Black race
Multiparity
Increased maternal age
Toxemia of pregnancy
Twin gestation

Prognosis varies considerably.

- In 50% of patients, an almost full recovery of cardiac
  function occurs within 6 months. For those with
  normalized cardiac function, further pregnancy is not
  contraindicated, but the patient should be closely
  monitored.
- In 50% of patients, diminished cardiac function
  remains or ventricular function declines further.
  Pregnancy should be discouraged in this group for
  fear of further decline in cardiac function.

Chemotherapeutic Drugs (see Chapter 14)

Infectious Agents

Infectious causes of DCM will be covered in greater
detail in the section on myocarditis, but in general any
class of infectious agent can cause cardiac injury.

Tachycardia-Mediated Dilated Cardiomyopathy

Cardiac dilatation and reduced systolic performance may
accompany chronic SVTs. Elimination of the tachycardia
may normalize systolic function.

Metabolic and Electrolyte Disorders

A variety of metabolic and electrolyte disorders are causally related to DCM.

- Endocrinopathies such as hyperthyroidism, hypothyroidism, diabetes mellitus, acromegaly, and pheochromocytoma have well-described effects on the heart.
- Thiamine deficiency (beriberi) and selenium deficiency (Keshan disease) are rare, but potentially reversible, forms of DCM.
- Electrolyte disorders such as hypocalcemia and hypophosphatemia are unusual, but potentially reversible, causes of DCM.

Clinical Presentation

History

Presenting complaints of DCM usually include:

Dyspnea on exertion
Fatigue
Weakness
Orthopnea
Cough
Peripheral edema

In approximately 15% to 20% of cases of DCM, a history of an antecedent viral-type illness is obtained.

Less frequent presenting complaints include:

Chest pain
Hemoptysis
Embolic phenomena

Symptoms of right heart failure such as increasing abdominal girth, anorexia, and nausea occur in advanced cases.

Physical Examination

- Pulse pressure is often narrowed reflecting diminished CO.
- Jugular venous distention is common.
- A diffuse, inferolaterally displaced apical impulse indicates LV enlargement.

- RV and LV precordial impulses are often palpable and ventricular gallop sounds are audible.
- Systolic murmurs of MR and less commonly TR are present.
- Additional findings include peripheral edema and pulmonary rales.

Diagnostic Testing

Chest X-Ray　The CXR demonstrates LV enlargement and in many cases generalized cardiomegaly. Pleural effusions and signs of pulmonary venous HTN are frequent.

Electrocardiogram　VPCs with grouped beats and AF are common. The ECG often shows:

- Nonspecific abnormalities of the T wave and ST segment
- Sinus tachycardia
- LVH
- LA enlargement
- Intraventricular conduction defects
- In some cases, complete LBBB

Radionuclide Ventriculography　DCM tested with radionuclide ventriculography universally shows evidence of chamber dilatation with reduced ejection fraction (<45%). Segmental wall motion abnormalities are not uncommon.

Echocardiography　Echocardiography reveals diffuse hypokinesis with LV dilatation and increased E-point to septal separation and reduced valve excursion consistent with a low CO.

- Other cardiac chambers may be enlarged to varying degrees.
- Regional wall motion abnormalities have been noted in up to 60% of patients, thus making echocardiographic differentiation from ischemic heart disease difficult.
- Pericardial and pleural effusions and intracardiac thrombi (especially at the apex of the LV) may be demonstrated.

- MR is present in greater than 95% of patients and TR in 40%.

Myocardial Perfusion Imaging   Normal perfusion of all myocardial segments is most commonly found in DCM. In some cases, focal areas of decreased radiotracer uptake, related to areas of patchy fibrosis, may be demonstrated.

Cardiac Catheterization and Coronary Angiography Cardiac catheterization and coronary angiography studies often mirror the findings of the noninvasive evaluation.

- PCWP and LVEDP are usually markedly elevated. Pulmonary HTN is frequent.
- Contrast ventriculography reveals a dilated chamber with globally poor contractile function. Regional wall motion abnormalities may be present.

Coronary arteriography should be performed in all patients presenting with chest pain or established risk factors for CAD. Among patients with idiopathic DCM, angiography often reveals no, or at most minimal, CAD. If CAD is present, its anatomical extent does not account for the impairment of LV function.

Endomyocardial biopsy of the RV may be helpful to identify suspected myocarditis.

Management

Appropriate management begins with recognition of underlying etiologic factor(s), contributing extra-cardiac disorders, and therapy of reversible causes to the extent possible. Once these factors have been addressed and corrected, the treatment becomes that of CHF (see Chapter 2).

- Adjunctive therapy includes sodium and fluid restriction along with restriction of activity to diminish cardiac work. Alcohol intake should be minimized or abolished. Obese individuals should be encouraged to lose weight.
- Due to its high prevalence, CAD must be excluded in the proper clinical setting. Revascularization

procedures should be performed for appropriate candidates.

Pharmacologic Therapy (see Chapter 2)

Diuretic Agents Diuretic agents are used to control edema and central congestive symptoms.

- Loop diuretics are often the agents of choice.
- In refractory cases the combination of a loop diuretic and a thiazide-type agent may be necessary.

Digitalis Glycosides Though digoxin has a neutral effect on long-term mortality, it improves symptomatic status and reduces hospitalizations for CHF. The beneficial effects of digoxin are likely due in part to its (relatively weak) positive inotropic effect and to its modulating effects on neurohormonal responses and the autonomic nervous system.

Vasodilator Agents Vasodilator agents are the drugs of choice in the therapy of LV systolic dysfunction.

- **ACE-inhibitors.** ACE inhibitors have well-documented beneficial effects on survival and functional status in chronic CHF. They are the vasodilator agents of choice for chronic CHF therapy.
- **Hydralazine and isosorbide dinitrate.** Hydralazine and isosorbide dinitrate in combination (in addition to digoxin and diuretics) have beneficial effects compared to placebo on symptomatic status and mortality. This combination is not superior to ACE-inhibitors for CHF therapy and should not be used as first-line therapy unless ACE-inhibitor allergy or intolerance is documented.
- **Angiotensin II receptor blockers.** Angiotensin II receptor blocking agents are a new class of vasodilator drugs. Though preliminary studies indicate benefit, large scale clinical trials are unavailable at this time.

Some patients may require a combination of vasodilator agents to improve symptomatic status.

Beta-Blocking Agents (see Chapter 2) Beta-blocking agents have shown beneficial effects on functional status, ejection fraction, exercise capacity, and filling pressures in select groups of patients with idiopathic DCM.

Calcium Channel Blockers (see Chapter 2)

Other Positive Inotropic Agents Other positive inotropic agents include dobutamine, milrinone, and amrinone.

- Dobutamine, milrinone, or amrinone can be administered IV for the acute treatment of severe CHF.
- Chronic, intermittent infusion of dobutamine or milrinone as an outpatient may stabilize clinical status and reduce hospitalizations for CHF.
- End-stage patients with severe CHF may require constant infusion of inotropic agents for survival prior to surgical therapy.

No positive inotropic agent given orally, with the exception of digoxin, has been shown to confer a significant therapeutic advantage in CHF.

Anticoagulants Anticoagulants should be prescribed for most patients with DCM and an acceptable risk/benefit profile due to these patients' high risk of cardiac thrombus formation and peripheral embolization, especially those with AF.

Anti-arrhythmic Agents Treatment of atrial arrhythmias, with the goal of maintenance of sinus rhythm and AV synchrony, is important for adequate CO in many cases (see Chapter 17).

- AADs should not be routinely prescribed in the setting of asymptomatic ventricular ectopy because randomized, controlled studies documenting a survival advantage are not available. The risk of an adverse effect (proarrhythmia) may exceed benefit.
- Patients with symptomatic ventricular arrhythmias should be referred for EP evaluation and individualized treatment.

Immunosuppressive Therapy Immunosuppressive therapy for chronic idiopathic DCM is generally not warranted. Exceptions include patients with biopsy proven, active myocarditis and inflammatory disorders such as sarcoidosis.

Surgical Therapy

Orthotopic Cardiac Transplantation Orthotopic cardiac transplantation (see Chapter 20) can be a highly beneficial therapeutic option among selected patients with refractory, end-stage CHF.

Dynamic Cardiomyoplasty Cardiomyoplasty (see Chapter 2) may be a surgical option in selected patients.

Implantable Left Ventricular Device (LVAD) LVADs are currently indicated for use as a bridge to transplantation. Long-term use of a circulatory support device as an alternative to transplantation may be possible as these devices become increasingly portable. A randomized trial is now ongoing to test this hypothesis.

Left Ventricular Diameter Reduction (Batista Operation) Reduction of ventricular volumes by surgical removal of dysfunctional LV myocardium, theoretically reducing wall stress and MR, has been performed in limited cases to date. Although enthusiasm for this procedure is increasing due to the limited number of organs available for transplantation, long-term follow-up data in a large patient cohort are not available at this time.

HYPERTROPHIC CARDIOMYOPATHY (HCM)

Pathology and Pathophysiology

Extensive ventricular hypertrophy, without valvular heart disease or preexistent systemic HTN, is characteristic of HCM. The LV cavity size is normal or small, and the RV may also be involved.

- Various patterns of hypertrophy have been noted and are divided into two groups: asymmetric and symmetric (concentric) hypertrophy. Asymmetric hypertrophy, the more common of the two, can be further subdivided into subgroups according to the primary involvement of the ventricular septum, mid-ventricular area, apical area, and the posterior and/or lateral wall.

- Microscopically, cellular hypertrophy, disorganized myofibers, and myocardial fibrosis are present. Partial or complete obstruction of the medium-sized intramural coronary arteries is noted in up to 80% of cases.

The pathophysiologic hallmark of the obstructive form of HCM (idiopathic hypertrophic subaortic stenosis) is the dynamic systolic pressure gradient. Controversy exists about the exact nature of this gradient, but it appears to be due to a combination of vigorous (hyperdynamic) contractile function and systolic anterior motion of the anterior mitral leaflet and chordae tendineae from the Venturi effect of the already narrowed outflow tract.

Prominent impairment of diastolic function, characteristic of this disorder, is secondary to the combination of interstitial fibrosis and impaired myocardial cellular relaxation.

Clinical Presentation

History

The vast majority of patients have a mild form of HCM and are usually asymptomatic or only minimally symptomatic. In addition, it is important to emphasize that not all forms of HCM cause LV outflow tract obstruction.

- Patients may come to clinical attention with symptoms related to diastolic dysfunction (CHF), outflow obstruction, or ischemia.
- The most common complaint is dyspnea due to elevated left heart filling pressure, followed by angina pectoris, fatigue, weakness, palpitation, near syncope, and syncope.
- Sudden death, especially after physical exertion, is not a rare presentation among younger patients.

Physical Examination

- As compared to valvular AS, the initial carotid upstroke with obstructive HCM is brisk, but as ejection proceeds, the pulse classically assumes a bifid contour in approximately 70% of patients.

- The heart sounds are usually normal except for a loud S_4.
- A systolic thrill at the left sternal border or apex is frequently present.
- A harsh systolic murmur at the left lower sternal border is the classic auscultatory finding of obstructive HCM. When present, the outflow tract gradient can be augmented by various maneuvers which alter preload, afterload, or contractility. Maneuvers such as straining against a closed glottis (Valsalva maneuver), standing from a squatting position, and administration of amyl nitrate can augment the gradient and thus transiently increase the intensity of the systolic murmur.

Diagnostic Tests

Electrocardiogram (ECG)   The ECG often reveals:

LVH

Nonspecific ST segment and T wave abnormalities

QRS complexes tallest in the mid-precordial leads (due to septal hypertrophy)

Q waves in the inferior, lateral, and/or precordial (V_2–V_6) leads (pseudo-MI patterns).

In the "Japanese form" of apical hypertrophic cardiomyopathy, giant negative T waves with high precordial QRS voltage are present.

Chest X-Ray (CXR)   The CXR may reveal cardiomegaly and LA enlargement.

Echocardiography   Echocardiography is the procedure of choice for noninvasive evaluation because it can differentiate HCM from aortic and mitral valvular pathology and provide an estimate of the severity of hemodynamic compromise.

M-mode echocardiographic criteria for diagnosis include:

1. Presence of LVH.
2. Ratio of interventricular septum to LV posterior wall thickness greater than 1.3:1.
3. Demonstration of systolic anterior motion (SAM) of the anterior mitral valve leaflet in cases of outflow tract obstruction.

• **Two-dimensional echocardiography.** 2D echocardiography better details the extent and localization of hypertrophy, the dynamic nature of the process, systolic cavity obliteration, SAM, and the morphology of the aortic valve.

• **Doppler echocardiography.** Doppler allows recognition of the intracavitary origin of the outflow tract gradient with characteristic "ski-slope" appearance of the late peaking systolic spectral envelope, quantification of MR, and evaluation of diastolic dysfunction.

Cardiac Catheterization and Coronary Angiography
Hemodynamic tracings reveal elevated LVEDP. With obstructive HCM, the gradient is dynamic in nature and certain provocative measures such as straining or administration of IV NTG can increase the outflow tract gradient. Induction of a VPC causes an increase in contractility with an increase in outflow tract gradient and diminution of pulse pressure of the following beat.

• Approximately 25% of patients exhibit evidence of pulmonary HTN.
• Ventriculography reveals vigorous LV contraction and evidence of MR.
• In the apical hypertrophic ("Japanese") variant, a characteristic "spade-like" ventricular shape is noted at end-diastole in the right anterior oblique projection.

Natural History

The prevalence of HCM is estimated to be 1 in 500 in the general population. Natural history studies of outpatient and elderly populations with HCM have documented a generally favorable prognosis in those patients who are asymptomatic or only minimally symptomatic.

Heredity
A genetic basis with autosomal dominant pattern of inheritance can be identified in 50% to 60% of patients. Variable penetrance may account for the varied clinical expression among family members.

• To date, mutations in a number of genes that encode for proteins of the cardiac sarcomeres or myosin light chains have been identified.

- Family members of an affected patient should be screened with a history, physical examination, and echocardiogram.

Sudden Death

An annual mortality rate of 2.5% to 4% for patients with outflow tract obstruction has been reported, primarily due to sudden death. This mortality rate, however, may significantly overestimate the true incidence of sudden death as these figures represent highly selected patient populations from referral centers.

The risk factors for sudden death include:

Severe symptoms
History of syncope
Family history of sudden death
Nonsustained ventricular tachycardia
Young age
Severe LVH

Complications

Other complications of HCM include:

- Development of AF leading to hemodynamic deterioration
- IE (5% lifetime risk)
- MR
- Myocardial ischemia
- LV systolic impairment with cavity dilatation ("burned-out phase") in up to 10% of patients

Therapy

- IE prophylaxis is recommended in all patients (see Chapter 7).
- Younger patients (less than 30 years old) with documented outflow tract obstruction should be instructed to avoid excessive physical activity due to their increased risk of sudden death.
- Asymptomatic patients (the majority of those with HCM) probably require no further therapy.

Pharmacologic Therapy

Mild to Moderate Symptoms Patients with mild to moderate symptoms should receive treatment to improve diastolic filling and reduce ischemia. Either beta-blockers or CCBs (verapamil preferred) are acceptable choices in this situation.

- Theoretically, verapamil-induced afterload reduction may increase the outflow tract gradient; therefore, it should be used with caution in patients with resting outflow tract gradients.
- In cases of treatment failure, other available agents include disopyramide, amiodarone, or the combination of a beta-blocker and CCB.

Atrial Fibrillation   AF may cause hemodynamic deterioration and should be aggressively treated. Treatment strategies include:

- Control of the HR with beta-blockers or verapamil.
- Medical therapy to convert the patient and attempt to maintain sinus rhythm (amiodarone often most effective).
- In refractory cases, AV node ablation with insertion of a permanent pacemaker.

Failed Pharmacologic Therapy

Surgery   For patients with refractory symptoms, the surgical options for those patients with documented outflow tract obstruction include septal myotomy and myectomy or mitral valve replacement. The mortality of surgery on the septum is 5%. In refractory cases without outflow tract obstruction cardiac transplantation is an option.

Dual chamber pacing   An alternative to surgical therapy for carefully selected patients with outflow tract obstruction who are refractory to drug therapy is dual chamber (DDD) pacing. RV pacing causes paradoxical motion of the interventricular septum which increases LV outflow tract dimensions, reduces outflow tract blood velocity, and results in less SAM of the anterior mitral leaflet and MR.

An initial report showed improved symptomatic status in 89% of patients, reduced outflow tract gradient, and significant thinning of the anteroseptum and distal anterior wall in 25% of patients. Subsequent reports have shown less favorable results.

Absolute ethanol   Another nonsurgical alternative is induced infarction of the subaortic portion of the interventricular septum by selective injection of absolute ethanol into the major septal branch of the left anterior descending coronary artery. Preliminary observations show a significant reduction in outflow tract gradient and mildly improved exercise capacity.

RESTRICTIVE CARDIOMYOPATHY (RCM)
Pathology and Pathophysiology

RCM is the least common form of cardiomyopathy (Table 12-2).

Gross pathologic examination reveals normal ventricular cavity sizes and mild to no increase in wall thickness. Biatrial enlargement and small pericardial effusions are common. Histology varies depending upon the

---

Table 12-2. The Restrictive Cardiomyopathies

I. Myocardial
   A. Infiltrative
   - Amyloid
   - Sarcoid
   - Hurler's disease
   - Gaucher's disease

   B. Noninfiltrative
   - Idiopathic
   - Scleroderma

   C. Storage Disease
   - Hemochromatosis
   - Fabry's disease
   - Glycogen storage disease

II. Endomyocardial
   Endomyocardial fibrosis
   Loffler's endocarditis
   Carcinoid syndrome
   Irradiation
   Metastatic malignancy
   Anthracycline toxicity

Adapted with permission from: Child JS, Perloff JK. The restrictive cardiomyopathies. Cardiology Clinics Vol 6 (2). Philadelphia: WB Saunders, 1988, p. 290.

specific etiology, but in general, interstitial fibrosis is the most prominent finding.

- Amyloid deposition, the most common cause in Western civilization, is characterized by frequent focal involvement of the cardiac valves, atrial thrombi, intramural vascular involvement, and fibrosis of the conduction system.
- Sarcoidosis is characterized by the presence of noncaseating granulomata and an affinity for the cephalad portion of the ventricular septum.
- Endomyocardial disease is characterized by marked endocardial fibrotic thickening of the apex and subvalvular regions of one or both ventricles.

The pathophysiologic hallmark of the RCMs is restriction to diastolic filling due to excessively stiff ventricular myocardium.

- Abnormal diastolic function is manifested by exaggerated early diastolic filling (rapid filling phase) and blunted filling during diastasis and atrial systole.
- Chronic constrictive pericarditis may present with similar physiologic findings, but can be most often differentiated on the basis of noninvasive testing and endomyocardial biopsy.

Clinical Presentation

History
Prominent early complaints caused by an inability to appropriately augment CO include symptoms such as:

Weakness
Fatigue
Exercise intolerance
Dyspnea

Later in the course, symptoms of right heart failure such as peripheral edema, abdominal bloating, and nausea predominate.

- Patients with amyloid involvement may present with orthostatic hypotension due to involvement of the autonomic nervous system, arrhythmias, and conduction system abnormalities.

- Sudden death, presumably due to advanced conduction system disease and ventricular tachyarrhythmias, is a common manifestation of myocardial sarcoidosis.
- Systemic or pulmonary embolism may be presenting complaint among patients with cardiac amyloid and endomyocardial disease.

Physical Examination
- Jugular venous distention with a prominent Y-descent and peripheral edema are common.
- An inspiratory increase in central venous pressure (Kussmaul's sign) may be appreciated.
- The S_1 and S_2 are normal. Ventricular gallop sounds are frequent.
- A diastolic knock is absent.
- In advanced cases, an enlarged pulsatile liver and ascites may be present.

Diagnostic Tests

Electrocardiogram (ECG) The ECG often reveals nonspecific findings:

Low voltage
Nonspecific ST segment and T wave changes
Interventricular conduction delay
Varying degrees of AV block

- Pseudo-infarction patterns may occur with amyloid or sarcoidosis.
- AF and other supraventricular arrhythmias may be present.

Chest X-Ray
- The CXR shows evidence of pulmonary venous HTN and pleural effusions.
- The cardiac silhouette shows no evidence of ventricular enlargement except in advanced cases.
- Biatrial enlargement is frequent.
- Patients with sarcoidosis may exhibit the full spectrum of mediastinal and pulmonary involvement characteristic of this disorder.
- Pericardial calcification is absent.

Echocardiography Echocardiography characteristically reveals normal to decreased ventricular cavity size, biatrial enlargement, small pericardial effusions, and evidence of AV valve regurgitation.

- Cardiac amyloidosis is characterized by increased ventricular wall thickness, AV valve thickening, thickening of the interatrial septum, decreased systolic LV function, and a "granular-sparkling" appearance of the ventricular myocardium.
- In sarcoidosis, regional wall motion abnormalities and localized aneurysm formation may be noted.
- Carcinoid cardiomyopathy characteristically causes thickening and restricted motion of the tricuspid and pulmonic valves.

• **Doppler echocardiography.** Doppler examination reveals evidence of impaired diastolic function and AV valve regurgitation. A restrictive pattern (tall E wave, rapid deceleration time, and small A wave) may characterize the mitral inflow.

Scintigraphy Scanning after injection of technetium-99m pyrophosphate may show diffuse myocardial uptake in advanced cases of cardiac amyloidosis.

Cardiac Catheterization Hemodynamic tracings reveal characteristic findings:

- Mean RA pressure is elevated, with a prominent Y-descent (reflecting rapid early diastolic ventricular filling) and a rapid X-descent yielding the classic "M" or "W" configuration.
- RV pressure tracing reveals an early diastolic dip and mid- to late diastolic plateau configuration with an elevated RV systolic pressure.
- LVEDP is usually more than 5 mm Hg higher than RV end diastolic pressure.
- PA systolic pressure is usually greater than 45 mm Hg.

In contrast, constrictive pericarditis is characterized by lower PA systolic pressure; RV diastolic pressure is usually at least one-third the peak RV systolic pressure; and the LV and RV end diastolic pressures are less than 5 mm Hg different.

Coronary arteriography reveals nonobstructive disease in the majority of cases.

Endomyocardial biopsy may be required to make a definitive diagnosis in certain cases.

Management

In general, the course of RCM is characterized by relentless progression. Maintenance of sinus rhythm is important to optimize ventricular filling.

Agents to Treat Congestive Symptoms

Symptomatic treatment of congestive symptoms with diuretic agents and use of digitalis is usually beneficial.

- Care must be taken not to administer excessive diuretic doses as these patients are preload dependent.
- Digitalis must be used with caution in patients with amyloidosis because of the increased risk of toxicity.

Anticoagulants

Anticoagulant therapy is indicated in those conditions associated with chronic AF and with cardiac thrombi, especially if pulmonary and/or peripheral embolic events have occurred.

Other Treatments

Specific treatments include:

- Corticosteroids in patients with sarcoidosis and hypereosinophilic syndrome.
- Phlebotomy and/or chelation therapy in hemochromatosis.
- Operative excision of fibrotic endocardium and MVR and/or TVR in those with endomyocardial fibrosis.

Transplantation

Cardiac transplantation is an option for refractory symptoms if a systemic disorder is not present.

ARRHYTHMOGENIC RIGHT VENTRICULAR DYSPLASIA/CARDIOMYOPATHY (ARVD)

ARVD is an unusual disease characterized by primary involvement of the RV free wall with myocardial atrophy and fatty or fibrofatty tissue replacement.

- LV involvement may occur. Involvement of the interventricular septum is unusual. Patchy myocarditis may be present.
- In addition to fibrous and fatty tissue replacement, aneurysms of the RV (primarily affecting the inferior wall) are common.

Etiology

The etiology of ARVD is unknown; however, a genetic component with autosomal dominant inheritance and variable penetrance is suspected.

Clinical Presentation

The clinical presentation is varied.

- ARVD often presents as sudden death among young, asymptomatic athletes.
- In some cases, palpitation, syncope, or ventricular ectopy may be presenting manifestations.
- In later stages, the presentation may be that of biventricular cardiac failure.

Diagnosis

Suspected diagnosis (Table 12-3) depends upon a constellation of clinical findings:

Family history
Results from imaging studies
ECG findings

At present, RV endomyocardial biopsy is required for histologic confirmation and definitive diagnosis.

ECG   ECG findings include:

- Negative (inverted) T waves in the right precordial leads in the absence of RBBB.
- VPCs and VT with LBBB morphology.
- Late potentials with signal averaging.

Echocardiography and MRI

- Echocardiography of the RV shows variable degrees of dilatation and hypokinesis. Aneurysms may be detected.
- MRI allows tissue characterization and may reveal

Table 12-3. Criteria for Diagnosis of Arrythmogenic Right Ventricular Dysplasia/Cardiomyopathy

I. Global and/or regional dysfunction and structural alterations*

Major

- Severe dilatation and reduction of RV ejection fraction with no (or only mild) LV impairment.
- Localized RV aneurysms (akinetic or dyskinetic areas with diastolic bulging).
- Severe segmental dilatation of the RV.

Minor

- Mild global RV dilatation and/or ejection fraction reduction with normal LV.
- Mild segmental dilatation of the RV.
- Regional RV hypokinesia.

II. Tissue characterization of walls

Major

- Fibrofatty replacement of myocardium on endomyocardial biopsy.

III. Repolarization abnormalities

Minor

- Inverted T waves in right precordial leads (V_2 and V_3) with people aged more than 12 years, in absence of RBBB.

IV. Depolarization/conduction abnormalities

Major

- Epsilon waves or localized prolongation (>110 ms) of the QRS complex in right precordial leads (V_1–V_3).

Minor

- Late potential (signal averaged ECG).

V. Arrhythmias

Minor

- LBBB–type VT (sustained and nonsustained) during ECG, Holter monitor, exercise testing.
- Frequent ventricular extrasystoles (more than 1000/24 hours) during Holter monitoring.

VI. Family history

Major

- Familial disease confirmed at necropsy or surgery.

Minor

- Familial history of premature sudden death (<35 years of age) due to suspected RV dysplasia.
- Familial history—clinical diagnosis based on present criteria.

---

* Detected by echocardiography, angiography, magnetic resonance imaging, or radionuclide scintigraphy. ECG = electrocardiogram; LV = left ventricle; RV = right ventricle.

Adapted with permission from: McKenna WJ, et al. Diagnosis of arrhythmogenic right ventricular dysplasia/cardiomyopathy. Br Heart J 1994;71:215.

the fibrofatty infiltration characteristic of ARVD. MRI has high specificity but low sensitivity.

Biopsy Biopsy specimens should preferentially be taken from the RV free wall because the interventricular septum is often not involved. Pathologic evaluation reveals two histologic patterns:

Fatty variety (40%)
Fibrofatty variety (60%)

Treatment

- Young athletes with ARVD should be restricted from strenuous activity.
- CHF and arrhythmias are treated in standard fashion (see Chapters 2, 17, and 18).

MYOCARDITIS

Myocarditis is an inflammatory process involving the myocardium. Although most commonly caused by an infectious agent, it may also be secondary to a variety of other processes (Table 12-4).

- In North America, viral agents are the most common cause.
- In South America, *Trypanosoma cruzi* (the agent causing Chagas' disease) is the leading cause.

Clinical Presentation

The clinical course of a patient with myocarditis ranges from an asymptomatic state to overwhelming myocarditis manifesting as severe CHF and sudden arrhythmic death.

- Nonspecific symptoms such as fever, fatigue, exertional dyspnea, and palpitation predominate. Most patients present with varying degrees of CHF.
- Approximately 40% of patients relate a history of a systemic viral syndrome.
- Some patients may present with chest discomfort reflective of an underlying myopericarditis.
- Rarely, a systemic embolus brings a patient to clinical attention.

Table 12-4. Causes of Myocarditis

Infective

Viral
  Coxsackievirus (A and B)
  Echovirus
  Adenovirus
  Influenza
  Varicella
  Poliomyelitis
  Mumps
  Viral hepatitis
  Epstein-Barr virus
  Cytomegalovirus
  Herpes simplex
  Human immunodeficiency virus (HIV)

Rickettsial
  Rocky Mountain spotted fever
  Scrub typhus (tsutsugamushi fever)
  Q fever (nine mile fever)

Bacterial
  Diphtheria
  Salmonella
  Tuberculosis
  Streptococcus
  Meningococcus
  Clostridium
  Legionella
  Brucella
  Bacterial endocarditis

Spirochetal

Fungal
  Aspergillosis
  Actinomycosis
  Blastomycosis
  Cryptococcus
  Candidiasis
  Histoplasmosis

Protozoal and Metazoal
  Trypanosomiasis
  Toxoplasmosis
  Malaria
  Schistosomiasis
  Cysticercosis
  Echinococcus
  Trichinosis

Table 12-4. (continued)

Table 12-4. (continued) Causes of Myocarditis

Noninfective
Drugs
  Cocaine
  Acetaminophen
  Lithium
  Catecholamines
  Doxorubicin
  Hypersensitive drug reactions
Chemicals
  Lead
  Arsenic
  Carbon monoxide
  Animal stings and bites
Physical Agents
  Radiation
  Hypothermia
  Hyperpyrexia
Systemic Illness
  Systemic lupus erythematosus
  Other collagen vascular disease
  Sarcoidosis
  Kawasaki's disease

Reproduced with permission from: Peters NS, Poole-Wilson PA. Myocarditis—continuing clinical and pathologic confusion. Am Heart J 1991;121:943.

On physical examination, tachycardia and fever are common. Pulmonary congestion and ventricular gallops are noted in the presence of CHF.

Diagnostic Tests

Electrocardiogram   The ECG often shows nonspecific ST segment and T wave changes and varying degrees of conduction abnormality.

- Often, ECG changes are transient.
- Atrial and ventricular arrhythmias may occur.
- Abnormal QRS complexes and LBBB are reported to be markers associated with a poor prognosis.

Chest X-Ray   The cardiac silhouette may be normal to enlarged. Pulmonary vascular congestion may be present.

Echocardiography   Echocardiography reveals ventricular systolic dysfunction, which may be segmental in location. LV mural thrombus is detected in 15% of cases.

Scintigraphy Radionuclide scanning may show focal areas of inflamed and necrotic myocardium.

Myocardial Biopsy Endomyocardial biopsy may allow for a specific diagnosis, but caution is indicated:

- Myocarditis can be focal in nature and, therefore, easily missed unless multiple biopsies are taken.
- The biopsy may not be performed at the time of maximal inflammatory activity.
- Considerable interobserver variability of biopsy interpretation exists and histopathologic criteria are not uniformly applied.

Only 10% of cases of recent onset severe CHF are explainable by myocarditis as defined by histopathologic criteria.

Natural History

A wide spectrum of disease is present. Myocarditis may be an acute or chronic process. The clinical expression ranges from an asymptomatic state to fulminant CHF and severe dysrhythmias.

- The majority of patients with acute myocarditis make a full recovery with resolution of myocardial dysfunction.
- Giant-cell myocarditis appears to have a worse prognosis than lymphocytic myocarditis. A higher incidence of VT and AV block requiring pacemaker insertion is observed with giant-cell myocarditis. In addition, giant-cell myocarditis has a more fulminant clinical course and may be rapidly fatal.
- Subsequent "idiopathic" DCM and CHF may be late manifestations of myocarditis.
- Subclinical myocarditis may account for cases of dysrhythmias in otherwise structurally normal hearts and also for chest pain in the setting of normal coronary arteries.

Management

Therapy for myocarditis remains largely supportive. Evidence from animal studies indicates that hypoxia and exercise may exacerbate myocardial injury, so rest and adequate oxygenation are of paramount importance.

- Patients should be closely observed for evidence of conduction abnormalities and ventricular arrhythmias with appropriate treatment as indicated.
- CHF is treated in standard fashion (see Chapter 2).

Immunosuppressives

For the majority of patients with myocarditis, routine use of immunosuppressive drugs is not indicated. Certain subgroups of patients (sarcoidosis, giant-cell myocarditis, hypersensitivity myocarditis) may favorably respond to immunosuppressive therapy.

- Corticosteroids have been noted to cause increased viral replication and tissue necrosis in experimental models, and thus have been felt to be detrimental in human myocarditis. Recent studies, however, indicate that high-dose steroid therapy may be safe in acute myocarditis.
- Other immunosuppressive agents have not proved useful in experimental myocarditis. A treatment regimen consisting of prednisone with either cyclosporine or azathioprine did not improve ejection fraction or survival compared to standard therapy.

Anti-inflammatory Agents

Nonsteroidal anti-inflammatory agents should not be used in early (within the first 2 weeks) viral myocarditis because increased myocardial necrosis has been noted.

Antiviral Agents

Antiviral agents, interferon, and monoclonal anti-T cell antibodies may have benefit in experimental myocarditis and remain under active investigation.

Transplantation

Cardiac transplantation may be beneficial in fulminant cases when all other therapy has failed, but myocarditis patients have a poorer 1-year survival compared to patients transplanted for other indications. Among patients with giant-cell myocarditis, recurrence of disease in the transplanted heart is possible. More frequent follow-up care is suggested for this group of patients.

SUGGESTED READINGS

Basso C, Thiene G, Corrado D, et al. Arrhythmogenic right ventricular cardiomyopathy. Dysplasia, dystrophy, or myocarditis? Circulation 1996;94:983–991.

Brown CA, O'Connell JB. Myocarditis and idiopathic dilated cardiomyopathy. Am J Med 1995;99:309–314.

Child JS, Perloff JK. The restrictive cardiomyopathies. In: Perloff JK, ed. Cardiology Clinics Vol 6: The cardiomyopathies. Philadelphia: WB Saunders, 1988:389–416.

Cooper LT Jr, Berry GJ, Shabetai R. Idiopathic giant-cell myocarditis—natural history and treatment. N Engl J Med 1997;336:1860–1866.

Davidoff R, Palacios I, Southern J, et al. Giant cell versus lymphocytic myocarditis. A comparison of their clinical features and long-term outcomes. Circulation 1991;83:953–961.

Dec GW, Fuster V. Idiopathic dilated cardiomyopathy. N Engl J Med 1994;331:1564–1575.

Fananapazir L, Epstein ND, Curiel RV, et al. Long-term results of dual-chamber (DDD) pacing in obstructive hypertrophic cardiomyopathy. Circulation 1994;90:2731–2742.

Homans DC. Peripartum cardiomyopathy. N Engl J Med 1985;312:1432–1437.

Kasper EK, Agema WRP, Hutchins GM, et al. The causes of dilated cardiomyopathy: a clinicopatholgic review of 673 consecutive patients. J Am Coll Cardiol 1994;23:586–590.

Knight C, Kurbaan AS, Seggewiss H, et al. Nonsurgical septal reduction for hypertrophic obstructive cardiomyopathy. Outcome in the first series of patients. Circulation 1997;95:2075–2081.

Kushwawa SS, Fallon JT, Fuster VF. Restrictive cardiomyopathy. N Engl J Med 1997;336:267–276.

Maron BJ. Hypertrophic cardiomyopathy. Lancet 1997;350:127–133.

Mason JW, O'Connell JB, Herskowitz A, et al. A clinical trial of immunosuppressive therapy for myocarditis. N Engl J Med 1995;333:269–275.

McKenna W, Thiene G, Nava A, et al. Diagnosis of arrhythmogenic right ventricular dysplasia/cardiomyopathy. Br Heart J 1994;71:215–218.

Parrillo JE, Cunnion RE, Epstein SE, et al. A prospective, randomized controlled trial of prednisone for dilated cardiomyopathy. N Engl J Med 1989;321:1061–1068.

Peters NS, Poole-Wilson PA. Myocarditis—continuing clinical and pathologic confusion. Am Heart J 1991;121:942–947.

Spirito P, Seidman CE, McKenna WJ, Maron BJ. The management of hypertrophic cardiomyopathy. N Engl J Med 1997;336:775–785.

St. John Sutton MG, Cole P, Plappert M, et al. Effects of subsequent pregnancy on left ventricular function in peripartum cardiomyopathy. Am Heart J 1991;121:1776–1778.

Richardson P, McKenna W, Bristow M, et al. Report of the 1995 World Health Organization/International Society and Federation of Cardiology Task Force on the definition and classification of cardiomyopathies. Circulation 1996;93:841–842.

Pericardial Disease

Dennis A. Tighe
Edward K. Chung

The normal pericardium is composed of two layers:

Parietal pericardium: the outer layer, composed of collagen and elastic fibers.
Visceral pericardium: the inner layer, a serosal membrane.

As much as 50 mL of clear fluid (derived from the visceral layer) can be normally found within the pericardial space. The functions of the pericardium include:

- Anatomical fixation of the heart.
- Reducing friction between the beating heart and surrounding thoracic structures.
- Prevention of excessive cardiac motion.
- Acting as a barrier to prevent extension of thoracic infection or malignancy to the heart.
- Contributing to ventricular interdependence.
- Prevention of acute cardiac dilatation.

This chapter reviews the major disease processes affecting the pericardium.

ACUTE PERICARDITIS

Etiology

Idiopathic Pericarditis

Idiopathic (nonspecific or benign) pericarditis is the most common form of acute pericarditis. The cause is unknown, but may be related to a viral process or hypersensitivity reaction. Idiopathic pericarditis is often preceded by an upper respiratory tract infection occurring days to weeks before signs and symptoms.

Infectious Pericarditis

Viral Pericarditis Viral pericarditis is the most common form of infectious pericarditis. The most common viruses causing pericarditis are:

Coxsackievirus types A and B
Echovirus, type A
Mumps
Cytomegalovirus
Infectious mononucleosis
Human immunodeficiency virus (HIV)

Bacterial Pericarditis Bacterial pericarditis is most commonly caused by local extension of an intrathoracic infection, such as pneumonia or empyema. It occurs less often as a result of septicemia or IE. The most common infecting organisms are:

Staphylococcus aureus
Pneumococcus
Streptococci
Gonococcus
Meningococcus
Haemophilus influenzae

Tuberculous (TB) Pericarditis TB pericarditis is less common today, primarily due to the availability and efficacy of antituberculous drug therapy.

- Among patients with HIV infection, the incidence of TB pericardial involvement is increased.
- Evidence of pulmonary TB is found in half of patients with TB pericarditis.

Other Infectious Agents
- **Fungi.** Histoplasmosis is the most common cause. Less common infections include coccidioidomycosis and aspergillosis.
- **Parasites.** Parasitic infections such as toxoplasmosis,

amebiasis, and echinococcosis are uncommon causes of pericarditis.
• **Other infectious agents.** *Actinomyces israelii* and nocardia are uncommon.

Pericarditis After Myocardial Infarction

Post-MI pericarditis can occur within the first few days, weeks, or months after infarction.

- Acute pericarditis is clinically evident in up to 40% of patients following transmural MI, presumably due to direct extension of inflammation resulting from subepicardial necrosis.
- Dressler's syndrome (post-MI syndrome) is an acute pericardial inflammation often associated with fever and pleuritis that occurs 10 days to several weeks following MI. An autoimmune mechanism is presumed.

Postcardiotomy Syndrome

Postcardiotomy syndrome can occur in 10% to 30% of patients following cardiac surgery or as a result of cardiac trauma.

- It appears 2 weeks to 2 months following cardiac manipulation.
- Fever, chills, malaise, and pleuritic chest pain are presenting complaints.

It is likely secondary to a hypersensitivity response to blood in the pericardium and/or to an autoimmune reaction to injured myocardium or pericardium.

Miscellaneous Causes of Pericarditis

Collagen Vascular Disorders Pericarditis can be observed in patients with collagen vascular disorders such as systemic lupus erythematosus, rheumatoid arthritis, and scleroderma.

Other Inflammatory Disorders The pericardium can be involved in sarcoidosis, inflammatory bowel disease, acute rheumatic fever, and amyloidosis.

Drug-Related Pericarditis Procainamide is the most common cause. Other implicated drugs include hydralazine, diphenylhydantoin, isoniazid, methysergide, minoxidil, and penicillin.

Uremic Pericarditis   Uremic pericarditis may be hemorrhagic, but the majority of patients are asymptomatic. The etiology is unknown.

Radiation Therapy   Greater than 40 Gy delivered to the heart may cause acute pericarditis and pericardial effusion. Constrictive pericarditis may be a subsequent complication.

Clinical Manifestations

In spite of its varied etiologies, the signs and symptoms of pericarditis are similar. In most cases, signs and symptoms persist for 2 to 6 weeks and may recur in 20% to 30% of patients.

• **Substernal, Pleuritic-type Chest Pain.** The hallmark of acute pericarditis, this symptom is exacerbated with the supine position. Characteristically, the pain is partially or totally relieved by sitting up or leaning forward.
• **Low to Moderate Grade Fever.** Fever, in the range of 100° to 103°F (37.8° to 39.4°C), is common. Higher fevers may be observed with purulent pericarditis.
• **Pericardial Friction Rub.** A friction rub is the characteristic sign of pericardial inflammation. The rub has a "leathery" scratching sound which results from the rubbing of the inflamed layers of the pericardium. Friction rubs may have one to three components, corresponding to:
1. Cardiac motion during atrial systole (presystole)
2. Rapid ventricular filling in early diastole
3. Ventricular systole
   • The loudest and most easily heard component is that associated with ventricular systole.
   • The rapid diastolic filling component is least likely to be detected.
   • Friction rubs are classically evanescent and change with alteration of body position.
• **Cardiac Arrhythmias.** Rhythm disturbances such as sinus tachycardia, paroxysmal AF or atrial flutter, and SVT occur in 20% of patients.

Diagnostic Tests

Electrocardiography (ECG) Serial ECG is the most helpful test to confirm the diagnosis. Abnormalities of ST segments and T waves are characteristic of acute pericarditis. PR segment alteration may also occur.

Four ECG stages are recognized:

Stage 1. Typically, this stage persists for several days but occasionally may last for a number of weeks.
- Diffuse, concave upward ST segment elevations in all leads except aVR and V1 (Fig 13-1). These changes are caused by diffuse epicardial inflammation and/or injury.
- Upward concavity of the ST segment and its elevation in many leads allows one to differentiate pericarditis from acute MI.
- The PR segment may be depressed or isoelectric.

Stage 2.
- ST segments return to baseline and the T waves flatten, usually several days after the onset of acute pericarditis.
- PR segment depression may be present.

Stage 3.
- Diffuse T wave inversion is noted.
- Isoelectric PR segments are present.

Stage 4. This stage occurs weeks to months following onset of acute pericarditis.
- T waves revert to normal and the PR segment is isoelectric.

"Low QRS voltage" may suggest an associated large pericardial effusion.

Chest X-Ray In the absence of significant pericardial effusion, the CXR is usually within normal limits. However, if radiographic evidence of thoracic malignancy or pulmonary infection is present, insight into the etiology of pericarditis may be provided.

Echocardiography Echocardiography is a sensitive technique to diagnose the presence of pericardial effusion, which may occur as a result of pericarditis.

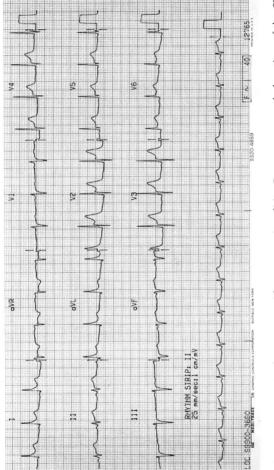

Figure 13-1. ECG of a patient with acute pericarditis. Concave upward elevation of the ST segment is present in many leads.

- In the presence of perimyocarditis, diffuse ventricular wall motion abnormalities may be present.

Tuberculosis Skin Testing TB skin testing should be performed in acute pericarditis of unknown etiology to screen for possible TB.

Cardiac Enzymes Cardiac enzymes are usually normal. The MB fraction of creatine phosphokinase or cardiac troponins may be elevated if significant epicardial (perimyocardial) inflammation is present.

Other Diagnostic Studies Other studies that may be indicated in the appropriate clinical situation include:

- Blood cultures if purulent pericarditis is suspected.
- Acute and convalescent serum viral titers in the setting of viral pericarditis.
- Serum BUN and creatinine if uremia is suspected.
- HIV testing if AIDS is suspected.
- Serum antinuclear antibody titer as well as serum rheumatoid factor if collagen vascular disease is suspected.
- Antihistone antibodies if procainamide-associated lupus is suspected.

Treatment

In the majority of cases, treatment consists of rest and alleviation of symptoms, as with:

Idiopathic pericarditis
Viral pericarditis
Pericarditis secondary to myocardial infarction
Postcardiotomy syndrome

If a treatable etiology is identified, specific treatment aimed at the underlying cause should be initiated:

Uremia
Bacterial infection
Tuberculosis

Standard Treatment for Nonpurulent Pericarditis
Bed rest is essential during the acute phase. Hospitalization is appropriate in the majority of cases because

cardiac tamponade has been reported to occur in up to 15% of patients.

Anti-inflammatory Therapy Anti-inflammatory therapy usually leads to a complete resolution of symptoms. Anti-inflammatory drugs should be tapered slowly after the patient has been pain free for several days.

Note: Anticoagulants should be avoided during the acute phase of pericarditis.

- **Mild Symptoms.** ASA, 650 mg orally four to six times daily, is appropriate therapy for the patient with mild symptoms.
- **Mild to Moderate Symptoms.** Nonsteroidal anti-inflammatory agents—such as indomethacin, 25–50 mg orally, or ibuprofen, 400–600 mg orally four times daily—usually bring relief of mild to moderate symptoms not relieved by ASA.
- **Severe, Nonresponsive Symptoms.** Prednisone (or its equivalent), 60–80 mg daily in divided doses given orally, may be used if symptoms are severe and not responsive to nonsteroidal anti-inflammatory drug therapy.
- **Other Analgesics.** In rare cases, opiates (morphine, meperidine) may be required to provide analgesia.

Treatment of Purulent Pericarditis
Surgical drainage of the infected pericardial space, often with pericardiectomy, is required.

- Antibiotic therapy, based on the specific infectious organism identified by pericardial fluid culture and sensitivity, should be given.

Surgery
- Pericardiectomy may be required for relief of symptoms when refractory, recurrent pericarditis occurs and medical therapy is not adequate.

PERICARDIAL EFFUSION

Pericardial effusion is an acute or chronic accumulation of fluid in the pericardial space. An effusion may be secondary to pericarditis of any etiology. Although pericardial effusion is often asymptomatic, it may result in pericardial tamponade.

Pericardial Tamponade

Pericardial tamponade occurs when intrapericardial pressure exceeds cardiac filling pressures. The occurrence of tamponade relates to the rate of fluid accumulation as well as the quantity of fluid within the pericardial space.

- Sudden accumulation of 150 to 200 mL of fluid may increase intrapericardial pressure sufficiently to cause tamponade.
- If the effusion accumulates slowly, allowing the pericardium to stretch, several liters of fluid may accumulate without a significant increase of intrapericardial pressure.

Etiology

Pericardial effusion may be secondary to any cause of pericarditis. The character of the fluid is related to the cause of the effusion:

Serosanguinous, exudative pericardial effusion: Neoplastic involvement of the pericardium, TB, idiopathic pericarditis, uremia, hypothyroidism, radiation pericarditis, or pericarditis due to MI.

Serous, transudative pericardial effusion: CHF or hypoproteinemia.

Bloody pericardial effusion: Cardiac trauma, rupture of an aortic aneurysm or aortic dissection into the pericardial space, coagulopathy, or cardiac rupture following MI.

Chylous pericardial effusion. Milky white in appearance, laboratory evaluation reveals high cholesterol, triglyceride, and protein content. It is associated with any cause of mechanical obstruction of the thoracic duct or its drainage into the left subclavian vein.

Clinical Manifestations

Clinical manifestations depend on the presence or absence of increased pericardial pressure.

- When pericardial pressure is not elevated, the patient is often asymptomatic. Some patients may complain of a dull chest ache.
- With increasing effusion size, symptoms may be related to local compression of adjacent structures; for example, dysphagia can be caused by esophageal compression or dyspnea secondary to pulmonary compression.
- Ewart's sign (dullness to percussion at the lung base below the angle of the left scapula) is noted when a large pericardial effusion with distended pericardial sac compresses the base of the left lung.
- Decreased heart sounds are often present when the pericardial effusion is very large.

Cardiac Tamponade

Cardiac tamponade, characterized by decreased diastolic cardiac filling and diminished CO, occurs when intrapericardial pressure is significantly elevated.

- Tamponade may be due to a large, uniform effusion or may be secondary to localized cardiac compression (e.g., after open heart surgery or trauma).
- Malignancy (especially carcinoma of the lung and breast) is now the most common cause of cardiac tamponade in medical patients.

Symptoms   The symptoms of cardiac tamponade are manifestations of diminished CO:

Dyspnea
Fatigue
Restlessness

Signs   The signs of cardiac tamponade are caused by external compression of the heart, causing systemic venous congestion, decreased diastolic cardiac filling, and decreased CO.

Jugular venous distention   Jugular venous distention with alteration of venous filling waves is the most common finding of cardiac tamponade.

Normal venous return to the heart occurs during ventricular ejection (systolic X-descent on venous pressure pulse) as well as during the opening of the TV during diastole (diastolic Y-descent of venous pressure pulse). With cardiac tamponade, venous return occurs only during ventricular ejection; therefore, the systolic X-descent of the venous pressure pulse is preserved or accentuated, while the diastolic Y-descent is diminished or obliterated.

Hepatic congestion and peripheral edema Hepatic congestion and peripheral edema may result from increased systemic venous pressure.

Hypotension and tachycardia Hypotension and tachycardia are signs of decreased CO.

Pulsus paradoxus Pulsus paradoxus—an inspiratory decline in systolic arterial pressure more than 10 mm Hg during normal breathing—may indicate pericardial effusion under pressure. A common, but not pathognomonic physical sign, it is an exaggeration of the normal 8 to 10 mmHg inspiratory decrease in systolic arterial pressure.

Laboratory Studies

ECG
ECG abnormalities are common:

- ST segment elevation and/or T wave inversion may be found when pericardial effusion is associated with acute or subacute pericarditis.
- Generalized low voltage of the QRS complex is common with moderate to large pericardial effusions.
- Electrical alternans—changing configuration of the P waves, QRS complexes, or T waves on every other beat or every third beat—may represent swinging of the heart amid a large pericardial effusion.

Chest X-Ray
An enlarged cardiac silhouette is present when the effusion is moderate to large in size. A "water bottle" or "pear-shaped" cardiac configuration may be observed if the effusion is large.

Echocardiography
Echocardiography can detect as little as 20 mL of fluid. It is the most sensitive test for diagnosis and semiquantitation of pericardial effusion.

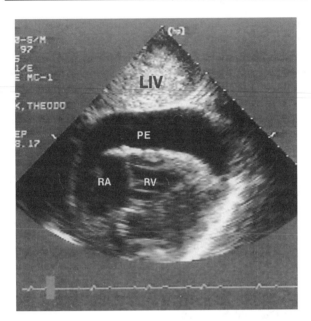

Figure 13-2. A large pericardial effusion (PE) is present. No compression of the right ventricle (RV) or right atrial (RA) free wall is noted. The etiology of this effusion was metastatic malignancy. (LIV = liver.)

Following cardiac surgery, localized effusion (especially adjacent to the RA) should be sought. If TTE is not adequate, a TEE should be performed.

Cardiac Tamponade   Cardiac tamponade is a hemodynamic phenomenon. The presence of a large pericardial effusion alone is not indicative of pericardial tamponade (Fig 13-2).

• **Two-dimensional and M-mode.** Signs of altered diastolic filling such as RV free wall collapse (Fig 13-3) or persistent RA free wall inversion strongly suggest cardiac tamponade. Plethora of the IVC without significant respiratory variation is frequently observed.
• **Doppler.** The Doppler findings characteristic of cardiac tamponade (Fig 13-4) are:

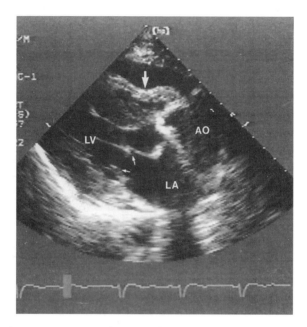

Figure 13-3. A medium-sized pericardial effusion under pressure is present. The large arrow demonstrates compression of the right ventricle during diastole. Small arrows point to open mitral valve. (AO = aorta; LA = left atrium; LV = left ventricle.)

- Diminished mitral E wave height immediately following inspiration.
- Diminished tricuspid E wave height immediately following expiration.
- Appreciable decrease in or total loss of diastolic forward flow during expiration in hepatic venous flow velocity profile.

Cardiac Catheterization
Invasive measurements can determine intracardiac pressures and document the hemodynamic effects. The classic hemodynamic findings of tamponade include:

- Elevation of mean RA pressure with prominent systolic X-descent and absence of diastolic Y-descent in the RA pressure tracing.

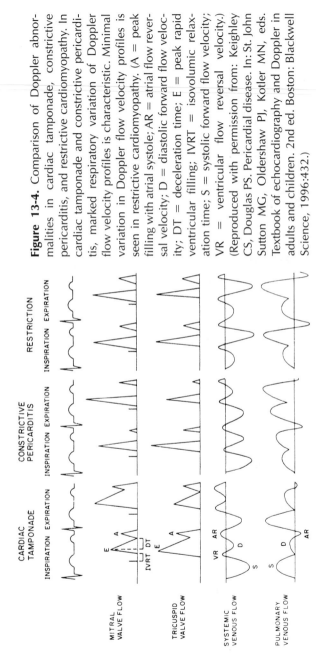

Figure 13-4. Comparison of Doppler abnormalities in cardiac tamponade, constrictive pericarditis, and restrictive cardiomyopathy. In cardiac tamponade and constrictive pericarditis, marked respiratory variation of Doppler flow velocity profiles is characteristic. Minimal variation in Doppler flow velocity profiles is seen in restrictive cardiomyopathy. (A = peak filling with atrial systole; AR = atrial flow reversal velocity; D = diastolic forward flow velocity; DT = deceleration time; E = peak rapid ventricular filling; IVRT = isovolumic relaxation time; S = systolic forward flow velocity; VR = ventricular flow reversal velocity.) (Reproduced with permission from: Keighley CS, Douglas PS. Pericardial disease. In: St. John Sutton MG, Oldershaw PJ, Kotler MN, eds. Textbook of echocardiography and Doppler in adults and children. 2nd ed. Boston: Blackwell Science, 1996:432.)

- Elevation and virtual equalization of diastolic pressures in all cardiac chambers as a result of the uniform external cardiac compression.
- Diminished CO.

Diagnosis

Pericardial Effusion

- The presence of a pericardial effusion should be considered in any patient with pericarditis.
- The diagnosis of pericardial effusion should be suspected in the patient who exhibits an enlarged cardiac silhouette on CXR without known cause.

  Echocardiography. Echocardiography is the most sensitive technique for identifying pericardial effusion.

Pericardial Tamponade

Pericardial tamponade should be suspected when elevated central venous pressure is associated with signs and symptoms of decreased CO. When volume depletion is present, elevation of central venous pressure may be subtle or absent.

Echocardiography. In suspected tamponade, urgent echocardiography should be performed.

- If there is no evidence of pericardial effusion, then pericardial tamponade cannot be the etiology of the clinical picture. TEE may be required if transthoracic windows are suboptimal or a localized collection is suspected.

Catheterization. If the diagnosis of tamponade remains unclear, invasive hemodynamic parameters as discussed above should be measured.

Treatment

Pericardial Tamponade

Removal of pericardial fluid is the treatment of pericardial tamponade. Prior to and during pericardial drainage, hypotension caused by external cardiac compression is treated by intravascular volume expansion.

Pericardiocentesis   Pericardiocentesis, using a needle or catheter to percutaneously enter the pericardial space,

is effective in treating acute tamponade when the pericardial effusion is large and anteriorly located. A drainage catheter may be left in place until significant drainage stops.

Surgery   Surgery should be considered to remove pericardial fluid when:

- Percutaneous pericardiocentesis is unsuccessful.
- Pericardial effusion is rapidly recurrent.
- Purulent pericarditis is present.
- Tamponade is due to small, posterior, or loculated effusion.

Surgical pericardial exploration is indicated when hemopericardium due to cardiac trauma is present.

The surgical approaches include:

- Subxiphoid pericardial window.
- Thoracotomy with creation of a pleuropericardial window.
- Thoracotomy with radical pericardiectomy.
- Placement of pericardioperitoneal shunt (in patients with symptomatic malignant pericardial effusion).

The subxiphoid pericardial window approach has the advantage of being performed under local anesthesia with a low rate of complications.

Percutaneous Balloon Pericardiotomy   Percutaneous balloon pericardiotomy is an option for patients with large symptomatic pericardial effusions. It is less invasive than the current surgical approaches. In the experience to date it has a high success rate.

Pericardial Effusion

Therapy directed at the underlying disorder is indicated for pericardial effusion without tamponade. Pericardial fluid should be removed by pericardiocentesis and undergo bacterial and cytologic analysis if the effusion is thought to be secondary to a nonviral infection (bacterial, fungal, mycobacterial) or malignancy.

- **Purulent pericarditis.** Purulent pericarditis requires surgical pericardial drainage and parenteral antibiotic therapy directed at the specific infecting organism.

- **Malignant effusions.** Malignant pericardial effusions are often recurrent and require repeated percutaneous drainage, surgical pericardiostomy with drainage, percutaneous balloon pericardiotomy, or pericardioperitoneal shunt placement.
  - Intrapericardial tetracycline or bleomycin instillation may be a helpful adjunctive therapy to sclerose the pericardial space and prevent recurrent effusion.
- **Viral, idiopathic, uremic pericarditis.** In the setting of viral, idiopathic, or uremic pericarditis, pericardial fluid should be obtained if the effusion does not respond to anti-inflammatory therapy or dialysis, or if tamponade occurs.

CONSTRICTIVE PERICARDITIS

Pericardial constriction is a disorder in which the pericardium thickens, undergoes scar formation, and becomes fibrotic following an inflammatory, infectious, or traumatic pericardial process. It may exist in several forms:

Chronic Constrictive Pericarditis. The chronic form obliterates the pericardial cavity with a rigid, sometimes calcified pericardium.

Subacute Constrictive Pericarditis. In the subacute form, the pericardium is less rigid or fibroelastic.

Effusive Constrictive Pericarditis. In this variant, pericardial effusion exists along with fibroelastic pericardial constriction.

The constrictive process usually affects the heart uniformly; however, localized constriction may be observed in rare cases.

Transient Constrictive Pericarditis. In this variant pericardial thickening may cause transient constrictive physiology that resolves spontaneously or with medical therapy of pericarditis.

Etiology

Idiopathic pericarditis. Idiopathic pericarditis is the most common cause.

Purulent pericarditis. Purulent pericarditis may result in pericardial fibrosis with constriction. In spite of effective antituberculous therapy, pericardial constriction occurs in 50% to 60% of patients treated for TB pericarditis.

Radiation. Mediastinal radiation therapy may result in constriction months to years following exposure.

Malignancy. Malignancy may cause cardiac compression by neoplastic pericardial thickening. Metastasis from breast or lung carcinoma is most commonly implicated. Malignant melanoma, lymphoma, and leukemia result in pericardial involvement less frequently.

Uremic pericarditis. Uremic pericarditis may progress to constriction an average of 6 months following the acute episode.

Surgery. Cardiac surgery may rarely result in pericardial constriction as early as 2 weeks, or months, or even years following surgery. Constriction may occur even if the pericardium is left open after surgery.

Trauma. Cardiac trauma, nonpenetrating or penetrating, may lead to pericardial constriction months to years following trauma.

Collagen vascular disease. Collagen vascular diseases are rare causes of pericardial constriction.

Pathophysiology

Constriction of the cardiac chambers with impaired diastolic filling is the primary pathophysiologic feature. Systolic function is usually preserved. The rigid, thickened pericardium leads to an impairment of ventricular filling during the latter two-thirds of diastole causing decreased CO and systemic venous congestion.

- In early diastole, when intracardiac volume is less than that defined by the rigid pericardium, ventricular filling occurs rapidly due to increased atrial pressure. This early diastolic filling corresponds to the steep Y-descent of the jugular venous and RA pressure waveforms and the early diastolic dip of the ventricular pressure waveform.
- Following the first third of diastole, cardiac filling is rapidly impeded by the constricting, noncompliant

pericardium. This is manifested by the diastolic pressure plateau of the ventricular pressure waveform.

Clinical Manifestations

Clinical features reflect the insidious increase of systemic and pulmonary venous pressure coupled with decreased CO. A high degree of clinical suspicion is required for proper diagnosis.

Symptoms

Exertional Dyspnea Dyspnea, the most common symptom, occurs in up to 80% of cases. Pulmonary venous HTN, decreased CO, pleural effusion, and limited diaphragmatic excursion due to ascites are possible causes.

Abdominal Fullness and Peripheral Edema Abdominal symptoms are often due to ascites. Fluid accumulation may appear as peripheral edema.

Nonspecific Symptoms Malaise, weakness, wasting, and fatigue are common nonspecific symptoms. These symptoms are the result of low CO and hepatic congestion.

Physical Examination
- The patient with subacute fibroelastic constriction has hemodynamic abnormalities and physical signs that are intermediate between those of cardiac tamponade and chronic, rigid pericarditis.
- Among patients with effusive-constrictive pericarditis, physical signs closely resemble those of cardiac tamponade.

Elevated Systemic Venous Pressure Elevation of jugular venous pressure occurs in almost all cases.

- Prominent X- and Y-descents of the venous pressure waveform occur in 95% of patients with chronic, rigid constriction.
- In subacute (fibroelastic) disease, the X-descent is prominent but the Y-descent may be minimal or absent.

Hepatomegaly, ascites, and peripheral edema occur in 70% to 90% of patients. These signs may initially be absent in rapidly developing cases.

Kussmaul's Sign   Kussmaul's sign (inspiratory distention of jugular veins) occurs in up to 40% of cases of chronic, rigid constriction. It indicates that the encased RV is unable to accept the increased venous return during inspiration.

Pericardial Knock   Pericardial knock is an early diastolic sound caused by a sudden cessation of ventricular filling at the end of the first one-third of diastole in the setting of rigid constriction.

- It occurs 0.09 to 0.12 seconds after S_2.
- It is higher in frequency and occurs earlier than S_3.

Pulsus Paradoxus   Pulsus paradoxus may be prominent with subacute (fibroelastic) disease, but it is rare with rigid constriction.

Diagnostic Studies

ECG   The ECG most often reveals nonspecific abnormalities of the ST segment and the T wave.

- Low QRS voltage and LA abnormality suggesting P-mitrale may be present.
- In long-standing disease, AF may develop.

Chest X-Ray
- Pericardial calcification (Fig 13-5) strongly supports the diagnosis of constriction, but is found in only 40% of cases.
- Pleural effusions are present 60% of the time.

Echocardiography   TTE is insensitive and nonspecific in documenting pericardial thickening. TEE may be superior to study pericardial thickness.

The altered diastolic hemodynamics characteristic of pericardial constriction are well documented by echocardiography:

- M-mode signs include abrupt posterior motion of the interventricular septum in early diastole (septal

Figure 13-5. Lateral chest x-ray demonstrating pericardial calcification (*arrows*) in a patient with rigid pericardial constriction.

bounce), LV posterior wall flattening, and premature diastolic opening of the pulmonic valve.
- 2D imaging also can show abnormal septal motion. In addition, dilation (plethora) of hepatic veins and IVC is prominent, and minimal respiratory variation in vena caval diameter is often observed.
- The Doppler hemodynamic findings in relation to respiratory events are similar to those noted in cardiac tamponade (see Fig 13-4).

Computed Tomography(CT) CT can determine the presence and extent of pericardial thickening and effusion. CT does not provide hemodynamic information.

Magnetic Resonance Imaging (MRI) MRI is a sensitive technique for evaluation of pericardial thickness. As with CT, MRI does not provide hemodynamic information.

Cardiac Catheterization Left and right heart catheterization verifies the hemodynamic features of constriction and is usually required for diagnosis.

Elevation and equalization (within 5 mm Hg) of mean

RA, RV diastolic, PA diastolic, mean LA (often represented by PCWP), and LV diastolic pressures occur because the constricting process most often affects all chambers equally (Fig 13-6).

- The RA waveform displays A and V waves of equal amplitude with rapid X- and Y-descents, giving the characteristic "M" or "W" appearance (Fig 13-7). An inspiratory increase in mean RA pressure (Kussmaul's sign) may be demonstrated.
- LV and RV pressure waveforms display a deep early diastolic dip (period of rapid ventricular filling), which rises rapidly to a diastolic plateau (cessation of ventricular filling due to external cardiac compression) producing the classic "square root sign" (Fig 13-8).
- In the presence of volume depletion, equalization of diastolic pressures as well as diastolic dip and plateau waveform may be absent. These characteristic hemodynamic findings may be elicited by rapid IV infusion of 1000 mL of 0.9% sodium chloride over several minutes.

As opposed to the findings of RCM, the RV and PA systolic pressures in constrictive pericarditis rarely exceed 60 mm Hg and most often are in the range of 30 to 40 mm Hg.

Diagnosis

The diagnosis of constrictive pericarditis should be strongly considered in the presence of the classic symptoms and signs previously discussed. A high index of suspicion is necessary. Documentation of pericardial thickening with diastolic cardiac dysfunction as described above is required for diagnosis.

Treatment

Complete pericardial resection is the definitive treatment for symptomatic chronic constrictive pericarditis. Following pericardiectomy, reversal of constrictive hemodynamics and resolution of symptoms may occur immediately or may be delayed for weeks or months.

Low-dose diuretic therapy may be used to treat the

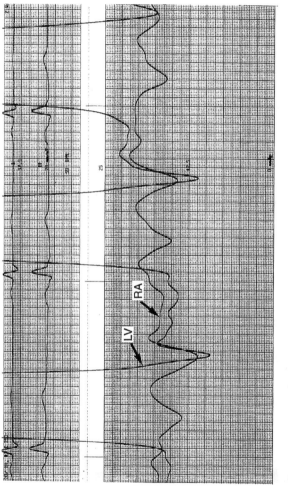

Figure 13-6. Simultaneous left ventricular (LV) and right atrial (RA) pressure tracings (0 to 25 mm Hg scale). An ECG tracing is provided at the top to allow timing of hemodynamic events in relation to electrical activity. Elevated and near-equal diastolic pressures are demonstrated.

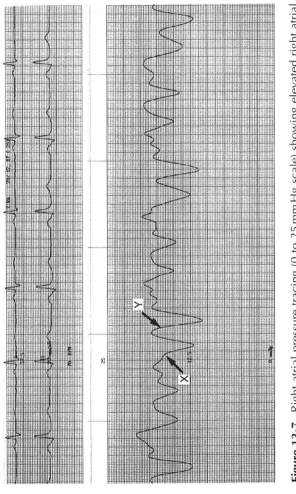

Figure 13-7. Right atrial pressure tracing (0 to 25 mm Hg scale) showing elevated right atrial pressure with rapid X- and Y-descents. The characteristic "M" or "W" configuration is present.

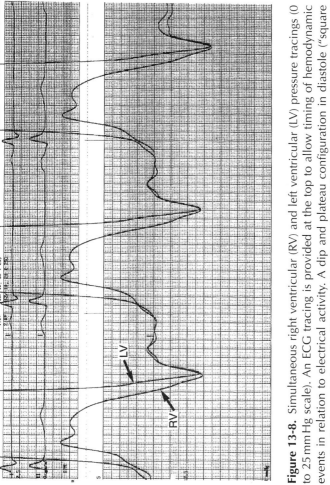

Figure 13-8. Simultaneous right ventricular (RV) and left ventricular (LV) pressure tracings (0 to 25 mm Hg scale). An ECG tracing is provided at the top to allow timing of hemodynamic events in relation to electrical activity. A dip and plateau configuration in diastole ("square root sign") characterizes the RV and LV tracings. In addition, elevation and equalization of ventricular diastolic pressures are present.

patient who is minimally symptomatic or whose only sign is mild peripheral edema.

SUGGESTED READINGS

Burstow DJ, Oh JK, Bailey KR, et al. Cardiac tamponade: characteristic Doppler observations. Mayo Clin Proc 1989;64:312–324.

Cameron J, Oesterle SN, Baldwin JC, Hancock EW. The etiologic spectrum of constrictive pericarditis. Am Heart J 1987;113:354–360.

Fowler NO. Tuberculous pericarditis. JAMA 1991;266:99–103.

Hancock EW. On the elastic and rigid forms of constrictive pericarditis. Am Heart J 1980; 100:917–923.

Lorell BH. Pericardial diseases. In: Braunwald E, ed. Heart disease. 5th ed. Philadelphia: WB Saunders, 1997:1478–1534.

Markiewicz W, Borovik R, Ecker S. Cardiac tamponade in medical patients: treatment and prognosis in the echocardiographic era. Am Heart J 1986;111:1138–1142.

McGregor M. Current concepts: pulsus paradoxus. N Engl J Med 1979;301:480–482.

Nishmura RA, Connolly DC, Parkin TW. Constrictive pericarditis: assessment of current diagnostic procedures. Mayo Clin Proc 1985;60:397–401.

Oh JK, Hatle LV, Mulvagh SL, Tajik AJ. Transient constrictive pericarditis: diagnosis by two-dimensional Doppler echocardiography. Mayo Clin Proc 1993;68:1158–1164.

Shabetai R, Fowler NO, Guntheroth W. The hemodynamics of cardiac tamponade and constrictive pericarditis. Am J Cardiol 1970;26:480–489.

Soulen RL, Stark DD, Higgins CB. Magnetic resonance imaging of constrictive pericardial disease. Am J Cardiol 1985;55:480–484.

Spodick DH. The normal and diseased pericardium: current concepts of pericardial physiology, diagnosis, and treatment. J Am Coll Cardiol 1983;1:240–251.

Vaitkus PT, Herrmann HC, LeWinter MM. Treatment of malignant pericardial effusion. JAMA 1992;272:59–64.

Wang N, Feikes JR, Mogensen T, et al. Pericardioperitoneal shunt: an alternative treatment for malignant pericardial effusion. Ann Thorac Surg 1994;57:289–292.

Ziskind AA, Pearce AC, Lemmon CC, et al. Percutaneous balloon pericardiotomy for the treatment of cardiac tamponade and large pericardial effusions: description of technique and report of the first 50 cases. J Am Coll Cardiol 1993;21:1–5.

Cardiac Tumors and Cardiovascular Aspects of Malignancy

Dennis A. Tighe
Edward K. Chung

The heart may be the site of a primary tumor or may be secondarily involved by metastatic disease. Cardiac neoplasms may produce a variety of symptoms, and a high index of suspicion must be maintained to make a proper diagnosis. Treatment of malignancies with chemotherapeutic agents and/or radiation therapy may have toxic effects on the heart. This chapter reviews the presentation, diagnosis, and treatment of tumors involving the heart as well as the effects of antineoplastic therapy on it.

PRIMARY CARDIAC TUMORS

Primary cardiac tumors are rare, occurring with a frequency of 0.017% to 0.33% in postmortem examinations.

Benign tumors. More than 75% of primary cardiac
tumors are benign.
- Cardiac myxomas comprise 30% to 50% of all benign tumors.
- Other benign cardiac neoplasms include rhabdomyomas, fibromas, lipomas, and papillary fibroelastomas.

Malignant tumors. Sarcomas are the most common malignant primary cardiac tumor. Angiosarcomas and

449

rhabdomyosarcomas are the predominant pathologic types.

BENIGN CARDIAC TUMORS

Myxoma

Epidemiology and Pathology
Myxoma is the most common primary cardiac tumor.

- Most myxomas occur sporadically; however, up to 10% may be familial.
- Myxomas have a female preponderance (70%).
- Myxomas are found in all age groups. The most common age at diagnosis is 30 to 60 years old. Familial myxomas often present at a younger age.

Myxomas can arise anywhere in the heart including the endocardial surface of the cardiac chambers, the chordae tendineae, or the valve leaflets.

- More than 75% occur in the LA.
- 8% to 25% occur in the RA.
- 4% to 8% occur in one or both ventricles.

Typically, myxomas occur as a single pedunculated mass (Fig 14-1) attached near the fossa ovalis of the interatrial septum. Myxomas are rarely sessile.

Multiple myxomas in a single chamber or those found in more than one cardiac chamber should suggest a genetic component.

Diagnosis

History and Symptoms
The widespread use of echocardiography has led to the earlier detection of myxomas, many of which are asymptomatic.

A variety of symptoms may be associated. Patients may present with one or more of the following triad:

- **Constitutional symptoms.** Fever, weight loss, fatigue, and/or anemia occur in up to 90% of patients at some time during the clinical course.
- **Embolism.** Embolic phenomena occur in 30% to 50% of cases.

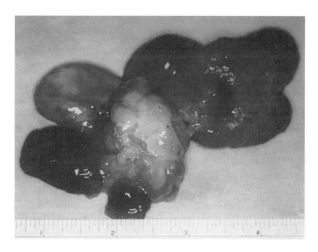

Figure 14-1. Pathologic specimen of an excised large cardiac myxoma. The tumor is multilobulated and has a glistening appearance.

- **Obstructive manifestations.** Intermittent occlusion of the MV or TV may cause transient symptoms mimicking MS or TS (dyspnea, CHF, syncope). Very large myxomas may obstruct the pulmonary or great veins.

Physical Examination

Jugular venous pressure may be elevated if there is obstruction of the TV orifice or SVC.

Auscultation Auscultatory features are associated with movement of the myxoma. Myxomas have no distinct auscultatory features unless they interfere with valve function.

- **Heart sounds.** S_1 and P_2 may be accentuated if there is pulmonary HTN due to obstruction of the mitral orifice.
- **Tumor plop.** An early diastolic sound ("tumor plop") caused by the sudden cessation of tumor movement may be heard in cases of LA myxoma 0.08 to 0.12 seconds after A_2. The low-pitched tumor plop may be confused with:

- Opening snap of MS—tumor plop occurs later than opening snap and is lower in frequency.
- S_3—tumor plop has higher frequency and occurs later than S_3.

Tumor plop may also be heard in cases of RA myxoma.

- **Murmurs.** Murmurs occur in 40% to 100% of cases.
- LA myxoma is associated with a diastolic murmur when obstruction to LV filling occurs. Classically, alteration of the body position changes the degree of obstruction and thereby alters the murmur.
- The murmur of MR is present when LA myxoma inhibits MV closure. RA myxomas may cause tricuspid diastolic and systolic murmurs by similar mechanisms.

Diagnostic Evaluation
- Elevated ESR, anemia, and leukocytosis are frequent.
- The CXR is often normal. It may exhibit chamber enlargement when the tumor is very large or significant valvar insufficiency or inflow obstruction is present.
- ECG is usually normal.

Echocardiography
Echocardiography is the diagnostic study of choice to evaluate cardiac masses.

M-mode echocardiography
- M-mode of LA myxoma typically reveals a mass of echoes behind the anterior leaflet of the MV during diastole which move into the LA during systole. Similar findings are noted with RA myxoma and the TV.

Two-dimensional Echocardiography (2TE)
2TE is superior to M-mode by allowing real time visualization of the cardiac chambers and valves and defining tumor size and attachment point.

- The echocardiographic appearance may help differentiate myxomas from other cardiac mass lesions (Table 14-1).
- It is very important to scan all cardiac chambers carefully for the presence of synchronous masses.

Table 14-1. Echocardiographic Features of Atrial Masses

Mass	Appearance	Attachment	Mobility	Comments
Myxoma	Gelatinous, friable	Interatrial septum	Mobile	Majority in left atrium
Thrombus	Irregular, layered appearance	Posterior atrial wall Atrial appendage	Usually not mobile	Mitral or tricuspid stenosis
Vegetations	Irregular	AV valve	Mobile	Associated valve abnormalities
Metastatic tumor	Large, irregular	Atrial wall	Immobile	Associated primary tumor

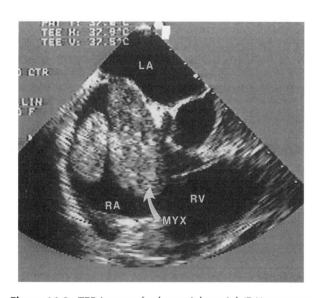

Figure 14-2. TEE image of a large right atrial (RA) myxoma (MYX). The tumor is attached at the fossa ovalis of the inter-atrial septum. (LA = left atrium; RV = right ventricle.)

Transesophageal Echocardiography (TEE) TEE provides high-resolution imaging without many of the limitations associated with TTE (Fig 14-2). TEE can provide precise anatomic information and should be used when TTE is suboptimal.

MRI Scanning   MRI is helpful to confirm the presence of an intracardiac mass and to estimate the extent of the tumor involvement. An advantage of MRI is its ability to characterize tissue density, which may enable identification of tissue type preoperatively.

Angiography   Angiography is rarely used today to diagnose or evaluate intracardiac masses. It has poor sensitivity and specificity with a diagnostic yield much lower than echocardiography or MRI.

Treatment

Once identified, myxomas should be surgically removed to avoid the risk of tumor embolization. The recurrence rate is:

1% to 5% for sporadic myxomas
12% to 22% familial and complex tumors

Other Benign Cardiac Tumors

Rhabdomyoma, lipoma, fibroma, papillary fibroelastoma, teratoma, and angioma comprise the majority of other benign primary tumors.

Clinical Presentation. These tumors are usually clinically silent. Symptoms may result from:
- Intracavitary obstruction (rhabdomyoma)
- Arrhythmias
- Conduction defects due to impingement on the conduction system (fibroma, lipoma)
- Peripheral embolization (papillary fibroelastoma)

Diagnosis
- Usually made by echocardiography.
- Biopsy is often required for tissue identification.
- MRI is a promising technique to aid in noninvasive tissue characterization and identification.

Treatment. Surgical excision is indicated when symptoms are present.

Rhabdomyomas

Rhabdomyoma is the most common primary cardiac tumor among infants and children.

- Nearly all are multiple and they occur with equal frequency in the LV and RV myocardium.
- Tuberous sclerosis is a common association.

Lipomas

Lipomas may present at any age.

- Lipomas are characteristically well circumscribed, encapsulated, and solitary.
- Lipomas may be subepicardial, subendocardial, or intramuscular in location. Lipomas may be massive in size.
- MRI can permit accurate diagnosis.

Fibromas

Fibromas occur predominantly in children.

- Fibromas most often involve the myocardium of the anterior wall of the LV or the interventricular septum.
- Fibromas tend to be large.
- Fibromas are associated with ventricular arrhythmia, sudden death, or obstructive symptoms.

Papillary Fibroelastomas

Papillary fibroelastomas are most often recognized in adults.

- Papillary fibroelastomas involve the ventricular surface of the semilunar valves and the atrial surface of the AV valves.
- Papillary fibroelastomas are characterized by a thin stalk and fronded head.
- Most papillary fibroelastomas are clinically silent and often are incidental findings during routine echocardiography.
- In some cases, peripheral embolization may occur.

MALIGNANT PRIMARY CARDIAC TUMORS

Pathology and Epidemiology

Approximately 25% of primary cardiac tumors are malignant, and almost all are sarcomas. Sarcomas are histologically classified as angiosarcoma, rhabdomyosarcoma, fibrosarcoma, osteosarcoma, and liposarcoma.

- Angiosarcoma and rhabdomyosarcoma are the most frequent types.
- Mesothelioma and lymphoma may rarely occur as primary cardiac tumors.

Most sarcomas involve the right heart and LA.

- Sarcomas grow rapidly and invade myocardium, valves, and pericardium.
- Lung metastases are common.

Clinical Presentation

Malignant cardiac tumors most often present between the ages of 30 and 70. Symptoms are caused by cardiac chamber infiltration, pericardial involvement, arrhythmia, compression, or obstruction.

- At the time of presentation, widespread tumor infiltration and/or metastases are present. A rapid and progressive downhill clinical course is characteristic.
- Mesothelioma may cause advanced AV block and sudden death.

Diagnosis
- Echocardiography or other noninvasive imaging study may strongly suggest the presence of a primary cardiac malignancy.
- Biopsy, which can be guided by TEE, is often required for histologic confirmation.

Treatment

Palliative treatment with tumor resection, radiation therapy, and chemotherapy may bring relief of symptoms, but these tumors are ultimately fatal. In rare instances, heart transplantation may be performed.

SECONDARY (METASTATIC) CARDIAC TUMORS
Epidemiology and Pathology

Secondary cardiac tumors are 20 to 40 times more common than primary tumors.

- Direct extension of intrathoracic malignancy to the pericardium is the most common mode of tumor dissemination. Metastasis to the myocardium via hematogenous or lymphangitic routes is less common. Direct extension of tumor to the heart via the pulmonary veins may also occur.
- Direct extension from the IVC may occur with abdominal tumors such as renal cell carcinoma, hepatocellular carcinoma, uterine leiomyosarcoma, or adrenal cell carcinoma.
- The cardiac valves are infrequently involved due to their relative avascularity.

In autopsy series, cardiac metastases have been found in:

Up to 60% of patients with malignant melanoma.
20% to 50% of patients with lymphoma, leukemia, or myeloma.
20% of patients with carcinoma of the lung, breast, esophagus, pancreas, kidney, or testicle.

Bronchogenic carcinoma and carcinoma of the breast account for the most frequently encountered tumor metastases to the heart.

Diagnosis

Among patients with known malignancy, any change in cardiac status should prompt a search for cardiac metastasis.

Clinical Presentation

Pericardial Involvement Pericardial involvement may result in:

Chest pain
Arrhythmias (especially AF)
Pericardial effusion, tamponade, or constriction (see Chapter 13)

Myocardial Involvement
Myocardial involvement may result in:

Atrial or ventricular arrhythmias
Conduction abnormalities

Diffuse tumor invasion resulting in myocardial damage may lead to heart failure.

• **ECG.** Myocardial tumor involvement is suggested by the presence of diffuse electrocardiographic ST segment and/or T wave changes. Tumor invasion may lead to Q waves on the electrocardiogram simulating an MI.

Intracavitary Tumors Intracavitary tumor invasion may result in manifestations of valve or chamber obstruction.

Superior Vena Cava Syndrome SVC syndrome usually results from caval compression by tumors of the mediastinum, lung carcinoma, or lymphoma. In some cases, caval thrombosis causes obstruction. Patients present with:

Facial, chest, or upper extremity edema
Headache
Distended neck veins

Diagnostic Studies
Echocardiography, CT, or MRI are the tests of choice.

Treatment

Pericardial Involvement
See Chapter 13.

Pericardial Tamponade Pericardial tamponade with hemodynamic instability is treated with emergency pericardiocentesis or subxiphoid pericardiotomy.

Pericardial Effusion Chronic treatment of documented malignant pericardial effusion depends on the etiology of the primary tumor.

• Hematologic malignancies are treated with systemic chemotherapy directed at the primary tumor tissue type and/or external radiation therapy.
• Solid tumor metastases are also often treated with systemic chemotherapy, but response rates are poor.

For patients with persistent, refractory pericardial effusion, pericardial sclerotherapy with instillation of sclerosing agents (tetracycline, bleomycin) into the pericardium leads to a significant decrease in effusion in up to 70% of cases.

Other options include subxiphoid pericardiotomy, which has 100% immediate efficacy and a 3% recurrence rate (many physicians perform this as initial therapy), a pleuropericardial window using a median sternotomy approach, or balloon pericardiotomy.

Pericardial Constriction Pericardial constriction is treated by radical pericardiectomy.

Myocardial Involvement
Radiation therapy and/or systemic chemotherapy in patients with responsive tumors may occasionally result in myocardial tumor regression.

Intracavitary Involvement
Surgical resection of obstructing lesions may diminish symptoms and prolong survival in a small number of patients who have intracavitary involvement.

Superior Vena Cava Syndrome
In the majority of cases, SVC syndrome is not a medical emergency. Chemotherapy or irradiation is usually the treatment of choice. Caval thrombosis is treated with antithrombotic agents.

CARDIAC EFFECTS OF ANTITUMOR THERAPY

Radiation Therapy

Mediastinal irradiation may lead to acute and/or chronic cardiac damage. The pericardium is the cardiac structure most sensitive to radiation. Less commonly the myocardium and endocardium are affected.

Most patients with radiation-induced cardiac dysfunction are asymptomatic.

Pericardium
Acute pericarditis occurs in up to 15% of patients with Hodgkin's disease who receive more than 40 Gy to the mediastinum. Radiation-induced pericarditis typically occurs within 9 months of mediastinal irradiation; however, cases have been reported to occur up to 10 years

following therapy. Radiation-induced pericarditis may occasionally result in pericardial tamponade or pericardial constriction.

- Shielding of the heart during radiation therapy significantly decreases the incidence of pericarditis.
- Treatment of radiation-induced pericarditis is similar to that for idiopathic pericarditis (see Chapter 13).

Myocardium

LV systolic function may acutely decrease during mediastinal irradiation and usually normalizes following cessation of therapy. Myocardial fibrosis, typically occurring 5 to 10 years following exposure, may be complicated by heart block or CHF.

Coronary Artery Involvement

Coronary stenosis may occur in patients treated with mediastinal radiation therapy within several months to many years following therapy. Treatment is similar to that for patients with atherosclerotic CAD.

Cardiac Valves

Radiation-induced papillary muscle dysfunction may lead to MR. AR may result from valvar endocardial thickening.

Chemotherapeutic Agents

Anthracyclines

Anthracyclines (doxorubicin, daunorubicin) are widely used in the treatment of sarcomas, lymphomas, and leukemias and tumors of the breast, lung, and thyroid. A major limiting factor is acute and/or chronic cardiac toxicity.

Acute Toxicity Acute toxicity may occur during IV infusion and is not related to drug dose. The ECG manifestations are:

ST segment elevation
T wave changes
Atrial arrhythmias
VPCs

These phenomena are rarely clinically significant and usually resolve within several days following therapy.

- Patients with preexisting severe LV dysfunction may develop acute CHF.
- Perimyocarditis related to acute administration may occur (rare).

Chronic Cardiac Toxicity Chronic cardiac toxicity is characterized by progressive LV dysfunction and cardiac dilatation due to cardiomyopathy.

- Although the toxicity is dose-dependent, significant variations in individual patient susceptibility have been noted.
- Advanced cardiomyopathy occurs in 2% to 20% of patients treated with cumulative doses of doxorubicin exceeding 500 mg/m^2.

The incidence of anthracycline-induced chronic cardiac toxicity is increased in the presence of one or more of the following situations:

Cumulative dose of doxorubicin in exceeding 450 mg/m^2
Cumulative dose of daunorubicin in exceeding 500 mg/m^2
Age greater than 70 years or less than 15 years
Prior mediastinal irradiation
Preexisting cardiac disease
Concomitant cyclophosphamide therapy

Prevention of Anthracycline-Induced Cardiac Toxicity Several strategies to prevent or reduce the risk of cardiac toxicity have been proposed:

- Administration by "slow infusion" (giving the drug continuously over 48 to 96 hours) or at a low dose on a weekly basis causes less cardiac toxicity than high-dose administration given as a single dose every 3 to 4 weeks because peak plasma levels of doxorubicin are reduced.
- Administration of pharmacologic adjuncts to therapy such as iron chelators (dexrazoxane), carnitine, coenzyme Q10, or probucol.
- Use of newer anthracyclines, epirubicin and idarubicin, associated with less cardiotoxicity.

Treatment of Anthracycline Toxicity Among patients receiving anthracycline therapy, the goal is to identify cardiac dysfunction in its preclinical phase and cease anthracycline administration prior to the onset of irreversible ventricular dysfunction.

- Radionuclide ventriculography is an effective method for determination of preclinical LV dysfunction. Table 14-2 lists guidelines for anthracycline administration based on LV ejection fraction.
- Some centers advocate serial RV endomyocardial biopsy in patients with a high cumulative anthracycline dose to evaluate for possible toxic cardiac side effects. If the biopsy indicates toxicity, then therapy must be stopped.

Table 14-2. Guidelines for Monitoring of Patients Receiving Doxorubicin

1. Perform baseline radionuclide angiography at rest for calculation of left ventricular ejection fraction (LVEF) prior to administration of $100\,mg/m^2$ doxorubicin.
2. Perform subsequent studies at least 3 weeks after the indicated total cumulative doses have been given, before consideration of the next dose.

Patients with Normal Baseline LVEF ($\geq$50%)
- Perform the second study after 250 to $300\,mg/m^2$.
- Repeat study after $400\,mg/m^2$ in patients with known heart disease, radiation exposure, abnormal electrocardiographic results, or cyclophosphamide therapy; or after $450\,mg/m^2$ in the absence of any of these risk factors.
- Perform sequential studies thereafter prior to each dose.
- Discontinue doxorubicin therapy once functional criteria for cardiotoxicity develop, i.e., absolute decrease in LVEF $\geq$10 EF units associated with a decline in LVEF to $\leq$50%.

Patients with Abnormal Baseline LVEF ($<$50%)
- Do not initiate doxorubicin therapy with baseline LVEF $\leq$30%.
- In patients with LVEF $>$30% and $<$50%, obtain sequential studies prior to each dose.
- Discontinue doxorubicin with evidence of cardiotoxicity: absolute decrease in LVEF $\geq$10 EF units and/or final LVEF $\leq$30%.

Adapted with permission of the publisher from: Schwartz RG, et al. Congestive heart failure and left ventricular dysfunction complicating doxorubicin therapy. Seven year experience using radionuclide angiocardiography. Am J Med 1987;82:1112. Copyright 1987 by Excerpta Medica Inc.

In the patient with ventricular dysfunction due to anthra-cycline toxicity, treatment is the same as for DCM (see Chapter 12).

Cyclophosphamide
Cyclophosphamide, an alkylating agent, is given in high doses for patient preparation prior to bone marrow trans-plantation or as part of an aggressive antineoplastic regimen.

- Cyclophosphamide administration can cause transient ECG changes, hemorrhagic myopericarditis, or CHF.
- Concomitant administration with doxorubicin can potentiate the toxic effects of doxorubicin.

5-Fluorouracil (5-FU)
5-FU is an antimetabolite commonly used for the treat-ment of breast, colonic, and head and neck tumors. 5-FU cardiotoxicity occurs in 1% to 2% of patients. The most common manifestations include:

Angina pectoris usually occurring with the first cycle of drug administration
Silent ischemic ECG changes
Arrhythmias
MI

The mechanism of 5-FU toxicity is uncertain; however, coronary artery spasm may play a role. Symptoms are usually responsive to NTG.

Paclitaxel
Paclitaxel is a taxene derivative used in the treatment of advanced ovarian and metastatic breast carcinoma. The most common cardiac side effects are:

Hypotension
Transient bradycardia
Nonspecific ECG changes (often asymptomatic)
MI and CHF (rare)

Interleukin-2 (IL-2)
IL-2 is approved for use in treatment of metastatic renal cell cancer. The most frequent cardiac side effects include:

Hypotension
Tachycardia
Reversible depression of LV systolic function

SUGGESTED READINGS

Bristow MR, Lopez M, Mason JW, et al. Efficacy and cost of cardiac monitoring in patients receiving doxorubicin. Cancer 1982;50:32–41.

Engberding R, Daniel WG, Erbel R, et al. Diagnosis of heart tumours by transesophageal echocardiography: a multicentre study in 154 patients. Eur Heart J 1993;14:1223–1228.

Frishman WH, Sung HM, Yee HCM, et al. Cardiovascular toxicity with cancer chemotherapy. Curr Prob Cardiol 1996;21:225–288.

Fujita N, Caputo GR, Higgins CB. Diagnosis and characterization of intracardiac masses by magnetic resonance imaging. Am J Cardiac Imag 1994;8:69–80.

Lancaster LD, Ewy GA. Cardiac consequences of malignancy and their treatment. Adv Intern Med 1984;30:275–293.

Press O, Livingston R. Management of malignant pericardial effusion and tamponade. JAMA 1987;257:1088–1092.

Reeder GS, Khandheria BK, Seward JS, Tajik AJ. Transesophageal echocardiography and cardiac masses. Mayo Clin Proc 1991;66:1101–1109.

Reyen K. Cardiac myxomas. N Engl J Med 1995;333:1610–1617.

Salcedo EE, Cohen GI, White RD, Davison MB. Cardiac tumors: diagnosis and management. Curr Prob Cardiol 1992;17:75–137.

Schwartz RG, McKenzie WB, Alexander J, et al. Congestive heart failure and left ventricular dysfunction complicating doxorubicin therapy. Seven year experience using radionuclide angiocardiography. Am J Med 1987;82:1109–1118.

Stewart JR, Fajardo LF. Radiation induced heart disease: an update. Prog Cardiovasc Dis 1984;27:173–194.

Tazelaar HD, Locke TJ, McGregor CGA. Pathology of surgically excised primary cardiac tumors. Mayo Clin Proc 1992;67:957–965.

15

Traumatic Heart Disease

Dennis A. Tighe
Edward K. Chung

Trauma is a leading cause of morbidity and mortality among persons younger than 40 years old. Cardiac injury may accompany trauma to the chest, neck, or upper abdomen. The major categories of cardiac injury are penetrating and nonpenetrating (blunt) trauma. This chapter provides an overview of the presentation, diagnosis, and treatment of traumatic heart disease.

PENETRATING CARDIAC TRAUMA

Etiology

Penetrating trauma to the heart is most often the result of:

Stab wounds from a knife, ice pick, other sharp objects
Missile injury from bullets, shrapnel, etc.

Other mechanisms of injury include:

- Displacement of fractured ribs or sternal fragments accompanying chest trauma.
- Iatrogenic injuries occurring with invasive cardiac procedures or cardiac surgery.

Penetrating cardiac injury is most often observed with wounds to the precordium. However, injury may also accompany wounds elsewhere to the chest, back, neck, proximal upper extremities, and upper abdomen.

- Penetrating wounds most often involve only the cardiac free wall. Chamber involvement correlates with the degree of exposure to the anterior chest wall (in order of frequency):
  1. RV (most frequently involved)
  2. LV
  3. RA
  4. LA (least frequently involved)
- Less commonly, injury to the interventricular septum, interatrial septum, cardiac valves, chordae tendineae, coronary arteries, or conduction system may occur.

Pathophysiology

The pathophysiologic consequences of penetrating cardiac injury are determined by the mechanism of injury; size, location, and extent of the wound; and the status of the pericardial wound.

- **Stab wounds.** Stab wounds usually result in discrete myocardial laceration without extensive cellular damage adjacent to the wound. Small transmural stab wounds to the LV may seal after injury because of apposition of myocardial fibers and/or clotted blood.
- **Gunshot wounds.** Gunshot wounds typically cause more extensive cellular damage and usually involve more than one cardiac chamber or structure resulting in non-sealing defects of the myocardium and pericardium.
- The pericardial wound may remain open, allowing blood to drain into the left hemithorax leading to hemorrhagic shock. If the pericardial wound is closed off by clotted blood or adjacent tissue, then blood accumulates in the pericardial space and may produce cardiac tamponade.
- **Iatrogenic injury**
- Perforation of the RA or RV by a pacing catheter usually results in a small, discrete perforation which, in most instances, is self-sealing because right heart pressures are low.
- Perforation of a coronary artery or iatrogenic dissection of the aorta during cardiac catheterization usually requires operative intervention.
- Rupture of a PA by a flow-directed catheter may

cause massive hemoptysis and require thoracotomy for control and repair.

Clinical Presentation

The clinical presentation of penetrating cardiac trauma ranges from hemodynamic stability to shock and cardiopulmonary arrest.

- A penetrating cardiac injury should be considered in any patient with a penetrating wound of the chest, upper abdomen, proximal upper extremities, or neck. A high index of suspicion must be maintained because concomitant injuries to the lungs and upper abdominal organs may be present, diverting attention from the cardiac injury.
- Cardiac penetration should also be considered in any patient who has undergone a recent invasive cardiac or great vessel diagnostic or therapeutic procedure and has developed unstable hemodynamic status.

Major Syndromes

Two major syndromes may occur with penetrating cardiac injury: hemorrhagic shock and cardiac tamponade.

Hemorrhagic Shock   If the pericardial wound *remains open,* then blood may drain freely into the pleural space (hemothorax). In this situation, the presentation is that of hemorrhagic shock. The physical findings include:

Hypotension
Tachycardia
Flat neck veins

Cardiac Tamponade   If the pericardial wound *seals,* then blood will not drain from around the cardiac wound and will accumulate within the pericardial space. Depending on the size and nature of the myocardial laceration, cardiac tamponade may develop over a period of minutes to several hours. The physical findings include:

Hypotension
Tachycardia
Paradoxic pulse
Distended neck veins

Diagnostic Evaluation

Imaging studies are often of limited value in the evaluation of patients with penetrating cardiac trauma.

Hemodynamically unstable patients. Among the hemodynamically unstable and those with obvious injury, no imaging studies should be performed. Definitive diagnosis is made at the time of surgery.

Hemodynamically stable patients
- CXR may identify intracardiac missiles, pneumothorax, hemothorax, or widened mediastinum (possibly indicating injury to a great vessel).
- Echocardiography can identify pericardial effusion, intracardiac foreign bodies, valvular lesions, and intracardiac shunts.

Treatment

A proposed management strategy for penetrating cardiac injury is presented in Table 15-1.

Urgent thoracotomy and cardiorrhaphy is the definitive treatment for penetrating cardiac injury. Survival is inversely proportional to the duration of time from injury to thoracotomy.

Preparation

1. Immediate resuscitation with full attention to airway, breathing, and circulation ("ABCs") is given highest priority.
2. Hypotension is treated with IV fluids (1 to 2 liters) and blood. Overadministration of IV fluids has been correlated with poorer outcome.
3. A chest tube is inserted when hemothorax and/or pneumothorax are suspected.
4. When pericardial tamponade is suspected, pericardiocentesis should be performed only if it can allow for a safer operation. Repeated attempts at pericardiocentesis may waste valuable time in transporting the patient to the operating room for definitive treatment and may fail to evacuate the pericardial space if clotted blood is present.

Table 15-1. Proposed Management Strategy for Penetrating Cardiac Injury at the Time of Hospital Presentation

Lifeless Patient (Category 1)
Unconscious, with no signs of life.
- Treatment should not be delayed by any diagnostic procedure. If signs of life were present for some time prior to hospital arrival, immediate intubation and thoracotomy are indicated in the emergency department.
- In a patient already lifeless at the scene of injury, any resuscitative attempt in the emergency department is futile.

Critically Unstable Patient (Category 2)
Signs of life present, but clinical picture dominated by profound hypotension and impending cardiac arrest.
- No diagnostic procedure is indicated. Immediate intubation and fluid resuscitation should be performed.
- Stabilized patients are transferred to the operating room.
- Patients remaining unstable with persisting hypotension undergo emergency department thoracotomy.

Patient with Cardiac Tamponade (Category 3)
Hypotension with increased central venous pressure.
- Subxiphoid pericardial window is indicated. If blood is recovered, then a full thoracotomy and cardiac repair are indicated.

Patient with Thoracoabdominal Injury (Category 4)
Presence of cardiac injury/tamponade, possibly obscured by abdominal penetration. A precordial wound may be present, or control of abdominal bleeding does not result in hemodynamic improvement.
- A transdiaphragmatic pericardial window before closure of the abdomen is indicated. If blood is recovered, then a full thoracotomy and cardiac repair are indicated.

Benign Presentation (Category 5)
Precordial wound, but without signs of cardiac tamponade or intrathoracic hemorrhage.
- Echocardiography or subxiphoid pericardial window is indicated to exclude hemopericardium.

Adapted from: Saadia R, et al. Penetrating cardiac injuries: clinical classification and management strategy. Br J Surg 1994;81:1572–1575.

Surgery

Emergency department thoracotomy should be performed on patients who reach the hospital in extremis, but who have not sustained irreversible brain damage.

1. Pericardial tamponade is relieved and lacerations are repaired at surgery.

- Missiles that are easily accessible should be removed.
- Missiles in the left heart should be removed to prevent future systemic embolism.
2. Major wounds to the coronary arteries are repaired or bypassed. Wounds involving vessels that supply a small amount of myocardium are ligated.
3. Penetrating injuries to the great vessels should be repaired.

Prognosis
- More than 50% of victims with penetrating cardiac injury succumb very shortly following injury.
- Of the patients reaching the hospital, reported survival rates vary widely (33% to 70%).

Favorable Prognostic Signs	Poor Prognostic Signs
Single chamber injury	Multisystem injury
Knife wounds	Gunshot wounds
Stable hemodynamic status on presentation	Unstable hemodynamic status on presentation
Absence of intracardiac septal defects	Cardiac injury to more than one structure

Delayed Complications of Penetrating Injuries

Up to 25% of patients surviving surgical repair of penetrating trauma will develop a structural cardiac abnormality. It is important to closely observe patients in the early postoperative period and following discharge for changes in hemodynamic status and symptoms of cardiac dysfunction.

Delayed complications include:

- VSD
- ASD
- Delayed cardiac tamponade
- Valvular injury (aortic valve most common) with secondary insufficiency
- Cardiac conduction defects
- Fistulae (systemic to PA, coronary artery to cardiac chamber)

- Ventricular aneurysm
- Pericarditis

Evaluation

Echocardiography is the procedure of choice to evaluate a change in clinical status. Some authors recommend routine echocardiography in the early postoperative period to assess cardiac status and identify intracardiac injuries that require repair.

Treatment

Hemodynamically significant septal defects, valvular insufficiency, and fistulae require early surgical repair.

NONPENETRATING (BLUNT) CARDIAC TRAUMA

Etiology

Blunt injury to the heart is most often caused by deceleration injury during an automobile accident. Other mechanisms of injury include falls from height, objects striking the chest, and forceful blows to the chest.

Pathophysiology

The heart can be injured during deceleration trauma by three mechanisms:

1. Compression by the sternum.
2. Impingement between the sternum and the spinal column.
3. Overdistention due to a marked increase of intravascular pressures secondary to abdominal or extremity compression.

Depending on the mechanism of injury and the severity of trauma, a wide spectrum of cardiac injuries may result. The most frequent blunt injuries include:

Cardiac contusion
Cardiac free wall rupture
Rupture of the interventricular septum
Cardiac valve injury
Pericardial rupture
Injury to the aorta and great vessels

Cardiac Contusion

Cardiac contusion is the most common injury. Except in cases of injury involving a coronary artery, the contused area corresponds to the mechanism and extent of injury rather than the distribution of coronary blood supply.

Myocardial contusion is pathologically characterized by cellular injury with patchy edema, necrosis, and hemorrhage. The extent of pathologic injury may vary from minor subepicardial or subendocardial injury to full thickness contusion.

- Based on pathologic criteria, approximately 16% of patients dying from major chest trauma have findings consistent with myocardial contusion at autopsy.
- The reported incidence of myocardial contusion on the basis of clinical findings varies from 8% to 67%. This wide range likely represents the lack of a diagnostic gold standard.

Etiology
- The most common cause of myocardial contusion is steering wheel deceleration injury during an automobile accident.
- Less common causes include blows to the chest of any cause and compression of the chest during CPR.

Pathophysiology

Cardiac Chambers
- The RV is most commonly injured due to its close proximity to the chest wall and sternum.
- Less commonly, the atria and LV are injured.

Heart Valves
- The aortic valve is most susceptible to injury. Mechanisms of injury include cuspal laceration or detachment and rupture of the annulus.
- MV injury due to rupture or tear of a papillary muscle or chordae tendineae and TV injury are less common.

Arteries   Direct injury to the coronary arteries is less common.

- The right coronary artery and the left anterior descending artery are vulnerable due to their anatomic position.
- Coronary artery thrombosis or laceration may result in MI.

Complications Ventricular aneurysm formation and pericardial constriction are late complications.

Clinical Presentation
The vast majority of patients suffering a cardiac contusion are asymptomatic. The diagnosis should be suspected in any patient presenting with blunt chest trauma.

- No physical findings are specific for cardiac contusion.
- In many instances, no obvious external chest injury is apparent.
- Cardiac injury may be obscured by injury to other chest or abdominal organs.

The major clinical manifestations of myocardial contusion are arrhythmias, chest pain, hypotension, and CHF.

- Hypotension with elevated jugular venous pressure suggests cardiac tamponade or RV injury.
- Acute CHF suggests disruption of the interventricular septum or injury to a left-sided cardiac valve. Characteristic murmurs of AR or MR may be present. (Traumatic TR is often asymptomatic, and the murmur is usually not pronounced.)
- Sinus tachycardia, most often caused by the stress of trauma, is common.
- APCs and VPCs are common, as are transient conduction abnormalities.
- A pericardial friction rub may indicate traumatic pericarditis.

Diagnostic Tests
No currently available diagnostic test can absolutely confirm the presence of myocardial contusion in all patients. Because the clinical significance of myocardial contusion is the hemodynamic compromise that may result from pump dysfunction and/or arrhythmias,

diagnostic tests are used to screen for injury and identify the patient at risk for development of these complications.

ECG ECG is the most commonly used screening test. No ECG finding is specific for myocardial contusion and its sensitivity is low. Right-sided ECG leads to identify RV injury have no proven utility.

- In the first few hours following injury, ECG abnormalities may reflect hypoxia, hypovolemia, acidemia, and/or electrolyte imbalance, so an abnormal ECG should be repeated after these conditions have been corrected.
- ECG changes, especially localized ST segment elevation with characteristic progression, can be a marker of myocardial contusion.
- Most often, nonspecific ST segment and T wave changes and sinus tachycardia are present. APCs, VPCs, and RBBB may commonly occur.

A normal ECG has an excellent negative predictive value.

Cardiac Enzymes

CPK-MB Measurement of CPK-MB is routinely performed in patients with suspected myocardial contusion to exclude myocardial necrosis.

- CPK-MB is also present to some extent in skeletal muscle, lung, pancreas, tongue, stomach, colon, diaphragm, small intestine, and liver. Though less CPK-MB is present in these organs on a percentage basis, injury to them may increase the CPK-MB level in the absence of a cardiac injury.
- CPK-MB levels have not been shown to correlate well with other markers of myocardial injury such as echocardiography or radionuclide angiography.

As with the ECG, normal CPK-MB has a high negative predictive value for significant cardiac injury.

Cardiac Troponin I (cTnI) Among patients with acute or chronic skeletal muscle injury or renal insufficiency, elevated cTnI has been shown to be a specific marker of myocardial injury. cTnI should be obtained in trauma patients when CPK-MB is elevated or as an alternative to CPK-MB.

Rhythm Monitoring   Significant arrhythmias occur in 25% of patients with anterior chest injury.

- Paroxysmal VT is the most common, and potentially lethal, significant rhythm disturbance.
- Arrhythmias following chest trauma may reflect myocardial injury.
- Rhythm disturbances may be secondary to hypoxemia, acidemia, electrolyte abnormalities, alcohol intoxication, drug intoxication, and high catecholamine state.

- **Stable condition.** The vast majority of patients with blunt trauma, stable hemodynamic status, and a normal ECG who subsequently develop arrhythmias do so within the first 12 hours of hospitalization. Monitoring may be limited to 24 hours or less in this group.
- **Unstable condition.** Patients with an abnormal ECG, hemodynamic instability, or arrhythmia should receive continuous rhythm monitoring until stabilized.

Echocardiography   Echocardiography should be used to evaluate symptomatic patients (CHF, significant arrhythmia, hypotension) with suspected contusion.

The RV apex, RV free wall, interventricular septum, and LV anteroapical segment are most often injured.

- Echocardiography can visualize wall motion abnormalities, pericardial effusions, and intracardiac thrombi and assess valvular structures.
- TEE provides an alternative window to the heart when inadequate TTE windows are present, as is the case in approximately 20% of patients (chest wall injury, chest tubes, etc.).

Contused myocardium can be identified on echocardiography by:

- Increased end-diastolic wall thickness
- Increased echogenicity of the ventricular wall
- Impaired regional systolic function

Radionuclide Imaging

- Radionuclide angiography may provide assessment of global and regional ventricular function.
- Technetium pyrophosphate can concentrate in areas of injured myocardium.
- Radionuclide studies have been demonstrated to be costly and of low yield in patients with suspected myocardial contusion. Their routine use is not recommended.

Management

Treatment of myocardial contusion is similar to that of recent MI. The major complications include arrhythmias, CHF, and hypotension.

1. Patients with documented contusion should initially be treated with bed rest for the first 24 to 48 hours. Ambulation is progressively increased thereafter among stable patients. Cardiac monitoring is performed for 2 to 5 days.
2. Symptomatic patients or those subsequently developing a complication should have prompt echocardiography to determine regional and global ventricular function, to check for presence of a pericardial effusion, and to assess for a structural abnormality (valvular dysfunction, VSD).
   - CHF is treated in standard fashion (see Chapter 2).
   - Cardiac tamponade is treated with urgent pericardiocentesis (see Chapter 13). Exploratory thoracotomy should be performed if pericardiocentesis is inadequate to reverse tamponade.
   - Hemodynamically significant structural cardiac defects should be surgically repaired.
   - Significant arrhythmias are treated in standard fashion (see Chapters 17 and 18).

Note: Anticoagulants should not be administered due to the risk of developing hemorrhagic pericardial effusion and cardiac tamponade.

Cardiac Rupture

Myocardial rupture is the most lethal complication of blunt cardiac trauma. Rupture of a cardiac chamber is usually fatal due to acute cardiac tamponade. The few survivors have usually ruptured a low-pressure chamber.

Ventricles and atria. The RV, due to its anterior location, is most susceptible to rupture. Among the patients surviving cardiac rupture, the RA is most often injured, followed in descending order by the LA, RV, and LV.

Other structures. Rupture of other cardiac structures, such as the interventricular septum and heart valves (the aortic valve being the most common), may also occur.

Clinical Presentation

The vast majority of patients die prior to hospitalization. The patient who survives cardiac rupture usually has suffered a deceleration injury. Less commonly, delayed rupture of necrotic myocardium as complication of an earlier cardiac contusion may occur.

- Most patients have associated lung, chest, abdominal, or head trauma.
- In some patients, rupture may not be immediately apparent. Delayed cardiac tamponade or constrictive pericarditis may be subsequently observed.
- If a pericardial laceration has occurred (10% of cases), the presentation is that of hemorrhagic shock due to exsanguination within the thorax. If no pericardial laceration is present, then cardiac tamponade may occur.
- Rupture of a left-sided cardiac valve or the interventricular septum is associated with a heart murmur and CHF. Traumatic rupture of the TV may present acutely with a minimal murmur and no signs of cardiac decompensation.

Diagnosis

Cardiac rupture should be suspected when signs of cardiac tamponade or intrathoracic bleeding are present. If time permits, urgent echocardiography is the procedure of choice to evaluate suspected myocardial rupture.

Treatment

Urgent pericardiocentesis followed by immediate thoracotomy and repair is the treatment of choice for patients with chamber rupture and cardiac tamponade.

- Patients with CHF and hemodynamic compromise due to valve disruption or rupture of the interventricular septum should have urgent echocardiography and/or cardiac catheterization followed by early surgery.
- Patients without hemodynamic compromise should be closely observed. In some cases, small VSDs may heal spontaneously.

BLUNT INJURY TO THE THORACIC AORTA AND GREAT VESSELS

Etiology and Pathophysiology

The thoracic aorta and innominate artery are the vessels most frequently injured by blunt trauma. The left carotid and subclavian arteries and the SVC are less commonly injured.

The mechanism of injury is most often deceleration; however, any blunt force applied to the chest may cause injury. Traction on the shoulder or sudden extension of the neck may also cause injury to the great vessels.

Rupture of the Aorta

Rupture of the aorta, the most frequent great vessel injury, accounts for 18% of deaths related to motor vehicle accidents. Complete aortic rupture usually results in death at the scene of the accident.

The most frequent sites of aortic rupture are the isthmus just distal to the left subclavian artery, where the mobile arch joins the relatively fixed descending thoracic aorta, and the ascending aorta just proximal to the origin of the innominate artery. A false aneurysm is formed at the site of rupture.

Clinical Presentation

Any patient sustaining blunt injury to the chest or abdomen or who has suffered deceleration injury should be suspected of having aortic rupture. Its presence is often obscured by coexisting serious injuries.

- 80% to 90% of traumatic aortic ruptures are immediately fatal.
- 10% to 20% of patients survive to reach the hospital.
- 40% of survivors die within 24 hours if surgery is not performed.

Because coexisting injuries often mask the presence of aortic injury, a high index of clinical suspicion must be maintained. Physical findings that may suggest traumatic aortic rupture include:

Upper extremity HTN with increased pulse amplitude
Diminished lower extremity pulse amplitude
Thoracic bruits

Diagnostic Studies

Chest X-Ray

A CXR is indicated to identify potential abnormalities of the mediastinum (Table 15-2).

- CXR findings have a sensitivity exceeding 90% for injury to the aorta and great vessels.
- CXR specificity (5% to 10%) and positive predictive accuracy (10% to 15%) are quite low.
- Up to 28% of patients with aortic rupture will have a "normal" CXR.

Table 15-2. Findings on Chest X-Ray Suggesting Injury to the Aorta and Great Vessels

Widened mediastinum (>8 cm)
Depressed left mainstem bronchus
Loss of aortic knob contour
Lateral deviation or anterior displacement of the trachea
Deviation of nasogastric tube in the esophagus
Calcium layering in the aortic arch
Large left hemothorax
Fracture of thoracic spine, clavicle, sternum, or scapula
Loss of paraspinal stripe
Loss of aorticopulmonary window
Left apical pleural cap (hematoma)

Aortography   Aortic angiography remains the gold standard procedure in most institutions to evaluate suspected aortic trauma.

Aortography advantages   Aortography provides excellent anatomic detail of the aorta, aortic arch, and the great vessels.

Aortography disadvantages
Removal of injured patient to the angiography suite
Prolonged (relatively) time period to complete the
    procedure
Invasive nature
Exposure to ionizing radiation
Risks of contrast dye administration

Transesophageal Echocardiography   Because the thoracic aorta lies in close proximity to the esophagus, TEE is an excellent technique to evaluate suspected aortic trauma. The entire thoracic aorta (except for a blind spot in the distal portion of the ascending aorta where the left bronchus overlies the aorta) can be imaged.

Findings   The findings specific to traumatic aortic disruption include:

A thick and mobile intraluminal flap usually confined to
    the area of the aortic isthmus
Evidence of a deformed aortic contour (representing a
    pseudoaneurysm)
Similar blood flow velocities on both sides of the flap
Mediastinal hematoma

These findings help to separate traumatic aortic disruption from aortic dissection (see Chapter 10).
   Based on TEE findings, two subsets of traumatic aortic injuries can be defined:

1. **Subadventitial traumatic aortic disruption.**
   Subadventitial traumatic aortic disruptions involve
   the aortic intimal and medial layers and are at high
   risk for rupture.
2. **Traumatic intimal tear.** Traumatic intimal tears are
   characterized by preserved integrity of the medial
   and adventitial layers. This lesion has been

documented to regress spontaneously. A conservative management strategy is indicated. Follow-up TEE is indicated prior to hospital dismissal.

CT Scanning CT cannot demonstrate the actual site of arterial disruption. The role of CT appears to be that of excluding mediastinal hemorrhage in patients with equivocal or abnormal CXR results (see Table 15-2) and moderate to low clinical likelihood of vascular injury. In this situation, CT may obviate the need for unnecessary angiography or TEE since the number of patients with actual aortic injury is small.

Patients with mediastinal bleeding on CT should undergo further investigation. A negative CT does not always exclude the possibility of an aortic laceration, but the likelihood of such injury is very low.

Management

Definitive treatment of aortic or great vessel laceration is surgical repair.

As for aortic dissection, medical therapy designed to control BP and reduce aortic shearing forces should be instituted while awaiting surgery (see Chapter 10).

COMMOTIO CORDIS

An increasingly recognized phenomenon is sudden death likely due to ventricular fibrillation following a seemingly inconsequential blow to the chest (commotio cordis) during sports activities among young athletes with otherwise normal hearts.

SUGGESTED READINGS

Asenio JA, Stewart BM, Murray J, et al. Penetrating cardiac injuries. Surg Clin North Am 1996;76(4):685–724.

Feghali NT, Prisant LM. Blunt myocardial injury. Chest 1995;108:1673–1677.

Ivatury RR, Shah PM, Ito K, et al. Emergency room thoracotomy for the resuscitation of patients with "fatal" penetrating injuries of the heart. Ann Thorac Surg 1981;32: 377–385.

Ivatury RR, Nallathambi MN, Stahl WM, Rohman M. Penetrating cardiac trauma. Quantifying the severity of anatomic and physiologic injury. Ann Surg 1987;205:61–66.

Karalis DG, Victor MF, Davis GA, et al. The role of echocardiography in blunt chest trauma: a transthoracic and transesophageal echocardiographic study. J Trauma 1994;36: 53–58.

Maron BJ, Poliac LC, Kaplan JA, Mueller FO. Blunt impact to the chest leading to sudden death from cardiac arrest during sports activities. N Engl J Med 1995;333:337–342.

Mattox KL, Limacher MC, Feliciano DV, et al. Cardiac evaluation following heart injury. J Trauma 1985;25:758–765.

Mattox KL, Feliciano DV, Burch J, et al. Five thousand seven hundred sixty cardiovascular injuries in 4459 patients. Epidemiologic evolution 1958 to 1987. Ann Surg 1989;209:698–707.

Morgan PW, Goodman LR, Aprahamian C, et al. Evaluation of traumatic aortic injury: does dynamic contrast-enhanced CT play a role? Radiology 1992;182:661–666.

Pandian NG, Skorton DJ, Doty DB, Kerber RE. Immediate diagnosis of acute myocardial contusion by two-dimensional echocardiography: studies in a canine model of blunt chest trauma. J Am Coll Cardiol 1983;2:488–496.

Pretre R, Chilcott M. Blunt trauma to the heart and great vessels. N Engl J Med 1997;336:626–632.

Rosenthal MA, Ellis JI. Cardiac and mediastinal trauma. Emerg Med Clin North Am 1995;13(4):887–902.

Roxburgh JC. Myocardial contusion. Injury 1996;27:603–605.

Saadia R, Levy RD, Degiannis E, Velmahos GC. Penetrating cardiac injuries: clinical classification and management strategy. Br J Surg 1994;81:1572–1575.

Symbas PN. Traumatic heart disease. In: Schlant RC, Alexander RW, eds. The heart. 8th ed. New York: McGraw-Hill, 1994:2031–2037.

Vignon P, Gueret P, Vedrinne JM, et al. Role of transesophageal echocardiography in the diagnosis and management of traumatic aortic disruption. Circulation 1995;92:2959–2968.

Noncardiac Surgery in the Patient with Cardiac Disease

Howard H. Weitz
Dennis A. Tighe

Each year about 10% of the adult American population undergoes noncardiac surgery. The risk of a serious perioperative cardiac event is significantly increased in patients with severe CAD, advanced age, decompensated CHF, and in those undergoing certain major surgical procedures. Frequently, the cardiologist/internist is called upon to evaluate "cardiac risk" prior to noncardiac surgery. The goal of the consultant is to risk stratify the patient prior to surgery by performing a detailed cardiovascular history and physical examination, identifying and correcting underlying conditions to the extent possible, implementing diagnostic and management strategies in the context of the patient's underlying cardiac condition so that risk may be reduced, and following the patient in the postoperative period so that problems may be identified and treated. This chapter will briefly review physiologic responses to surgery and anesthetic considerations, strategies to assess cardiovascular risk, treatment strategies, and management considerations in patients with specific cardiovascular conditions.

PHYSIOLOGIC RESPONSES TO SURGERY

- Surgery places hemodynamic and metabolic stresses upon the cardiovascular system, which must compensate to maintain homeostasis.

- In response to the stress of surgery, a physiologic increase in circulating catecholamine and aldosterone levels occurs to increase CO, maintain intravascular volume, and preserve vital organ perfusion. Myocardial oxygen demand, afterload, and sodium and water retention are increased.
- In the patient with marginal cardiac reserve, these stresses may lead to clinical deterioration if compensation is inadequate.
  1. Patients with significant CAD may experience myocardial ischemia due to increased myocardial oxygen demand.
  2. Patients with impaired ventricular function or a limited CO may experience retention of salt and water along with increased afterload which may lead to CHF.

ANESTHETIC CONSIDERATIONS

Various anesthetic approaches are available depending upon the planned operative procedure and patient characteristics. Monitoring capabilities, anesthetic techniques, and availability of IV medications to maintain intra-operative homeostasis have improved significantly over the past two decades.

Anesthetic Agents

The choice of anesthetic agent and its delivery clearly belongs to the anesthesiologist. The role of the consultant is to advise the anesthesiologist of the severity of any underlying cardiovascular disease prior to surgery. In addition, the consultant should have a basic understanding of the cardiovascular effects of anesthesia in order to optimally manage the patient in the perioperative period.

Inhalation agents (nitrous oxide, halothane, isoflurane, enflurane) produce dose-dependent myocardial depression.
- Nitrous oxide produces less myocardial depression than the other agents and its use is associated with a reflex increase in SVR.
- Halothane causes the greatest degree of myocardial depression and peripheral vasodilatation. It may

also sensitize the myocardium to catecholamines and predispose to arrhythmia.

- Enflurane and isoflurane also cause peripheral vasodilatation but are less arrhythmogenic than halothane.
- Hypotension caused by inhalation agents may be exacerbated in the presence of vasodilator agents and/or intravascular volume depletion.

Narcotic agents (morphine, fentanyl) may cause peripheral vasodilatation, hypotension, and bradycardia.

Muscle relaxants (pancuronium, vecuronium, succinylcholine) have variable cardiovascular effects.

- Pancuronium has a vagolytic action which may lead to tachycardia.
- Succinylcholine may rarely cause bradycardia, but in general has few cardiac side effects.
- Type IA AADs may prolong the action of muscle relaxants resulting in temporary postoperative skeletal muscle paralysis.

Short-acting IV agents are used for induction of general anesthesia.

- Benzodiazepines (Valium, midazolam) have minimal hemodynamic side effects.
- Barbiturates cause a direct negative inotropic effect along with peripheral vasodilatation. Hypotension may occur when reflex increases in sympathetic nervous system tone are blunted by alpha- or beta-blockers.

Mode of Anesthesia Delivery

- Many studies have shown no difference in the rate of cardiovascular complications relating to the delivery of regional versus general anesthesia. Regional anesthesia may be preferred when severe respiratory disease and/or LV dysfunction is present.
- Spinal anesthesia is relatively contraindicated in patients with fixed CO states (severe AS, severe LV dysfunction, obstructive HCM) due to the risk of peripheral vasodilatation, hypotension, and inability to augment CO.
- General anesthesia may be preferred in patients in

whom anxiety and high catecholamine levels may have an unfavorable impact upon the myocardial oxygen supply-demand relationship.

METHODS TO ASSESS CARDIAC RISK

Multifactorial Cardiac Risk Indexes

Goldman Cardiac Risk Index

- Nine clinical or historical features (Table 16-1) were retrospectively found to be associated with increased risk of a cardiac complication following noncardiac surgery.
- Risk points were assigned by multivariate analysis to allow an estimate of total risk and stratification to

Table 16-1. Multifactorial Index of Cardiac Risk in Noncardiac Surgery

Risk Factor	Points
History	
Myocardial infarction within six months	10
Age older than 70 years	5
Physical Examination	
S3 or jugular venous distention	11
Significant aortic stenosis	3
Electrocardiogram	
Rhythm other than sinus or sinus plus atrial premature beats on preoperative electrocardiogram	7
More than five ventricular premature contractions per minute at any time prior to surgery	7
Medical Status	
Poor general medical status	3
(potassium <3 mEq/l or HCO$_3$ <20 mEq/l	
BUN >50 mg/dl or creatinine >3 mg/dl	
pO$_2$ <60 mm Hg or pCO$_2$ >50 mm Hg)	
Evidence of abnormal liver function	
Patient bedridden	
Surgical Procedure	
Abdominal, thoracic, or aortic surgery	3
Emergency operation	4
Total	**53**

Adapted from: Goldman L, et al. Multifactorial index of cardiac risk in noncardiac surgical procedures. N Engl J Med 1977;297:847.

Table 16-2. Cardiac Complications Determined by the Multifactorial Index

Class	Points	Life-Threatening Complications or Cardiac Death (%)
I	0–5	1
II	6–12	7
III	13–25	13
IV	≥26	78

Adapted from: Goldman L, et al. Multifactorial index of cardiac risk in noncardiac surgical procedures. N Engl J Med 1977;297:847.

one of four risk groups (Table 16-2). The higher the score, the higher the predicted risk.

- This index was derived in a population undergoing general surgery. It is less reliable in stratification of patients with CAD, as well as those having vascular surgery.

Modified Cardiac Risk Index

- The Goldman index was modified by Detsky (Table 16-3) to include more variables associated with CAD such as angina and remote MI (>6 months). The scoring system was also simplified into three classes of risk.
- This index improved predictive accuracy among higher risk patients as compared to the Goldman index.
- Similar to the Goldman index, the modified cardiac risk index is less effective in estimating risk in a homogeneous population, such as those undergoing vascular surgery and among those at "low risk."

Mangano and Colleagues

- Mangano and colleagues used multivariate analysis in men with CAD or at high risk for it undergoing elective noncardiac surgery to show that early postoperative myocardial ischemia was the best predictor of perioperative MI.
- No other clinical, historical, or perioperative variable (including cardiac-risk index) was independently associated with ischemic events.

Table 16-3. Modified Multifactorial Index

Multivariate Cardiac Risk Indicator Variables	Variable	Points (n)	Post-Test Probability (%)
Age	>70 years	5	
CAD	MI within 6 months	10	
	MI more than 6 months	5	
	CCS Class III	10	
	CCS Class IV	20	
	Unstable angina within 6 months	10	
Alveolar pulmonary edema	Within 1 week	10	
	Ever	5	
Valvular heart disease	Critical aortic stenosis	20	
Arrhythmias	Other than sinus or APCs	5	
	>5 VPCs at any time	5	
Medical status	Poor general status*	5	
Nature of operation	Emergency	10	
Scores and post-test probability	Class I	0–15	5
	Class II	20–30	27
	Class III	>30	60

Adapted from: Palda VA, Detsky AS. Perioperative assessment and management of risk from coronary artery disease. Ann Intern Med 1997;127:318.
APCs, atrial premature contractions; CCS, Canadian Cardiovascular Society; VPCs, ventricular premature contractions.
*Poor general status as defined in multifactorial (Goldman) cardiac index.

Eagle Criteria

- Patients with peripheral vascular disease have a high incidence of coexisting CAD.
- Five clinical factors (age >70, Q waves on the ECG, diabetes mellitus, history of ventricular arrhythmias requiring treatment, and history of angina) were found to be independent correlates of postoperative cardiac events in patients undergoing major vascular surgery.

- Patients with one or two risk factors (intermediate risk) were best stratified with preoperative dipyridamole-thallium scanning. Patients without thallium redistribution may safely proceed to surgery while those with redistribution should be considered high risk (see below).
- Low-risk patients (no risk factors) may proceed directly to vascular surgery without further evaluation. High-risk patients (three or more risk factors) should be considered for coronary arteriography and appropriate coronary revascularization or modification or cancellation of the planned surgery.

American College of Cardiology/American Heart Association Consensus Guideline

- The ACC/AHA Consensus Guideline (Fig 16-1) emphasizes assessment of clinical markers, consideration of functional status, surgery-specific risk, and history of coronary evaluation or treatment. Preoperative cardiac testing should depend upon clinical situations where results of testing will indicate that treatment will have an impact on outcome.
- Clinical markers are classified as:

    Major: Recent MI (<30 days) with residual ischemic myocardium, or unstable or severe angina, decompensated CHF, significant arrhythmias, severe valvular heart disease.

    Intermediate: Mild angina, prior MI, compensated or prior CHF, diabetes mellitus.

    Minor: Advanced age, abnormal ECG, rhythm other than sinus, low functional capacity, history of stroke, and uncontrolled HTN.

- Functional capacity is quantified by evaluating the patient's daily activity. Perioperative cardiac risk is increased in patients unable to reach or exceed an aerobic demand of 4 METS (climbing a flight of stairs).
- Surgery-specific risk is determined by the type of surgery (Table 16-4).
- If the patient has undergone coronary evaluation during the preceding 2 years or coronary

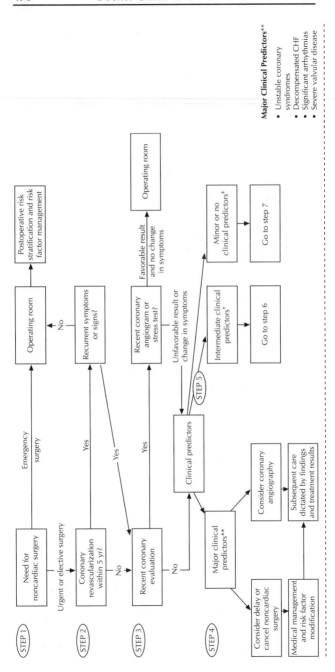

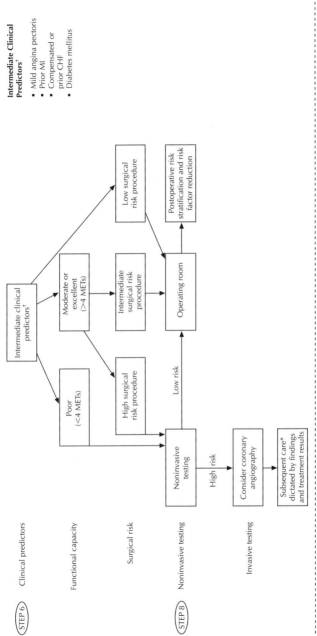

Intermediate Clinical Predictors[†]
- Mild angina pectoris
- Prior MI
- Compensated or prior CHF
- Diabetes mellitus

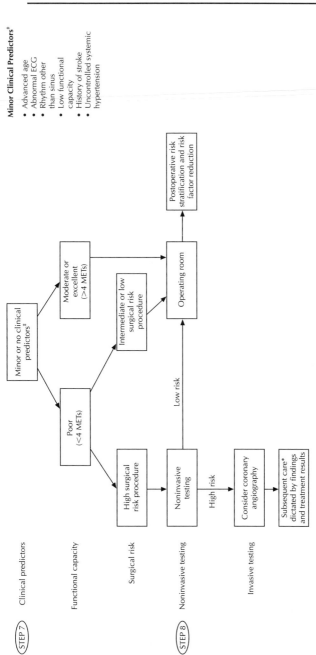

Minor Clinical Predictors‡

- Advanced age
- Abnormal ECG
- Rhythm other than sinus
- Low functional capacity
- History of stroke
- Uncontrolled systemic hypertension

Figure 16-1. Stepwise approach to perioperative cardiac assessment as recommended by the ACC/AHA Task Force Report. Reproduced with permission of the American College of Cardiology from: Eagle KA, et al. Guidelines for perioperative cardiovascular evaluation for noncardiac surgery. J Am Coll Cardiol 1996;27:921.

Table 16-4. Surgery-Specific Risk for Cardiac Complications of Noncardiac Surgery

High	(Reported cardiac risk often >5%)
	• Emergent major operations, particularly in the elderly
	• Aortic and other major vascular
	• Peripheral vascular
	• Anticipated prolonged surgical procedures associated with large fluid shifts and/or blood loss
Intermediate	(Reported cardiac risk generally <5%)
	• Carotid endarterectomy
	• Head and neck
	• Intraperitoneal and intrathoracic
	• Orthopedic
	• Prostate
Low	(Reported cardiac risk generally <1%)
	• Endoscopic procedures
	• Superficial procedure
	• Cataract
	• Breast

Adapted from: Eagle KA, et al. Guidelines for perioperative cardiovascular evaluation for noncardiac surgery. J Am Coll Cardiol 1996;27:919.

revascularization during the prior 5 years and has no symptoms or signs of myocardial ischemia during physical activity that exceeds 4 METS, he or she may be considered at low risk for perioperative MI.

- Because of the relatively high incidence of restenosis during the 6 months following PTCA, patients must be assessed carefully prior to noncardiac surgery performed during this time period.

Special Considerations in Risk Assessment

- Canadian Cardiovascular Society (CCS) class III angina (walking up one flight of stairs or while walking one to two blocks on level) during the 3 months prior to noncardiac surgery suggests a risk of perioperative cardiac complication similar to that of a patient who had an MI during the 6 months prior to surgery. Class IV angina (angina with any activity) likely doubles this risk.
- ACC/AHA guidelines assign history of a recent MI as a major risk predictor and history of MI any more

remote than 30 days as an intermediate risk predictor. Following an MI, if post-MI risk stratification suggests low risk (preserved LV function, absence of significant ectopy), then cardiac risk relating to noncardiac surgery is probably low. The consensus for this low-risk group is that elective surgery should be delayed for 4 to 6 weeks following the MI.

• In the patient with a structurally normal heart without evidence of myocardial ischemia, nonsustained ventricular arrhythmias are probably not a significant risk for cardiac complication in the perioperative setting. Significant risk would be estimated if the patient had ischemic or structural heart disease.

INVASIVE HEMODYNAMIC MONITORING

Patients most likely to benefit from perioperative invasive hemodynamic monitoring are those who are at high risk for perioperative hemodynamic complication. This group would include:

• Patients with recent MI with LV dysfunction and/or significant CAD undergoing surgical procedures associated with significant hemodynamic stress; significant valvular heart disease that places them at risk for CHF (critical AS, MR with ventricular dysfunction).

• Patients with ongoing or recent CHF who are undergoing surgery associated with significant volume shifts.

PERIOPERATIVE CARE OF THE PATIENT WITH ISCHEMIC HEART DISEASE

• Chronic stable angina is not a risk factor for cardiac complication related to noncardiac surgery.

• The patient with CAD or at high risk for it should be treated with beta-blockers during the surgery and for several days thereafter. When used in this fashion, atenolol has been shown to be associated with a significant reduction in cardiac events for 2 years following surgery.

- Topical or IV nitroglycerin is used in the perioperative period for the patient who is chronically maintained on nitroglycerin.
- Elective noncardiac surgery should be avoided in the patient with CCS class III, VI, or unstable angina. If surgery is not elective, then cardiac catheterization with coronary artery revascularization (if indicated) should be considered in this group. If surgery is deemed an emergency it should be performed with the patient receiving an appropriate anti-ischemic regimen in the perioperative period.
- Although no prospective randomized trial has been performed, a protective effect of previous CABG surgery is suggested.
- ACC/AHA guidelines suggest that the patient with high-risk coronary anatomy (three-vessel CAD with LV dysfunction, two-vessel disease involving the left anterior descending artery, or greater than 50% stenosis of the left mainstem) undergo revascularization before a noncardiac surgical procedure of intermediate or high risk.
- There are no data from randomized prospective studies regarding the impact of PTCA or coronary stenting on the risk of subsequent perioperative cardiac complications.

Perioperative Myocardial Infarction

- More than 60% of patients who sustain perioperative MI do not have accompanying anginal pain.
- Presenting symptoms include arrhythmias, pulmonary edema, hypotension, hyperglycemia, and, in the elderly, alteration of mental status.
- The peak incidence of perioperative MI is 24 to 48 hours following surgery.

The optimal surveillance strategy for perioperative MI is uncertain. It is suggested that high-risk patients have an ECG immediately after surgery and on the first 2 post-operative days. Cardiac enzyme measurements are best used in high-risk patients with ECG changes or evidence of cardiac dysfunction.

Hypertension

- Preoperative diastolic blood pressure (DBP) exceeding 110 mm Hg is a risk factor for a perioperative cardiac complication.
- Chronic antihypertensive therapy should be continued in the perioperative period. Parenteral agents are substituted until oral intake resumes.
- Acute perioperative hypertension (HTN) occurs at one of four time periods:
  1. During intubation secondary to sympathetic stimulation
  2. During the surgical procedure
  3. Immediately after termination of anesthesia due to intravascular volume overload, hypothermia, hypoxia, or pain induced sympathetic stimulation
  4. Forty-eight hours following surgery secondary to mobilization of fluid from extravascular sites
- Reversal of precipitating factors will reverse many cases of perioperative HTN. Caution must be taken in the treatment of HTN that does not normalize with reversal of precipitating factors, as too rapid or aggressive HTN control may result in hypotension and myocardial or cerebral hypoperfusion.

Perioperative Hypotension

- Perioperative hypotension may result in cerebral or myocardial ischemia.
- The most common causes of perioperative hypotension are intravascular volume depletion and excessive vasodilatation.
- Other causes include pulmonary embolus or sepsis.

Valvular Heart Disease

Aortic Stenosis
- Symptomatic critical AS is a risk factor associated with a cardiac mortality rate up to 13%. Patients with

asymptomatic AS and normal LV function can tolerate anesthesia with a low risk of complication.
- For the patient with symptomatic critical AS, aortic valve replacement should be considered prior to major noncardiac surgery.
- Aortic balloon valvuloplasty may be considered as a temporizing measure for the person with critical AS and either hemodynamic compromise or shock who is not a candidate for AVR but requires urgent noncardiac surgery.
- Maintenance of sinus rhythm is important in the perioperative period because the hypertrophied LV is often noncompliant and highly dependent on the atrial contribution to ventricular filling.

Aortic Regurgitation
- Operative risk depends on the degree of LV dysfunction.
- Vasodilatation and spinal anesthesia are usually well tolerated.
- In the perioperative period, hemodynamic factors may increase the degree of valvular regurgitation. Examples include vasopressor-induced increases in peripheral vascular resistance, and bradycardia because it leads to an increase in diastolic filling time with subsequent increased regurgitant volumes.

Mitral Stenosis
- Patients with severe MS are sensitive to perioperative changes of intravascular volume.
- Small increases in intravascular volume may lead to marked elevation of PCWP and resultant pulmonary edema.
- Decreases in intravascular volume may result in impaired ventricular filling and decreased CO.
- Bradycardia with its associated increase in diastolic filling time is usually well tolerated. Conversely, tachycardia may contribute to the development of pulmonary edema.

Mitral Regurgitation
- LV dysfunction may be subclinical and ejection fraction only minimally decreased even in the

presence of severe ventricular dysfunction because the LV ejects blood into the "low pressure" LA, as well as the systemic circulation.
- Vasodilatation is usually well tolerated.

Hypertrophic Cardiomyopathy

- HCM is typically accompanied by LV diastolic dysfunction.
- In some patients dynamic LV outflow obstruction occurs. Outflow tract obstruction may be made worse by catecholamines and reductions in preload or afterload. In the perioperative period factors to be avoided include use of catecholamines (dobutamine, dopamine), digoxin, excessive volume loss, or loss of sinus rhythm (preload reduction).
- Invasive hemodynamic monitoring should be considered for the patient whose surgery and perioperative period is associated with volume shifts.
- Perioperative hypotension should be treated with volume administration; if that is insufficient, then peripheral vasoconstrictors (phenylephrine) are used.

Prosthetic Heart Valves

Care must be taken to avoid prosthetic valve thrombosis in the perioperative period, given the need for temporary withholding of anticoagulants. Options include:

- For many minimally invasive procedures (e.g., dental procedures) surgery may be safely performed with anticoagulation at low therapeutic levels.
- For patients with mechanical aortic valves we recommend discontinuation of warfarin 2 to 3 days before surgery. Surgery is performed when the INR is less than 1.4. Anticoagulation is resumed as soon as possible following surgery.
- Prosthetic mitral valves are more prone to thrombosis than are aortic valves. For a patient with a prosthetic mitral valve, warfarin is stopped 48 hours before surgery. Full-dose heparin is begun, usually in the hospital, once the INR is subtherapeutic. Heparin is stopped 6 to 12 hours before surgery and restarted 12 to 48 hours following surgery when hemostasis is

stable. Warfarin is restarted when the patient is able to tolerate oral medications.

IE prophylaxis is indicated for all patients with prosthetic heart valves who undergo surgical procedures associated with a significant risk of bacteremia (see Chapter 7).

Cardiac Arrhythmias and Conduction Disturbances

Preoperative Cardiac Arrhythmias
- Although preoperative VPCs have been found to be a risk factor for perioperative cardiac complication, it is when they are a marker of underlying cardiac disease that they truly increase cardiac risk.
- Underlying structural or ischemic heart disease, as well as electrolyte abnormalities, should be looked for when VPCs are identified prior to surgery.

Perioperative Cardiac Arrhythmias
Perioperative cardiac arrhythmias are common (occurring in up to 80%). The majority are clinically insignificant and require no treatment.

- Sinus tachycardia is often a result of catecholamine release due to pain or stress, anemia, or hypovolemia.
- Sinus bradycardia may be caused by medications (e.g., narcotics) or pain-related vagal stimulation.

Some cardiac arrhythmias may persist despite correction of provoking factors.

- SVT that causes hemodynamic instability should be treated with synchronized DC cardioversion.
- Narrow complex SVT that is hemodynamically stable should be treated by vagal stimulation (e.g., carotid sinus massage) or IV adenosine or verapamil.
- The rapid ventricular response of AF usually slows with IV digoxin, propranolol, diltiazem, or verapamil.
- Patients whose AF persists for more than 48 hours should undergo warfarin anticoagulation for 3 weeks before and 4 weeks following cardioversion.
- Atrial flutter usually responds to low energy DC cardioversion.

- Ibutalide has been shown to be effective for the rapid conversion of AF and atrial flutter. Its use in the perioperative period is not yet defined.
- VPCs, as well as nonsustained VT, are usually a result of reversible factors including hypoxia, hypercarbia, electrolyte abnormality, or myocardial ischemia.
- RV catheters may cause ventricular ectopy via trauma to the RVOT. This resolves with repositioning or withdrawal of the catheter.
- Hemodynamically unstable sustained VT or VF should be treated immediately with DC cardioversion and adjunctive AAD therapy (see Chapters 17 and 19).

Perioperative Conduction Abnormalities

- Asymptomatic chronic uni- or bifascicular heart block rarely progresses to complete heart block in the perioperative period.
- A temporary cardiac pacemaker should be placed prior to surgery if the patient meets criteria for a permanent pacemaker but has not yet had the device implanted.
- Placement of a PA catheter is associated with up to 5% incidence of transient RBBB. For the patient with chronic LBBB this may result in complete AV block. A means for temporary pacing should be available for the patient with chronic LBBB who undergoes placement of a PA catheter.

Permanent Pacemaker and ICD Management

See Chapter 18.

Congestive Heart Failure

- Patients with chronic stable CHF should have their medical therapy continued. If oral intake is a problem, parenteral medications can be substituted (see Chapter 2).
- Perioperative CHF occurs at two distinct time periods:
  1. The peak occurrence is during the first 60 minutes after cessation of anesthesia due to intraoperative

fluid overload, postoperative HTN, anesthesia-induced myocardial dysfunction, and termination of positive-pressure ventilation related preload reduction.

2. The second peak is 24 to 48 hours after surgery resulting from mobilization of interstitial fluid.

• Treatment of perioperative CHF is directed toward resolution of the precipitating factor(s), diuretics when volume overload is the cause, and anti-ischemic therapy when myocardial ischemia is a causative factor.

SUGGESTED READINGS

American College of Physicians. Clinical guidelines for assessing and managing the perioperative risk from coronary artery disease associated with major vascular surgery. Ann Intern Med 1997;127:309–312.

American Society of Anesthesiologists Task Force on Pulmonary Artery Catheterization. Practice guidelines for pulmonary artery catheterization. Anesthesiology 1993;78:380–394.

Detsky AS, Abrams HB, McLaughlin JR, et al. Predicting cardiac complications in patients undergoing non-cardiac surgery. J Gen Intern Med 1986;1:211–219.

Eagle KA, Brundage BH, Chaitman, BR. Guidelines for perioperative cardiovascular evaluation for noncardiac surgery. Report of the American College of Cardiology/ American Heart Association Task Force on Practice Guidelines (Committee on Perioperative Cardiovascular Evaluation for Noncardiac Surgery). J Am Coll Cardiol 1996;27:910–948.

Eagle KA, Coley CM, Newell JB, et al. Combining clinical and thallium data optimizes preoperative assessment of cardiac risk before major vascular surgery. Ann Intern Med 1989;110:859–866.

Goldman L, Caldera DL, Nussbaum SR, et al. Multifactorial index of cardiac risk in noncardiac surgical procedures. N Engl J Med 1977;297:845–850.

Mangano DT, Browner WS, Hollenberg M, et al. Association of perioperative myocardial ischemia with cardiac morbidity and mortality in men undergoing noncardiac surgery. N Engl J Med 1990;323:1781–1788.

Mangano DT, Goldman L. Preoperative assessment of patients

with known or suspected coronary disease. N Engl J Med 1995;333:1750–1756.

Mangano DT, Layug EL, Wallace A, et al. Effect of atenolol on mortality and cardiovascular morbidity after noncardiac surgery. N Engl J Med 1996;335:1713–1720.

Palda VA, Detsky AS. Preoperative assessment and management of risk from coronary artery disease. Ann Intern Med 1997;127:313–328.

Wong T, Detsky AS. Preoperative cardiac risk assessment for patients having peripheral vascular surgery. Ann Intern Med 1992;116:743–753.

Anti-arrhythmic Drug Therapy

James R. Cook
Dennis A. Tighe
Edward K. Chung

The diagnosis and management of cardiac arrhythmias have improved significantly owing to advances in the understanding of basic cellular electrophysiology and the testing of this knowledge in large clinical trials. The best therapeutic results can be anticipated when a precise diagnosis and electrophysiologic mechanism for an arrhythmia is entertained because certain drugs are more effective and even specific for certain arrhythmias. This chapter discusses individual anti-arrhythmic drugs (AADs) and management strategies for various cardiac arrhythmias.

CLASSIFICATION OF ANTI-ARRHYTHMIC DRUGS

Classification schemes have been devised to highlight the differences in AAD actions and effects.

Vaughan-Williams classification. The Vaughan-Williams classification scheme is based on the main action of the drug on the myocardium (Table 17-1). This classification has proven useful clinically, but it must be emphasized that no two drugs are identical and that some agents have several actions rendering the class distinctions somewhat ambiguous.

Sicilian gambit. Recently, an improved operational

Table 17-1. Pharmacology of Oral Anti-arrhythmic Drugs

	Dose	Half-life	Clearance	Therapeutic Plasma Levels	Drug Interactions
Class IA					
Quinidine	Sulfate: 200–400 mg t.i.d. Gluconate: 324–648 mg t.i.d.	5 to 8 hours	70% to 90% hepatic 10% to 30% renal	2–5 ug/mL	Digoxin Barbiturates Phenytoin Cimetidine
Procainamide (PA)	Short-acting: 500–1000 mg every 4 to 6 hours Long-acting: 1000–2500 mg b.i.d.	Procainamide: 1.5 to 3 hours NAPA: 6 to 7 hours	60% renal Hepatic acetylation to active NAPA	Procainamide: 4–10 ug/mL PA + NAPA: 6–30 ug/mL	None known
Disopyramide	Short-acting: 100–200 mg t.i.d. Long-acting: 150–300 mg b.i.d.	5 to 8 hours	70% renal 15% hepatic 15% GI	2–5 ug/mL	Rifampin Phenytoin
Class IB					
Mexiletene	200–400 mg t.i.d. 10% unchanged in urine	8 to 12 hours	90% hepatic	N/A	None known
Phenytoin	300–400 mg/day in divided doses	24 hours (quite variable)	Hepatic	10–20 ug/mL	Quinidine Disopyramide Cimetidine
Class IC					
Flecainide	50–200 mg b.i.d.	16 hours (quite variable)	50% hepatic 30% unchanged in urine	500–1000 ug/mL	Cimetidine Digoxin

Drug	Dosage	Half-life	Metabolism/Elimination	Therapeutic level	Drug interactions
Propafenone	150–300 mg t.i.d.	6 to 10 hours	Hepatic	N/A	Digoxin, Cimetidine, Warfarin
Moricizine	200–300 mg t.i.d.	3 to 12 hours	Hepatic	N/A	Cimetidine
Class II					
Propranolol	10–80 mg t.i.d. or q.i.d.	4 to 6 hours	Hepatic	N/A	None known
Acebutolol	100–300 mg t.i.d.	8 hours	Hepatic	N/A	None known
Class III					
Sotalol	80–240 mg b.i.d.	6 to 18 hours	Renal	N/A	None known
Amiodarone (PO)	Loading: 400–1200 mg/day for 7 to 10 days; Maintenance: 200–600 mg/day	Up to 120 days	Hepatic	1–2 ug/mL	Digoxin, Warfarin, Beta-blockers
Class IV					
Diltiazem	Short-acting: 30–120 mg t.i.d. to q.i.d.; Long-acting: 120–480 mg/day	4 to 10 hours	Hepatic; Extensive first-pass effect	50–200 ng/mL	Cimetidine, Beta-blockers, Digoxin, Carbamazepine
Verapamil	Short-acting: 80–160 mg t.i.d.; Long-acting: 120–480 mg/day	4.5 to 12 hours	Hepatic; Extensive first-pass effect	125–400 ng/mL	Beta-blockers, Digoxin, Quinidine
Other					
Digoxin	0.125–0.5 mg/day	36 to 48 hours	70% renal	1.0–2.0 ng/mL	Quinidine, Verapamil, Amiodarone, Propafenone

framework (the Sicilian gambit) has been posited to incorporate information on clinical effects, cellular mechanisms, and molecular targets for AADs. It remains to be seen how this newer scheme will affect the perception, use, and development of AADs.

CLASS I ANTI-ARRHYTHMIC DRUGS

Class I agents possess local anesthetic and membrane stabilizing effects. Their predominant action is to bind to sodium channels and impede sodium influx during phase 0 of the action potential, resulting in depression of intra-cardiac conduction.

Class I drugs can be further subclassified into IA, IB, and IC agents based on their effect on cardiac tissue refractoriness and conduction:

- Class IA agents prolong ventricular refractoriness and the QT interval.
- Class IB agents are less potent sodium channel blockers and at high tissue concentrations shorten action potential duration (APD) and refractoriness.
- Class IC agents are potent sodium channel blockers that markedly slow conduction with very little effect on repolarization.

Class IA Anti-arrhythmic Drugs

Quinidine

Quinidine has been used extensively for the management of atrial and ventricular arrhythmias. The drug depresses myocardial excitability, conduction velocity, and contractility.

The direct effect of quinidine on the heart is complicated by an indirect anticholinergic action, an effect that can result in facilitated AV conduction during AF.

Pharmacokinetics
- Quinidine is rapidly and almost completely absorbed from the gastrointestinal (GI) tract.
- Quinidine is removed by both the liver and the kidneys. Approximately 80% is metabolized by the liver.
- The half-life is 5 to 8 hours.

Drug interactions Drug interactions have been documented with:

Digoxin
Barbiturates
Phenytoin
Rifampin
Cimetidine

Major side effects
GI upset (most notably diarrhea)
Immune-mediated thrombocytopenia
Rash
Proarrhythmia from QT interval prolongation
Cinchonism

Dosing Oral and parenteral forms are available.

Oral
Quinidine sulfate: 600–1000 mg loading dose, and then 200–300 mg every 6 to 8 hours (maximum dose 2.4 gram/day)
Quinidine gluconate: 324–648 mg loading dose, followed by 324–648 mg every 8 hours.

Intravenous Parenteral quinidine is available as a gluconate (80 mg/mL) or hydrochloride (200 mg/mL) compound. The drug should be infused at the rate of 16 mg/minute with continuous ECG monitoring.

- The infusion should be stopped if excessive QT prolongation is noted (>25% of baseline).
- Careful attention must be paid to the BP as the drug is an alpha-blocker that can cause hypotension.

When given orally, the plasma concentration is maximal in about 60 to 90 minutes.

Serum quinidine levels may be useful when obtained after 4 to 5 half-lives. Therapeutic plasma levels are 2–5 mg/L.

Clinical Results

Supraventricular arrhythmias Quinidine is most extensively used for treatment of AF. It is often the first agent chosen for attempted chemical cardioversion.

- A recent meta-analysis showed that 50% of patients on quinidine remained in sinus rhythm at 1 year. However, a small but statistically significant increase in overall mortality was seen in treated patients.
- Quinidine has been reported to be effective in the prophylaxis of recurrent attacks of supraventricular tachycardia (SVT) due either to atrioventricular nodal reentry or to atrioventricular reentry.

As is common to virtually all AADs, the EP changes produced by quinidine are largely reversible by catecholamines. When quinidine is used to treat paroxysmal SVT, the addition of a beta-adrenergic blocker to quinidine is often the best approach.

Ventricular arrhythmias In patients with chronic, stable VPCs, quinidine produces a greater than 80% suppression of arrhythmia in approximately half of patients treated. Studies using EP testing have found the drug effectiveness to range from 20% to 40%.

The drug may also be used in combination with other AADs. Mexiletine (class IB) is often combined with quinidine for synergistic EP interaction. The advantage of this combination is that lower doses of each agent may be used to avoid excessive side effects.

Procainamide
Procainamide has EP effects similar to those of quinidine. Procainamide has an indirect vagolytic action; despite direct effects to slow AV conduction, the drug may actually facilitate conduction in low doses.

Pharmacokinetics
- Procainamide is rapidly and almost completely absorbed from the GI tract. When given orally, its plasma concentration is maximal in about 60 minutes.
- The drug is slowly hydrolyzed by plasma esterases. The biological half-life is 3 to 4 hours.
- The major metabolite, *N*-acetylprocainamide (NAPA), has a 6- to 7-hour half-life.
- Procainamide and NAPA are excreted primarily (approximately 60%) by the kidneys and should not be used in patients with significant renal disease.

Neither procainamide nor NAPA is readily dialyzable.

Side effects
GI upset
Neurologic toxicity
Proarrhythmia
CHF
Drug-induced systemic lupus erythematosus
Agranulocytosis

Dosing

Oral
Short-acting preparation: 1–2 gram loading dose, followed by 500 to 1000 mg every 4 to 6 hours.
Long-acting preparation: 1000–2500 mg, twice a day. Maximum dose is 50 mg/kg per day.

Serum drug levels are available and should be followed:

• The therapeutic range for procainamide is 4–10 mg/L. That for combined procainamide and NAPA is 6–30 mg/L.

Intravenous *Note*: Hypotension and excessive prolongation of the QT interval are limiting factors.

Loading dose: 10–20 mg/kg in 200 cc of D5W to infuse over 40 to 60 minutes.
Maintenance dose: 2–4 mg/min.

Clinical Results

Supraventricular arrhythmias Procainamide seems to have similar efficacy as quinidine for AF, but some investigators have found it less effective.

• IV dosing with conversion to an oral equivalent gives procainamide a distinct clinical advantage.
• The high conversion of patients to ANA positivity and the development of drug-induced lupus limit the long-term tolerability.

Ventricular arrhythmias Procainamide was found comparable to quinidine for the suppression of ventricular ectopic activity in the ESVEM (Electrophysiologic Study Versus Electrocardiographic Monitoring) trial.

- A 50% efficacy was predicted by Holter monitoring and 26% by EP testing; however, the probability of recurrence of arrhythmia or death at 1 year among the group predicted as effectively treated was 50%.
- Quinidine and procainamide had the highest percentages of patients with adverse effects requiring discontinuation of the drug during long-term therapy (approximately 31% for each).

Disopyramide

Disopyramide is electrophysiologically similar to quinidine. The drug also has significant anticholinergic effects which have made it popular for AF secondary to excessive sinus bradycardia (athletic heart).

Drug Interactions Drug interactions with disopyramide have been described with:

Rifampin
Phenytoin

Side Effects Disopyramide is a potent negative-inotropic agent that can substantially worsen LV function and provoke CHF.

Other side effects include:

Anticholinergic effects: urinary hesitancy and retention, constipation
Neurologic toxicity
Hypoglycemia
Rash
Proarrhythmia

Dosing

Oral

Short-acting preparation: 100–200 mg three or four times daily.
Long-acting preparation: 150–300 mg two times a day.

Clinical Results

Supraventricular arrhythmias Disopyramide is as effective as quinidine for treatment of AF.

- Disopyramide, like the other class IA drugs, should *not* be used for the management of AF unless the ventricular rate has already been controlled with a beta-blocker, CCB, digoxin, or a combination of these drugs.

- Disopyramide has a vagolytic action that may increase conduction through the AV node and, when combined with a slowing of the atrial rate, can result in rapid increases in ventricular response and hemodynamic compromise.

Ventricular arrhythmias Disopyramide has been shown to suppress ventricular ectopic activity in 70% to 80% of patients and prevent the induction of sustained ventricular arrhythmia in up to 35% of patients (some of whom were refractory to other class IA agents).

Class IB Anti-arrhythmic Drugs

Lidocaine
Lidocaine is considered the first-line parenteral agent for treatment of serious ventricular arrhythmias.

- Lidocaine shortens APD and repolarization but does not prolong ventricular refractoriness or affect conduction velocity. The intervals on the surface ECG are not significantly affected.
- Lidocaine has very little effect on the atria, but sinus node arrest may be a complication of therapy.

Pharmacokinetics
- Lidocaine is readily absorbed from the GI tract. However, it undergoes an extensive first-pass hepatic metabolism, thus necessitating parenteral administration.
- Approximately 90% of an administered dose of the drug is metabolized by the liver, with the remaining 10% excreted unchanged via the kidneys.
- Significant liver dysfunction or conditions that decrease hepatic blood flow (CHF, hypotension, cardiogenic shock, advancing age) decrease lidocaine metabolism and clearance and increase its plasma concentration.

Side effects Side effects are infrequent and are mainly limited to the CNS:

Dizziness
Drowsiness and confusion
Seizures
Perioral numbness

Dosing

Intravenous
For the initiation of therapy: injection of 75–100 mg of
lidocaine hydrochloride (1.0–1.5 mg/kg).

- A second dose may be required 5 to 10 minutes later
  (first-pass effect).
- Total doses should not exceed 750 mg.
- No more than 300 mg should be administered during
  a 1-hour period.

Intramuscular When IV injection is not immediately
feasible, 200–300 mg of lidocaine may be given IM into
the deltoid muscle.

- An additional IM injection may be administered 60
  to 90 minutes later if necessary.

Continuous infusion A continuous IV infusion at a
rate of 1 to 5 mg/min is frequently used to maintain adequate serum levels for 24 to 48 hours.

- Therapeutic serum level ranges vary, but levels
  <6 mg/L are most widely accepted.

Clinical Results Lidocaine is effective for the treatment of ventricular arrhythmias in various clinical settings. It remains the drug of choice for emergency therapy
because of the rapidity with which therapeutic plasma
concentrations can be achieved and the low incidence of
significant hemodynamic complications. The efficacy of
lidocaine in the treatment of ventricular ectopic activity
and VT due to ischemia has been reported to be 50% to
75%.

- Prophylactic treatment with lidocaine for patients
  with acute MI is not recommended (see Chapter 1).
- Lidocaine is not effective and should not be used for
  the treatment of atrial arrhythmias.

Mexiletine

Mexiletine is structurally and pharmacologically similar to lidocaine. The drug has proved effective for the suppression of ventricular ectopic activity in patients with CAD and MI.

Pharmacokinetics

- Mexiletine is well absorbed from the GI tract and has a bioavailability of 80% to 90% in healthy individuals.
- Peak plasma levels are observed in 2 to 4 hours, and 70% of the drug is protein bound.
- The drug is metabolized predominantly by the liver, and less than 10% is excreted unchanged in the urine.
- The half-life is 8 to 12 hours in healthy individuals, and is significantly prolonged in patients with acute MI, hepatic disease, or renal failure.

Side effects The most common side effects are neurologic and GI:

Drowsiness, tremors
Vertigo, confusion, and nystagmus
Nausea, vomiting, and indigestion
Rash
Thrombocytopenia
Hepatitis
Positive ANA

Dosing The recommended dose range is 200–400 mg three times a day (10–15 mg/kg per day).

Clinical Results Efficacy for the suppression of ventricular ectopic activity is in the range of 40% to 60%. When using serial EP testing to study effects of drugs in the treatment of sustained VT or VF, less than 15% of patients are found to be responsive to mexiletine therapy alone.

When studied in patients with a recent MI, mexiletine was effective in suppressing VPCs. However, at the end of 12 months there were more deaths in the mexiletine-treated group (7.6%) than in the placebo group (4.8%). This finding reinforces the conclusion of the Cardiac Arrhythmia Suppression Trial (CAST): the treatment of asymptomatic or minimally symptomatic complex ventricular ectopy with AADs in patients following an MI is *not* indicated.

The principal clinical application of mexiletine appears to be in combination with a class IA agent in the treatment of ventricular arrhythmias. Mexiletine and quinidine are frequently combined.

Phenytoin

Phenytoin has a chemical structure similar to barbiturates. Like lidocaine, it neither depresses the excitability nor prolongs the effective refractory period (ERP) of cardiac tissues. In isolated Purkinje tissue, the APD is abbreviated but the ERP is not diminished in proportion, resulting in an increased ERP/APD ratio.

Pharmacokinetics

- Phenytoin is 70% to 95% bound to plasma proteins and is widely distributed to all tissues.
- It is almost exclusively metabolized by hepatic microsomal enzymes and has a variable half-life that averages 24 hours.

Side effects

CNS: drowsiness, tremor, depression
Gingival hyperplasia
Purpura
Eosinophilia

Dosing

Oral

200 mg loading dose, followed by 100 mg three to four times a day.

Intravenous

50 to 100 mg over 1 to 3 minutes; repeat the dose every 10 to 15 minutes as necessary to a maximum of 10 to 15 mg/kg.

A maintenance infusion is not practical.

Clinical Results

- Numerous studies emphasize the almost specific effect of phenytoin in digitalis intoxication.

- The drug is of little use in the treatment of AF and flutter.

Class IC Anti-arrhythmic Drugs

Class IC agents are potent fast sodium channel blockers.

In the CAST study, flecainide was associated with more presumed proarrhythmic deaths than placebo. Due to these concerns it is recommended that this class of AADs should *not* be used in patients with structural heart disease.

Flecainide

Flecainide is FDA approved for the treatment of supraventricular and ventricular arrhythmias.

Pharmacokinetics

- Approximately 50% of an oral dose is metabolized in the liver with 30% excreted unchanged in urine and 5% in feces.
- The bioavailability of flecainide is high (~95%) and peak plasma levels occur at 2 to 4 hours.
- The plasma half-life is long (mean of 16 hours) in healthy people, and longer in elderly individuals and those with renal or cardiac disease.

Side effects

- Flecainide is a potent negative inotropic agent and may precipitate CHF.
- Flecainide can occasionally provoke serious ventricular arrhythmias in patients with minimal structural heart disease being treated for AF.

Other side effects include:

CNS: diploplia and dysgeusia
GI
Cardiac: incessant VT (proarrhythmia)

Dosing

Oral Flecainide is only available as an oral preparation:

50–200 mg twice daily.

Clinical Results

Supraventricular arrhythmias   In a double blind, crossover study of patients with paroxysmal AF, flecainide significantly decreased symptoms and the incidence of paroxysmal AF when compared to placebo.

Ventricular arrhythmias   Flecainide has been shown to suppress ventricular ectopic activity in approximately 80% to 90% of patients. It has also been shown to prevent the induction of sustained VT at programmed ventricular stimulation.

Propafenone
Propafenone has similar EP effects as flecainide. In addition to direct effects, propafenone also possesses significant beta-blocker activity, which plays a role in the anti-arrhythmic activity. Propafenone is FDA approved for the treatment of supraventricular and ventricular arrythmias.

Pharmacokinetics
- The drug is metabolized almost exclusively by the hepatic system with only 1% excreted unchanged in the urine.

Drug interactions   Significant drug interactions have been described with:

Digoxin
Cimetidine
Warfarin

Side effects
GI: nausea, vomiting, constipation
Neurologic: weakness, fatigue, tremor, and blurred vision
Cardiovascular: arrhythmias, CHF

Dosing

Oral
150–300 mg three times a day.

- Propafenone is only available as an oral preparation.
- A single loading dose of 600 mg may be useful to terminate recent onset AF.

Clinical Results

Supraventricular arrhythmias In one study, propafenone was evaluated in 26 patients with AF who had cardiovascular disease and had not responded to or were intolerant of a mean of 2.7 previous anti-arrhythmic drugs. Twelve patients with AF (46%) were maintained in normal sinus rhythm with a mean follow-up of 15.6 months.

Ventricular arrhythmias Propafenone has been evaluated by several investigators using either serial EP testing or ECG monitoring and found to be effective in suppressing ventricular arrhythmias.

In the ESVEM study, propafenone was found effective in suppressing ventricular ectopic activity 48% of the time, but only 14% of the time when efficacy was assessed by EPS.

Although propafenone was not included in CAST, other IC agents increased arrhythmic mortality. Therefore, it has found limited use for ventricular arrhythmias.

Moricizine

Although classified as a class I anti-arrhythmic agent, moricizine does not clearly fit into a IA, IB, or IC category.

The drug was evaluated in the Cardiac Arrhythmia Pilot Study (CAPS) and found to suppress ventricular ectopic activity in 66% of the patients tested. It was most effective in patients with severely depressed LV ejection fractions.

Moricizine was studied in CAST II, and found to impart an early risk of proarrhythmia and no survival benefit when suppressing ventricular ectopy after MI.

Pharmacokinetics The pharmacokinetics of moricizine are complex and poorly understood.

- The drug is completely absorbed from the GI tract.
- The half-life ranges from 3 to 12 hours, but may be longer in patients with low CO.

Side effects The drug tends to be well tolerated. In the CAPS trial there was no significant increase in any side effect over that found with placebo.

Dosing Standard doses: 600–900 mg/day in divided doses (every 8 to 12 hours).

Clinical Results Moricizine suppresses spontaneous ventricular arrhythmias comparably to class IA agents. The drug is well tolerated, but only modestly effective in preventing inducible sustained VTs. It may be preferable in patients with CHF and a reduced LV ejection fraction. However, CAST and CAST II have changed the treatment strategies of patients with ventricular ectopy after MI.

CLASS II ANTI-ARRHYTHMIC DRUGS

Beta-Blockers

At clinically prescribed doses, the beta-blockers do not exert any significant direct effects on the myocardial membrane. Beta-blocker actions are mediated principally by blockade of myocardial beta receptors, resulting in antagonism of catecholamine effect on myocardial EP properties. Thus, they are most effective in the presence of elevated circulating catecholamines and an activated sympathetic nervous system.

Two beta blockers are FDA approved for arrhythmia management: propranolol and acebutolol. Unlike propranolol, acebutolol is cardioselective and has ISA. The anti-arrhythmic effects imparted by these medications are related to the degree of beta-blockade, and other beta-blockers are probably equally effective. Further discussion on beta-blocker therapy can be found in Chapter 1.

Dosing

Propranolol
Oral: 10–80 mg three to four times per day.
Intravenous: 0.1–0.15 mg/kg in 1 mg doses every 5 to 10 minutes to a maximum of 10 mg.

Acebutolol
Oral: 100–300 mg three times a day.

Clinical Results
Beta-blockers have a favorable effect on supraventricular arrhythmias and can revert a reentrant SVT to normal

sinus rhythm. They can control the ventricular response to AF and atrial flutter as monotherapy or in combination with digitalis or CCBs. They are useful in patients with arrhythmias due to MVP and the congenital long QT syndrome.

- A recent meta-analysis suggests that a greater than 80% suppression of benign ventricular arrhythmia is attained in 40% to 60% of patients treated with a beta-blocker alone.
- In patients with malignant ventricular arrhythmias, beta-blockers play an important adjunctive role in combination with other AADs.

CLASS III ANTI-ARRHYTHMIC DRUGS

The class III agents share the properties of prolonging the APD and repolarization of cardiac tissues.

Sotalol

Sotalol is both a nonselective and water-soluble beta-blocker. It prolongs the action potential duration and delays repolarization. This results in slowing of the HR and an increase in the QT interval.

Pharmacokinetics
- Sotalol is metabolized exclusively by the kidneys.
- The half-life varies from 6 to 18 hours.

Drug interactions   There are no known drug interactions.

Side effects
CNS
Cardiovascular
Proarrhythmia: a dose-dependent incidence of torsades de pointes
CHF

Dosing

Oral
80–240 mg, twice a day.

- Sotalol is only available in oral form.
- No loading dose is needed.

Clinical Results

Supraventricular Arrhythmias Sotalol is a more effective AAD than other beta-blockers. Overall, the drug is well tolerated. In a recent trial, sotalol was as effective as quinidine in maintaining sinus rhythm when used for the treatment of AF.

Ventricular Arrhythmias The ESVEM study identified sotalol as the only treatment to predict independently a reduced risk of recurrent ventricular arrhythmia and a correlation with a reduced mortality.

Amiodarone

Amiodarone is a complex AAD with multiple effects. It is also an effective anti-anginal agent and both a coronary and systemic vasodilator. The major anti-arrhythmic effects result from prolongation of APD and repolarization. The drug also produces mild sodium channel blocking activity and is a noncompetitive beta-blocker and CCB. In addition, amiodarone contains substantial amounts of iodine and may exert some anti-arrhythmic activity by effects on thyroxin metabolism.

Pharmacokinetics
- Amiodarone is cleared by hepatic metabolism.
- It has a large volume of distribution and an exceedingly long half-life (>6 weeks).

Drug Interactions Numerous drug interactions have been described:

Digoxin
Warfarin
AADs
Beta-blockers
CCBs
Anesthetic agents

Side Effects
Pulmonary toxicity: early and insidious pulmonary fibrosis, adult respiratory distress syndrome
Thyroid abnormalities: both hypo- and hyperthyroidism
Hepatic: transaminase elevation
GI: anorexia, constipation

Ophthalmologic: corneal deposits, optic neuritis
Dermatologic: photosensitivity, bluish skin discoloration

Dosing

Oral
Loading dose: 600–1800 mg per day, for a total of 8–10 grams.
Maintenance dose: 200–800 mg per day.

Intravenous For the treatment of drug-resistant VT:
150 mg at 15 mg/min (~10 minutes);
followed by 1.8 mg/mL (900 mg in 500 cc) at 1 mg/min (33.3 mL/hr) for the next 6 hours;
followed by 1.8 mg/mL (900 mg in 500 cc) at 0.5 mg/min, until oral intake is feasible.
Additional bolus doses of 150 mg may be necessary to control recurrent episodes of VT.

Clinical Results

Supraventricular Arrhythmias Substantial data exist supporting the efficacy of amiodarone in the treatment of atrial arrhythmias. It appears 70% effective in treating paroxysmal SVT or paroxysmal AF or flutter. It may be the single most effective agent for the prophylaxis of AF, and it compares very favorably with the effectiveness of class IA agents, class IC agents, and beta-blockers.

Ventricular Arrhythmias In patients with VT or VF, amiodarone has provided response rates of >60%. In a study of 462 patients with recurrent VT or VF refractory to an average of 2.6 anti-arrhythmic drugs per patient, the reported recurrence rate for VT was 19% at 1 year, 33% at 3 years, and 43% at 5 years.

Ibutilide

Ibutilide is considered a class III agent due to its predominant action of prolonging APD and refractoriness of myocardial cells. However, its EP profile is distinct from other class III agents. Rather than acting on potassium channels, the drug activates a slow, predominantly sodium current which serves to increase the APD.

- Ibutilide exhibits a dose-related prolongation of the QT interval but little other effect on the surface ECG.
- Ibutilide has been approved as an IV agent for the treatment of acute AF and flutter.

Pharmacokinetics
- Ibutilide is cleared via hepatic metabolism.
- The half-life averages 6 hours.

Drug Interactions   There are no clinical data on the safety and efficacy of combining the drug with other AADs for the treatment of AF.

Side Effects
Proarrhythmia: polymorphic VT in up to 2.4% of patients

Dosing

Intravenous
1 mg over 10 minutes; may be repeated once after 10 to 15 minutes.

- Ibutilide is available intravenously only.
- Pretreatment with 2 grams of IV magnesium may decrease the incidence of polymorphic VT.
- Patients should have continuous ECG monitoring during drug administration and for at least 4 hours after infusion.

Clinical Results
Several double blind placebo controlled trials using ibutilide for AF and flutter have proven the drug to be quite effective with conversion to sinus within an hour in 50% to 70% of patients. Atrial flutter is more likely to respond than is AF.

Bretylium

Bretylium tosylate is a parenteral agent indicated for the treatment of life-threatening, drug-resistant VT and VF. It is an adrenergic neuron blocking agent. An initial "sympathomimetic" effect may result in HTN and paradoxical worsening of the ventricular arrhythmia. Progressive catecholamine depletion at the adrenergic nerve terminal membranes reduces the BP and is also antiarrhythmic.

Bretylium also appears to have a direct membrane

effect on cardiac tissue. It prolongs the APD and ERP of the Purkinje fibers and ventricular myocardium.

Pharmacokinetics

The primary route of elimination is via the kidneys, with 80% to 90% excreted unchanged in the urine.

Side Effects

Hypotension
Nausea
Transient sympathomimetic effect

Dosing

IV bolus of 5–10 mg/kg, repeated 15 to 30 minutes later if necessary.

- Continuous maintenance infusions of 1–2 mg/min may follow the bolus doses.
- IM administration of 5–10 mg/kg every 6 or 8 hours may follow the bolus dose.

Clinical Results

Bretylium is considered primarily an antifibrillatory agent with only modest suppression of ventricular ectopic activity. It is considered as effective an antifibrillatory agent as lidocaine in the setting of an acute MI.

CLASS IV ANTI-ARRHYTHMIC DRUGS

Calcium Channel Blockers

The CCBs have been shown to be clinically useful for ventricular rate control in patients with SVTs and AF. Both diltiazem and verapamil increase the refractory period and the conduction time of the AV node. CCBs have been shown to impart a frequency dependent effect on AV nodal conduction, such that these drugs are more effective at higher stimulation rates.

Diltiazem

Diltiazem is available in both oral and IV formulations. IV diltiazem is highly effective for the rapid control of the ventricular rate in AF.

Pharmacokinetics

- Diltiazem undergoes hepatic metabolism.
- Its half-life is 3.5 hours.

Drug interactions   Drug interactions have been noted with:

Beta-blockers
Cimetidine

Side effects
Mild hypotension
Bradycardia
AV block
Peripheral edema

Dosing

Oral
Short-acting preparation: 60–90 mg three to four times daily.
Slow-release form: 240–360 mg once a day.

Intravenous
20 to 25 mg (0.25 to 0.35 mg/kg), followed by 10 to 15 mg/hour infusion.

Clinical Results   In a double blind study of 113 patients with AF or flutter and a ventricular rate ≤120 beats per minute, 75% of patients responded to 0.25 mg/kg diltiazem (given over 2 minutes) with at least a 20% reduction in HR or a reduction in the ventricular rate to less than 100 bpm. The median time from drug infusion to rate control was 4.3 minutes.

Verapamil

Verapamil is effective in slowing the ventricular response rate of AF and flutter and in slowing or abolishing SVTs that use the AV node as part of a reentrant circuit.

Pharmacokinetics
- Verapamil undergoes hepatic metabolism.
- The half-life is quite variable (4.5 to 12 hours).

Drug interactions   Significant drug interactions have been noted with:

Beta-blockers
Digoxin
Disopyramide
Quinidine

Side effects
Hypotension
Bradycardia
AV block
Constipation
Peripheral edema

Dosing

Oral
Short-acting preparation: 80–160 mg three to four times
    daily.
Long-acting preparation: 120–480 mg daily.

Intravenous
5–20 mg in 5 mg increments over 30 seconds (serum
    half-life is 15 to 20 minutes).
Although not frequently used, a constant infusion of
    0.005 mg/kg per minute may be given.

Clinical Results   IV verapamil is highly effective for
slowing the ventricular rate in AF. A maximal response is
seen within 2 to 3 minutes after drug administration, an
effect that appears to be independent of the level of sympathetic tone.

MISCELLANEOUS ANTI-ARRHYTHMIC AGENTS

Adenosine

Adenosine is an endogenous nucleoside that depresses AV
nodal conduction and decreases sinus node automaticity.

Pharmacokinetics
- Adenosine is metabolized by red blood cells and
  endothelium.
- The half-life is less than 10 seconds.

Side Effects
- Adenosine shortens the APD in atrial tissue and may
  precipitate short bursts of AF.
- Adenosine should not be used in patients with a
  known history of bronchospastic lung disease.
- Adenosine has no effect on ventricular myocardium.

Other known side effects include:

Transient flushing
Chest pain
Dyspnea
Hypotension

Dosing
6 mg by rapid IV push, followed by a saline flush to promote "bolus" effect.

If no response is obtained with the 6 mg dose, repeat with 12 mg rapid IV push in 1 to 2 minutes.

3 mg should be the initial dose if a central venous line is used.

Clinical Results
Adenosine (6/12 mg) has been shown to terminate 90% to 95% of episodes of AV nodal reentrant tachycardia and is similarly effective for orthodromic AV reciprocating tachycardia. One report found adenosine to shorten the antegrade refractory period of an accessory pathway in WPW syndrome.

Digoxin

Digoxin is a cardiac glycoside that has been used for the treatment of CHF and the management of AF. It is the most frequently used drug for management of chronic AF and is administered primarily for control of the ventricular rate.

Digoxin primarily works in an indirect manner to impart a vagotonic effect that is easily reversed by enhanced sympathetic tone. Thus, drug actions are quite attenuated in high catecholamine states or in patients with reduced autonomic function (diabetes mellitus, cardiac transplant). However, the positive inotropic effects of digoxin make the drug useful for ventricular rate response to AF in patients with LV dysfunction and CHF.

Although digoxin is often administered for the acute termination of AF, the drug has no proven benefit for this condition.

Pharmacokinetics
- Digoxin is cleared primarily by the kidneys.
- The half-life is 36 to 48 hours.

Drug Interactions Drug interactions have been described with:

Quinidine
Propafenone
Flecainide
Verapamil
Amiodarone

Side Effects

Cardiac arrhythmias: VT, paroxysmal atrial tachycardia with AV block
GI upset
CNS

Dosing

Oral

0.125–0.50 mg daily.

Intravenous

0.5 mg over 2 to 3 minutes, followed by 0.25 mg every 6 hours for a total of 1.0 mg loading dose.

MANAGEMENT STRATEGIES FOR THERAPY OF CARDIAC ARRHYTHMIAS

Supraventricular Tachycardias

SVTs can be separated into two categories:

Atrioventricular nodal-dependent: SVTs requiring AV nodal conduction for maintenance of the arrhythmia. Atrioventricular nodal reentrant tachycardia (AVNRT) and AV reentry (using a bypass tract as part of the circuit) comprise the AV nodal-dependent tachycardias.

Atrioventricular nodal-independent: SVTs in which the AV node conducts impulses from the atrium to the ventricle but is not required for maintenance of the arrhythmia. AV nodal-independent tachycardias include AF, atrial flutter, multifocal atrial tachycardia, and sinus node reentrant tachycardia.

Atrioventricular Nodal-Dependent Tachycardias

AV nodal-dependent tachycardias are most effectively treated with therapies targeted at the AV node.

Acute Therapy

Vagal maneuvers   The AV node has vagal innervation; maneuvers that increase vagal tone are useful in terminating these arrhythmias.

Carotid sinus massage or the Valsalva maneuver should be tried in hemodynamically stable patients, as these may successfully terminate the tachycardia.

Drug therapy
- IV adenosine (first-line drug therapy after vagal maneuvers):
  6–12 mg by rapid IV push
- IV verapamil:
  2.5–5.0 mg IV over 2 to 3 minutes, may repeat for total of 20 mg.

Chronic Therapy
Beta-blockers
Digoxin
Flecainide and propafenone have also shown efficacy
Radiofrequency catheter ablation (see Chapter 18)

Atrioventricular Nodal-Independent Tachycardias

Atrial Fibrillation   AF is an extremely common cardiac arrhythmia whose prevalence increases dramatically with age. The morbidity due to AF may be substantial. The major problem is that of a reduced functional capacity due to symptoms, including palpitations, fatigue, and dyspnea, or worsening of symptoms of preexisting cardiac conditions, such as angina pectoris and CHF. In addition, among patients older than 49 years with CHF, HTN, cardiac enlargement, or LVH by echocardiograpy, an increased risk of embolic stroke is found.

Acute management
1. **Hemodynamically stable patients.**

- *AV nodal blocking agents.* Drugs that limit the ventricular response by blocking AV nodal conduction are the initial treatment of choice in hemodynamically stable patients. AV nodal blockers should not be given to patients with AF and ECG evidence of preexcitation (WPW syndrome).

Digoxin

Digoxin: 0.5 mg IV, followed by 0.25 mg every 4 to 6 hours. Note that several hours may lapse before significant control of ventricular response occurs.

Beta-blockers. Available IV agents are effective for the acute control of the ventricular rate during AF.

Propranolol: 0.5–1.0 mg IV every 5 minutes up to a total of 0.15 mg/kg.

Metoprolol: 5 mg IV every 5 minutes for a total of 15 mg.

Esmolol: 0.5 mg/kg per minute load over 1 minute, followed by a constant IV infusion of 0.05–0.3 mg/kg per minute.

Calcium channel blockers

Diltiazem: Diltiazem is effective and its short term administration is well tolerated by patients with ventricular dysfunction.

- The initial dose for most patients is 20 mg (0.25 mg/kg) IV over 2 minutes.
- A second bolus of 25 mg (0.35 mg/kg) should be given if an inadequate response to the first bolus occurred.
- A maintenance infusion of 10–15 mg/hr is then started until an adequate oral regimen is achieved.

Verapamil. Verapamil is effective but its use may be associated with hypotension.

- 2.5–20 mg IV in 5 mg increments.

- *Oral maintenance therapy after initial rate control.* As 44% to 78% of patients with new onset AF may spontaneously revert to sinus rhythm, oral maintenance therapy may not be required in a significant number of patients. Patients with structural heart disease, advanced age, and AF of long duration (>1 month) are unlikely to spontaneously revert to sinus rhythm.

Digoxin. 0.125–0.5 mg per day.

Beta-blockers

Propranolol: 40–320 mg per day.

Metoprolol: 50–200 mg per day.

Calcium channel blockers
  Diltiazem: 120–480 mg per day.
  Verapamil: 120–480 mg per day.

2. Hemodynamically unstable patients.

- ***DC Cardioversion.*** If the patient is clinically unstable (hypotension, unstable angina, severe dyspnea, or pulmonary edema), urgent DC cardioversion is the treatment of choice.

Once the HR is controlled, investigation should begin to determine the underlying cause of the arrhythmia (see Chapter 3).

3. Subsequent management: restoration and maintenance of sinus rhythm with attendant heart rate control.

Several small randomized clinical trials have demonstrated the ability of individual AADs to increase the proportion of AF patients who remain in sinus rhythm at the expense of varying degrees of constitutional side effects.

Small studies in highly selected groups of patients have also demonstrated hemodynamic benefit from restoration and maintenance of sinus rhythm.

No trial has demonstrated other tangible benefits, such as reduction in stroke or embolic risk, but current trials such as AFFIRM (Atrial Fibrillation Follow-up Investigation of Rhythm Management) will address these issues.

- **Class IA agents.** The IA drugs have similar efficacy to the other anti-arrhythmics studied for AF. However, several recent studies such as the Stroke Prevention in Atrial Fibrillation trial (SPAF-I) identified an increased mortality in patients with a history of CHF treated with the class IA drugs in a nonrandomized fashion.
  Procainamide
    10–20 mg/kg IV over 45 to 60 minutes, followed by 2–4 mg/min.
  Only IV procainamide is available for the acute management of AF. IV procainamide is the treatment of choice for patients with AF and ECG evidence of preexcitation (WPW syndrome).
- **Class IC agents.** Investigations of propafenone or flecainide in patients with AF have shown these

agents to be quite effective. Flecainide was evaluated in a study of over 900 patients with paroxysmal AF and found to be well tolerated and effective at maintaining sinus rhythm in 63% of cases at 9-month follow-up.

Flecainide

300 mg orally as a single dose in a monitored setting has been shown to convert AF acutely.

50–150 mg orally twice a day as chronic therapy.

Propafenone

600 mg orally as a single dose.

150–300 mg orally three times a day as chronic therapy.

- **Class III agents**

Sotalol

80–160 mg orally two times a day as chronic therapy was found to be as effective as quinidine.

Not useful for the acute management of AF.

Amiodarone

600 mg/day for 14 days, followed by 200 mg/day.

Not useful for the acute management of AF.

Ibutilide

1 mg IV over 10 minutes, repeat once if no effect.

Effective for termination of AF acutely.

4. Anticoagulation treatment.

- **Heparin:** Because of the increased risk of LA appendage thrombus formation and peripheral embolization, IV heparin should be initiated to achieve full anticoagulation when AF persists ≤48 hours' duration.

  Therapeutic heparinization is recommended even when DC cardioversion with TEE guidance is planned because LA stunning following cardioversion may lead to thrombus formation and embolization.

- **Warfarin:** It is currently recommended that warfarin (INR 2.0 to 3.0) be given for 3 weeks prior to elective cardioversion (if TEE is not done at time of cardioversion) with patients who have been in AF for ≤48 hours. Warfarin should be continued until normal sinus rhythm has been maintained for at least 4 weeks.

Atrial Flutter   Atrial flutter usually occurs in the presence of structural heart disease.

Management   Management is similar to that for AF.

- Overdrive pacing with a temporary transvenous pacing wire may be feasible ("flutter-version").
- DC cardioversion may be accomplished with lower synchronized energies (25 to 100 joules).
- Previously, anticoagulation was not felt to be as important as with AF, but recent evidence strongly supports full anticoagulation if the duration of the arrhythmia exceeds 24 to 48 hours.

Multifocal Atrial Tachycardia (MAT)   MAT frequently occurs in patients with chronic pulmonary disease and metabolic abnormalities.

Management   Treatment of the underlying problem is the most effective therapy.

- DC cardioversion is often ineffective, as the arrhythmia tends to recur without effective treatment of the underlying disorder.
- Small studies have shown verapamil or beta-blockers are most effective. However, many patients with this arrhythmia have significant lung disease which may prohibit the use of a beta-blocker.
- Digitalis has little role in the treatment of MAT.

Ventricular Arrhythmias

Several recent clinical trials have helped to clarify the indications for drug therapy in various subgroups of patients with ventricular arrhythmias.

Ventricular Ectopic Activity

After Myocardial Infarction   Following MI there is no current indication to treat isolated VPCs.

- **CAST** (Cardiac Arrhythmia Suppression Trial). The suppression of ventricular ectopic beats with flecainide, encainide, and moricizine was associated with an increased risk of mortality.
- **BASIS** (Basel Anti-arrhythmic Study of Infarct Survival). This is the only study supporting the suppression of ventricular ectopy with AADs after MI. Amiodarone

therapy was associated with an improved survival even after the drug was discontinued. Most experts, however, do not recommend amiodarone for the treatment of isolated ventricular ectopy.

• **IMPACT** (International Mexiletine and Placebo Antiarrhythmic Coronary Trial). Mexiletene, given prophylactically after MI, decreased the frequency of ventricular ectopy but increased mortality.

• **CAMIAT** (Canadian Amiodarone Myocardial Infarction Arrhythmia Trial). The use of amiodarone after MI in patients with ventricular ectopic activity was associated with a decrease in sudden death. However, this study was not powered to show an improvement in survival.

Congestive Heart Failure   At present, there is no conclusive evidence that treatment of isolated ventricular ectopy in the presence of CHF is beneficial.

• **CHF-STAT** (Survival Trial of Antiarrhythmic Therapy in Congestive Heart Failure). Treatment with amiodarone was effective in suppressing ventricular ectopy but did not result in a substantial reduction in the combined endpoint of cardiac death or hospitalizations for CHF.

• **GESICA** (Grupo de Estudio de la Sobrevida en la Insuficiecia Cardiaca en Argentina). Treatment with amiodarone resulted in a 28% risk reduction for mortality, attributable to both arrhythmic death and progressive heart failure. These results are divergent from those of CHF-STAT, however, and at present no consensus exists to treat isolated ventricular ectopy in CHF patients.

Nonsustained Ventricular Tachycardia
Nonsustained VT is considered an independent predictor of mortality after an MI. Treatment in certain groups may improve survival.

• **MADIT** (Multicenter Automatic Defibrillator Implantation Trial). Among post-MI patients with LVEF <35%, nonsustained VT, and inducible but not suppressible sustained VT at EP study, a 50% reduction in mortality was observed with ICD therapy as compared to therapy with AADs.

• **MUSTT** (Multicenter Unsustained Tachycardia Trial). Nonsustained VT and inducible sustained VT at EP study in patients with CAD and LVEF <35% will be treated with EP-guided anti-arrhythmic therapy (including the ICD) versus standard care. Enrollment is complete but results are not available at the time of this writing.

Sustained Ventricular Arrhythmia

- **AVID** (Antiarrhythmics Versus Implantable Defibrillators). Survivors of cardiac arrest or symptomatic VT were randomized to ICD therapy or anti-arrhythmic therapy (amiodarone or sotalol). A statistically significant 28% reduction in death was associated with ICD therapy.
- **ESVEM** (Electrophysiologic Study versus Electrocardiographic Monitoring). Survivors of cardiac arrest, symptomatic VT, or syncope with inducible arrhythmia at EP study and ventricular ectopic activity (>10 VPCs/hr on 24-hour ECG monitoring) were randomized to VPC suppression (24-hour ECG and ETT) or noninducibility at EP study with seven anti-arrhythmic drugs. Neither strategy was superior for predicting arrhythmia recurrence or death, but sotalol appeared to be a superior AAD.

Less Common Forms of Ventricular Tachycardia

Long QT syndrome (LQTS) LQTS is a heterogeneous syndrome characterized on the molecular level by genetic alterations of cardiac ion channels. It often manifests clinically as syncope due to a malignant ventricular arrhythmia, which may result in cardiac arrest and sudden death. The onset of arrhythmias is often related to physical or emotional stress.

Therapy. Therapy is often aimed at modulation of the autonomic nervous system.
- Beta-blockers are the mainstay of therapy.
- Specialized centers may perform left-sided cardiac sympathetic denervation.
- Pacing therapy may be useful for pause mediated arrhythmias.
- ICD therapy may be considered in high risk patients or patients refractory to other therapies.

Arrhythmogenic Right Ventricular Dysplasia/Cardiomyopathy (ARVD) ARVD is primarily a disorder of the RV myocardium ranging from isolated focal thinning to profound RV dilatation and loss of myocardium (see Chapter 12). The LV may also be involved.

Therapy. ICD therapy is the treatment of choice.

Bundle branch reentry Bundle branch reentry is a form of monomorphic VT that often occurs in the setting of a DCM.

Therapy. The bundle branch reentry form of VT may be cured with radiofrequency catheter ablation.

Repetitive monomorphic ventricular tachycardia (RMVT) RMVT is a monomorphic VT that occurs in the absence of structural heart disease. RMVT usually arises from the RV outflow tract. The VT is characteristically associated with an ECG pattern of LBBB with an inferior axis.

Therapy. The tachycardia mechanism is not felt to be due to reentry; thus, standard antiarrhythmic therapy is not usually employed. In symptomatic patients, the following treatments have been employed:
- Beta-blockers are effective since this arrhythmia is catecholamine-sensitive.
- CCBs have been used successfully.
- Adenosine may be useful for acute therapy.
- Radiofrequency ablation has been used for cure (see Chapter 18).

SUGGESTED READINGS

The AVID Investigators. A comparison of antiarrhythmic-drug therapy with implantable defibrillators in patients resuscitated from near-fatal ventricular arrhythmias. N Engl J Med 1997;337:1576–1583.

Berns E, Rinkenberger RL, Jeang MK, et al. Efficacy and safety of flecainide acetate for atrial tachycardia or fibrillation. Am J Cardiol 1987;59:1337–1341.

Burkart F, Pfister M, Kiowski W, et al. Effect of antiarrhythmic therapy in survivors of myocardial infarction with asymptomatic complex ventricular arrhythmias: Basel Antiarrhythmic Study of Infarct Survival (BASIS). J Am Coll Cardiol 1992;16:1711–1718.

Cairns JA, Connolly SJ, Roberts R, Gent M. Randomized trial

of outcome after myocardial infarction in patients with frequent or repetitive ventricular premature depolarisations: CAMIAT. Lancet 1997;349:675–682.

The Cardiac Arrhythmia Suppression Trial (CAST) Investigators. Preliminary report: effect of encainide and flecainide on mortality in a randomized trial of arrhythmia suppression after myocardial infarction. N Engl J Med 1989;321:406–412.

The Cardiac Arrhythmia Suppression Trial II Investigators. Effect of the anti-arrhythmic agent moricizine on survival after myocardial infarction. N Engl J Med 1992;327:227–233.

Coplen SE, Antman EA, Berlin JA, et al. Efficacy and safety of quinidine therapy for maintenance of sinus rhythm after cardioversion. A meta-analysis of randomized controlled trials. Circulation 1990;82:1106–1116.

Echt DS, Liebson PR, Mitchell LB, et al. and the CAST investigators. Mortality and morbidity in patients receiving encainide, flecainide or placebo. The Cardiac Arrhythmia Suppression Trial. N Engl J Med 1991;324:781–788.

Flaker GC, Blackshear JL, McBride R, et al. Stroke Prevention in Atrial Fibrillation Investigators. Anti-arrhythmic drug therapy and cardiac mortality in atrial fibrillation. J Am Coll Cardiol 1992;20:527–532.

Gosselink ATM, Crijns HJGM, Van Gelder IC, et al. Low-dose amiodarone for maintenance of sinus rhythm after cardioversion of atrial fibrillation or flutter. JAMA 1992;267: 3289–3293.

IMPACT Research Group. International mexiletine and placebo antiarrhythmic coronary trial I. Report on arrhythmia and other findings. J Am Coll Cardiol 1984;4: 1148–1163.

Juul-Moller S, Edvardsson N, Rehnquist-Ahlberg N. Sotalol versus quinidine for the maintenance of sinus rhythm after direct current conversion of atrial fibrillation. Circulation 1990;82:1932–1939.

Laupacis A, Albers G, Dalen J, et al. Antithrombotic therapy in atrial fibrillation. Chest 1995;108:352S–359S.

Mason JW, for the Electrophysiologic Study versus Electrocardiographic Monitoring Investigators. A comparison of electrophysiologic testing with Holter monitoring to predict antiarrhythmic-drug efficacy for ventricular tachyarrhythmias. N Engl J Med 1993;329:445–451.

Mason JW, for the Electrophysiologic Study versus Electrocardiographic Monitoring Investigators. A comparison of seven antiarrhythmic drugs in patients with ventricular tachyarrhythmias. N Engl J Med 1993;329: 452–458.

Moss AJ, Hall WJ, Cannom DS, et al for the Multicenter Automatic Defibrillator Implantation Trial Investigators. Improved survival with an implanted defibrillator in patients with coronary disease at high risk for ventricular arrhythmia. N Engl J Med 1996;335:1933–1940.

Pritchett ELC. Management of atrial fibrillation. N Engl J Med 1992;326:1264–1271.

Task Force of the Working Group on Arrhythmias of the European Society of Cardiology. The Sicilian gambit. A new approach to the classification of anti-arrhythmic drugs based on their actions on arrhythmogenic mechanisms. Circulation 1991;84:1831–1851.

CHAPTER 18

Electrical Therapy of Cardiac Arrhythmias

James B. Kirchhoffer
Dennis A. Tighe

Electrical therapy encompasses pacemakers, cardioversion/defibrillation (both external and internal using implanted devices), radiofrequency (RF) catheter ablation/modification, and arrhythmia surgery. This chapter reviews aspects of the care of patients with permanent pacemakers and implanted cardioverter-defibrillators (ICDs), and discusses catheter-based procedures for arrhythmia control, arrhythmia surgery, and cardioversion.

PERMANENT PACEMAKERS

Indications for Implantation

Acquired AV Block

AV block may be symptomatic, observed on some form of monitor or persist after acute MI (see Chapter 1). Indications for permanent pacing include symptomatic bradycardia, documented asystole (≤3.0 sec) or any escape rate <40 beats per minute regardless of symptoms, requirement for medications that result in symptomatic bradycardia, postoperative AV block not expected to resolve, and following catheter ablation of the AV junction. A prolonged HV interval (>100msec) in the presence of symptoms (syncope or lightheadedness) would also be considered an indication for a pacemaker.

Symptomatic Sick Sinus Syndrome (SSS)

SSS is diagnosed using clinical criteria such as symptomatic pauses or inability to maintain appropriate HR response because of required medical therapy. Diagnosis may also be made by finding abnormalities at EP study (prolonged sinus node recovery times, etc.) in patients with syncope or lightheadedness.

Pacemaker Implantation Techniques

Transvenous versus Epicardial

- Almost all primary implants are transvenous.
- Epicardial implants may be considered in still-growing pediatric patients or in patients with prosthetic TV replacements because leads cannot be passed through a mechanical valve.

Vascular Access

The preferred vascular access route is a cutdown to the cephalic vein in the deltopectoral groove. This approach is associated with lower risks of hemothorax, pneumothorax, and lead crush.

Pacing Lead Technology

The pacing lead(s) carries electric current from the pulse generator to the heart. The lead consists of the tip, the insulation, and the conducting wire.

Tip The lead tip is kept in place at the endocardium by either passive or active fixation.

- **Passive leads.** Passive leads have small tines, which nestle in the trabeculations and become fibrosed to the endocardium.
- **Active leads.** Active leads have a screw tip that extends into the endocardium. Active fixation is useful in patients with extensive endocardial scarring and those who have had previous cardiac surgery because these leads do not depend on trabeculations to stay in place. Fibrosis is more extensive, so thresholds tend to be higher.

The tip may be impregnated with a long-acting steroid to prevent excessive scar formation at the tip/endocardium interface. This keeps the pacing threshold (and consequently, battery drain) as low as possible.

Leads and Conducting Wires

Pacing Lead The pacing lead may be unipolar or bipolar.

Unipolar devices The unipolar configuration has one conducting wire surrounded by its insulator.

Path. The path of the electric current in a unipolar device:
1. Starts at the pulse generator.
2. Stimulates the heart muscle at the tip of the lead.
3. Returns to the battery by passing current through body tissues.

The long path through the body can cause diaphragmatic or pectoral muscle twitching as well as cardiac contraction.

Bipolar devices The path of the electric current in the bipolar configuration traverses much less of the body, thus there is no chance of pectoral stimulation and less chance of diaphragmatic stimulation.

Path. The path of electric current in a bipolar device:
1. Starts at the pulse generator.
2. Exits at the tip of the lead.
3. Stimulates the myocardium.
4. Returns to the pulse generator using a second conducting wire which has a ring electrode on the lead separated from the tip by a small distance.

Bipolar leads are less susceptible to electromagnetic interference, but more susceptible to insulation and conducting wire problems.

Device identification
- **X-Ray.** Unipolar leads can be distinguished from bipolar leads on CXR.

Electrode:
- Unipolar leads have a single tip electrode.
- Bipolar leads have a tip electrode and a ring electrode.

Connector:
- Unipolar leads have a single connector to the pulse generator.
- Bipolar leads have two connectors to the pulse generator.

• **ECG.** On the ECG, the device currents create distinctive spikes.

Unipolar. The long current path causes a large spike.

Bipolar. Spikes from a bipolar device may be either very small or not visible on the surface ECG.

Pacing Lead Positioning

Ventricular Lead

The ventricular lead is most commonly positioned in the RV apex.

- A QRS complex stimulated by the pacemaker from this location will have LBBB morphology. If the ventricular lead is actively fixed in the RV outflow tract, the LBBB morphology will have a different axis.
- If a paced beat has RBBB morphology, then the lead may have perforated the interventricular septum and be pacing the LV, or have perforated the RV apex, entered the pericardium, and be stimulating the LV epicardium.
- Left-sided diaphragmatic pacing may occur if the output on the ventricular lead stimulates muscular contraction of the diaphragm as well as the heart. This does not necessarily imply perforation, and can happen merely because of the proximity of the infero-apical portion of the RV and the dome of the diaphragm.

Atrial Lead

The atrial lead is most commonly positioned in the RA appendage. If the RA appendage has been amputated during previous cardiac surgery, other areas of the RA can be used.

- Lateral placement of the lead tip may stimulate the phrenic nerve and cause right-sided diaphragmatic contraction.

Complications of Pacemaker Implantation

Early Complications

Early complications are most often due to vascular problems or lead migration.

Vascular Access Problems Difficulty with vascular access may lead to pneumothorax, hemothorax, and backbleeding into the pocket. Standard practice is to obtain a CXR, either immediately after implantation or the following morning, to document lead position and absence of a pneumothorax.

• **Pneumothorax.** Small leaks can be observed, but a larger one or a pneumothorax in a patient with limited pulmonary reserve will require closed tube thoracostomy until the leak resolves. Tension pneumothorax is unusual, but should be considered if a postoperative patient becomes acutely dyspneic.

• **Bleeding.** Bleeding complications are much more likely to occur in patients who require early postoperative anticoagulation.

• Minor pocket hematomas will resorb over several weeks and should be managed conservatively. A needle should not be blindly introduced into the pocket in this situation.

• Tense, large, painful pocket hematomas may require opening of the pocket, evacuation, and identification and control of the bleeding site.

Dislodgment Lead migration occurs most frequently in the first 24 to 48 hours after surgery. Active fixation leads are less likely to move. Atrial leads dislodge more frequently than ventricular leads.

• Dislodgment may be obvious, with failure of capture or sensing and abnormal appearance on chest film.

• "Microdislodgment" is said to occur when the lead position on CXR is appropriate, but thresholds or sensing are unacceptable.

Either type of dislodgment requires opening the pocket and repositioning the lead.

Symptoms Migration can cause a variety of symptoms, including:

Diaphragmatic pacing
Alteration of the QRS morphology
Chest pain (usually pleuritic)
Embolic stroke, if the ventricular lead perforates the
    septum, lodges in the LV, and stimulates clot
    formation

Late Complications

Late complications include lead migration, lead fracture, insulation breakdown, subclavian vein thrombosis, alteration of the lead/endocardium interface, and infection of the pacing system.

Lead Migration Late lead migration may be due to "twiddler's syndrome," which occurs when a patient flips the pacemaker over and over in the pocket—the patient's "twiddling" causes the leads to wrap around the pacemaker and retract from the endocardium.

Lead Fracture Lead fracture is most common where the lead enters the subclavian vein and is crushed by muscular contractions. Lead fracture can occasionally be detected by careful inspection of the CXR.

Insulation Breakdown Insulation breakdown occurs in the same area as lead fracture. It is manifested by a decrease in lead resistance. Insulation breakdown is difficult to detect because the findings of decreased impedance may be intermittent.

Subclavian Vein Thrombosis Subclavian vein thrombosis is frequently subclinical and requires no treatment. If it is symptomatic, the usual treatment is elevation of the arm, anticoagulation, and pain control until collaterals form and swelling resolves.

Alteration of the Lead/Endocardium Interface Alteration of the lead/myocardium interface may be due to microdislodgment or exuberant scar formation. Both events lead to increased pacing threshold.

Infection of the Pacing System Infection of the pacing system can occur due to failure of sterile technique or when the pacing system is seeded during a systemic infection.

- **Primary infections.** Staphylococcal infections (accounting for 80% of pacing system infections) may start from leakage from the skin into the pocket and spread through the entire pacing system. Documented infection requires removal of the entire pacing system.
- **Secondary infections.** Secondary infection can occur during bacteremia, which can seed the pocket or settle in fibrotic tissue which grows around the lead. TEE may be required to document pacing lead vegetations.

Metabolic alterations Drug treatment and metabolic or structural abnormalities can alter the pacing threshold.

- The threshold can be increased by most AADs, hyperkalemia, acidosis, and MI.
- The threshold can be decreased by steroids and isoproterenol.

Pacemaker Code and Pulse Generator Selection

Pacemaker Code (NASPE/BHEG)

The pacemaker code is designed to identify the type of device and its function.

1. The first letter of the code refers to the chamber paced.
2. The second letter refers to the chamber sensed.
3. The third letter refers to the manner of response to native electrical activity.
4. A fourth letter, "R," is added when the device is rate adaptive.

- **Single-Chamber Pacemakers.** Single-chamber pacemakers are labeled in the box as SSI, indicating that only one chamber can be paced:
  AAI—the device lead is placed in the atrium.
  VVI—the device lead is placed in the ventricle.
- **Dual-Chamber Pacemakers.** Dual-chamber pacemakers are DDD because they pace both chambers,

sense both chambers, and have physiologic response to native electrical occurrences.

• **Rate Adaptive Pacemakers.** A rate adaptive pacemaker has a sensor (most often motion through a piezoelectric crystal, sometimes transthoracic impedance or blood temperature) that senses changes in body functions induced by physical activity. The pacing rate will increase when the sensor detects increased body activity, giving a more physiologic HR.

VVI versus DDD

The choice between a dual-chamber or a single-chamber device is influenced by price, complexity, patient characteristics, and the patient's native rhythm.

• Single-chamber devices (VVI or VVIR) are appropriate for patients with chronic AF.
• Dual-chamber devices (DDD or DDDR) are appropriate for patients with AV block or only paroxysmal AF.

The addition of automatic mode switching to DDD pacemakers has made them more frequently used, as reprogramming is not necessary when AF occurs.

Pacemaker Electrocardiography

Response to Magnet Application

Placing a doughnut magnet over the pacemaker disables sensing functions.

• A VVI pacemaker becomes VOO, and paces regardless of the native rhythm.
• A DDD pacemaker becomes DOO, pacing both chambers without sensing either.

Each manufacturer has a different policy for the rate the pacemaker assumes during magnet application (the "magnet rate").

Battery Life

The rate at which the pacemaker discharges during magnet application is an indication of how much battery life remains.

Single-Chamber Devices

A VVI pacemaker has limited functions: it can sense a native QRS or fail to sense one; it can pace appropriately or fail to pace. Magnet application will make the pacemaker send out electrical stimuli at a constant rate.

- If there are pacing spikes outside of the ventricular refractory period with a QRS complex following the spike, then the pacing system is capable of stimulating the myocardium.
- If there are pacing spikes without a subsequent QRS, then failure to capture is the diagnosis. This can be caused by insulation breakdown, lead fracture, high thresholds, or lead migration.

Since failure to sense and failure to capture are the most common pacemaker malfunctions, elimination of one of these possibilities by magnet application rapidly leads to narrowing down the possible differential diagnosis.

Dual-Chamber Devices

The same techniques for single-chamber devices apply to the evaluation of a dual-chamber pacemaker. The physician must take into account both atrial and ventricular activity when evaluating a dual-chamber device.

Upper Rate Limit Behavior

The most confusing situation in pacemaker electrocardiography is "upper rate limit behavior." In this situation, a dual-chamber pacemaker will pace the ventricle at a rapid rate, and atrial activity will not be visible because of the wide paced QRS complexes.

- Upper rate limit behavior can occur when the pacemaker is tracking an atrial arrhythmia.
- An unusual cause of upper rate limit behavior is "pacemaker-mediated tachycardia." This frequently starts with a VPC, a retrograde P wave, antegrade conduction through the pacemaker, and then another retrograde P wave generated by the paced beat.

Differentiation of these causes is easily accomplished with magnet application. With the dual-chamber pacemaker functioning in the DOO mode, an underlying atrial arrhythmia can be identified or the pacemaker-mediated tachycardia terminated (magnet application stops the sensing and interrupts the endless loop).

Routine Pacemaker Follow-Up

Medicare guidelines suggest transtelephonic monitoring every 1 to 3 months and office visits every 6 months.

Transtelephonic Monitoring

Transtelephonic monitoring is usually performed by a commercial service.

1. The service calls the patient on a predetermined schedule.
2. Pacemaker strips are recorded with and without magnet application. This allows for determination of battery life indicators, and gives early detection of atrial arrhythmias or failure of sensing or pacing.
3. The tracings are interpreted by the service and reviewed by either the implanting physician or the follow-up physician of record.

Pacemaker Clinic Functions

Office visits are generally performed every 6 months.

- The patient is connected to an ECG monitor, and the device is interrogated using the appropriate programmer.
- Interrogation and testing allow for determination of pacing thresholds, lead impedances, and battery data. The output can be adjusted to maximize battery longevity, and the recorded data from the pulse generator can be retrieved.

Troubleshooting Suspected Pacemaker Malfunction

History

1. Obtain the pacemaker identification card.
2. Determine if the patient has attended a follow-up visit recently, as this may have resulted in inadvertent reprogramming.
3. Question the patient regarding sources of electromagnetic interference with the device. Sources of interference may include:

- Electrocautery from an operating room procedure or a visit to a dermatologist's office.
- Intense magnetic fields generated in certain manufacturing environments.
- Interference from cellular phones (very unusual unless the body of the phone is placed directly over the pacemaker). Interaction with microwave ovens is no longer a serious consideration due to improvements in shielding in both devices.
- On rare occasions, trauma to the device or the patient's chest may cause lead fracture or dislodgment.

4. Determine if the patient has a lead or pulse generator that has had a history of malfunction, information that is readily available through the manufacturer. Some leads are known to have an increased failure rate, and a very small number of pulse generators have shown consistent problems.

Physical Examination

The physical examination is often not helpful in evaluating suspected pacemaker malfunction. Exceptions include:

- If the pacing system is grossly infected, then the pocket may be fluctuant, erythematous, or draining fluid.
- If lead migration has occurred, there may be diaphragmatic pacing.
- If perforation with pericardial bleeding has occurred, the patient will be in extremis, with classic signs of cardiac tamponade.

Pacemaker ECG

The ECG with and without magnet application should be inspected in a systematic fashion. Each chamber should be assessed for appropriate sensing and pacing. Examining each beat, determine if the P wave is sensed or paced and if the QRS complex is sensed or paced.

- Failure to sense a P wave will lead to atrial spikes closely following a surface P wave.
- Capture of the atrium by a pacing spike depends on the atrial refractory period and the pacing threshold.

- Failure to sense combined with failure to capture is most frequently due to lead migration.
- Failure to sense with appropriate capture may imply that the P wave amplitude has become too small to be detected or that there is an intermittent lead fracture or insulation breakdown.

Magnet application will help differentiate the questions about capture, since it guarantees there will be pacing stimuli leaving the pulse generator. Failure to capture once a stimulus has left the pulse generator may be due to lead fracture, insulation breakdown with a shortened circuit, or an intervening increase in the pacing threshold due to metabolic or anatomic changes.

Chest X-Ray
The chest film will be revealing in a small number of cases.

Lead Migration　　Lead migration should be obvious on CXR.

- **Passive atrial lead tip.** The tip of a passive atrial lead generally slips out of the appendage, allowing the lead to retract into the atrium, float freely, and occasionally migrate up into the SVC.
- **Active atrial lead tip.** The tip of an active atrial lead generally pulls free of the endocardium and moves into the middle of the atrium if it has a performed J configuration, or it points straight down into the IVC (occasionally RV) if it does not have a performed J.
- **Ventricular leads.** Ventricular leads can retract into the atrium or advance through the septum or myocardium. These changes should be obvious if the lead was initially positioned in the RV apex. If the lead was placed in the outflow tract and slips into the apex, the change may be less obvious unless the original position was documented.

Insulation Breakdown　　Insulation breakdown will not be obvious on an x-ray because the materials used are relatively radiolucent. Fracture of the conducting coil will only be apparent if there is separation of the two segments. Carefully examine the area where the lead enters the subclavian vein, the most common site for lead fracture to occur. The lead may be fractured without the flaw being visible, as this is frequently an intermittent or nearly microscopic phenomenon.

Interrogation with the Programmer

Interrogation of the device using the appropriate programmer documents if the pacemaker is functioning appropriately in nearly all cases. The initial interrogation displays the currently programmed pacing parameters and measured values. The measured numbers include pacing lead impedances, which may be diagnostic.

- If the pacing lead impedance is low, it implies that the current path is short, so there is an insulation breakdown.
- If the pacing lead impedance is high, it implies that the circuit is not complete, so there is conducting coil fracture.

These changes are diagnostic when present, but the abnormalities are not excluded if they are absent. Both lead fracture and insulation breakdown can be intermittent, so repeated measurements may be necessary.

If the situation is not clear, then clinical judgment would dictate changing the lead. It is very unusual to have to open the pocket and interrogate the leads manually to diagnose lead malfunction.

Most programmers can display intracardiac electrograms in both chambers. This will be very helpful if interference or other abnormalities are visualized on the intracardiac tracings. Displaying the atrial electrogram may be the final word on whether an atrial arrhythmia is causing the problem.

Pacemaker Patients Undergoing Operative Procedures

The pacing system can be affected during operative procedures.

Noncardiac Procedures

Leads. It is unusual for the leads to be affected during noncardiac procedures.

Pacemaker. During noncardiac procedures, the pacemaker can be affected by electrocautery. When extensive electrocautery is planned:

1. The pacemaker should be programmed to an asynchronous mode and the cautery return pad placed as far from the chest as possible, usually on the thigh or calf.
2. The pacemaker should be interrogated after the operation. If the pacemaker has gone into the reset mode, the programmer will identify the problem and reprogramming will restore the device to normal function, provided the device has not been permanently damaged.

Cardiac Procedures

Leads. The atrial lead can be dislodged during cardiac procedures when the apparatus for the bypass machine is introduced into the RA.

Pacemaker. If a pacemaker patient is scheduled for a cardiac procedure, the pacemaker should be removed from the pocket at the start of the procedure and replaced when the use of electrocautery has been completed.

IMPLANTABLE CARDIOVERTER DEFIBRILLATORS (ICD)

Indications for ICD Therapy

The standard treatment of patients with malignant ventricular arrhythmias has evolved rapidly as ICD technology has changed. Drug therapy guided by EP testing is now appropriate in only a small subset of VT/VF patients. The results of multicenter trials suggest that treatment with amiodarone or an ICD is appropriate and safe. In some cases, both drug and ICD therapy are necessary.

The standard indications for ICD therapy are:

- Out-of-hospital cardiac arrest without precipitating cause
- Drug resistant VT or inability to use or tolerate clinically appropriate medications
- Patients with prior MI, ejection fraction ≤35%, and nonsustained asymptomatic VT (high risk for sudden cardiac death); the presence of inducible VT at EP study not suppressed by IV procainamide (findings of the MADIT trial)

ICD Implantation Techniques

The introduction of transvenous technology has radically changed ICD implantation techniques.

Formerly, defibrillator implants required sewing defibrillating patches directly onto the heart or pericardium. This was accomplished using sternotomy, subxiphoid, subcostal, or thoracotomy approaches. The leads were then tunneled to an abdominal pocket and attached to the pulse generator.

The development of transvenous leads and significant reduction of the pulse generator size now make ICD implants technically similar to pacemaker implants. The lead is positioned in the RV apex, and the size of the intrinsic QRS complex measured. The lead is anchored to the fascia of the pectoral muscle. The lead may have one defibrillating coil in the RV, or two, with one in the RV and one situated more proximally so that the coil lies in the SVC.

The pocket is usually formed in the pectoral region. However, if there is insufficient tissue in the pectoral region, the lead may be tunneled to an abdominal pocket for the pulse generator.

ICD Functions

Early generation ICDs sensed rate alone. When the patient's rate exceeded the programmed limit, the device detected the tachycardia (whether it was AF with rapid ventricular response, sinus tachycardia, or a ventricular arrhythmia), charged, and shocked. Refinements have been made to this simple algorithm, but the overall function is similar. ICDs now have multiprogrammable settings for detection and treatment parameters, extensive memory, and many diagnostic tools.

Zones

Present generation devices can be programmed to diagnose different arrhythmias at different rates, usually referred to as *zones*. For example, a two-zone device would be programmed to detect VT if the HR exceeded 165 bpm, and VF if it exceeded 220 bpm. This is clinically useful since therapy can be different for slower VT rates.

Algorithms   Modern ICDs can be programmed to treat different arrhythmias with distinct algorithms. Anti-tachycardia pacing is often effective in terminating episodes of monomorphic VT. The device detects the rate of VT, and then introduces pacing stimuli at a rate faster than the VT. When programmed correctly, the pacing stimuli will capture the ventricle at the rate faster than the VT (entrainment).

1. When the technique is successful, the reentrant loop is disrupted, and termination of the pacing results in return to sinus rhythm.
2. If the technique was unsuccessful, the device recognizes continued VT and steps up to the next therapy, typically low energy cardioversion (1 to 5 joules).
3. If VT continues, cardioversion with the full energy of the device (27 to 42 joules) is the next treatment.
4. As antitachycardia pacing can cause acceleration of VT to a faster rate instead of termination, treatment algorithms will continue unless the rate exceeds the upper end of the zone, when the therapy for the next zone will kick in.

Complications of ICD Implantation

Early Complications

Early complications are similar to those of pacemaker implantation. Problems with vascular access, cardiac per-foration, and subclavian vein thrombosis are possible.

Late Complications

The late complications are also similar to pacemaker complications.

• The infection rate is probably higher because of the increased mass of hardware installed.
• Lead fracture or insulation breakdown have different sequelae than with pacemaker leads. Failure to sense and failure to capture during paced beats can occur, but they are not symptomatic.

Lead Migration   Patients who have ICD leads migrate may suffer inappropriate shocks if the lead lodges across the TV and counts both P waves and QRS complexes.

If the lead migrates to the IVC, the device may not detect ventricular arrhythmias, leading to complications of VT/VF events.

Lead Fracture

• **Shocking coil.** Lead fracture of the shocking coil may be difficult to detect, as the lead resistance is measured only during a shock. A fractured shocking coil will not deliver energy to the heart, leading to failure to defibrillate.

• **Rate-sensing lead.** Lead fracture of the rate-sensing lead can cause underdetection if the separation of the two pieces of conductor is complete; overdetection may occur if the two pieces of conductor rub together, creating tiny amounts of electricity that the device interprets to be VT. Patients may receive numerous asymptomatic shocks when rate-sensing lead fracture occurs.

Routine ICD Follow-Up

Patients with ICDs are usually seen in the office every 3 or 6 months to check device function. At these visits, the device is interrogated with the appropriate programmer. Rate-sensing lead resistance and threshold, electrograms from the leads, and battery status are all recorded.

• The device records the episodes of ventricular arrhythmias, saving the time, date, and recorded electrogram for review. This allows the physician to detect asymptomatic shocks and early changes in lead resistance and to follow the status of the battery.

• Most batteries last about 5 years. Battery changes can be performed as an outpatient procedure. At the time of the battery replacement, the leads are inspected, tested, and replaced if they show signs of premature wear.

Troubleshooting ICDs

Patients with ICD problems usually present with frequent discharges or failure of the device to discharge.

Frequent discharges. Patients with frequent discharges may have appropriate or inappropriate shocks. If each shock is preceded by palpitations or pre-syncope, the patient is most likely experiencing frequent episodes of VT. However, the device may have trouble distinguishing AF with rapid ventricular response from VT.

Failure to discharge. If the patient presents with sustained VT or cardiac arrest, the device may be undersensing due to lead fracture, or the rate of the VT may be lower than the programmed detection rate.

History and Physical Examination

The history and physical examination of an ICD patient may be helpful in detecting the cause of malfunction.

- First, obtain the device identification card.
- If a patient has recently started an AAD (such as amiodarone), the rate of VT may have been lowered by drug effect to less than the detection rate.
- Exposure to intense electrical fields, cautery, cellular phones, or strong magnets may disable or reprogram the device.
- Acute traumatic injury is unlikely to cause damage to the ICD.

ECG   ECG is less often useful in ICD patients than it is in pacemaker patients. Newer ICDs have DDD pacemakers, so the ECG is more helpful in this situation.

Chest X-Ray   Examination of the CXR is important. The film may reveal evidence of lead fracture or lead migration. In patients with older devices, there may also be folding up of the patches which can lead to ineffective defibrillation.

Interrogation with Programmer   Placing the programming head over the device and instructing the programmer to interrogate will provide information from the device on lead resistances, battery status, and history of recent episodes.

Magnet Application   Application of a doughnut magnet directly over the pulse generator will disable therapy for ventricular arrhythmias with devices from all present manufacturers. Bradycardia pacing therapy will continue, but antitachycardia pacing and shocking will cease.

- Magnet application when a patient is receiving clinically inappropriate shocks for oversensing from a lead fracture or a rapid ventricular rate due to atrial arrhythmias or sinus tachycardia is the first step in treatment.

Care of Patients with ICDs Undergoing Surgical Procedures

The ICD is susceptible to electrical and magnetic interference.

- ICD patients cannot have MRI examinations.
- ICD patients should not be exposed to electrocautery. The electrical discharge from the cautery can cause damage to the ICD circuitry with complete loss of function, or can be detected as cardiac electrical activity, interpreted as VT, and generate multiple defibrillator discharges.

Elective Procedures

If an ICD patient is scheduled for an elective procedure, the ICD should be programmed to inactive in the pre-operative holding area. The patient should be continuously monitored, and the ICD reactivated in the recovery area.

If the patient is at risk for postoperative atrial arrhythmias, especially after cardiac or thoracic surgery, then the time to reactivate the device may be delayed until the patient is clinically stable.

Emergency Surgery

If an ICD patient must undergo emergency surgery and the programmer is not available, taping a magnet over the device will disable detection and therapy of VT and most likely protect the device from electrical damage and the patient from multiple discharges.

RADIOFREQUENCY (RF) CATHETER ABLATION

The use of RF catheter ablation has greatly expanded the role of invasive EP in the electrical treatment of arrhythmias. In many cases, the RF procedure can be curative, and the burden of the arrhythmia can be removed.

The principle behind RF application is simple. If the area of the heart that is causing the rhythm disturbance can be localized, RF energy can be applied to that area through the tip of a percutaneously introduced electrode catheter, causing local tissue desiccation with subsequent loss of electrical function. The amount of cardiac tissue rendered nonfunctional during the procedure is so small (in the adult) that there is no significant change in overall cardiac function.

Success rates vary depending on the type of rhythm disturbance, but frequently exceed 90%.

Complications are unusual and are most frequently related to vascular access. However, excessive RF application to pathways close to the AV node can lead to complete AV block and require permanent pacemaker implantation. The small risk of sudden cardiac death after ablation of the AV junction has decreased since RF energy has replaced DC shock as the ablative technique.

Treatment of Specific Arrhythmias with RF Ablation

Atrial Fibrillation

Curative RF catheter ablation for AF is possible in only a very small number of patients. Several case reports have demonstrated that RF delivered to a specific site responsible for atrial irritability can eliminate AF. In most cases, however, more extensive RF is necessary to treat AF.

• **Catheter maze procedure.** Application of RF along lines in the LA and RA can cause sufficient scarring to prevent multiple wavefront reentry, preventing AF from sustaining itself ("catheter maze procedure"). This technique is receiving extensive evaluation at this time, but will most likely require changes in RF catheter technology to become widely applicable.

• **Palliative radiofrequency catheter ablation.** Palliative RF catheter ablation for AF is much more widely used. When applied to patients with inappropriately rapid ventricular response who cannot tolerate medications, measurable changes in quality of life can occur. The two techniques are modification and complete ablation.

Modification of the AV node. Modification of the AV node by RF application can limit the ventricular response without causing symptomatic bradycardia. The ventricular response can be estimated in the EP laboratory by isoproterenol infusion, so the amount of RF application can be titrated appropriately.

Complete ablation of the AV node. Complete ablation consists of RF application to the AV node/His bundle region, creating complete AV block. A rate-responsive VVI pacemaker is then implanted to provide rate support. Patients may be rendered pacemaker-dependent by this procedure.

Recent investigations have focused on the utility of AV node ablation for paroxysmal AF. Complete ablation of the AV junction with implantation of a DDD pacemaker with automatic mode switching can decrease the amount of medication necessary to control symptoms and improve the quality of life.

Atrial Flutter

The common variety of atrial flutter is a reentrant arrhythmia with an endless loop of electrical activity circling the junction of the IVC and RA. Interruption of this circuit by RF of the floor of the RA has been useful.

A line of RF lesions extending from the TV annulus across the isthmus to the IVC leads to block in the loop so that the circling wavefront cannot complete the loop. The procedure is most likely to be successful in patients who do not have significant structural heart disease and who demonstrate classic "saw-tooth" flutter waves on the ECG.

Complications

- Complications are usually related to vascular access.
- When the patient has episodes of AF that are not preceded by atrial flutter, the chance of maintaining sinus rhythm decreases.
- Atypical atrial flutter may be due to anatomic abnormalities in different areas of the atrium or

functional areas of block in diseased atrial tissue. The success rate with atypical atrial flutter is lower.

• When the AV node is located in an unusual position or when the catheter slips during RF application, complete AV block may occur.

Ectopic Atrial Tachycardias

The utility of RF in ectopic atrial tachycardias is limited. Mapping of the irritable focus during tachycardia can demonstrate the site of origin of the tachycardia, but there are frequently multiple sites so that the success rate is decreased. The focus can be located in either the RA or LA, so both sides may have to be explored.

Many tachycardias are not inducible in the EP laboratory, so complete ablation of the AV junction with pacemaker implantation is an option in drug-resistant patients.

Reentrant Supraventricular Tachycardias (SVT)

The two classic forms of reentrant SVTs are AV node reentry and atrioventricular reciprocating tachycardia utilizing an accessory atrioventricular connection (bypass tract, or forms of WPW).

The use of RF catheter ablation in treating patients with these tachycardias is frequently curative. The associated complications are usually limited to problems with vascular access or inadvertent creation of complete heart block. Cardiac perforation with rapid onset of tamponade during catheter manipulation is a rare but dramatic complication, which is usually diagnosed during or immediately following the procedure.

AV Node Reentry The indications for RF for reentrant SVT are not clear cut.

• Patients who have drug-resistant SVT are obviously candidates. (The definition of drug resistance varies in different clinical categories.)
• Women of child-bearing age may choose to undergo RF prior to pregnancy to avoid the possibility of drug effects on the fetus.
• Patients with high-risk vocations or avocations may choose RF as first-line therapy to avoid SVT when

they do not have access to immediate medical intervention.
- Older patients with other medical problems who require drug therapy for other illnesses may be best served by medical treatment.

Atrioventricular Reciprocating Tachycardia The indications for EP evaluation of patients with obvious preexcitation on an ECG are more clear.

Bypass tract   Patients with symptomatic SVT using a bypass tract may have the reentrant SVT convert to AF. If the bypass tract has a very short refractory period, AF can cause very rapid ventricular response by stimulation of the ventricle via the bypass tract instead of the AV node, leading to the chain of events in which AF induces VF. Therefore, patients with symptomatic preexcitation syndromes should undergo EP evaluation for risk stratification for sudden cardiac death.

Wolff-Parkinson-White syndrome   The overall incidence of sudden cardiac death in WPW syndrome is low, but increased over the general population. If a patient is involved in a high-risk vocation or avocation, some authorities recommend EP evaluation even for asymptomatic preexcitation.

Ventricular Tachycardia
The use of RF catheter ablation for VT is developing rapidly as catheter technology improves. The applications are more clearly defined for VT that is not caused by ischemic heart disease than for the more common CAD scar-related VT.

VT in structurally normal hearts most frequently occurs in patients at younger ages than patients with VT from CAD because of the obvious differences in natural history of the diseases. The three most common types of non-CAD VT include:

1. Repetitive monomorphic VT from the right ventricular outflow tract (RVOT)
2. Arrhythmogenic right ventricular dysplasia (ARVD)
3. Idiopathic left ventricular tachycardia (ILVT)

Right Ventricular Outflow Tract Patients with VT from the RVOT may have bursts of VT separated by periods of sinus rhythm. They may be asymptomatic or have palpitations and lightheadedness. VT from the RVOT is commonly precipitated by physical or emotional stress, and may be treated successfully with beta-blockers or verapamil.

RVOT-related VT is frequently curable by RF catheter ablation, so the trial of medical management may be limited depending on the clinical situation. The RF catheter can be advanced into the RVOT, and mapping by either activation sequence or pacing can identify the focus of the VT. Application of RF at the sites is curative, in some series greater than 90% of the time.

Arrhythmogenic Right Ventricular Dysplasia (ARVD) Ventricular tachycardia in patients with ARVD is not benign. There are frequently many different sites from which the VT originates, and some of the VT episodes may lead to syncope or sudden cardiac death.

This form of VT can be approached with RF catheter ablation, but with a lower success rate. In addition, the anatomic abnormality of the RV makes the tissue more friable, thus the incidence of perforation is higher.

Idiopathic Left Ventricular Tachycardia Patients with ILVT are more like those with RVOT than those with ARVD, but the VT originates in the LV, thus displaying an RBBB morphology (VT originating from the RV displays an LBBB morphology).

Patients with ILVT are candidates for RF catheter ablation if they fail medical management; the ILVT may have multiple morphologies, and the site of the VT may be more difficult to reach than the relatively easily accessible RVOT.

CAD-Related VT Patients with VT from CAD are very different from the non-CAD group. Their scar-related VTs leave them with significant LV dysfunction, underlying CAD, and a significantly increased risk for sudden cardiac death.

Treatment of these patients usually involves AADs (frequently amiodarone), ICDs, or both. In selected cases, RF may be curative.

The RF catheter is advanced into the LV, and mapping is performed to localize the site of the scar-related focus of VT. Careful localization is necessary, because there may be a long reentrant circuit and radiofrequency catheter ablation of only a small portion will lead to cure. The VT must be monomorphic, and the patient hemodynamically stable during VT to allow for mapping without frequent cardioversions or deterioration into VF.

ARRHYTHMIA SURGERY

Surgery for Ventricular Arrhythmias

Since the introduction of the ICD, surgery for VT has seen a dramatic decrease in frequency. The surgical technique involves concurrent CABG (if necessary), opening the LV, and resecting the scar tissue which includes the VT focus. Mapping with computer-enhanced techniques has made the success rate high. Most series continue to be complicated by relatively high mortality rates and postoperative CHF. However, in well-selected cases, VT can be cured.

Ideal Candidate

The ideal candidate for VT surgery has:

- Monomorphic, hemodynamically tolerated VT
- A well-defined ventricular aneurysm
- Preserved systolic function in the nonaneurysmal portions of the LV

The patient can be mapped preoperatively in the EP lab, then intraoperatively, with scar resection and ventricular remodeling using one of several effective techniques. Patients with these characteristics should be identified when there is evidence of a previous anterior MI and monomorphic VT.

Poor Candidates

Patients are more likely to have better results with ICD or drug therapy if they have:

- Unstable VT
- Heterogeneous rather than homogeneous scar tissue
- Poor systolic function in unaffected areas

Surgery for Supraventricular Arrhythmias

The first cures for patients with WPW syndrome were surgical. Careful preoperative localization of the bypass tract in the EP lab followed by mapping and separation of the accessory connection at surgery leads to cures. In the last decade, catheter-based techniques have virtually eliminated surgery for reentrant SVT.

Surgery for Atrial Fibrillation

The EP mechanism for AF implies multiple reentrant circuits. As reentrant SVT can be cured by interrupting the loop, the concept was applied to the treatment of AF. Using this technique, several linear incisions are made in the atria to limit the amount of atrial tissue available for reentry (the maze procedure). When the procedure is properly performed, the incidence of AF is markedly reduced. The risks are relatively low in carefully selected patients when the operation is performed as a primary procedure.

SYNCHRONIZED CARDIOVERSION FOR ATRIAL FIBRILLATION

Indications for Cardioversion

The indications for urgent cardioversion for AF are clear if the onset of AF leads to acute hemodynamic compromise, as in pulmonary edema or an acute coronary syndrome.

- Cardioversion can be performed with little risk of an embolic event if the duration of AF is less than 24 hours, and is indicated if medical treatment is unsuccessful in reversing the acute hemodynamic effects.
- Cardioversion for AF of unknown duration is currently controversial. Once sinus rhythm is restored, individual patients may notice symptomatic improvement. However, there is an approximately

50% recurrence rate despite AAD therapy, even with amiodarone, after 1 year.

It is important to make a careful clinical decision about the advisability of returning the patient to sinus rhythm. There are many risk factors for recurrence of AF, including atrial dimensions, age, and severity of underlying heart disease. Lone AF (in patients with no structural heart disease) may respond more favorably to medical treatment.

Embolic Events and Atrial Fibrillation

Anticoagulation
See Chapter 17.

Cardioversion for Atrial Fibrillation
There is a clearly recognized increased risk for LA thrombus formation and subsequent systemic embolization in patients with AF. The onset of the increased risk is estimated at 24 to 48 hours after the onset of AF. Thus, if a patient has AF of unknown duration, is hemodynamically stable, and the clinical decision has been made to pursue the return to sinus rhythm, anticoagulation to reduce the risk of emboli should be considered.

Transesophageal Echocardiography   In some patients the waiting period during anticoagulation therapy may present clinical difficulties. Recent studies suggest that TEE imaging of the LA appendage demonstrating absence of thrombus can safely shorten the waiting period. The patient should be adequately anticoagulated at the time of TEE-guided cardioversion to prevent LA thrombus formation soon after the procedure.

After any cardioversion (medical or electrical), return of atrial electrical function precedes return of mechanical function by days to weeks, and the risk of embolic events continues. Consequently, even if TEE shows absence of LA thrombus, anticoagulation for at least 4 weeks after cardioversion should be undertaken.

Anti-arrhythmic Drug Therapy

See Chapter 17.

Techniques for Cardioversion of Atrial Fibrillation

- A typical patient for cardioversion has been anticoagulated for at least 3 weeks after the discovery of AF.
- In some cases, loading with an AAD has taken place. The decision whether loading is performed as an inpatient or an outpatient remains controversial.

The risk of proarrhythmia in patients with significant heart disease is elevated, and many authorities favor hospitalization for several days of therapy followed by cardioversion if medical treatment does not result in return to sinus rhythm.

Sedation for the Procedure
Patients for cardioversion should be kept NPO after midnight the night before the procedure. Adequate sedation for the procedure is vital. Practices differ, with some preferring conscious sedation, and others calling for brief periods of general anesthesia. This choice is most often made by the anesthesiologist.

Placement of Cardioversion Electrodes
- Careful skin preparation is necessary to prevent burns and deliver the desired energy appropriately. The use of pre-gelled adhesive electrodes is common.
- The large pads can be placed anteriorly, with one on the upper right sternal border and the second at the cardiac apex. They can also be placed anterior-posterior, with one over the apex and the second at the inferior border of the right scapula.
- Regular paddles are still frequently used. They are usually placed anteriorly, one at the sternum and the other at the cardiac apex, both over conducting pads. Appropriate pressure must be exerted, and can be measured with the paddles on modern systems.

Energy for Cardioversion
Considerable controversy exists about the initial energy for synchronized cardioversion of AF. Some practitioners advocate using the least amount of energy possible, and may start with as few as 50 joules, then work up to higher

levels if unsuccessful. Others advocate starting at higher levels if the patient is adequately sedated, with a few starting at 360 joules to minimize the number of attempts.

If the initial cardioversion attempt is unsuccessful, a second shock should be delivered rapidly during the period of decreased transthoracic impedance caused by the first shock.

If the highest energies fail, then other methods may be used. Additional AAD therapy may decrease cardioversion energy requirements, so having the patient return after a loading period is reasonable. If this fails, internal cardioversion can be considered.

Internal Cardioversion   In internal cardioversion, an EP catheter is inserted into the heart and connected to the defibrillator as one of the cardioversion electrodes. When the shock is triggered, the current flows from the intracardiac catheter to a pre-gelled electrode pad on the patient's back. This technique requires the use of fluoroscopy and is useful in resistant cases.

SUGGESTED READINGS

Calkins H, Sousa J, El-Atassi R, et al. Diagnosis and cure of the Wolff-Parkinson-White syndrome or paroxysmal supraventricular tachycardias during a single electrophysiologic test. N Engl J Med 1991;324:1612–1618.

Cosio FG, Goicolea A, Lopez-Gil M, Arribas F. Catheter ablation of atrial flutter circuits. PACE 1993;16:637–642.

Ewy GA. Optimal technique for electrical cardioversion of atrial fibrillation. Circulation 1992;86:1645–1647.

Fatkin D, Kuchar DL, Thorburn CW, et al. Transesophageal echocardiography before and during direct current cardioversion of atrial fibrillation: evidence for "atrial stunning" as a mechanism of thromboembolic complications. J Am Coll Cardiol 1994;23:307–316.

Gregoratos G, Cheitlin MD, Conill A, et al. ACC/AHA Guidelines for implantation of cardiac pacemakers and antiarrhythmia devices. J Am Coll Cardiol 1998;31: 1175–1209.

Furman S. Pacemaker syndrome. PACE 1994;17:1–5.

Jackman WM, Beckman KJ, McClelland JH, et al. Treatment of supraventricular tachycardia due to atrioventricular reentry by radiofrequency catheter ablation of slow pathway conduction. N Engl J Med 1992;327:313–318.

Jackman WM, Wang X, Friday KJ, et al. Catheter ablation of accessory atrioventricular pathways (Wolff-Parkinson-White syndrome) by radiofrequency current. N Engl J Med 1991;324:1605–1611.

Klein LS, Shih H-T, Hackett FK, et al. Radiofrequency catheter ablation of ventricular tachycardia in patients without structural heart disease. Circulation 1992;85:1666–1674.

Klug D, Lacroix D, Savoye C, et al. Systemic infection related to endocarditis on pacemaker leads. Circulation 1997;95:2098–2107.

Morady F, Harvey M, Kalbfleisch SJ, et al. Radiofrequency catheter ablation of ventricular tachycardia in patients with coronary artery disease. Circulation 1993;87:363–372.

Moss AJ, Hall WJ, Cannom DS, et al. Improved survival with an implanted defibrillator in patients with coronary disease at high risk of ventricular arrhythmias. N Engl J Med 1996;335:1933–1940.

Petersen P, Boysen G, Godtfredsen J, Andersen ED, Andersen B. Placebo-controlled, randomised trial of warfarin and aspirin for prevention of thromboembolic complications in chronic atrial fibrillation: the Copenhagen AFASAK study. Lancet 1989;1:175–179.

Ritchie JL, Cheitlin MD, Garson A, et al. Guidelines for clinical intracardiac electrophysiological and catheter ablation procedures. J Am Coll Cardiol 1995;26:555–573.

Stroke Prevention in Atrial Fibrillation Investigators. Stroke prevention in atrial fibrillation study: final results. Circulation 1991;84:527–539.

Sweeney MO, Ruskin JN. Mortality benefits and the implantable cardioverter-defibrillator. Circulation 1994;89: 1851–1858.

Winkle RA, Mead RH, Ruder MA, et al. Long-term outcome with the automatic implantable cardioverter-defibrillator. J Am Coll Cardiol 1989;13:1353–1361.

Zipes DP, DiMarco JP, Gillette PC, et al. Guidelines for clinical intracardiac electrophysiological and catheter ablation procedures. Circulation 1995;92:673–691.

Cardiopulmonary Resuscitation

Dennis A. Tighe
Edward K. Chung

CAD accounts for approximately 700,000 deaths annually in the United States. The majority are sudden (occurring within 2 hours of symptom onset), and approximately 1000 prehospital sudden deaths occur each day. Public education, risk factor modification, and advances in the diagnosis and treatment of cardiovascular disease have led to a 30% decline in mortality from CAD and stroke. However, sudden cardiac death remains a major public health concern.

External "closed" chest compression was introduced in 1960 and was subsequently coupled with mouth-to-mouth ventilation to form the components of basic cardiopulmonary resuscitation (CPR). These developments have offered the hope that the number of cases of sudden death can be diminished and that patients can survive to receive more definitive care (advanced cardiac life support).

This chapter reviews emergency cardiac care (ECC) guidelines as applied to the adult victim and also discusses recent developments of clinical concern.

MANAGEMENT OF AIRWAY OBSTRUCTION

Airway obstruction can occur from intrinsic or extrinsic etiologies. Large, poorly chewed pieces of meat (café coronary) are the most common cause of obstruction.

Other etiologies include trauma or obstructions by the tongue, epiglottitis, regurgitated gastric contents, mass lesions, bleeding, and other foreign bodies.

Airway obstruction may be partial or complete. Partial obstruction may progress to complete blockage. Once complete obstruction occurs and the victim's reflexes (coughing) to expel or relieve the obstruction are compromised, oxygen desaturation leading to unconsciousness and death may occur rapidly.

Heimlich Maneuver

The *Heimlich maneuver* (abdominal thrusts) is the recommended technique for relieving foreign body obstruction. This maneuver is designed to elevate the diaphragm, increasing intrathoracic pressure, and forcing air from the lungs to clear the obstruction.

The Heimlich maneuver can be performed with the victim standing, sitting, or lying down; it can even be self-administered by the victim. In the unconscious victim, the airway should be opened and any foreign body removed (sometimes requiring a finger-sweep technique).

Heimlich Sequence
1. With the victim sitting or standing, the rescuer places his or her arms around the victim's waist (staying clear of the xiphoid process), slightly above the navel.
2. The thumb side of the fist is pressed in an inward and upward direction into the victim's abdomen with a thrusting motion (Fig 19-1).
3. The maneuver is repeated until the obstruction is cleared or the victim becomes conscious.

Chest Thrusts
Chest thrusts are an alternative technique to relieve airway obstruction, but they are recommended only in victims with marked obesity and advanced pregnancy.

If adequate rescue breathing cannot be performed, the rescuer straddles the victim (Fig 19-2) and with one hand placed on top of the other, delivers up to 5 mid-abdominal thrusts in an inward and upward direction followed by a finger sweep and reattempt at rescue breathing. This sequence should be repeated as long as necessary.

Figure 19-1. Heimlich maneuver administered to conscious victim of foreign-body airway obstruction who is sitting or standing. (Adapted with permission from: Guidelines for cardiopulmonary resuscitation and emergency cardiac care. JAMA 1992;268:2193.)

CARDIOPULMONARY ARREST

Cardiopulmonary arrest is the sudden loss of effective cardiac and/or pulmonary function leading rapidly to a state of unconsciousness and ultimately death if not reversed. The leading cause in the adult population is malignant ventricular arrhythmia associated with underlying CAD. Irreversible central nervous system (CNS) damage can occur within 4 minutes if effective ventilation and circulation are not restored.

The survival of arrest victims receiving CPR is only 5% to 15%. Survival in localities with large numbers of trained bystanders and a highly organized emergency medical system (EMS) is higher.

Management of the arrest victim can be divided into stages:

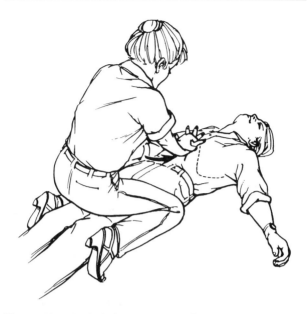

Figure 19-2. Heimlich maneuver administered to unconscious victim of foreign-body airway obstruction who is lying down. (Adapted with permission from: Guidelines for cardiopulmonary resuscitation and emergency cardiac care. JAMA 1992;268:2193.)

1. Initial evaluation
2. Basic life support (BLS)
3. Advanced cardiac life support (ACLS)
4. Post-resuscitation management

INITIAL EVALUATION

The goal of the initial evaluation is to determine whether the cause of the collapse is a cardiopulmonary arrest. Common noncardiac causes of unconsciousness include the post-ictal state following a seizure, hypoglycemia, drug-toxin ingestion, head trauma, cerebral infarction or hemorrhage, and psychiatric conditions.

A brief history-taking can be useful to elucidate these underlying conditions, but the first priority should be to examine the victim and determine if spontaneous respi-

ratory movements and major arterial pulsations are
present.

- If the victim is hemodynamically stable, there is time
  to explore the underlying etiology and perform a
  more detailed diagnostic evaluation.
- In the absence of spontaneous respiratory efforts and
  pulse, BLS should be initiated promptly. The highest
  hospital discharge rate has been achieved when CPR
  was initiated within 4 minutes of the arrest.

BASIC LIFE SUPPORT

The goal of BLS is to maintain adequate flow of blood
and oxygen to the heart, CNS, and other vital organs until
ACLS can be initiated.

It is imperative that BLS be initiated as rapidly as possible once the rescuer determines that the victim has suffered a cardiopulmonary arrest. Activation of the EMS
system must be given the highest priority, because early
defibrillation is the most important factor in patient survival—80% to 90% of adult cardiac arrest victims are
found to be in VF on the initial ECG.

Technique and Sequence of BLS

The sequence of one- and two-rescuer BLS is outlined in
Table 19-1. BLS should be continued until the victim is
able to receive more definitive care.

Indications for BLS

- **Cardiac Arrest**
- **Respiratory Arrest.** Respiratory arrest has a diverse
  etiology including foreign body obstruction,
  drowning, stroke, epiglottitis, drug overdose, smoke
  inhalation, and trauma. Despite the lack of
  respiration, the circulation may remain intact for
  several minutes. Establishing an adequate airway and
  providing rescue breathing if necessary can provide
  adequate oxygenation and prevent cardiac arrest.

Determine Unresponsiveness

The rescuer should determine if the patient is unconscious by tapping the victim or gently shaking the victim

Table 19-1. Sequences of CPR Performed by One Rescuer or Two Rescuers

CPR Performed by One Rescuer
1. Determine unresponsiveness.
2. Activate EMS system if unresponsive.
   Airway: Position victim and open airway.
   Breathing: Determine breathlessness.
   - If spontaneous breathing is present: place victim in recovery position and maintain open airway.
   - If no respiration present: deliver initial breaths.
   - If unable to ventilate the victim: reposition the head and reattempt ventilation.
   - If still unable to ventilate: suspect foreign-body obstruction and perform maneuvers to relieve the obstruction (repeat sequence until relieved).
   - If no spontaneous respiration is present, but an adequate pulse is present: perform ventilation at 10 to 12 breaths per minute.
   Circulation: Determine pulselessness.
   - If no pulse present: perform 15 external chest compressions at a rate of 80 to 100 per minute and then two ventilations.
   - Perform 4 complete cycles of 15 compressions and 2 ventilations.
3. Reassessment: Check for return of carotid pulse (2 to 5 seconds) after 4 cycles of compressions and ventilations.
   - If pulse absent: resume CPR sequence
   - If pulse present: check for breathing
   - If breathing and pulse present: monitor closely
   - If breathing absent: perform rescue breathing at 10 to 12 breaths per minute.

CPR Performed by Two Rescuers
In two-rescuer CPR, activation of the EMS system and assessment of airway, breathing, and circulation are similar to the recommendations for one-rescuer CPR.

First rescuer: Performs chest compressions.
Second rescuer:
- Maintains an open airway.
- Provides ventilation.
- Assesses the effectiveness of chest compressions.
- Monitors periodically for return of spontaneous respiration and pulse.

The second and first rescuers exchange positions when fatigue occurs.

Specific recommendations for two-rescuer CPR
- Compression rate of 80 to 100 per minute.
- Compression-ventilation ratio of 5:1 with a 1.5 to 2 second pause for ventilation.
- Reassessment at the end of the first minute and every few minutes thereafter.

Adapted from: Emergency Cardiac Care Committee and Subcommittees, American Heart Association. Guidelines for cardiopulmonary resuscitation and emergency cardiac care, II: adult basic life support. JAMA 1992;268:2184–2198.

and asking, "Are you OK?" A brief inspection for obvious head and neck trauma should be performed before the victim is moved.

Activate EMS System

Prior to any further attempts at resuscitation, the EMS system must be activated immediately because the majority of adult, nontraumatic cardiac arrest victims are in VF.

Airway

Position the Victim and Rescuer

Victim position: For effective CPR, the victim should be positioned supine on a flat and firm surface. In the hospital setting, a board should be placed under the victim. If head and neck injury is suspected, the head and neck should remain in the same plane as the torso and the body should be rolled as a unit.

Rescuer position: The rescuer should be at the victim's side to deliver effective BLS.

Open the Airway In the unconscious victim, the tongue is the most common cause of airway obstruction. Moving the lower jaw forward will lift the tongue away from the back of the throat and open the airway.

Two procedures for opening the airway of a unconscious victim have been developed: the head tilt–chin lift and the jaw-thrust.

Head tilt–chin lift maneuver. This maneuver is the technique of choice in the victim without suspected head and neck trauma because it is simple, safe, and effective.

1. Place one hand on the victim's forehead with firm backward pressure applied with the palm to tilt the head back.

2. Place the fingers of the second hand under the bony portion of the lower jaw close to the chin and lift to bring the chin forward and the teeth almost to occlusion (Fig 19-3).

3. Gently remove any visible foreign material to the extent possible.

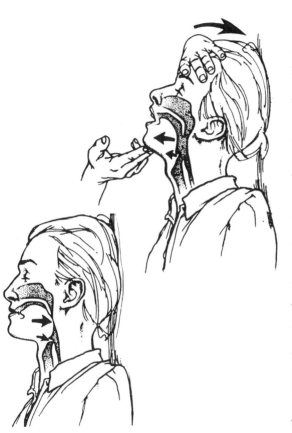

Figure 19-3. Opening the airway. **Top:** Airway obstruction produced by tongue and epiglottis. **Bottom:** Relief by head-tilt-chin-lift maneuver. (Adapted with permission from: Guidelines for cardiopulmonary resuscitation and emergency cardiac care. JAMA 1992;268:2186.)

Jaw-thrust maneuver. This technique is the safest initial approach to opening the airway in the victim with suspected head and neck injury.

1. Place the rescuer's elbows on the same surface upon which the victim is lying.
2. Grasp the angles of the victim's lower jaw and lift with both hands, one on each side, displacing the mandible forward and tilting the head backward.

Breathing

Determine Breathlessness During a period not exceeding 5 seconds, the rescuer should:

LOOK for the chest to rise and fall.
LISTEN for air to escape during exhalation.
FEEL for airflow.

If, after this period, spontaneous respiration is present and the patient has not sustained neck injury, the victim should be placed in the recovery position.

Rescue Breathing Rescue breathing is indicated in the absence of spontaneous respiration after the airway has been adequately opened.

If adequate rescue breaths cannot be delivered, the rescuer should attempt to reposition the victim to ensure adequate opening of the airway and then reattempt rescue breathing. If ventilation remains inadequate, a foreign body obstruction should be suspected and maneuvers to clear the airway should be employed.

Techniques Mouth-to-mouth rescue breathing is the most common technique. With mouth-to-mouth breathing, the rescuer maintains an open airway and pinches the nose closed with the thumb and index finger of the hand on the forehead to prevent the escape of air during his or her rescue breath. A tight seal is created by the rescuer's lips with the victim's mouth and two slow breaths are delivered.

Timing Two initial breaths delivered over 1.5 to 2.0 seconds each should be given. Sufficient time for these two initial breaths diminishes the risk of gastric distention and allows adequate time to observe the rise and fall of the chest (tidal volume of 800 to 1200 cc needed). Adequate ventilation is indicated by observing the chest rise and fall and hearing and feeling air escape during exhalation.

CPR Breaths During CPR breaths should be delivered at a rate of 10 to 12 per minute.

- For one-rescuer CPR, a pause for ventilations should occur after the 15th chest compression.
- In two-rescuer CPR, it should occur after the 5th chest compression.

Circulation

Determine Pulselessness The presence of a pulse should be determined for a period of 5 to 10 seconds in a central pulse.

- The most accessible is the carotid artery.
- The femoral artery pulse may be used, but it is difficult to locate on a fully clothed victim.

Chest Compressions Chest compressions provide circulation as a result of a generalized increase in intrathoracic pressure and/or direct compression of the heart. An optimally performed chest compression only achieves 25% to 33% of the pre-arrest CO.

Positioning the victim Effective chest compression can only be accomplished if the victim is placed supine on a firm surface with the rescuer alongside.

Proper hand position The rescuer places the heel of one hand over the lower half of the victim's sternum. The rescuer's other hand is placed on top of the first hand, with both hands along the long axis of the sternum to minimize the risk of rib fracture. The fingers should be kept off the chest.

Proper compression technique
1. The rescuer's elbows should be locked and the arms straightened, with the shoulders directly over the patient's sternum to direct the thrust in a straight, downward direction (Fig 19-4).
2. The sternum should be depressed 1.5 to 2.0 inches in

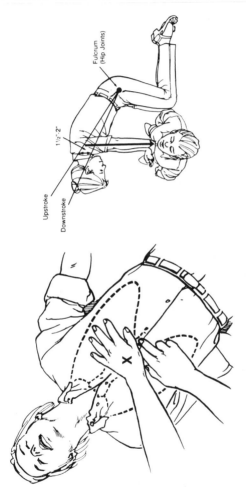

Figure 19-4. External chest compression. **Left:** Locating the correct hand position on the lower half of the sternum. **Right:** Proper position of the rescuer, with shoulders directly over the victim's sternum and elbows locked. (Adapted with permission from: Guidelines for cardiopulmonary resuscitation and emergency cardiac care. JAMA 1992;268:2190.)

the normal-sized adult. Adjust the depth of the sternal compression by palpation of the carotid or femoral pulse to assess the peripheral perfusion pressure.

3. Chest compression should occur at a rate of 80 to 100 per minute and be coordinated with rescue breathing.
   - During one-rescuer CPR, 15 external chest compressions are delivered for every 2 rescue breaths.
   - In two-rescuer CPR, 5 external compressions are delivered for each 1 rescue breath. The second rescuer maintains an open airway, assesses adequacy of compression by palpation of the carotid pulse, provides rescue breathing, and relieves the compressor upon fatigue.

Reassessment

After four cycles of compressions and ventilation in one-rescuer CPR and 1 minute in two-rescuer CPR, the victim should be reevaluated for return of circulation by palpating the carotid or femoral pulse for 3 to 5 seconds.

- If a pulse is absent, CPR should be resumed.
- If a pulse is palpable, then breathing is reassessed.

In the event that CPR is continued, the victim should be reassessed every few minutes. CPR should be terminated when:

1. A physician determines that resuscitative efforts should cease.
2. Reliable criteria for death are apparent.
3. The rescuer is too exhausted to continue.
4. The situation is determined to be medically "futile."
5. A valid no-CPR order is present.

ADVANCED CARDIAC LIFE SUPPORT (ACLS)

The outcome of adult cardiac arrest patients is clearly related to the initial cardiac rhythm and, most importantly, time to defibrillation. Therefore, early delivery of ACLS is important.

Formerly, the delivery of ACLS was restricted to the hospital environment, but in many communities advanced EMS systems allow this technique to be administered in the field.

Universal Algorithm for Adult Emergency Cardiac Care

The universal algorithm for adult ECC (Fig 19-5) represents the starting point for all rescue situations. Once it is determined that the victim is unresponsive, the EMS system should be activated immediately, prior to assessing the airway.

1. If the airway is patent and a pulse is absent, CPR should be initiated until the cardiac rhythm is known and/or a defibrillator is present.
2. Defibrillation of ventricular tachyarrhythmias with sequential shocks of progressively increasing energy levels (to a maximum of 360 joules) should assume primary importance and precede attempts at IV access and intubation of the airway.
3. At this point, the victim is reassessed and the individual algorithm most appropriate is followed.

Individual Algorithms
Individual algorithms for VF and pulseless VT, pulseless electrical activity (PEA), asystole, bradycardia, and tachycardia are presented in Figures 19-6 to 19-10.

Drug Treatments
Suggested doses of cardiac drugs for adult arrest victims are listed with the individual algorithms (see Figs 19-6 to 19-10).

- All IV medications should be followed immediately by a 20–30 mL bolus of fluid. If a peripheral vein is used, the extremity should be lifted to facilitate return to central circulation.
- Several medications (epinephrine, lidocaine, and atropine) can be administered via the endotracheal route. A dose of 2.0 to 2.5 times the IV dose should be used.

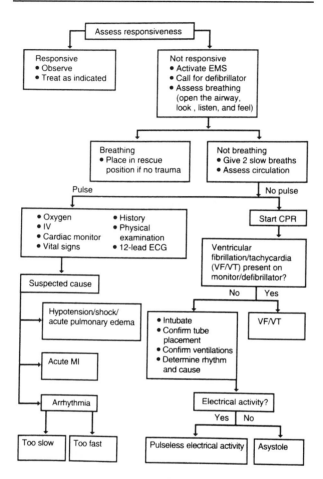

Figure 19-5. Universal algorithm for adult emergency cardiac care. The rescuer is directed to the appropriate algorithm based on clinical assessment. (Adapted with permission from: Guidelines for cardiopulmonary resuscitation and emergency cardiac care. JAMA 1992;268:2216.)

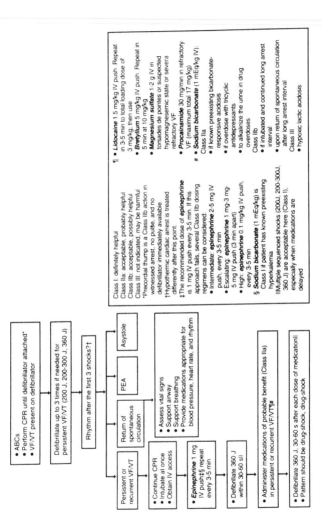

Figure 19-6. Algorithm for VF and pulseless VT. (Adapted with permission from: Guidelines for cardiopulmonary resuscitation and emergency cardiac care. JAMA 1992;268:2217.)

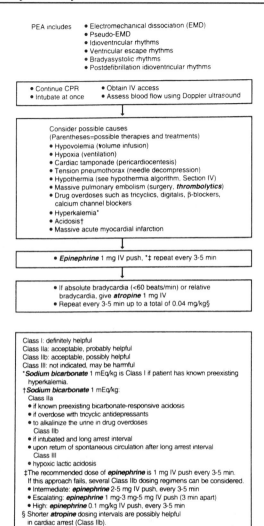

PEA includes
- Electromechanical dissociation (EMD)
- Pseudo-EMD
- Idioventricular rhythms
- Ventricular escape rhythms
- Bradyasystolic rhythms
- Postdefibrillation idioventricular rhythms

- Continue CPR
- Intubate at once
- Obtain IV access
- Assess blood flow using Doppler ultrasound

Consider possible causes
(Parentheses=possible therapies and treatments)
- Hypovolemia (volume infusion)
- Hypoxia (ventilation)
- Cardiac tamponade (pericardiocentesis)
- Tension pneumothorax (needle decompression)
- Hypothermia (see hypothermia algorithm, Section IV)
- Massive pulmonary embolism (surgery, ***thrombolytics***)
- Drug overdoses such as tricyclics, digitalis, β-blockers, calcium channel blockers
- Hyperkalemia*
- Acidosis†
- Massive acute myocardial infarction

- ***Epinephrine*** 1 mg IV push, *‡ repeat every 3-5 min

- If absolute bradycardia (<60 beats/min) or relative bradycardia, give ***atropine*** 1 mg IV
- Repeat every 3-5 min up to a total of 0.04 mg/kg§

Class I: definitely helpful
Class IIa: acceptable, probably helpful
Class IIb: acceptable, possibly helpful
Class III: not indicated, may be harmful
****Sodium bicarbonate*** 1 mEq/kg is Class I if patient has known preexisting hyperkalemia.
†***Sodium bicarbonate*** 1 mEq/kg:
  Class IIa
  - if known preexisting bicarbonate-responsive acidosis
  - if overdose with tricyclic antidepressants
  - to alkalinize the urine in drug overdoses
  Class IIb
  - if intubated and long arrest interval
  - upon return of spontaneous circulation after long arrest interval
  Class III
  - hypoxic lactic acidosis
‡The recommended dose of ***epinephrine*** is 1 mg IV push every 3-5 min. If this approach fails, several Class IIb dosing regimens can be considered.
  - Intermediate: ***epinephrine*** 2-5 mg IV push, every 3-5 min
  - Escalating: ***epinephrine*** 1 mg-3 mg-5 mg IV push (3 min apart)
  - High: ***epinephrine*** 0.1 mg/kg IV push, every 3-5 min
§ Shorter ***atropine*** dosing intervals are possibly helpful in cardiac arrest (Class IIb).

Figure 19-7. Algorithm for pulseless electrical activity (PEA). (Adapted with permission from: Guidelines for cardiopulmonary resuscitation and emergency cardiac care. JAMA 1992;268:2219.)

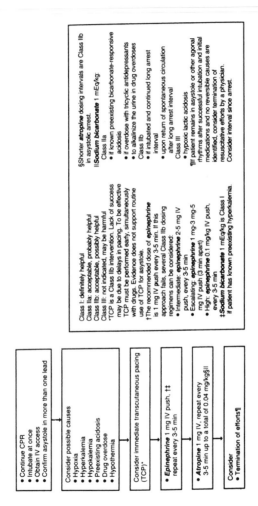

- Continue CPR
- Intubate at once
- Obtain IV access
- Confirm asystole in more than one lead

Consider possible causes
- Hypoxia
- Hyperkalemia
- Hypokalemia
- Preexisting acidosis
- Drug overdose
- Hypothermia

Consider immediate transcutaneous pacing (TCP)*

- *Epinephrine* 1 mg IV push, ‡‡ repeat every 3-5 min

- *Atropine* 1 mg IV, repeat every 3-5 min up to a total of 0.04 mg/kg§||

Consider
- Termination of efforts¶

Class I: definitely helpful
Class IIa: acceptable, probably helpful
Class IIb: acceptable, possibly helpful
Class III: not indicated, may be harmful

*TCP is a Class IIb intervention. Lack of success may be due to delays in pacing. To be effective TCP must be performed early, simultaneously with drugs. Evidence does not support routine use of TCP for asystole.

†The recommended dose of *epinephrine* is 1 mg IV push every 3-5 min. If this approach fails, several Class IIb dosing regimens can be considered:
- Intermediate: *epinephrine* 2-5 mg IV push, every 3-5 min
- Escalating: *epinephrine* 1 mg-3 mg-5 mg IV push (3 min apart)
- High: *epinephrine* 0.1 mg/kg IV push, every 3-5 min

‡*Sodium bicarbonate* 1 mEq/kg is Class I if patient has known preexisting hyperkalemia.

§Shorter *atropine* dosing intervals are Class IIb in asystolic arrest.

||*Sodium bicarbonate* 1 mEq/kg:
Class IIa
- If known preexisting bicarbonate-responsive acidosis
- If overdose with tricyclic antidepressants
- to alkalinize the urine in drug overdoses
Class IIb
- if intubated and continued long arrest interval
- upon return of spontaneous circulation after long arrest interval
Class III
- hypoxic lactic acidosis

¶If patient remains in asystole or other agonal rhythms after successful intubation and initial medications and no reversible causes are identified, consider termination of resuscitative efforts by a physician. Consider interval since arrest.

Figure 19-8. Algorithm for asystole. (Adapted with permission from: Guidelines for cardiopulmonary resuscitation and emergency cardiac care. JAMA 1992;268:2220.)

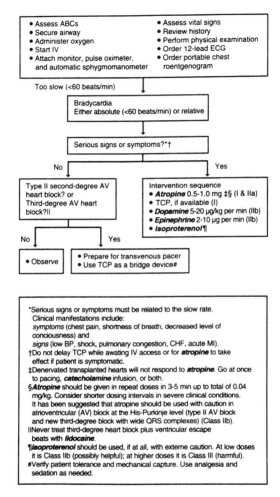

Figure 19-9. Algorithm for bradycardia. (Adapted with permission from: Guidelines for cardiopulmonary resuscitation and emergency cardiac care. JAMA 1992;268:2221.)

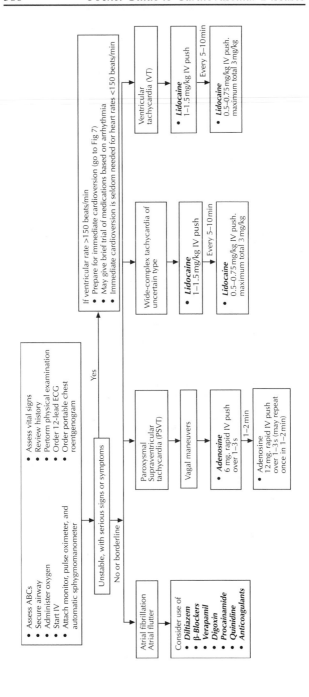

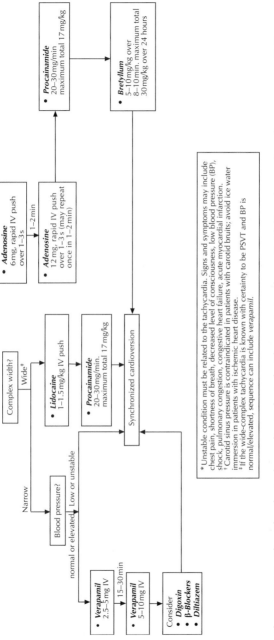

Figure 19-10. Algorithm for tachycardia. (Adapted with permission from: Guidelines for cardiopulmonary resuscitation and emergency cardiac care. JAMA 1992;268:2223.)

Post-resuscitation Management

The immediate goals following a successful resuscitation include:

- Identification and correction of precipitating cause(s).
- Stabilization and optimization of the victim's hemodynamic status.
- Transport to an emergency care facility if the patient suffered arrest outside of hospital, with subsequent transfer to an appropriately equipped critical care unit.
- Prophylactic therapy to prevent a recurrence.

A complete evaluation of the victim is essential with special emphasis placed upon the respiratory, cardiovascular, and central nervous systems.

Recent Issues in Adult Resuscitation

Epinephrine Dosage in Adult Resuscitation

Epinephrine exerts its beneficial effect by selectively increasing arterial BP, thereby helping to maintain pressure gradients for myocardial and cerebral blood flow.

- Experimental studies suggest that epinephrine's beneficial effects may be dose related, with a larger dose (0.2 mg/kg) improving cerebral and myocardial blood flow and resuscitation rates.
- Randomized studies have demonstrated no benefit to high dose versus standard dose (0.02 mg/kg) epinephrine in rates of survival and neurologic outcome in adult arrest victims.

High-dose epinephrine is not currently recommended for adult resuscitation as initial therapy, but may be "possibly helpful" in patients not responding to the standard dose.

Buffer Therapy

Acidemia has been demonstrated to decrease contractility and attenuate the hemodynamic response produced by catecholamines.

Earlier protocols recommended sodium bicarbonate

therapy to buffer the acids produced during cardiac arrest, but recent animal experiments have shown that buffer agents may be detrimental:

- Sodium bicarbonate is hypertonic and decreases aortic pressure during CPR therapy, reducing the myocardial perfusion gradient.
- Bicarbonate metabolism generates carbon dioxide, which can penetrate cells if not adequately removed and may paradoxically worsen intracellular acidosis while improving the blood pH.

The primary means to improve acid-base balance should be to increase alveolar ventilation. Bicarbonate therapy should be reserved for patients with preexisting metabolic acidosis. It may be beneficial after prolonged resuscitative efforts.

Calcium Chloride

Calcium therapy has not been shown to improve outcome in adult cardiac arrest victims and is potentially harmful because of the role of calcium accumulation in the mitochondria during irreversible ischemic cell injury. Calcium can only be recommended in cases of hyperkalemia, CCB toxicity, and hypocalcemia.

Elderly Victims

Successful outcomes of CPR in the elderly are less frequent than in younger populations. For elderly arrest victims (both in and out of hospital), those likely to survive to hospital discharge were those who:

1. Functioned independently with a normal mental status.
2. Suffered a witnessed cardiac arrest.
3. Had an initial cardiac rhythm of VT/VF.
4. Responded within 5 minutes to CPR techniques.
5. Regained consciousness promptly.

Elderly patients with underlying severe, chronic diseases and an initial cardiac rhythm of PEA, asystole, or an agonal (chaotic ventricular) rhythm have a less than 1% chance of surviving to leave the hospital. It is therefore imperative to discuss resuscitation decisions in advance with elderly patients and their families.

Continued In-Hospital Resuscitation

Less than 1% of non-hospital cardiac arrest victims who do not respond to appropriately delivered ACLS in the field receive any benefit from continued resuscitative efforts in the hospital.

Pneumatic Vest CPR

The rationale behind effective CPR stems from the observation that raising intrathoracic pressure can increase coronary and cerebral perfusion pressure and improve survival. Standard manual CPR changes thoracic volume and alters intrathoracic pressure by producing a large anteroposterior displacement at one point, which can increase the risk of thoracic trauma.

Circumferential application of a pneumatic vest can theoretically cause uniform, circumferential compression of the thorax, efficiently reducing thoracic volume and therefore generating larger changes in vascular pressure while producing less trauma as compared to standard manual CPR.

Preliminary Results

Preliminary observations in human cardiac arrest victims show that compared to standard manual CPR, pneumatic vest CPR produces significantly increased peak aortic pressure and coronary artery perfusion pressure.

In a recent study, more patients in the pneumatic vest CPR group as compared to those receiving standard manual CPR had return of spontaneous circulation and were alive 24 hours after attempted resuscitation. However, in both groups, no patient survived to leave the hospital. These observations should be considered preliminary; further study is required before this technique is used on a widespread basis.

The disadvantages of pneumatic vest CPR include its complexity of operation, delays encountered in system setup, and high equipment cost.

Active Compression-Decompression CPR

Active compression-decompression CPR converts the decompression phase of CPR from a passive process to an active one. This technique is performed with a small, hand-held device that consists of a corrugated silicone rubber cup, central stainless steel piston, and reinforced polyamide fiber-glass handle. An extension spring and force transducer allow various levels of force to be applied to the chest, depending on patient size and chest stiffness, such that compression depths of 1.5 to 2.0 inches can be achieved. Compression rates are performed in accordance with AHA guidelines for standard manual CPR.

The exact mechanism of improvement in cardiopulmonary circulation with this device is unknown, but may include enhanced venous return to the heart due to greater chest expansion and more efficient chest compression.

Preliminary Results

Preliminary results in human cardiac arrest victims indicate statistically superior initial rates of improvement in return of spontaneous circulation, 24-hour survival after resuscitation, and initial neurologic outcome in arrest survivors as compared to standard manual CPR. Survival to hospital discharge and intact neurologic function at hospital discharge were not significantly altered. These preliminary results need to be verified in larger clinical trials before this device can be a recommended adjunct to standard manual CPR.

Interposed Abdominal Counterpulsation during CPR

When performed as an adjunct to standard manual CPR, this technique can theoretically augment diastolic aortic pressure and coronary artery perfusion pressure. It is performed by delivering abdominal compressions over the umbilical area coinciding with the early relaxation phase of chest compression ("CPR diastole"). The abdominal compression rate is equal to the chest compression rate recommended in the AHA guidelines.

The exact mechanism by which interposed abdominal compression improves cardiopulmonary circulation is not known, but postulated mechanisms include hemodynamic augmentation of aortic DBP leading to greater retrograde coronary and cerebral blood flow, augmentation of venous return, and higher compression force as compared to standard manual CPR.

Preliminary Results

Preliminary observations have shown significantly improved return of spontaneous circulation, 24-hour survival, and survival to hospital discharge as compared to standard manual CPR. No significant differences in neurologic function were noted among survivors.

Advantages of interposed abdominal compression include ease of delivery and lack of apparent increases in damage to abdominal organs. Its disadvantage is that two operators must perform compressions while a third operator delivers ventilations.

Intravenous Amiodarone

Amiodarone has recently been approved for IV use in patients with ventricular tachyarrhythmias resistant to standard medications (see Chapter 17). This medication may prove useful in the victim of cardiopulmonary arrest in the appropriate clinical setting; however, at the time of this writing it is not formally included in ACLS guidelines.

Suggested Readings

Bedell SE, Delbanco TL, Cook EF, Epstein FM. Survival after cardiopulmonary resuscitation in the hospital. N Engl J Med 1993;309:569–576.

Cohen TJ, Goldner BG, Maccaro PC, et al. A comparison of active compression-decompression cardiopulmonary resuscitation with standard cardiopulmonary resuscitation for cardiac arrest occurring in the hospital. N Engl J Med 1993;329:1918–1921.

Emergency Cardiac Care Committee and Subcommittees, American Heart Association. Guidelines for cardiopulmonary resuscitation and emergency cardiac care. JAMA 1992;268:2171–2302.

Gray WA, Capone RJ, Most AS. Unsuccessful emergency medical resuscitation: are continued efforts in the emergency department justified? N Engl J Med 1991;325: 1393–1398.

Halperin HR, Tsitlik JE, Gelfand M, et al. A preliminary study of cardiopulmonary resuscitation by circumferential compression of the chest with use of a pneumatic vest. N Engl J Med 1993:329:762–768.

Murphy DJ, Murray A, Robinson BE, Campion EW. Outcomes of cardiopulmonary resuscitation in the elderly. Ann Int Med 1989;111:199–205.

Neimann JT. Cardiopulmonary resuscitation. N Engl J Med 1992;327:1075–1080.

Sack JB, Kesselbrenner MD, Bregman DB. Survival from in-hospital cardiac arrest with interposed abdominal counterpulsation during cardiopulmonary resuscitation. JAMA 1992;267:379–385.

Stiell IG, Hebert PC, Weltzman BV, et al. High dose epinephrine in adult cardiac arrest. N Engl J Med 1992;327:1045–1050.

Tucker KJ, Galli F, Savitt MA, et al. Active compression-decompression resuscitation: effect on resuscitation success after in-hospital cardiac arrest. J Am Coll Cardiol 1994;24:201–209.

CHAPTER 20

Heart Transplantation

Howard J. Eisen
Ileana L. Piña

Congestive heart failure (CHF) is a leading cause of morbidity and mortality and is the one cardiovascular disease whose prevalence is increasing. In recent years, important strides have been made in improving the prognosis and quality of life in patients with CHF. New therapies are available that are effective in slowing or reversing the progression of CHF. Some patients, however, either fail to improve with standard medical therapy or, after a period of improvement, deteriorate. For these patients, long-term survival is dramatically diminished; their only chance of survival is cardiac transplantation. This chapter discusses the current state of cardiac transplantation as therapy for end-stage CHF.

INDICATIONS FOR CARDIAC TRANSPLANTATION

Every effort should be made to ensure that the patient is taking maximal medical therapy prior to being considered for cardiac transplantation.

Failure of Standard Drug Therapy

Patients who should be considered for cardiac transplantation are those who are failing standard medical therapy, including maximal doses of ACE-inhibitors, diuretics, digoxin, and perhaps other agents such as beta-blockers and other vasodilators (ARBs, hydralazine, and nitrates).

Functional Class

Patients can be stratified prognostically using NYHA Functional Class (see Chapter 2). Patients in Class 3 (dyspnea during simple activities of daily living) and Class 4 (dyspnea at rest) have a dramatically decreased prognosis.

- Patients in Class 3 have a 1-year survival of approximately 50%.
- Class 4 patients have a 1-year survival substantially less than this.

The prognosis of these patients compares unfavorably to that of patients who undergo cardiac transplantation, who have an 85% to 90% 1-year survival; therefore, functional Class 3 and 4 patients are transplantation candidates.

Other Cardiac Conditions

Other patients who are potential candidates for cardiac transplantation include:

- Patients with severe diffuse CAD and continued angina despite maximal medical therapy and who are not candidates for revascularization.
- Patients with primary cardiac tumors that cannot be completely resected but have not metastasized.
- Patients with malignant arrhythmias who have failed all of the therapeutic modalities.

CARDIAC TRANSPLANT EVALUATION

Once patients are deemed to be sick enough for cardiac transplantation, they undergo transplant evaluation.

Cardiovascular Evaluation

Respiratory Gas Assessment

One of the major diagnostic tests for objectively determining the functional class of patients with CHF is the exercise stress test with respiratory gases. Using this approach, the maximal oxygen consumption (VO_2) can be obtained. Patients with $VO_2 \leq 14\,mL/kg/min$ have a survival that is substantially less than that of cardiac transplant survivors; therefore, these are patients who should be considered for cardiac transplantation.

Myocardial Viability

Positron emission tomography (PET), resting thallium scintigraphy, or dobutamine echocardiography offer potential assessments of myocardial viability.

Endomyocardial Biopsy

Endomyocardial biopsy is generally not recommended unless one is attempting to diagnose cardiac sarcoidosis (a potentially treatable cause of cardiomyopathy).

Hemodynamic Assessment

Many patients are referred for cardiac transplantation with severely decompensated hemodynamics. For these patients, performing an exercise stress test with respiratory gas analysis may not be possible. A right heart catheterization can assess cardiac hemodynamics.

The adverse prognostic indicators that can be determined from cardiac hemodynamics at the time of right-heart catheterization include:

Elevated PA pressure
PCWP
Diminished CO and CI
PA saturation

Elevated PVR of the time of transplantation is a predictor of post-operative RV failure and poor prognosis. If the PVR is greater than 6 Wood units, efforts should be made using vasodilators such as nitroprusside, prostaglandin E1, or losartan to bring it down.

Additional Evaluative Tests

In addition to the cardiac tests, a number of other tests are necessary during the evaluation of potential transplantation patients.

Evaluation of Function of Other Organs

1. Thyroid function tests
2. Liver function tests
3. Pulmonary function tests
4. 24-hour urine for creatinine clearance and total protein
5. CXR

Serologies
1. Cytomegalovirus (CMV) titers
2. Epstein-Barr virus (EBV) serologies
3. HIV antibody serologies
4. Hepatitis B antibody serologies
5. Hepatitis C antibody serologies

Immunologic Tissue Typing Studies
1. Blood type
2. HLA testing
3. Preformed reactive antibodies

The presence of preformed reactive antibodies is important to determine before a transplant, as these may bind to the HLA antigens of donors:

- Hyperacute rejection may occur very early after transplantation.
- Chronic humoral rejection, a form of noncellular cardiac allograft rejection, may result in allograft dysfunction.

Additional Evaluations
1. Psychiatric/psychological testing
2. Social worker's evaluation
3. Dental assessment
4. Neurological evaluation (if there is a prior history of the neurologic disease)
5. Financial assessment
6. Age-related exams
   - Sigmoidoscopy/colonoscopy
   - Prostate-specific antigen
7. Female patients
   - Mammography
   - Gynecologic exam
8. History of peptic ulcer disease
   - Upper endoscopy

CONTRAINDICATIONS FOR CARDIAC TRANSPLANTATION

The following diseases and/or conditions are considered contraindications for cardiac transplantation.

- Any illness that would shorten long-term survival, such as malignancy or severe collagen vascular disease.
- Active infection, except in patients with infections related to ventricular assist devices (VADs).
- Brittle diabetes (small vessel disease, gangrenous digits) and/or recent episodes of diabetic ketoacidosis.
- Active peptic ulcer disease.
- Irreversible pulmonary, hepatic, or renal disease. Patients with irreversible diseases of these organs may be considered for combined transplants such as heart-lung or heart-kidney transplants.
- Elevated PVR above 3 Wood units despite vasodilators.
- Recent cerebrovascular accident (within 6 weeks) or severe neurologic dysfunction.
- Significant alcohol, drug, or tobacco addiction.
- Active psychiatric disease.

DONOR ORGANS

Organ Matching

Organs are matched according to the following criteria:

Blood type
Body size
Priority on the waiting list
Time on the waiting list

Occasionally patients with preformed reactive antibodies may need prospective cross-matches, and this will enter into determination of which recipient gets a particular donor heart.

Patient Priority Status
Patients are divided into three "status" rankings:

Status 1. Patients with the highest priority, either those who have VADs or IABPs.
- Patients with VADs do not necessarily need to be in the ICU or even in the hospital to maintain Status 1 ranking.
- Patients in ICUs are considered Status 1 patients.

Status 2. All other patients on the transplantation waiting list, whether in the hospital or not.

Status 7. Patients who have been inactivated. These patients do not lose time on the list, but they do not receive offers of new organs.

Donor Evaluation

Donor organs must be evaluated very carefully. Effort must be made to select organs that either function normally or have a reasonable likelihood of functioning normally in the recipients.

- Organs generally are not obtained from donors above age 55, although in rare circumstances this may be necessary.
- Organs with significant CAD are not routinely procured.
- Organs from donors who had significant risk factors for CAD such as age, smoking, coronary event history, and prior diabetes should undergo cardiac catheterization prior to the organ being used for transplantation.

Donor Body Size

In the past, a close match between donor and recipient size was often mandated. It is now known that in many cases recipients can receive undersized donor hearts from donors who are up to 50% smaller in body size than the recipient.

Donor Infection

Additional issues to be evaluated in donors include the presence of HIV, hepatitis C, and hepatitis B. Organs from donors positive for CMV should not be transplanted into CMV-negative recipients, given the high likelihood and potential severity of primary CMV infection in these patients.

VENTRICULAR ASSIST DEVICES (VADs)

A growing number of patients ultimately fail inotropic therapy with dobutamine and/or milrinone to support their circulation while they wait for cardiac transplantation. VADs are used as bridges to cardiac transplantation to ensure the survival of these patients until an organ to transplant becomes available. These devices can include LVADs and total artificial hearts.

Indications for VADs

The hemodynamic indications for VADs should be obtained while patients are receiving maximal inotropic support with IV dobutamine and/or milrinone. The indications for the use of VADs include:

- CI less than 2.0 liters/min/m^2
- Systemic BP of less than 80 to 90 mm Hg
- PCWP greater than 25 mm Hg
- PA saturation of less than 50%

Complications of VADs

The major complications of the LVAD include:

- Mechanical failure.
- Infection at the site of device placement. Patients with active VAD-related infections should undergo transplantation as soon as possible, as this removes the foreign body and allow the surgeons to clean out the area of infection.
- Bleeding and/or thromboembolic events at the time of surgery or shortly afterward. Thromboembolic events are extraordinarily rare.

SURGICAL TECHNIQUE FOR CARDIAC TRANSPLANTATION

Biatrial Anastomosis

Biatrial anastomosis is the standard technique for cardiac transplantation. This technique involves bisecting the donor and recipient atria.

Bicaval Anastomosis

The bicaval technique involves anastomosing the recipient's SVC and IVC to the donor's SVC and IVC, as well as anastomosing a small cuff of recipient's LA around the pulmonic veins to the donor's LA.

- The bicaval anastomosis is more challenging technically, but allows greater preservation of the conduction system.

- The percentage of patients requiring pacemakers who have undergone bicaval cardiac transplants is less than 1%, compared to 10% of patients undergoing the biatrial procedure.
- Exercise tolerance may be improved with the bicaval technique.

POST-TRANSPLANT IMMUNOLOGY

The major cause of morbidity and mortality among cardiac transplantation patients is the recipient's immune response to the donor organ.

Rejection Immune Responses

Transplant recipients face a number of immune responses to the donor organ.

Hyperacute rejection. Hyperacute rejection is an antibody-mediated disease. Careful management, such as ensuring that donor organs do not violate ABO blood group compatibilities and that patients with preformed reactive antibodies undergo prospective cross-matching, has made this disease extraordinarily rare today.

Cellular rejection. Cellular rejection, the T cell–mediated response of the recipient immune system to the donor major histocompatibility (MHC) antigens, is the major form of rejection seen clinically.

Chronic rejection. Chronic rejection, as transplant coronary arteriopathy or graft vasculopathy, presents as diffuse transplant CAD and can occur from 9 months to years after transplantation.

Acute Allograft Rejection

The most common form of rejection in cardiac transplant recipients is acute cellular rejection, a T cell–mediated phenomenon that occurs in the majority of patients undergoing cardiac transplantation. Transplant recipients experience an average of 2.2 episodes of allograft rejection in the first year. Rejection is most likely to occur in the first 3 months after transplantation. The next most common period is months 4 through 6 after transplantation, followed by months 7 through 12.

Mechanism of Rejection CD4+ and CD8+ T cells proliferate in response to stimulation from alloantigens. These cells produce a number of cytokines. Among these are interleukin (IL)-2 which further stimulates activation and proliferation of T lymphocytes, as well as, cytokines such as tumor necrosis factor alpha and interferon gamma, which increase expression of the donor MHC antigens on the endothelial and parenchymal allograft cell surfaces. This has the effect of further increasing the immunogenicity of the transplanted organ.

Cellular rejection can involve immune recognition in two forms.

Classic recognition. In the classic form, peptide fragments of the donor MHC are presented to the CD4+ T cells of the recipient by the recipient's macrophages. This is in conjunction with elaboration of IL-1. These cells then express IL-2 receptor, and this results in proliferation and activation of these cells, as well as both activation and proliferation of the CD 8+ positive cytotoxic T cells.

Direct recognition. An alternative pathway of recognition involves direct recognition by the recipient's CD4+ T cells of the foreign MHC class 2 antigens, as well as direct recognition by the CD8+ cytotoxic T cells of the donor's MHC class 1 antigen. This direct recognition also results in activation of the T cells in a similar manner to the classic form of recognition.

Severity of Rejection

Rejection is graded according to the system developed by the International Society of Heart and Lung Transplantation in 1990 (Table 20-1). This nomenclature defines the severity of rejection according to the degree of the lymphocytic infiltration and extent of myocyte necrosis in the allograft myocardium.

Grade 1. Grades 1A and 1B rejections are not treated with enhanced immunosuppression unless there is evidence of hemodynamic compromise (see grade 4 treatment).

Grade 2. Grade 2 rejections are not treated with

Table 20-1. ISHLT Nomenclature for Grading of Cellular Rejection

Grade		Histologic Features
0		No rejection.
1	A	Focal perivascular lymphocytic infiltrate with no myocyte necrosis.
	B	Diffuse lymphocytic infiltrate without necrosis.
2		One focus of aggressive infiltration and focal necrosis.
3	A	Multifocal aggressive infiltrates and myocyte necrosis.
	B	Diffuse inflammation with necrosis.
4		Diffuse polymorphous infiltrates with edema, hemorrhage, and necrosis.

enhanced immunosuppression unless hemodynamic compromise occurs (see grade 4 treatment). Data from several groups show no significant difference in resolution between patients with grade 2 rejection treated with corticosteroids and those with grade 2 rejection who are not treated.

Grade 3. Grades 3A and 3B rejections are treated with enhanced immunosuppression.

- Grade 3A rejection without hemodynamic compromise receives enhanced doses of corticosteroids, given either orally (3 mg/kg of prednisone QID for 3 days) or IV (500 mg to 1 gm of methylprednisolone daily for 3 days). Endomyocardial biopsies are obtained on a weekly basis afterward.
- Grade 3B rejections without hemodynamic compromise are treated similarly to grade 3A.

Grade 4. Grade 4 rejection—and any episode of rejection, regardless of grade, with hemodynamic compromise—receives aggressive immunosuppressive therapies to reverse the rejection.

Endomyocardial Biopsy

Endomyocardial biopsy is the gold standard for the diagnosis of cardiac allograft rejection. This is a well-tolerated but invasive procedure with a low morbidity and mortality. It involves obtaining several samples of cardiac tissue and staining these for presence of lymphocytes and the degree of myocyte necrosis.

The major side effects of endomyocardial biopsy include localized bleeding, infection, arrhythmias (usually self-limited), and (rarely) cardiac tamponade.

Alternative noninvasive approaches have been investigated, including echocardiographic, radionuclide, and cytoimmunologic screening, but none of these has proven as successful as endomyocardial biopsy in detecting rejection.

Pharmacologic Management of Rejection

The approach to prevention of rejection has been to use agents that inhibit T cell activation or T cell recognition. The two broad approaches used for immunosuppression have been triple therapy and induction therapy.

Triple Therapy
The major approach for preventing rejection used today is "triple therapy," with the immunosuppressive agents cyclosporine, prednisone, and azathioprine.

Cyclosporine
Cyclosporine is a relatively specific immunosuppressive agent that binds to cyclophilin in the cytoplasm and inhibits the expression of the IL-2 gene. This results in at least partial inhibition of proliferation and activation of T lymphocytes.

Administration
• **Before transplantation.** Cyclosporine is initially given just prior to cardiac transplantation. In many cases it is given IV or orally through a nasal gastric tube in doses up to 10 mg a day in divided doses. Cyclosporine doses are monitored using TLC or radioimmunoassays.
• **After transplantation.** Over time, the dosage of cyclosporine can be decreased. Efforts are directed at maintaining a level in the first 2 months of 350–450 ng/ml; this can be reduced to 250–350 ng/ml in months 4 through 6 after transplantation; and further reduced to 100–150 ng/ml beyond the first year after transplantation.

- **Maintenance.** Patients receiving cardiac transplants must be maintained on life-long cyclosporine.

Side effects The major side effects of cyclosporine are:

- Acute tubular necrosis may occur at the time that it is first used.
- Chronic renal insufficiency.
- HTN is a common occurrence after transplantation and is present in over 90% of cardiac transplant recipients taking cyclosporine.
- Neurologic manifestations such as seizures.
- Hepatic dysfunction (occurs primarily in pediatric populations).

Azathioprine Azathioprine is an antiproliferative that inhibits purine synthesis in lymphocytes and other dividing cells.

Administration Azathioprine is titrated to maintain a white cell count between 4000 and 8000.

Side effects The side effects of azathioprine include:

Leukopenia
Hepatitis
Pancreatitis

The dosage should be decreased if the patient's white cell count falls.

Prednisone Prednisone has numerous anti-inflammatory effects, including immune recognition, elaboration of cytokines, and lymphocytolysis.

Administration Prednisone is initially started at a very high dosage: up to 125 mg every 8 hours during the first to second days after transplant. The dosage is later lowered to 50 mg two times a day, and later is lowered even more.

A number of groups have shown that steroids can be reduced to very low doses (2.5–5.0 mg daily) by 6 months after cardiac transplantation. In many cases, they can be withdrawn entirely without adverse effects at 6 months to 1 year after transplantation.

Side effects Prednisone has numerous side effects, including:

Cushing's syndrome
Diabetes
Hyperlipidemia
HTN
Osteoporosis
Cataracts

Induction Therapy (Aggressive Immunosuppression)

In the past, many transplant centers used induction therapy with either OKT-3 or antithymocyte globulin in the first 2 weeks after transplantation. The goal was to try to preserve renal function and improve electrolyte management by delaying the use of cyclosporine in the early post-transplant period.

Although evidence exists that use of this induction therapy delays the timing of the first rejection after transplantation, there is no evidence that this approach improves survival or reduces the prevalence and severity of rejection. In addition, some data suggest that some patients receiving induction therapy may be more likely to develop infections such as CMV.

OKT-3 or antithymocyte globulin remains potential aggressive therapy for grade 4 rejection or any rejections exhibiting hemodynamic compromise.

OKT-3

OKT-3, a monoclonal antibody preparation, binds to the CD3 protein located around the T cell receptor. As a result, the T cell receptors are internalized, while other T cells are opsonized by macrophages. Thus, T cells are either destroyed or rendered unable to recognize foreign antigens.

Side effects   A major side effect of OKT-3 use is a diffuse release of tumor necrosis factor alpha, which can result in a clinical picture resembling septic shock. This condition can be severe and life threatening, necessitating ICU monitoring and premedication with corticosteroids, histamine blockers, and anti-inflammatory agents.

Antithymocyte Globulin

An alternative therapeutic approach to OKT-3 is the polyclonal antibody preparation antithymocyte globulin (ATGAM). This agent binds to a number of T cell receptors and results in opsonization of the T lymphocytes, rendering them ineffective.

Side effects   The side effects of antithymocyte globulin include:

Leukopenia
Thrombocytopenia
Serum sickness with arthralgias and palpable purpura

Infections

Cardiac transplant patients are at an increased risk of infection from both common pathogens and opportunistic organisms as a result of immunosuppression therapy. These infections are most likely to occur within the first 6 months after transplantation when the amount of immunosuppression used to prevent rejection is at its highest. These episodes are also likely to occur after treatments of acute cellular rejection when patients have received enhanced amounts of immunosuppressive therapy.

Bacterial Infections

Bacterial pathogens, such as gram-negative organisms and gram-positive cocci, can cause infections in cardiac transplant recipients. These pathogens are found in hospitals and most often occur in nosocomial infections of hospitalized patients, generally during the peri- and post-transplant period.

The sites of infection can include surgical wounds, the respiratory system (pneumonias), urinary tract, infections through disruption of skin such as IV catheters (line infections), and GI infections, such as cholecystitis.

Treatment   Bacterial infections in transplant patients should be treated aggressively because these patients are immunosuppressed. This would include broad spectrum antibiotics covering gram positive cocci and gram negative rods until the infecting organism has been identified. Although cardiac transplant recipients are prone to opportunistic infections, it is bacterial infections such as pneumonias, urinary tract and wound infections, as well as *C. difficile* colitis which are most commonly encountered. Once the specific organism and its antimicrobial sensitivities are known, then specific antibiotic therapy can be given.

Viral Infections

Transplant recipients are prone to infections from viral agents.

Cytomegalovirus CMV is the most common infecting virus. The earliest time of CMV infection usually begins 1 month after cardiac transplantation. This virus is ubiquitous and can cause a mononucleosis-type syndrome of fatigue, fever, and leukopenia, or tissue-invasive disease such as CMV pneumonitis, myocarditis, and colitis.

Treatment CMV infections can often be delayed or prevented by use of specific anti-viral agents such as ganciclovir, given IV or orally within the first few weeks after cardiac transplantation.

Once CMV infection has occurred, it can be treated with ganciclovir. If the patient does not tolerate ganciclovir or if the virus is resistant against ganciclovir, then foscarnet can be used.

Herpes Virus Herpes simplex can cause oral and vaginal ulcers, and herpes zoster can result in shingles.

Treatment Both herpes simplex and herpes zoster infections can be treated with oral or IV acyclovir, depending on the severity of the disease.

Pneumocystis carinii *Pneumocystis carinii* was first observed in cardiac transplant recipients. It presents as a pneumonia, which can be quite severe and cause severe hypoxemia or death.

Treatment The use of prophylactic antibiotics such as trimethoprim-sulfamethoxazole or aerosolized pentamidine minimizes the occurrence of this infection.

Fungal Infections

Fungal agents can cause pneumonitis or infections of other organs, including endocarditis and neurologic infections. *Candida* and *Aspergillus* sp. are the most frequently encountered fungal pathogens.

Treatment *C. albicans* infections can often be treated with fluconazole. The other species of *Candida* and *Aspergillus* often require amphotericin. *Aspergillus* is a particularly difficult fungal pathogen to treat with a mortality of 50%.

Transplant Coronary Arteriopathy

The major cause of mortality after transplantation is transplant coronary vasculopathy. This is a poorly defined, poorly understood disease that histologically resembles restenosis after angioplasty. It is characterized by diffuse coronary artery intimal and smooth muscle cell hyperplasia with marked narrowing of the coronary artery lumen.

The disease usually begins to occur 9 months after cardiac transplantation and can either be localized, with an appearance that resembles nontransplant CAD, or can be more diffuse, including marked involvement of the distal arteries.

In its worst form, it is characterized by severe diffuse triple-vessel CAD with poor collateralization. Histologically, the arteries have very little in the way of lipid deposition and are characterized far more by proliferation of smooth muscle and intimal cells.

Etiology

The exact etiology of transplant coronary vasculopathy is unknown, but it appears to be related at least in part to an immunologic assault on the transplant coronary arteries. Evidence supporting an immunologic etiology includes:

- Activated T lymphocytes can be found in the artery blood vessel wall.
- Activation of endomyocardial biopsies is a predictor of transplant coronary arteriopathy.
- Enhanced expression of cell adhesion molecules is found in the arteries of patients who have this disease.
- Enhanced expression of HLA DR is found both in endomyocardial biopsies of patients who subsequently develop this disease and in the arteries of patients who actually develop the disease.
- Patients who have continued immune activation such as continued high serum levels of soluble IL-2 receptor are at higher risk for subsequently developing and dying from transplant arteriopathy.

CMV Infection Among the factors that have been correlated with transplant arteriopathy is an association with CMV infection. It is known from studies of restenosis that patients who undergo atherectomy and then subsequently develop restenosis afterward are more likely to have CMV genome in the arterial wall. One of the CMV proteins may inhibit the protein p53, an antiproliferative protein; thus, CMV infection may block some of the brakes to proliferation of cells that respond to damage from immunologic injury.

Coronary Risk Factors The relationship of transplant arteriopathy to the classic coronary artery risk factors is not as close as with nontransplant CAD. However, there is likely to be some contribution from hyperlipidemia as well as HTN.

Clinical Manifestation
The clinical manifestations of transplant coronary vasculopathy are often very subtle, as transplant patients have denervated hearts. Consequently, these patients seldom present with chest pain, but rather with catastrophic manifestations such as MI, CHF, arrhythmias, or sudden cardiac death.

Diagnosis Because transplant patients have denervated hearts, an effort should be made to detect this disease including noninvasive approaches such as dipyridamole thallium stress testing or dobutamine stress echocardiography. Given the importance of making this diagnosis, we recommend that intravascular ultrasound be performed, especially in patients at risk or with clinical manifestations that suggest ischemia.

Intravascular ultrasound (IVUS) Transplant coronary arteriopathy is often difficult to diagnose by standard coronary angiography as the disease may diffusely affect the coronary arterial tree. Consequently, other approaches including quantitative coronary angiography and IVUS have been used to attempt to make the diagnosis.

Information obtained from IVUS—including the extent of intimal thickening and the degree of luminal narrowing—has been shown to be predictive of subsequent adverse cardiac events, so this test may be useful not only in making the diagnosis of transplant coronary arteriopathy, but also for prognostic purposes.

Treatment
The treatment of transplant coronary arteriopathy is difficult.

Pharmacologic Therapy A few clinical studies support use of diltiazem for reducing the prevalence of this disease. Data support HMG-CoA reductase inhibitors for reducing the prevalence and severity of this disease.

There is evidence in experimental animals to support the utility of a number of agents for preventing transplant arteriopathy. Whether some of the new immunosuppressive agents may prevent this disease is not clear.

Surgical Therapy Many patients who have discrete coronary artery lesions are candidates for standard therapy with PTCA or atherectomy.

For patients who have severe triple-vessel arteriopathy, the only option may be retransplantation. The 3-year survival for patients with severe triple-vessel coronary disease is 6%. Many patients with milder disease have a good prognosis.

Post-transplant Lymphoproliferative Disorder

Post-transplant lymphoproliferative disorder, which is largely unique to transplant patients, appears to be caused in many cases by the EBV. EBV infection causes a proliferation of B cells, resulting in a polyclonal malignancy.

The patients most likely to develop post-transplant lymphoproliferative disorder are those who have received more extensive courses of immunosuppression, including several courses of OKT-3.

Treatment
- In many cases, this disease can be reversed by decreasing the amount of immunosuppression the patients are receiving.
- Certain forms of the disease may be monoclonal, and

with these forms the prognosis is worse. These patients may need to be treated with chemotherapy.

REHABILITATION AFTER CARDIAC TRANSPLANTATION

We recommend continued cardiac rehabilitation both for patients awaiting transplantation, either as inpatients or outpatients, and for patients who have undergone transplantation.

In the post-transplant setting, while the patient's sternum heals and the effects of high postoperative doses of corticosteroids wear off, rehabilitation should comprise:

1. Postoperative incentive spirometry
2. Postoperative pulmonary toilet
3. Early ambulation
4. Progression to resistive exercise
5. Full cardiopulmonary rehabilitation

Studies of cardiac transplant recipients who have participated in cardiac rehabilitation programs have demonstrated improvements in VO_2 from 16.7 to 20 mL/kg/min after 10 weeks of outpatient exercise training.

Long-Term Management and Care

The 1-year survival for cardiac transplant recipients is currently 85% to 90% and continues to improve. This is a dramatic improvement over the less than 50% 1-year survival of patients who have severe class 3 and class 4 CHF. The 5-year survival rate for cardiac transplant patients is reported to be 65% to 75%.

The quality of life of these patients largely resembles that of the general population. However, issues that may adversely affect the patient's survival after cardiac transplantation include older age of the donor organ, the presence of preformed reactive antibodies, and the use of a ventilator prior to transplantation.

The major causes of morbidity and mortality after transplantation are temporally dependent:

- In the first 30 days, the major causes of death include technical problems such as primary graft failure and rejection and infection.

- From the beginning of the second month to the end of the first year, the major causes of death are rejection and infection.
- After the first year the major causes of death include transplant CAD and malignancy, in addition to rejection and infection.

Although rejection generally occurs in the first year it can occur at other times as well. Thus, a major long-term management issue after transplantation centers on the need for these patients to be maintained on lifelong medications such as cyclosporine and the side effects accompanying the long-term use of these drugs. After the first year, the potential for transplant CAD is a continuing issue for transplant patients as well.

SUGGESTED READINGS

American College of Cardiology. 24th Bethesda Conference: Cardiac Transplantation. J Am Coll Cardiol 1993;22:1–64.

Mancini DM, Eisen H, Kussmaul W, et al. Value of peak exercise oxygen consumption for optimal timing of cardiac transplantation in ambulatory patients with heart failure. Circulation 1991;83:778–786.

Miller LW. Long-term complications of cardiac transplantation. Prog Cardiovasc Dis 1991;33:229–282.

Murali S, Uretsky B, Reddy S, et al. Reversibility of pulmonary hypertension in congestive heart failure patients evaluated for cardiac transplantation: comparative effects of various pharmacologic agents. Am Heart J 1991;122:1375–1380.

Renlund DG, Taylor DO, Ensley RD, et al. Exercise capacity after cardiac transplantation: influence of donor and recipient characteristics. J Heart Lung Transplant 1996;15: 16–24.

Saxon LA, Stevenson WG, Middlekauff HR, et al. Predicting death from progressive heart failure secondary to ischemic or idiopathic dilated cardiomyopathy. Am J Cardiol 1993;72:62–65.

Stevenson LW, Fowler MB, Schroeder JS, et al. Poor survival of patients with idiopathic cardiomyopathy considered too well for transplantation. Am J Med 1987;83:871–876.

Stevenson LW, Tillisch J, Hamilton M, et al. Importance of hemodynamic response to therapy in predicting survival with ejection fraction less than or equal to 20% secondary to ischemic or nonischemic dilated cardiomyopathy. Am J Cardiol 1990;66:1348–1354.

Turco M, Pina IL, Margulies KB, et al. Comparison of corticosteroid immunotherapy to absence of therapy for focal moderate (ISHLT II) rejection. J Heart Lung Transplant 1995;14:S47.

Vagelos R, Fowler MB. Selection of patients for cardiac transplantation. Cardiol Clin 1990;8:23–38.

Index